UITGAVEN VAN HET
NEDERLANDS HISTORISCH-ARCHAEOLOGISCH INSTITUUT TE ISTANBUL

Publications de l'Institut historique-archéologique néerlandais de Stamboul
sous la direction de

Machteld J. MELLINK, J. de ROOS,
J.J. ROODENBERG et K.R. VEENHOF

LXXXIV

TRADE AND FINANCE IN ANCIENT MESOPOTAMIA

Cover illustration: from the so-called Rassam Obelisk of Ashurnasirpal II (BM 118800).
From: C.J. Gadd, *The Stones of Assyria*, pl. 6.

TRADE AND FINANCE IN ANCIENT MESOPOTAMIA

(MOS STUDIES 1)

PROCEEDINGS OF THE FIRST MOS SYMPOSIUM
(LEIDEN 1997)

edited by

J.G. DERCKSEN

NEDERLANDS HISTORISCH-ARCHAEOLOGISCH INSTITUUT
TE ISTANBUL
1999

Trade and Finance in Ancient Mesopotamia;
Proceedings of the First MOS Symposium (Leiden 1997) / ed. by J.G. Dercksen.
Istanbul: Nederlands Historisch-Archaeologisch Instituut;
Leiden: Nederlands Instituut voor het Nabije Oosten [distr.].
(Uitgaven van het Nederlands Historisch-Archaeologisch Instituut te Istanbul; ISSN 0926-9568; 84)
ISBN 90 6258 085 8

Printed in Belgium

PREFACE

This volume is the first in a series published in the context of a post-doctoral research project on the *Economy of Ancient Mesopotamia*, financed by The Netherlands Organization for Scientific Research (NWO) in the framework of a special 'Middle Eastern Studies Programme' (MOS Programme) conducted by A.C.V.M. Bongenaar and J.G. Dercksen, both Leiden University, and R.M. Jas, Vrije Universiteit Amsterdam, and supervised by G. van Driel, M. Stol, and K.R. Veenhof. This project investigates three main themes: natural resources, notably agriculture, organization, in particular institutional production and management, and interregional and international overland trade. The focus is on data from the second and first millennia B.C. Each of the three themes is also the subject of an international symposium. The first dealt with the question how Mesopotamia was able to import goods from abroad, the second with the interdependency of institutions and private entrepreneurs with the focus on the Neo-Babylonian material, and the last with rainfall and agriculture in Northern Mesopotamia.

On 19-20 December 1997, the first one on *Trade and Finance in Ancient Mesopotamia*, organized by the editor of this volume, was held in Leiden and the present volume contains the revised version of the papers presented on that occasion. Unfortunately, four of the contributions for various reasons could not be included, *viz.* the one by J. Renger elaborating on his article in *Rätsel Geld* (Renger 1995), M. Stol's comments on the use of silver during the Old Babylonian period, the paper by M.T. Larsen on the relevance of the Old Assyrian text material for the understanding of Mesopotamian economic history, and A. Verhoogt's outline of trade in Ptolemaic Egypt.

I gratefully acknowledge the generous financial support received from the following institutions: Leiden University, both from the Research School CNWS (School of Asian, African, and Amerindian Studies) as well as from the Department of Near Eastern Studies (TCNO), The Netherlands Organization for Scientific Research (NWO), the Koninklijke Nederlandse Akademie van Wetenschappen, and the Leids Universiteits Fonds (LUF). I further wish to thank Leiden University for the facilities it made available to the symposium. Thanks are also due to the Board of Directors of the Nederlands Instituut voor het Nabije Oosten (NINO) for publishing this book in the series PIHANS.

J.G. Dercksen
April, 1999

TABLE OF CONTENTS

INTRODUCTION

An agrarian-based civilization with urban centres developed in Ancient Mesopotamia in spite of this region lacking many raw materials. In particular metals, stone, and wood had to be imported. These commodities reached Mesopotamia largely by means of trade in exchange for locally manufactured products. The way this was done and the manner in which this was financed from the Third Dynasty of Ur until the Achemenid period forms the topic of this book. Points of interest are:

– the way capital was formed which could be used to buy imported goods;
– the institutional or private role of merchants and how they acquired the assets to conduct trade;
– the availability and use of commodities that could function as money.

It proved impossible to treat each of these aspects for the entire period under consideration. Old Babylonian, Middle-Assyrian, Middle-Babylonian, and Nuzi material had to be omitted, although the aspect of money has been treated in two recent publications (Renger 1995; Powell 1996).

The opening contribution deals with money, markets, and merchants. Marvin A. Powell discusses the theoretical premises used by J. Renger in his articles on Mesopotamian society and economy. According to Renger, Babylonian society was dominated by large institutions who possessed the land where agriculture was possible and created a redistributive system from which its dependents lived. That part of the population which did not belong to such an institution lived as small farmers on subsistence level. Under such conditions, the use of money was restricted to the institutions. Outside institutions, money played a marginal role as there was little need for its use.

M.A. Powell takes issue with Marxist and substantivist theories which have affected students of Mesopotamian economy. The substantivist theory, developed by K. Polanyi and his school, has influenced, among others, J. Renger. Notably Polanyi's denial of the existence of markets and of a form of "market economy" with a drive for profit and supply and demand determining prices and trade, can be countered by evidence from Assyrian and Babylonian documents. Powell summarizes his position regarding the evidence for the use of money, particularly in the form of silver, and its role in Mesopotamian economy since the mid-third millennium. He further addresses the problems surrounding the weighing methods employed, the quality or purity of the metals used as money and the existence of coins.

The Capital

One can distinguish two forms of agriculture: enough rainfall permits a rainfed agriculture in the North, while the South, ancient Sumer and Babylonia, depends on an intricate irrigation system derived from the rivers Euphrates and Tigris. Whereas the irrigation-based agriculture demands more organizational skill and labour, it enables better and more reliable yields and hence surplusses than that depending on rainfall.

The socio-economic situation during the Third Dynasty of Ur is marked by the preeminence of the temple institutions which were integrated in the central administration. G. van Driel investigates the thesis that these institutions accumulated capital in order to invest. A large part of the agricultural production is realized by institutions organized as a religious household. The mere existence of these temples implies the existence of surplusses. They were managed by the central administration and exploited for central ends. The city-state of Lagaš is an example of how the local resources, mainly land and labour, were exploited. The bureaucrats were aware of the under-use of their assets and made calculations how to increase the yield of their land, but their own means to realize this were limited. They had enough land at their disposal but lacked the necessary manpower to bring it under cultivation. The institutions were unable to exploit their assets fully by their own means and sought help from outside their organization, thus providing an opportunity for private entrepreneurs. This will be a constant feature of Mesopotamian institutions until the Neo-Babylonian period. As a rule, the institutions managed their assets ineffectively. For these agricultural organizations, the surplus served partly for the creation of a buffer stock for periods of bad harvests, and as a means of payment for personnel and goods. The way in which the remaining capital was used for investment with the purpose of increasing production is difficult to ascertain, because the necessary documentation is often lacking. The bookkeeping practice does not permit the clear identification of reserved capital. Furthermore, a considerable portion left the institution and went to the central administration. In the course of Mesopotamian history, an ever increasing use of assets can be discerned.

The Traders and the Financing of their Activities

The trader (DAM.GÀR, *tamkārum*) under the Third Dynasty of Ur has long been regarded as a commercial agent in the service of a palace or temple, both institutions supposedly possessing a commercial monopoly. More recently, he is seen rather as a private entrepreneur who could also trade on behalf of the central administration, similar to the Old Assyrian and Old Babylonian *tamkārum*. H. Neumann emphasizes that merchants formed a heterogeneous social group within the private sector of the economy, ranging from those fully employed by an institution to those that were largely active privately. There was a close relationship between the state and the private economic spheres. Important is the documentation available from Umma, where the so-called "balanced accounts" detail the deliveries during a specific period of time by a merchant to the central administration and the means of payment. To facilitate the balancing of the commodities all are valued in silver, in a system of internal equivalences. The current discussion focuses on the relationship between these traders and the state and how these goods actually reached the state offices. Neumann argues that the limited number of merchants involved in this procedure were able to deliver the goods requested from what they had in stock and that their commercial activities were independent from the requirements of the administration.

The rich evidence from the Old Assyrian trading archives is dealt with by K.R. Veenhof and J.G. Dercksen. Veenhof discusses the use of silver in this period, which facilitated the transactions and made a swift turnover possible. Special attention is furthermore given to the mechanisms and legal devices regarding the borrowing of money, for instance from the *bēt tamkārim*, the role of credit, and securities.

Investments in Old Assyrian firms form the subject of the contribution by Dercksen. Beside the well-known *naruqqum* or "sack capital", there existed other forms of partnership which provided traders with the necessary funds. This paper also investigates the terminology used to differentiate between "own" and "foreign" assets and aspects of bookkeeping.

A detailed investigation of the role played by merchants in the Neo-Assyrian period is presented by K. Radner. The *tamkārum* is seen as a royal trade agent, who supplies the court with imported goods. Not only Assyrians, also merchants belonging to other ethnic groups within the Empire were engaged in this kind of trade. Some merchants cooperated closely with the Assyrian army in collecting and forwarding the goods. An important source for private commercial enterprises are the *bēl ḫarrāni*-texts from Assur, dealing with the financing of trade ventures. By reviewing the professions of the type *ša X-šu*, the documentary evidence for peddling trade in first millennium Assyria is examined.

Commerce in the Neo-Babylonian period is discussed by F. Joannès. Both private and temple archives shed light on this topic. Temples do not have their own commercial structure, but rely on the services of outsiders, in this case of *tamkārum*'s, to sell part of their surplus or to acquire necessities not locally available. This situation, in which the temple organization itself does not include merchants, is probably paralleled in the palace sphere, where the "merchant of the king" supplies goods to the palace or sells on its behalf without being part of the palace. The sale of surplus is one method to obtain silver, an aspect further discussed by A.C.V.M. Bongenaar.

Commercial activities in the private sphere are reflected in the so-called *ḫarrānu*-texts which deal with partnerships formed for production, financing, or trade purposes. Although these documents do not describe how the trade was carried out, they do show that silver circulated. The demand for agricultural products is manifest in the sale of these goods by merchants such as Iddin-Marduk (see Wunsch 1993). There were markets of some form where the goods changed hands, but the way in which payments were made for relatively small amounts remains unclear. Merchants like Iddin-Marduk were engaged in more types of business than a *tamkārum*, but a superior level is formed by wealthy families who manage the production of the institutions. The sale of agricultural products is a form of local trade, which also includes various forms of retail trade. The results of international trade are apparent in the purchase in Babylon of necessary goods by temple officials from the Ištar-temple in Uruk, or trading agents. If not of local or regional origin, most of these goods were imported from the West (*Eber nāri*). Elaborating on A.L. Oppenheim's discussion of two texts from Uruk, F. Joannès discusses the ways the Uruk-temple ordered goods from merchants who probably travelled to the West themselves to obtain goods. The existence in Babylonia of representatives of western trading-firms is likely, although undocumented.

The Role of Money

The question whether money existed in Ancient Mesopotamia has divided assyriology in two opposed camps. In his article, A.C.V.M. Bongenaar reviews the theories which have influenced and dominated assyriological discussion and then compares these with the outcome of a discussion of the data for the use of money in Neo-Babylonian texts from two large institutions.

Polanyi's theory of a Mesopotamian non-market economy without money has been both criticized and applauded. He formulated a set of criteria a good should fulfil in order to be called "money". J. Renger concluded that silver was the only commodity worthy of this title. He also argued that the functions performed by these types of money were only valid in certain economic spheres. Reciprocity in villages and also in cities would make the use of money superfluous. Silver was mainly used by institutions and by those of the elite having contacts with them. The largest part of the population, represented by tenants working on temple or palace land, lived close to subsistence level and hence had little means to acquire money. Mainly a small number of entrepreneurs in the cities used silver as money. The opposite view is taken by Powell, who distinguishes between low- and high-range money, depending on its use.

It appears from the Neo-Babylonian temple archives from Uruk and Sippar that silver as such was effectively used as a high-range money. It was coming into the administration, even as the payment for rent, and was used for various purposes, for example to pay for goods the institution obtained through commerce. But the existence of money does not imply the existence of a free market where prices were fixed by the laws of demand and supply. The issue of price-making, the meaning of the "rate of exchange" (*maḫīru*), and the data contained in the *Astronomical Diaries* of Babylon are referred to by F. Joannès and K. Radner.

K. Radner explores the Neo-Assyrian letters and legal texts for a chronological assessment of the question which metals served as money. Copper, bronze, and silver were used as means of payment. Silver is the most popular money during the seventh century, probably as a result of increased availability of this metal. Several weight standards were used. Most of the metals functioning as money entered the Empire as a result of military activity.

Wir müssen alle unsere Nische nutzen: MONIES, MOTIVES, AND METHODS IN BABYLONIAN ECONOMICS

MARVIN A. POWELL (DEKALB)

The title of my paper I owe, once more, to a bardic comment by my friend Manfred Krebernik, during the course of our communal worship of Ninkasi. My original commission from the organizers of "Trade and Finance" was to present a paper on the use of commodities as money, on the weighing system and its accuracy, and on the purity of metals. As I pointed out in the version of my paper printed in the symposium reader, this could easily be the subject for a book, and, in fact, even a book would not be able to satisfactorily answer a lot of the questions pertaining to these problems. In the present version of my paper I have tried to provide a succinct summary of what I think I know about these topics and to recast the paper in the light of the issues, evidence, and points of view presented at the Leiden symposium.

1. *J. Renger and Mesopotamian Economy*

On the whole, papers of the symposium and discussion of the evidence and its interpretation supported the general picture sketched out by me in previous papers (Powell 1996, 1990, 1989-90, 1979, 1978b, 1977) about money and the physical means of transferring money - by weight in the case of metal monies - in the Mesopotamian economy. Essentially that position is: 1. Money that is sufficiently like our money to permit legitimate use of the term can already be seen in Babylonia by the mid-third millennium. 2. By this time the economy had developed sufficiently to need something like money, and that need is reflected throughout, not just in so-called "private" transactions, even though a description of Babylonia as a "money" economy is hardly justified. 3. By ca. 2500 silver is already in the process of becoming the primary definition of economic value and retains and develops that function in a continuous and cummulative fashion (except for a hiatus at the end of the Bronze Age) until the cuneiform sources gradually disappear toward the end of the first millennium BC. 4. That the fundamental motive governing economic activity is self interest, which manifests itself in the profit motive, particularly - but not exclusively - in transactions involving silver.

None of these premises can be proved beyond doubt. The reason for this is quite simple: even though we seem to have lots of texts, in most cases the outstanding feature in any pattern of evidence is the lacunae. We are perforce constrained to bridge these gaps by quantum leaps that, at bottom, can only be intuitive.

Significantly, the Old Assyrian specialists at the symposium (J.G. Dercksen, M.T. Larsen, and K.R. Veenhof) presented compelling evidence for the point of view that has long been held by scholars specializing in the study of Old Assyrian economics, namely, that Old Assyrian trade operated primarily on the basis of supply and demand, that profit was, if not the only motive, the driving force behind economic activity, and that risk was something one accepted as a fact of economic life but which one sought to avoid or minimize if one had the option. Likewise, K. Radner (on later Assyria), M. Stol (on Old Babylonian), and A.C.V.M. Bongenaar (Neo-Babylonian) all pointed to evidence for wide circulation of silver. Particularly noteworthy, is the fact that H. Neumann's study, which summarized and elaborated upon his own extensive experience with merchant activity and motives in the Ur III period, supports the assumption of a continuity between Ur III and Old Babylonian. Finally, G. van Driel presented a general theory of economic development in Babylonia that largely corresponds to assumptions that underlie my treatment of money in the Mesopotamian economy.

Counterpoised to this general consensus of opinion is the methodological and epistemological problem raised by J. Renger's essay titled "Subsistenzproduktion und redistributive Palastwirtschaft: Wo bleibt die Nische für das Geld?" (Renger 1995) reprinted in the symposium reader as a basis for discussion. The title encapsules three theoretical premises that J. Renger has discussed in this and other works: 1. that "redistributive" economy was a primary feature of ancient Babylonia; 2. that "subsistence" economy was widespread; 3. that "money" is elusive and essentially a fantasy of modern scholars who do not understand how to properly interpret the evidence.

If these premises were all true, especially the last, there would be no point in discussing money, since the cumulative implication of Renger's arguments is that there is no real "niche" for money in ancient Babylonia. Before proceeding to a discussion of this, we should note that a great deal of what Renger says in this and other essays he has written over the last decade or so, insofar as it concerns concrete matters, will find few opponents among Mesopotamian specialists. After all, none of us debate his competence as an Assyriologist. Where many of us, however, are not prepared to follow are the theoretical paths charted out by Renger in applying terms like redistribution, reciprocity, and subsistence to the economy and in the striking tendency to deny that silver functioned as money or that profit motive or supply and demand played any significant role in the economy.

Renger and others who represent this point of view - particularly R. K. Englund, who devoted much space in his book on the Ur III fisheries to an attempt to demonstrate that all merchants were essentially dependents of the state whose economic activities were motivated, like virtually everybody else in the Ur III state according to Englund, by fear of punishment rather than economic self interest (Englund 1990) - are, of course, not unaware that the vast majority of Mesopotamian specialists do not agree with them. That does not restrain them, however, from making theoretical statements that suggest to non-specialists that the rest of us just fell off the turnip truck or, in any event, are operating with anachronistic models. It is true, of course, that the criticisms Renger makes of non-specialist pronouncements about ancient Mesopotamia are mostly legitimate: non-specialists usually do not know what they are talking about, but neither did K. Polanyi, to whom I am coming shortly. Englund goes further and rejects as unfounded opinions like those of J. D. Muhly (1980) and N. Yoffee (1981), because, says Englund, it is precisely the reading of Ur III texts that makes Polanyi's theory likely,[1] implying, of course, that

---

1 Englund 1990, 16.

the rest of us who do not agree with him have not actually read the texts (an attitude that is not unique to this passage) or are merely indulging in "misleading speculation".[2]

Any scholar who either knows J. D. Muhly or N. Yoffee personally or has read their published works will recognize the strained nature of Englund's argument in asserting that their view of ancient Mesopotamian economy was essentially determined by taking over uncritically ("Kritiklos": Englund 1990, 17 n. 58) the theory sketched out by me at the 1976 Rencontre Assyriologique (Powell 1977). While Muhly's formulation (1980, 174) that the "Ancient Near Eastern economy was also a market economy" surely overstates the case, his further points that Polanyi was ignorant in general about early Mediterranean economy, that there is evidence for markets and market forces in ancient Mesopotamia, and that the evidence presented in M. T. Larsen's contribution to the 1976 Rencontre Assyriologique (which Muhly was reviewing) "brings the Old Assyrian period into a world understood by any modern capitalist", are legitimate and found further confirmation in the evidence presented at the Leiden symposium.

That others who have also read many Ur III texts[3] can reach rather different conclusions from those reached by Englund[4] underscores two basic features of the problem with which we are dealing: 1. the evidence of the documents is often ambiguous; 2. the conclusions one draws from that evidence are shaped by the methodological ideology with which one approaches the evidence. Even D. C. Snell, whom Englund cites[5] as being critical of my idea that markets and profit motives played a role in the economy of the third millennium, has now, in a review of theories about ancient society and economy (Snell 1997, 145-158), come to a position that differs sharply with the positions enunciated by either J. Renger or R. K. Englund. A thoughtful critique rejecting the point of view represented by Renger and Englund is that of M. van de Mieroop[6] in his discussion of trade in southern Babylonia in the era following the collapse of the Ur III empire.

This is not to say that the conclusions of Renger or Englund are necessarily all wrong. Quite the contrary, as I have said there is much to agree with in Renger's overall picture of the Babylonian economy and some of Englund's specific interpretations are legitimate (along with a lot that are debatable). What is most dubious is the tendency to ignore counterindications.

I am not objecting to theory. Facts are, at bottom, theory, and "history" itself is a tissue of theory that can rarely hope to closely resemble the reality it purports to describe. The historical "facts" that we talk about cannot, from an epistemological point of view, be separated from how we know them. In this context, I assume sufficiently self-evident as to not require philosophical justification that, in the process of seeking to know the past, use of "models" or "paradigms" created by persons who were themselves essentially ignorant of that evidence we are trying to interpret and through which we seek to "know" the past are not inherently more likely to bring us closer to reality than are theories worked out by those more familiar with the evidence to be interpreted.

---

2 Englund 1990, 201.

3 Cf., *e.g.*, H. Neumann's symposium paper and Neumann 1979, 1992a, 1992b, 1993; Zettler 1992; Sallaberger 1994.

4 Englund 1990, 199-201.

5 Englund 1990, 17.

6 Van de Mieroop 1992, 188-203.

2. *Polanyi and the Evidence for Markets*

Over the last couple of generations, in addition to ad hoc theories worked out by Assyriologists and Mesopotamian archaeologists, two theoretical models have been consciously applied to the Mesopotamian evidence. First, the Marxist theory, represented chiefly by scholars within the penumbra of the Russian Empire in its Soviet incarnation, and second the "substantivist" economic theories represented by Karl Polanyi and his disciples. I do not intend to comment on Marxist interpretation of ancient Mesopotamian history except to note that Marx's theory is demonstrably wrong at both ends. According to Marx, "history" should have proceeded in a nice, neat fashion from slaveholding societies, through feudalism and capitalism, to communism. The problem on the early end was that the kind of slave system posited by Marx as characteristic of the beginning phase of this process was an anomaly characteristic above all of the Roman Empire from about 200 BC to about 100 AD. The contortions through which Marxist scholars put themselves to try to save the theory with the "Asiatic mode of production" are indicative of the underlying troubles. And then the collapse of the "great experiment" in the years following 1989 demonstrated, if that was needed, that the end of the theory did not work either. It is hardly necessary to add that Marx's vision of the "middle" bears so little resemblance to what mediaevalists at the end of the 20th century think they know about that vast and diverse world lying between antiquity and modernity that a candid observer would probably be reluctant to believe that they are even talking about the same thing.

Obviously, we are in no danger of seeing a rush of Assyiologists to use the Marxist model. It has failed. But its implications are still with us: virtually every use of the words capital, capitalist, capitalism, and related concepts has been infected with Marxist theory, even when used by the most adamant opponents of Marxism. This remains a serious problem of historical terminology: "capitalism" as the description either of an economic system or of a historical era is an intellectual construct. So is the related concept of "market economy" that played a major role in the thinking of K. Polanyi. As intellectual tools for understanding what really happened in the past they are more obfuscating than clarifying.

Karl Polanyi, like Karl Marx, wanted the world to be better (at least for humans) than it really is and therefore discovered "redistributive" economy. The criticisms made over two decades ago by rational historians of the ancient Near East like J. D. Muhly[7] and N. Yoffee[8] are still valid, and today there is even more reason to wonder whether the evidence itself on which the theory was erected was sound.[9] Although majority opinion is an unreliable criterion of validity, Polanyi's paradigm is far from commanding the allegiance of the majority of anthropologists.

Be that as it may, the acid test of a historical theory is whether it accounts for all the evidence. The specific shibboleth over which Polanyi's theory fatally stumbles is the evidence from Old Assyrian trade. That Polanyi's model does not work for Old Assyrian was adequately demonstrated by K.R. Veenhof almost three decades ago,[10] and it was specifically Veenhof's formulation of the problem to which both Muhly and Yoffee

7 Muhly 1980, 174.

8 Yoffee 1981, 4-6.

9 Cf. Snell 1997, 149-151.

10 Specifically Veenhof 1972, 348-351.

referred in rejecting Polanyi's theory as a useful tool for studying Mesopotamian history. For good reason: it is an elementary principle of historical method that one key mistake in an overarching historical theory is a good indication that the rest of the theory is liable to contain serious flaws.

In the mid-1970s, after returning from my first extended stay in the Soviet Union and being not entirely satisfied with the Marxist version of Mesopotamian history worked out by Soviet scholars, I decided to work through the literature pertaining to Polanyi's theory and to test it on the Mesopotamian evidence. I discovered that two key elements could not be made to fit: markets and merchants. I called attention to this problem in two papers (1977, 1978a) of which I reiterate here the main points, because they are still valid.

Polanyi made the following assumptions and assertions about Mesopotamian markets:[11] 1. Herodotus, who visited Babylon in the middle of the 5th century BC, reported that the Persians had no markets. 2. Babylonian documents reveal no essential economic changes between Old Babylonian and Persian periods. 3. Marketplaces, if they had existed in the time of Hammurabi (Old Babylonian), would have still existed in the time of Herodotus. 4. In Palestine, archaeology revealed no open spaces in towns that could reasonably be interpreted as marketplaces. 5. Cuneiform descriptions of Babylon fail to mention a marketplace. 6. No word for marketplace exists in cuneiform sources. 7. According to A. Leo Oppenheim, archaeological evidence does not favor the existence of marketplaces inside of cities throughout the whole Near East.

Points 1 and 3 are fallible, because they rest upon a misinterpretation of Herodotus, who was talking, not about Babylon, but rather about an ethnic characteristic of the Persians, the well known disdain of the Persian, horse-riding, warrior class for mundane matters like trade. Points 2, 5, and 6 are demonstrably false, and 3 and 6 rest on misinformation and misconceptions.

That the Akkadian word *maḫīru* (from a root with meanings in the semantic range of "come face to face", "correspond", "receive") has both the meaning of "market-rate" and "market-place" makes it inherently probable that marketplaces existed in Babylonia, and no historian without an axe to grind who reads through the evidence presented by W. Röllig in his essay on the ancient Mesopotamian market (1976) and by the Akkadian dictionaries (*CAD* M/1, 92-99; *AHw* 583f.) will fail to recognize that Röllig and the dictionaries are right and Polanyi wrong.

Moreover, point 5, about the topography of Babylon having no mention of a market, is now explicitly refuted in the excellent edition of topographical texts by A. R. George, where the "Market Gate", located in the eastern part of the city (*i.e.*, on the eastern side of the river) is used as a key orientation point for defining city quarters: "from the Market Gate to the Grand Gate is called Eridu, from the Market Gate to the Uraš Gate is called Šuanna".[12] Moreover, George has been able to make a probable case for dating the origin of this landmark to the Old Babylonian period, tentatively located in the southeastern section of the city but inside, of course, the city wall of the first millennium,[13] and, in this context it is worth recalling the instruction in an Old Babylonian letter (F. R. Kraus AbB 1 60:14-18) to buy "two good sacks" at the Market Gate (KÁ GANBA = *bāb maḫīrim*). Since we know from another Old Babylonian text (CT 6 29a left edge) that the cost of

11 See Powell 1978a, 133-134.

12 George 1992, 69f. = Tintir V 92f.

13 George 1992, 18-20, 372f.

one such sack was reckoned at two-thirds shekel of silver, this makes the prospective purchase entirely within the range of mass (*i.e.*, 1.5 shekels) at which one would expect actual transfers of silver on a commercial basis (see below on this subject). The evidence assembled by the dictionaries (particularly *CAD* M/1, 98 under *bāb maḫīri*) makes it clear that market gates were a feature not only of northern Mesopotamia but also of Babylonia from the early second millennium through the Macedonian period, and, in a number of cases, they gave their names to the adjacent city quarter.

Moreover, as Röllig rightly pointed out (1976, 293), *kāru* is another term that is directly parallel to *maḫīru* in that it also denotes both an exchange rate and a place where business took place (cf. *CAD* K, 231-237; *AHw* 451f.). This is pertinent to the question whether markets existed in the third millennium. The word *kāru* is a Sumerian loan into Akkadian and denotes in both Old Assyrian and Old Babylonian a community of merchants and in Old Babylonian also the derived sense of "exchange rate" and the original Sumerian sense of embankment or harbor. It seems unlikely that these semantic developments could have taken place if at least the rudimentary paradigm of a community or concentration of merchants involved in commerce had not been present in Sumerian cities in the third millennium. The "break" between Ur III and Old Babylonian does not seem to have been as profound as sometimes assumed.

The archaeological evidence, both that from surveys and from pottery typology (*e.g.*, Adams 1981, 171), does not seem to support the picture of a radical hiatus between Ur III and Old Babylonian sometimes drawn on the basis of texts.[14] The break seems to lie in the political area, *i.e.*, initially among elites, and this does not support the assumption that merchants in the Old Babylonian period operated under entirely different conditions and motives than those in the Ur III period. Indeed, the real hiatus in Babylonia - cultural and economic, as well as political - may have begun toward the end of Samsuiluna's reign, as has been argued in a recent work which uses archaeological, textual, and astronomical evidence to posit dates about a century lower than the widely used Middle Chronology.[15]

Another Akkadian term that seems to be linked in some way with Sumerian prototypes is *bābtu*, which means both "city quarter" and "outstanding goods", and "deficit/loss" (*CAD* B, 9-14; *AHw* 94f.). While it is quite true that the relationship between "city quarter", which is certainly associated with *bābu*, "gate", and "obligation" is not entirely clear, it seems rather likely that the connection lies in some kind of commercial procedure. In any case, it is remarkable that this and similar commercial terms seem to be collectively connected to "gates", "embankments", and "streets", *i.e.*, precisely where we would suspect market activity to have taken place and where the relatively sparse evidence indeed indicates that it did.

In view of the Arabic word *sūq* that has been borrowed into a number of European languages in the meaning "market" or "bazaar", the Akkadian word *sūqu*, "street", is a likely candidate for market-related terms. W. Röllig argued in favor of this,[16] and K.R. Veenhof also called attention to it in his essay on "hungry silver" and related terms.[17] It is to Claus Wilcke, however, that we owe the most penetrating observations about this problem, and I am particularly indebted to him for pointing out to me during a discussion

---

14 Arguing for continuity: Snell 1997, 57; van de Mieroop 1987, 86f., 118f.; 1992, 241f.

15 Gasche *et al.* 1998; cf. Adams 1981 ch. 4.

16 Röllig 1975-76, 291f.

17 Veenhof 1987, 65.

of the general problem of motive and markets (January 31, 1999) that I had overlooked his comments on market streets. Since Wilcke's discussion[18] is not where most economic historians are likely to look for such information on markets, I summarize his main points here.

There are two liver omen texts from Babylon dated in a single year near the end of the reign of Samsuiluna. Both must have been discovered at the time of the German excavations at Babylon, but somehow only one wound up in Berlin, with the other finding its way into the collections at Yale. B. Landsberger (1967) knew the Yale text and recognized its commercial importance but partly misinterpreted it. F. R. Kraus, in a discussion of omen texts,[19] recognized that the Yale text and the, at that time recently published, Berlin text belonged together and evidenced an interest in profit. Wilcke points out that a person named Kurû made at least two sacrifices of lambs within 27 days in order to discover whether the omens were favorable for making profit and that the person who is so anxious to know whether he is going to make a profit must be identical with "Kurû the merchant (*tamkārum*)" attested in two other contemporary texts from Babylon. Wilcke further calls attention to the fact that the significance of these texts has not been fully recognized by the dictionaries. Both texts refer to prospective sales in the market: *ina sūqī šīmāti*, literally, "in the buying-streets", and Wilcke rightly stresses that the use of the plural points to a complex market spread out over a number of streets (Arabic *ʾaswāq*) and that *sūqī šīmāti*, "market streets", and *maḫīru*, "market", are therefore probably two terms for the same thing, as long ago suspected by K. R. Veenhof.[20] One of these texts asks whether Kurû is going to make a profit (*nēmelu*) on some kind of (gem?) stone, whereas the other asks the same about the sale of goods, "market/trade goods", *saḫirtu*, another term for which the dictionary definitions need revision.

To summarize: there is good reason to believe that both market places and markets in the sense of economic mechanisms existed in Babylonia and that they were shaped by supply and demand like contemporary markets in Anatolia. Thus, we have here one answer to J. Renger's question: where was the "niche" for money? Among merchants and in markets. Similar conclusions have been reached by M. van de Mieroop regarding the Old Babylonian city of Ur.[21]

Now, I want to be clear that I do not imagine Babylonian markets as an ancient version of Wall Street. And, to what extent we can posit the type of small goods and commestibles markets that gradually came into existence in the fifth century BC in the eastern Mediterranean after the development of low value coinage remains quite uncertain. Nevertheless, something was there, and to deny this any economic significance is as unhistorical as trying to turn a Babylonian market into the Chicago commodities exchange. Moreover, Claus Wilcke's main point about the merchant Kurû deserves emphasis: he would hardly have made the relatively expensive investments in lambs and divination if the potential for lucrative profit had not been real.[22]

This clear connection between streets and markets, together with the lack of real evidence for a fundamental break between Ur III and Old Babylonian, suggests that the

---

18 Wilcke 1990, 302-304.

19 *JCS* 37 (1985), 155.

20 Veenhof 1972, 354.

21 Van de Mieroop 1992, 188-208.

22 Wilcke 1990, 304.

concrete background of the difficult Sumerian expression sila-a gál-la, which means, more or less literally, "that which exists on the street", may lie in some kind of commercial procedure that already existed in the Ur III period. In any case, the fact that the Sumerian term is equated with not only *bābtu* but also with its closely related but not identical synonym *qīptu* seems to point to a technical meaning something on the order of this: assets which have been (by one or more customary and therefore legally binding procedures) entrusted or invested with someone and which therefore constitute a debt obligation to the investor by the party with whom the assets are invested.

The Sumerian expression seems to be linked to the similar phrase sila-a se_{12}-a, "which live (plural, animate) on the street". The verbs gál and se_{12} belong to a semantic family (suppletive paradigm) meaning broadly "live, exist, be in existence", in which gál is the inanimate component (singular and plural) and se_{12} (= SIG_7) is the plural of both human and non-human animates, with /lug/ (= LUL) and /til/ (= TI) functioning respectively as the singular animate/non-human and the singular human components.[23]

In Ur III texts, sila-a gál-la / se_{12}-a clearly mean something on the order of the "entrusted assets" implied in *bābtu/qīptu*. There were filing categories (tablet baskets) for both sila-a se_{12}-a (BRM 3 173: oxen and sheep) and sila-a gál-la (UET 3 1781: barley), and merchants also seem to have kept accounts of this type, to judge by an Ur III protocol from Umma (Nik 2 447). This interesting text and its relationship to another text (Snell 1982 no. 1) has been competently analyzed from a philological point of view by R. K. Englund,[24] but these two texts do not support Englund's argument that merchants were dependents of the state without private property but rather the opposite.

The earliest of these (Snell 1982 no. 1) is a brief balanced account compiled at the end of Amar-Suen's second year after the death of Ur-silaluḫ the merchant. The outstanding assets entrusted to the merchant consisted of the following: a first receipt of 49 gur of barley reckoned at the rate of 1.333 shekels per gur, a second receipt of 2.5 gur of barley at the rate of 1.25 shekels per gur, 22 strings of some type of figs and 26 sila of some type of apples reckoned together as worth 147.5 barleycorns of silver, plus 2 shekels of silver from another person for a total indebtedness of 71 shekels and 50 barley corns of silver. Payments to the accounting agency came to 60 shekels in silver paid directly by the merchant and documented by sealed tablets, plus 2.5 shekels of silver credited to his account for bitumen for which there was no sealed document, and 6 shekels "received" by a third party for which the merchant's account was also credited, leaving a debit balance of 2 shekels and 140 barleycorns.

There are several points worth noting before proceeding to the other text. First, what is he going to do with all that barley? He needs something over 15 cubic meters of storage space for it, and apparently he had access to considerable storage space in his market warehouse, as the other text makes clear. But beyond that: is he going to load it on a boat and send it down river or is he planning to sell it locally for a profit? The latter looks probable. Both price ratios are above the Ur III mode value of 1 shekel of silver per gur. As R. K. Englund has extensively argued,[25] the state/temple was not a charitable institution and held its creditors responsible for their debts with life and property. Why

---

23 Literature in P. Steinkeller, *ASJ* 7 (1985), 195; cf. M. Sigrist Drehem 1992 112f. and Veenhof 1987, 42 + 65 n. 4.

24 Englund 1990, 38-42.

25 Englund 1990, 42-48.

would a merchant be willing to accept barley at such high prices? Obviously because he intended to make a profit out of it. The fact that the first consignment is very large and also very pricey suggests that this consignment took place in winter when everybody was running out of barley. The second consignment which is relatively small and also cheaper suggests that it may have come close to the time of the harvest when there was less possibility of profitably disposing of it.

The other text (Nik 2 447) underscores how little the texts actually tell us about what merchants were doing. It is dated 11 months later and records the results of legal proceedings that took place in the presence of ten witnesses, the first of whom is the governor of Umma and the last the "overseer of merchants" (most of the rest are officials of one kind or another). It establishes that the wife of a man (only he is identified by name) opened the market warehouse, é ganba / *bīt maḫīri*, of Ur-silaluḫ after it had been sealed by a messenger of the governor, and further that she "opened" 45 gur of barley, 4 jugs of oil, and two tablet filing baskets, one of which contained "hand tablets" (dub šu) and the other account tablets recording outstanding assets (im dub sila-a gál-la), and further that the husband of the woman and the woman herself (never identified by name) had removed either forcibly or deceitfully (á dar) property of Ur-silaluḫ from the market warehouse of Ur-silaluḫ. The court proceeding does not refer to Ur-silaluḫ as a merchant, presumably because, being dead, he no longer is a merchant, but identification of both "property" and "market warehouse" as being "of Ur-silaluḫ" makes it likely that this Ur-silaluḫ is identical with Ur-silaluḫ the merchant who died in the previous year. These seem to be the only published texts that record his merchant activity. That the property mentioned is private, *i.e.*, not state or temple capital, is indicated by absence of remarks typifying seizure by the state of property to which it had a right as owner or creditor that have recently been discussed by W. Heimpel (1997).

These two texts relating to the merchant Ur-silaluḫ encapsule in a nutshell the problems we face in trying to interpret merchant activity in the Ur III period. Unanswered, if my theory about the reason for the prices and sizes of the barley consignments is correct, is: why are there still 45 gur of barley in the merchant's market warehouse? Perhaps the reason is that the merchant died a month or so before the end of the year Amar-Su'en 2, and the actions of the woman and her husband took place immediately after his death. But then one has the problem of explaining why the court proceeding is not recorded until 11 months into the next year. Moreover, Lu-Nanna the overseer of merchants seems to be otherwise unattested in surviving documents, unless he happens to be identical with Lu-Nanna the merchant who appears in another court proceeding some ten years later.[26] Obviously, if our records were even minimally adequate, we would have some information about such an important person in the Umma merchant community.

There are innumerable questions about merchant activity in the Ur III period for which the evidence provides no answers, but the protocol text shows, as one would expect, that merchants also kept records of their own business. The precise nature of the distinction between dub šu and im dub sila-a gál-la cannot be established, but the latter probably refers to *bābtu*/*qīptu* type of debts owed to the merchant. It is also worth emphasizing in this context that these records were obviously kept by the merchant in his é ganba / *bīt maḫīri*, "market warehouse". This does not support the arguments of those

26 A. Falkenstein, *NG* II no. 62.

who claim that é ganba is merely a storehouse, deny any connection between é ganba and markets, and ignore the fact that ganba (KI.LAM) is the Sumerogram for *maḫīrum* "market, market-rate, market-place". It is obviously also a place of business. Moreover, in his symposium paper, M. Stol called attention to an unpublished Old Babylonian tablet in Philadelphia which mentions purchase of an é ganba of ca. 108 square meters followed by the purchase of another three times as large (*i.e.*, ca. 324 square meters) bordering on the property of the overseer of the merchants and located near the Gate of Šamaš, from which he rightly concludes that this sounds like a marketplace. Noteworthy also are the sizes of these properties, which are large for urban real estate in the Old Babylonian period. M. van de Mieroop has made similar arguments, partly on the basis of archaeological evidence, for the existence of a market center in Old Babylonian Ur.[27]

Whether the expression sila-a gál-la means that we also have to look for a commercial significance in the name of the third Umma month in Ur III, iti še kar-ra gál-la, "month that barley is on the embankment" cannot be determined for lack of contextual occurrences, but the possibility cannot be excluded.

3. *Money*

To turn now to the question of what constituted money (I am not going into how one defines it again, as I have said all that can reasonably be said on that point in Powell 1996), silver seems to have been the primary money of Babylonia from the mid-third millennium on except for the end of the Bronze Age, when it is temporarily replaced by gold.[28] It must be emphasized, however, that the published sources for this period remain sparse and do not represent a good geographical sample. Gold may have been more accessible in this period, since the large amounts of gold discovered in Mycenaean context in the eastern Mediterranean contrasts sharply with previous eras. Problematic, however, is that the basic price ratio of gold to silver does not seem to be much different than in preceding eras (see below).

In two of my previous papers (1990, 1996), I have made the point that cheap metal monies (tin, bronze or copper, and lead) came very close to forming, along with silver, a pre-coinage money system in northern Mesopotamia. K. Radner in her symposium contribution assembled lots of evidence for the Assyrian Empire which resembles the picture in Babylonia in that silver is pretty clearly the primary money throughout, but metals are more important in Assyrian context and in some cases payment in silver is accompanied by other cheap metal money. In Babylonia, on the other hand, for some centuries from about mid-third millennium (Fara to Akkad period) bronze or copper functioned like a cheap money. This is mostly attested in the land sale and quasi legal documents.[29] Copper or bronze seems to have gone out of use as money by the Ur III period, being replaced by barley,[30] which remains the primary low value money, though occasionally dates show a similar function in the Neo-Babylonian period. It is important to note that the price equivalencies in the Laws of Eshnunna are not necessarily to be

27 Van de Mieroop 1992, 188-190.

28 Powell 1990, 93f.

29 Gelb *et al.* 1991, chapter 8 + plates 87-166; see now Wilcke 1996 with literature.

30 Cf. Steinkeller 1989, 92-97 on weighing silver and pages 133-138 on prices in barley and silver.

interpreted as evidence for the use of bronze as a money in the sense that silver and, to a lesser degree, barley functioned as money but are probably intended as guidelines for judges in assessing fines or payments, and that these equivalencies have nothing to do with the "abundance encomia".[31]

In Babylonia, rather than calling barley (or dates) a cheap money, it would perhaps be better to say that it functioned like a cheap money, because the evidence as a whole points to silver as the ultimate standard of liquidity. Nor do I imagine people hauling around baskets of barley on their heads to buy a few heads of garlic. J. Renger's point that a substantial number of the inhabitants got some (and in some cases perhaps all) of their necessities from the large estates (temple or palace) with which they were associated and that some got these from their own production is something that I think most of us agree on. What remains quite uncertain is how much of the necessities were provided for in this way.

A small independent farmer raising barley is not necessarily going to be in the position to raise and process sesame. Where did they get their oil from? This is one of the key dark areas in Renger's theory, because, particularly in the case of oil, we have no evidence that all requirements for oil could be met without some type of market exchange. In this context, it is worth recalling that four storage jars of oil, probably each about the size of an amphora (*i.e.*, in the 30 liter range) were part of the deceased merchant Ur-silaluḫ's property that were "opened" by the woman in the Ur III court proceeding. The same is true of cloth (wool). We simply do not have in any era documentation that would permit us to assert that all of these needs are covered by institutional mechanisms or by self production.

A good case is beer, which is especially interesting, because it relates to the problem of how things were paid for and how the money system functioned. I have already discussed some aspects of this,[32] and Mesopotamian specialists are familiar with the evidence as a whole, but let me just repeat the essence of it. Paragraph 108 of the Laws of Hammurabi (cf. R. Borger TUAT I/1, 55) regulating tavern keepers prescribes that a tavern keeper ("alewife") who is convicted of refusing to accept barley in payment for beer and collecting silver from her customer by using a weight stone that is above standard weight and thereby cheating him is to be "thrown into the water".

There are several points of interest here. First, this is a clear case where someone did not get all one wanted or needed via "redistributive" mechanisms. Second, one can see why the tavern keeper might not want barley. She may have enough already to do her malting, and, if it is summer after the harvest, she will have to store it until the temperature drops low enough to do malting in the fall. So, cash is called for. However, there is a third aspect to this that I discussed in trying to deal with the problem of standards. The Laws of Hammurabi obviously do not presuppose the existence of a standards bureau and an enforcement police. What it legislates against is using a heavier weight stone to measure the customer's silver so that the tavern keeper gets proportionately more silver than she would have gotten if grain had been measured out. In other words, it is presupposed that the going rate (*maḫīru*) for beer in both barley and silver is common knowledge to both tavern keeper and customer. She, however, insists on silver. In this case, the deceit probably consisted of putting, let us say, a half-shekel stone in the balance

31 Powell 1990, 82, 93.

32 Powell 1979, 83-86.

pan instead of, say, a one-third shekel (or more likely at some lower unit of mass). This could have easily happened in Old Babylonian transactions, because the vast majority of small weights are not marked at all, and it is probably what is implied in the expression *aban kīsi šutēnû*, "to switch the stone of the bag" (attested in participle form in the great hymn to Shamash: Lambert 1960, 132:108). The parallel law ("P": R. Borger TUAT I/1, 54) regulating similar crimes by merchants may refer to two sets of weights and measuring vessels.

These laws also have a bearing on the problem of how and how much and how frequently silver passed from hand to hand in Babylonian society. That the laws exist shows that some silver at least did circulate in this way in Old Babylonian times despite the inherent possibilities for fraud. And to judge by the substantial number of lines devoted to merchants and commerce - about ten per cent - in the great hymn to Shamash,[33] the phenomenon of money and buying and selling cannot have been as uncommon as the redistribution-reciprocity theorists would have us believe.

This is not to say that buying and selling by weight did not entail some problems. The smallest weight stone that I have seen and weighed is a tiny duck in the Oriental Institute (Chicago), which has a mass of only 0.2923 gram,[34] but the Babylonians obviously thought they could measure to finer degrees of accuracy, since the basic lexical series that deals with material culture and economic matters records a weight-stone series going from a talent (ca. 30 kg.) to one-third barleycorn, which is only about 0.015 gram.[35] The heaviest surviving weight from Babylonia is the two-talent duck weight (60555 grams; cf. Powell 1971, 249) of Ur-Ningirsu, ensi of Lagash, who presumably ruled one or two generations before the beginning of the Ur III period. Its mass incorporates a norm that is virtually identical with the shekel norm on which the Persian daric was based, but it is important to keep in mind that in any group of weights from any era, one will inevitably find significant deviations in mass in all units lower than the shekel, and the margin of error rises, not unexpectedly, as the mass decreases, which is a general rule in weights of all sizes.

Based on calculation of standard deviation in Old Babylonian precision weights, I postulated (Powell 1979, 82f.) that the margin of error in small weights was about three per cent of the total mass. At the mass of a shekel, this would amount to about a day's pay in silver, so it is obvious that exchange of cheap commodities or small amounts of commodities for silver is not something to be expected. However, once the mass rises to the level of a shekel, which for Old Babylonian times represented a month's pay, the inhibitions to buy something for silver are naturally going to be less. After all, a month's pay was not a small amount of money, and someone who could fork out that amount had their eye on whatever it was they wanted and the value of the intended purchase to them. I do not think, therefore that inaccuracies in the weighing system would inhibit those who could afford to buy something for a shekel or more. But I also think that these were a rather small minority of the total population, and, consequently, as I have said repeatedly (since Powell 1979, 86f.), I cannot imagine silver circulating from hand to hand on a daily basis throughout the whole populace - including rural areas - in the Old Babylonian period or in any later period. That, however, is not the same thing as saying that its role in

33 Lambert 1960, 122f. + 132-135; cf. Hallo 1992, 355f.

34 Powell 1979, 107.

35 J. G. Westenholz, *MSL* 10 (1970), 49-50.

the economy was insignificant, and I think that is the main point on which not only I but a lot of other Mesopotamian specialists disagree with J. Renger.

When one turns to the problem of balances, one is, by contrast with weight specimens, faced with an almost complete lack of evidence. We do not, in fact possess any intact surviving balances from ancient Mesopotamia, and they are relatively rare from antiquity as a whole, though a considerable number of steelyards has survived from the Roman period.[36] It is therefore not possible to actually control the accuracy of Mesopotamian balances, but, as I have just said, deviation in the weight specimens themselves indicates that balances as a whole weighed more accurately where heavier masses were concerned. The two-talent weight of Ur-Ningirsu referred to above is evidence that balances capable of weighing this substantial mass already existed before the end of the third millennium.

Only two representations of balances from Mesopotamia are known to me, both Assyrian (9th/8th century), and show the weighing of prismatic and spherically shaped ingots. Thus, the material evidence for balances (both illustrated in K. Radner's symposium contribution) has not changed much since F. Delitzsch published a composite drawing of them in his popular booklet *Handel und Wandel*.[37] There is also a Syro-Hittite relief in the Louvre of unknown provenance showing a merchant holding in his right hand a balance and carrying in his left what must be the leather bag in which merchants transported their weight stones and also their silver.[38]

That Assyrian balances were capable of weighing masses as heavy as the two-talent duck weight of Ur-Ningrisu mentioned above is indicated in a letter (ABL 292) sent by Ashurbanipal to the governor and people of Nippur in which he urges them to capture an enemy and promises to put him in a balance (*ina zibānīti*) and to use him as a counterweight to measure (*ḫâṭu*) his weight in gold and give it to whomever killed or delivered the enemy, just as Sennacherib had done in silver for capture of another enemy. Moreover, the two-talent duck weight of Ur-Ningirsu shows that this capability must have been in existence already in the third millennium. Balances and their parts are treated in ten entries in the lexical series ḪAR-ra = *ḫubullu*,[39] but, like many technical terms, most of them are somewhat obscure, with the exception of the terms for balance itself (giš.erin$_2$/*gišrinnu*) and balance pans (dilim/*itqurtu*). The question, therefore, of how old weighing was in Mesopotamia is not easily answered: neither the archaeological nor textual evidence is sufficient. However, for what it is worth, the earliest clearly reconizable weights, which are shaped a bit like a pair of sheep testicles and are pierced at the top for attaching to the arm of the balance, seem to come from around the mid-third millennium or a bit later. The only published one is inscribed "mana of wool rations: Dudu the sanga" and weighs 680.485 grams.[40] The heavy norms, special norms for wool, and the fact that the weights are pierced may imply an early stage in systematic weighing, and therefore would fit with the fact that our first evidence for systematic

---

36 Kisch 1965; Skinner 1967; Powell 1971, 182-184.

37 F. Delitzsch, *Handel und Wandel in Altbabylonien* (Stuttgart 1910), 30-33.

38 *CAD* K, 430-432; A. Salonen, *Hausgeräte der alten Mesopotamier* (1965), 191f. + pl. XCVII; J. B. Pritchard, *ANEP*, fig. 117 + p. 263 = Louvre AO 19221 / 9th century; Kisch 1965, 29-31 fig. 3.

39 *MSL* 6, 60f.; Powell 1971, 238-242.

40 Langdon, *JRAS* (1921), 575-577; Powell 1971, 255, and note that this Dudu is distinct from the later Dudu, also sanga, with a mina of 497.5, contrary to Powell's assumption on page 198.

weighing and paying in metals comes from the Fara period. About all one can presently say is that it is there by about mid-third millennium, and textual evidence reveals a progressively refined system with fractions of the shekel (one-sixth, one-third, one-half, etc.) evolving into practically the equivalent of monetary units by the Akkad period.[41]

4. *The Great Estates and Mesopotamian Economy*

I think it is safe to say that from its first securely attested appearance in the third millennium, money was always important in all segments of the economy. Naturally, the picture we get from the economy of the great estates is different, but, as G. van Driel emphasized in his symposium contribution, they, too, needed and used money. After all, we should expect this: they probably owed their origins and certainly their continued survival to economic factors as much as to any set of socio-cultural factors.

These great estates seem to go back into the fourth millennium, so there is little chance that one will ever have the kind of evidence necessary to reconstruct their origins except in the most general sort of way. However, wherever one can more or less see what they are doing in later periods, their organizational principle is fundamentally self interest, and wealth is shared by the elite in these institutions only insofar as unavoidable custom and economic necessity demands. There is no reason to expect it to be otherwise: their size and success is probably to be attributed primarily to economic causes.

Agriculture was the basic economic activity in ancient Babylonia. Independent subsistence farming, which can be carried on by a relatively small group of people under dry farming conditions, was not a viable option in Babylonia. Annual rainfall in Babylonia today varies widely from about 50 to 150 milliliters. Most of it comes in the planting-growing season (roughly November-March), but actual precipitation varies greatly. Rain could not be depended upon even to provide enough moisture for germination, which had to be done artificially by damming a channel of the river or of a major canal to raise the water level, and sufficient water for maturation of the crop had to be supplied. This cannot be done independently, and responsibility for control fell naturally to the temples and later to the crown. The same is true of flood control in the spring.

Moreover, Babylonia was characterized by monoculture. The ubiquitous dependence upon barley is one of the reasons it comes to function like money. Diversification is extremely difficult in a monocultural agricultural regime that is absolutely dependent upon irrigation. Indeed, evidence for diversification comes only from the large estates. The bulk of the agricultural population seems to have raised and consumed primarily barley.

All small holdings are somewhat unstable in an agricultural economy and the degree of instability rises with the tendency toward monoculture, because monoculture increases the risk of failure and starvation. Large estates like the temples in ancient Babylonia were, in spite of their own dependence on grain agriculture, more "diversified" because some of their lands had a chance of a making a crop even in a very bad year. They could also undertake a late fall planting, or a summer planting of sesame or millet. And they had much more extensive storage options and could if need be ride out a difficult year or even

41 Powell 1989-90, 508-517.

several. These factors favor ownership of agricultural land by large economic entities and tenancy rather than ownership among individual farmers.

This also explains why land appears to be cheap. Agricultural land is valuable precisely for that: agriculture. The value of the potential crop determines the value of the land. This is one reason we see so little evidence of private ownership of farmland in ancient Babylonia: there is not much point in owning it unless one is able to cultivate it on a regular basis.

Moreover, labor is a major problem for all agricultural regimes that operate under conditions of low level technology, in any case, outside of the tropics. Successful farmers in the United States are usually overcapitalized in machinery. Modern farm machinery has a very high relative cost because of the limited period during which it is used. Successful agricultural regimes in antiquity, on the other hand, tended to be overcapitalized in labor - whether in slaves or dependent tenants. The reason for both phenomena is at bottom the same: all agricultural regimes have optimum periods in which certain things must be done as quickly as possible to maximize success. Lack of labor, a broken plow, lack of oxen - all these blueprints for disaster were avoided with relative ease by large estates but not by small, independent farmers. Even where subsistence agriculture could be practiced - not a viable long-term option in Babylonia - survival demanded constant preparation. Here the voice of wisdom is Hesiod.

It is therefore natural that the great estates dominated the economy in Babylonia. This is a far cry, however, from saying that they control everything directly or that they are the only significant economic factor in the society. The precise relationship between any particular individual and the temple or crown is impossible to reconstruct fully, not only because we never have all of the once existing documentation but also because it is quite certain that even if we did have it there would still be vast blank areas due to the principle enunciated by Miguel Civil of not recording the obvious. It is assumed here as a methodological principle that the data about prices and the like that stem from the accounting procedures of the temple and palace must be taken seriously and evaluated on their merits in each individual case. In other words, the prices that we see, even in the Ur III temple/palace records, reflect some underlying economic reality and are not simply imposed without concern for quality or supply and demand. Having stated this methodological principle, which cannot in my opinion be refuted by the textual evidence, let us turn to a consideration of the problem of money "purity".

5. *The Problem of Purity and Forms of Money*

If the just stated premise were not true, there would be no point whatever in discussing money itself, to say nothing of its purity. Even so, assessing the "purity" of silver (or any other metal money) in any particular situation where it functions as money is, in most cases, an intractable problem. The reasons behind this are similar to those that have occasioned such differing reconstructions of merchant activity: the texts never tell us all we need to know. I have called attention in my last paper to the possible existence of systematic alloying in the Chaldean and Persian periods.[42] How radically different the problem appears when one or two key assumptions are changed will become apparent

42 Powell 1996, 232f.

when we come to consider P. Vargyas's new theory about silver in the early Achaemenid period (see below). For earlier periods, the extensive collection of evidence by Karin Reiter (1997) now enables us to get a better grasp of the problem, but in most cases defining the quality or purity of metals used as money remains difficult.

As an example of the possibilities and limitations imposed upon us by our sources, the evidence for gold is well suited. The only usable criterion for the purity of gold is its price in silver, whereby one can already see that we can never come entirely free of circular reasoning. Gold prices in Babylonia prior to the Ur III period are extremely rare, but it is worth noting that one text explicitly states the ratio as being 1 shekel of gold to 8 of silver and moreover transforms "one-third mina minus one-third shekel of gold" into "two and a half minas seven and one-third shekels of silver" (ITT 2 4647). I am now inclined to believe that this is very close to the "standard" rate for "pure" gold and "pure" silver throughout most of the Bronze Age. This may sound strange, considering that silver:gold price ratios running from about 2:1 to 21:1 are attested,[43] however, let us first consider the Kassite evidence before trying to deal with the problem of what the wide spread of gold equivalencies means.

Thanks to K. Reiter's discussion of "red gold" and "bright/silvery gold",[44] a plausible explanation of the same Kassite terms, kug.gi sa_5 versus kug.gi babbar can be attempted. The Kassite silver ratios with "red" and "silvery" gold were 8:1 and 4:1, and, as I pointed out in my paper on long-term price trends, the 8:1 ratio seems to represent pure gold to pure silver, being near the top of the range for gold values throughout the Bronze Age.[45] I was unable, however, to propose a solution for the 4:1 value of "silvery gold". Reiter's study of the problem now allows the reasonable postulate that "silvery gold" represents a consciously intended alloy of silver and gold. The problem then becomes: 1. what are the percentages of silver and gold in the alloy? and 2. how would the ancient metallurgist have approached the problem using contemporary units of mass? If we proceed from the given that 1 shekel of gold = 8 of silver, then each one-eighth shekel of gold would correspond to one shekel of silver, and determination of the alloying ratio in "silvery" gold becomes a matter of calculating how much pure gold and pure silver must go into one shekel in order for it to equal four shekels in pure silver. This must, however, agree with the metrological system (summarized in Powell 1989-90, 511-513), because alloying presupposes actual measurement rather than just reckoning. The closest one can approximate these ratios in Babylonian terms is this:

pure gold		buys	pure silver
10 *girû* =	75 še		3 šql + 60 še
+	2.5 še		20 še
pure silver		buys	pure silver
13 *girû* =	97.5 še		97.5 še
+	2.5 še		2.5 še
total weight:			
23 2/3 *girû* = 177.5 še			3 šql + 180 še
(= 1 šql minus 2.5 še)			(= 4 šql exactly)

43 Now easily accessible in Reiter 1997, 19-35.

44 Reiter 1997, 36-42, 53-59.

45 Powell 1990, 80f. + n. 43.

As one can see, the shekel of alloy is missing 2.5 barleycorns. One would expect that a self-interested moneyer would not fill up the missing weight with gold but rather with silver. We cannot, however, be sure about such things, even if the theory underlying this reconstruction is essentially correct. One might also have built the whole system on the basis of the *girû*, "carat", and figured 11 carats of gold to 13 of silver, which is a richer alloy than the one sketched out above. On the other hand, it could have been 10 gold to 14 silver. There is no way to decide such questions, because we have no way of controlling what was going on. Much finer approximations of the 1:4, gold:silver, ratio are possible if alloys were calculated at the mina or talent range of mass. In any case, the precise 2:1 ratio between "silvery" gold and pure gold in Kassite texts makes it clear that we have got to reckon with the possibility of consciously produced alloys that served for money.

To what degree this was also the case in earlier eras is impossible to say. However, I must repeat that the fine distinctions that occur in Ur III texts cannot be explained as fineness grades, because there was no way for ancient technology to distinguish such minute differences in quality without destroying the objects in question.[46] They have to represent "added value", and as I have also said in my study of price trends,[47] while labor costs were relatively low, nothing in the textual record justifies assuming, because one particular account document seems to equate wool with cloth, or bread with flour or barley, that they were in fact treated as equal, unless one can exclude compensation somewhere else. This is the problem of trying to analyze the temple and palace economies in a nutshell: we can never reconstruct the whole situation. K. Reiter has arrived at similar conclusions.[48]

So what do we do about the "purity" problem? At the moment, the best thing is to keep an open mind and try to figure out what is going on. How profoundly all of our assumptions can be affected by the change in one key assumption is illustrated in a brilliant piece of historical detective work by P. Vargyas to be published soon in the *Zeitschrift für Assyriologie*. Since Vargyas's theory has such profound implications for the whole array of issues discussed at the Leiden symposium, I summarize here his main points that pertain to money in Babylonia: 1. *kaspu ginnu*, "*ginnu*-silver" is indentical with *kaspu peṣû ša ina ištēn šiqli bitqa*, "white silver in which there is one *bitqu* (= one-eighth part alloy) per shekel", and both of these are names for the early Achaemenid silver sigloi! 2. Introduction of this begins only under Cyrus, when there was apparently, a prohibition against melting down or cutting them up in the way that silver transactions had been carried out for centuries. 3. Darius abandoned this policy and used the sigloi as propaganda. 4. *kaspu lā ginnu* "silver which is not *ginnu*", probably refers to Greek, *i.e.*, non-Achaemenid coins, and represents the same purity, *i.e.*, .875 fine.

The most persuasive aspect of Vargyas's theory is that it enables us to make sense of the evidence. As I pointed out in my last paper,[49] Xenophon and the Greek soldiers who went to Babylonia with Cyrus the Younger in 401 BC must have used coins to pay for their purchases. Moreover, Xenophon likewise attests the existence of market mechanisms: in the region around Assur, enterprising Mesopotamians were even willing to transport the commodities across the river! When one considers the implications of

---

46 See already Powell 1990, 80f.

47 Powell 1990, 81f. n. 17.

48 Reiter 1997, 26-29.

49 Powell 1996, 234.

crossing over to sell wine and food to an army of ten thousand Greek soldiers, it will be apparent that the "capitalist" motives so apparent in Old Assyrian documents were still alive and well.

This is exactly as we should expect. It has long been known from the fragmentary Babylonian chronicle describing the troubled years following the murder of Seleukos I in 280 B.C., that Greek copper (bronze) coins were used in Babylon to transact business, presumably as a result of the scarcity of silver due to the extraordinary taxes imposed by Antiokhos I.[50] The term for coin is *zīpu* (*zeʾpu*), and it is instructive about how much cuneiform texts hide from us that this usage is not attested prior to the Seleucid period. Like markets, coinage was there before the Greeks. Neither are mentioned, because it was not necessary to state the obvious. Besides, the only significant difference that coinage makes in money transactions is the guarantee of quality: in Babylonia, as elsewhere, silver coins were cut up just like other silver and put in the balance pan. P. Vargyas's paper brings a lot of additional arguments in favor of this theory that I have long advocated[51] and which is now increasingly assumed for the early stages of Mediterranean coinage.

We may conclude by discussing a case from the early Achaemenid period which illustrates how profoundly the correct or incorrect definition of one element can clarify or distort the rest of the picture. Two texts dating to the last year of Cambyses (year 7, perh. month 8, day 26: Hecker Giessen 47) and the first month of Bardiya/Smerdis (Strassmaier *ZA* 4, 123ff. Sm. 2) connect Itti-Marduk-balāṭu of the Egibi family and Marduk-šuma-uṣur, one of his business associates, with the town of Humadēšu in southwestern Iran.[52] The earlier of these (Hecker Giesen 47) records the transfer by Marduk-šuma-uṣur of 12 minas of "white silver of which there is a *bitqu* in each shekel" and specifies that Itti-Marduk-balāṭu will deliver (perhaps 3 months later) to Marduk-šuma-uṣur's brother in Babylon "this silver, 12 minas, 12 *šibirtu* (kug.PAD.DU) of 1 mina each".

Looking at these descriptions of silver without the perspective introduced by Vargyas's identification of *kaspu ginnu* with silver coins and further with an alloy of "3 *girû*/carats", one is almost doomed to conclude that *šibirtu*, which should mean "broken up", actually denotes an ingot of some sort.[53] However, the context of this text and the closely related text dated perhaps five months later to Smerdis 1, both of which were written in the same Iranian town, clearly show this cannot be the case. If the *šibirtu* had been composed of scrap silver collected here and there, it would require an incredibly complex para-theory to explain how all of it could be defined by the same purity grade. Clearly, Vargyas is right: these are coins, and, moreover, the twelve *šibirtu* of one mina each are likewise not ingots but coins that have been weighed and put into twelve bags and sealed up. What was this profitable business that took an old man like Itti-Marduk-balāṭu off to southwestern Iran, hundreds of miles away from Babylon? Doubtless the motive was some lucrative business, but, in any case, part of it had to do with the slave trade in women.[54]

---

50 Smith 1924, 150-159.

51 Powell 1978b, 217-219.

52 R. Zadok, *RGTC* 8 (1985), 165: perhaps 130 km. southeast of Shiraz.

53 Cf. Powell 1996, 237.

54 Cf. Camb 388 and M. Dandamaev, *Slavery in Babylonia* (1984), 197 + 353f.

One more related example of how minor misperceptions can distort the whole picture. In Tiglath-Pileser I's account of the revolt and submission of Milidia/Melitene, he says: "one 'ass' of lumps of lead as tribute, year after year without stopping, I fixed for them".[55] One will naturally come to rather curious conclusions about the shape of these "lumps" (*kirbānu*) if one does not realize that an "ass" is a volumetric measure, probably to be read *amaru* (the reading amar is probable in Ur III and even earlier texts), and used for a pile of bricks. In a nutshell: getting at the "forms" in which metals changed hands is not easy.

To sum up: money played an important role in the economy of ancient Babylonia, and there is good reason to believe that this goes well back into the third millennium. Profit motives are clearly attested in the Old Babylonian evidence, and there is no reason to think that the third millennium was radically different. Silver was the money par excellence from the mid-third millennium onward, and, as in the early centuries of coinage in the Mediterranean, silver was weighed rather than counted. To what extent markets served the function of economic distribution is difficult to determine due to the lacunae in the records and the fact that the cuneiform documents never tell us many things that were simply assumed by them. The new theory of P. Vargyas, which identifies silver containing three carats of alloy with early Achaemenid sigloi not only solves an extremely difficult problem with elegance (as the mathematicians say) but also is an eloquent testimony to the difficulties we face in trying to recreate the real world of ancient Mesopotamia.

55 See Reiter 1997, 143 for literature.

CAPITAL FORMATION AND INVESTMENT IN AN INSTITUTIONAL CONTEXT IN ANCIENT MESOPOTAMIA

G. VAN DRIEL (LEIDEN)

I. *Introduction*

The commissioning title carries an implicit statement and there is little sense in attempting to escape from the consequences by proclaiming that this hidden assertion is anachronistic. Whether "capital" or "investment" are terms applicable to Ancient Mesopotamia is questionable, although, it will be argued, defensible, provided the context is not lost out of sight. In order to develop a more realistic discussion the word "asset" will often be used instead of "capital".[1] It seems more appropriate in a world where land, people, tools, seed, and herds of cattle and sheep constituted not only the principal forms of capital, but were also, in themselves, the primary objects of investment.[2]

Rightly or wrongly, the proposition to be explored is that Ancient Mesopotamian institutions purposefully accumulated, perhaps created, capital in order to invest. If no direct answer can be obtained, an indirect approach becomes unavoidable.

1. *The Institutions*

The Mesopotamian institutions are the Palace and the Temple, - in which we follow A.L. Oppenheim - and we can continue with the suggestion that these institutions can be represented in the shape of households, - in which we follow I.J. Gelb.

Both types of institution appear in recognisable form towards the end of Prehistory in the Southern alluvium. Their emergence is as yet incompletely understood but probably went through a long period of development, made possible because the stage of simple subsistence production had been left behind by a number of Mesopotamian societies already in the fourth millennium. At any rate in Eridu, an obvious temple has been excavated which can be traced back to virtually the first period from which settled life in

---

1 . Two ordinary dictionary entries, which usually are helpful, indicate that in this case such definitions are of limited value. "Capital" is:
a. *Webster's New Twentieth Century Dictionary*, 2nd Edition (1974), 268: *Money or wealth used in trade, in manufacture or in any business.* This translates in our case as "wealth used in an (agrarian) institutional context for agrarian ends", which is next to meaningless.
b.. *Concise Oxford Dictionary*, 5th Edition (1964), 177: *Accumulated wealth used in producing more.* This excludes the investing in security, hoarding, both material and immaterial, which I presume to be an important aspect of Mesopotamian institutional accumulation of wealth.
It is in any case gratifying to note that both definitions use the concept "wealth", which encompasses the concept "assets" which I prefer to "capital" in the "practical" sphere.

2 The other main assets, barley, dates and wool constituted both vital sustenance, essential reserves and, with silver, liquid capital.

the alluvium is at present known. In Uruk, seal impressions of around 3000 BC depict a person who behaves like a prince in cult, war and hunt. This is not sufficient for a confident claim that temple and palace were separate institutions, with separate purposes, around 3000 BC. The prince has an obvious cultic role. That the institutions, or the society in which they had come into existence produced a surplus, had certain means to invest, is, however, beyond doubt.

I will at any rate avoid speculation about the period before the Fara texts, around the middle of the third millennium, and will concentrate on evidence from the periods and text groups which are better known and reasonably accessible. In all documented cases in Ancient Mesopotamia both types of institution work in tandem. In fact, from the moment we can understand the texts, the temple is economically spoken a tool of the local ruler and, later on, of the central government.

When we reach the period with "understandable information" the institutions operate in such a way that their assets serve the purposes of the local prince and his retinue, in which the necessities required for the cult are an essential element of the political and economic system. As far as we can see it makes little practical difference whether the goddess Bau or the princely spouse Šaša is the (nominal) head of the Emi in Pre-Sargonic Lagaš.

Indeed much of the (known) agrarian production takes place in institutions organised as religious households. These households are organised into regional blocks, which in the Ur III period are, if not being exploited, at least managed by central organisations for central purposes. Though we have been conditioned into regarding the Akkad hegemony as the first recognisable supra-regional system of this type of extraction, there is no reason to suppose that there were no earlier attempts at such types of exploitation. If the city-state is regarded as a phase through which all Southern political-religious systems had to go, Lagaš (as a territorial "state") is a typical, relatively well-documented, example where such a system had stabilised into one containing several sub-systems managed by a central authority, which, in the Ur III period could be used to tap local resources by influencing the institutional use of assets, especially as regards land and manpower. In other "states" the same will have been the case, though on a different scale.

From the start of our "usable" documentation the "household" in which our "formation of capital" takes place is therefore organised institutionally to extract this "capital" for central purposes. To put it crudely, "capital" created locally finances a central superstructure. On its own, Mesopotamia never managed to create a single unified system. Only the Achaemenids succeeded in subjugating, perhaps even integrating,[3] the subsystems effectively into parts of a single organisation, which, if we can believe Herodotus, was very effective in creaming off the capital the system was able to create. In a sense, the political history of Ancient Mesopotamia could be taken as the tale of the growth of a system which, to the benefit of the central authority siphons off the surplus created not only by the documented institutions, but, of course, also by other, less well-known, means. That a politically independent Mesopotamia could not effectively create such a unified system on its own must have a bearing on the Ancient Mesopotamian economy. This constitutes an important difference with Egypt.

---

3 The participation of Southern institutions in the rearing of sheep in the Syrian-Mesopotamian steppe zone dates back at least to Chaldean times.

We must add that already in the (late) third millennium BC there are signs that these institutional households have begun a process of hiving off departments, which acquire a more or less independent position and no longer possess the essential autarkic characteristics of a household in that they do not produce their own sustenance.[4] Non-household, but institutional, are types of "military" organisation in which the members receive land for service and other obligations, though this can be combined with partial maintenance by a central institution.[5] In a certain sense the system invests in communications and other services and in the specialised production which is required for the diplomatic and honorific "giving of gifts" and which also serves military requirements. At least by 2000 BC the institutional system had grown to a size which compelled it to invest in communications and crafts production, but the process started much earlier to all probability. The household model is out-moded by this time. This will not be elaborated here.

Though, especially by the late period, but not exclusively so, people could participate as sleeping partners in commercial associations not only in trade, but also in production, this possibility requires no elaboration in the institutional sphere proper as there are no signs of it. Similar involvement of private persons in a type of rent farm as known in the Neo-Babylonian period, and in the margins of the institutions, in the production of those products required from certain prebendaries, could be envisaged for earlier periods. Investment in trained slaves employed in this type of production certainly occurred. I will, however, restrict myself to the institutions proper. Involvement of outsiders in institutional matters is less a sign of strength than one of a structural inability to realise the best possible exploitation of assets available with internal means.

My point is that from the later third millennium onwards, Mesopotamian institutions, if they created capital (that is: knew how to obtain a share in the surplus produced), did so not for their own purposes alone, but were primarily elements in a much larger system, that could easily be beheaded and redirected. The Mesopotamian institution, palace or temple, already in the third millennium and possibly earlier, does not work as a household which serves its own ends, it is an organisation which serves outside purposes. This service is done with all the available assets, but the means used were obviously not very efficient. This implies that a share of the wealth created was dissipated in gathering and

---

4 I am thinking of the Ur III post stations. They were funded by the organisation led by the ensi in Lagaš and Umma and were not self-supporting. The organisations from which the Ur and Isin crafts archives derive constitute a similar case. The possibility that similar separate institutional departments existed earlier should be considered. The existence of special weaving establishments with additional personnel for the finishing of the products within household confines is an important first step towards specialisation, milling is a less skilled occupation. As the personnel made available to these establishments is constantly being used for other types of work, especially in agriculture and for transport, I prefer to regard the weaving and milling establishments as an organisational devise which made a more intensive use of (female) labour feasible, rather than that we are dealing in these cases with non-household organisations proper.

Ur III Drehem is also a special "institution", the outlines of which are not very clear to me, but which I would not primarily regard as a household. It, at any rate, does not seem to produce its own sustenance.

5 *E.g.* military personnel being fed "from the king's table" during a tour of duty, cf. also, in another context, the Emi personnel receiving rations during part of the year only as in texts of type I-A-1 of Selz 1989, 40.

forwarding it: palace and temple *Geschäfte* in the Old Babylonian period and "rent farm" in the Neo-Babylonian period are relatively well-known. Perhaps it is possible to put a certain "economic gloss" on this phenomenon by claiming that stimulation of the "private sector" will have been a positive aspect of a process which in essence meant that a huge slice of the results of all productive efforts ended up in a few hands.

As has been argued above, already in the third millennium the institutions were in general not free agents, but increasingly became the executive organs of a centralising monarchy which operated on a regional or country-wide basis. This fact is of major importance for our subject.

If we can speak of policies, these policies are imposed from above, as is reasonably clear for both the Ur III institutions and the Neo-Babylonian "temples".

2. *The General Economic and Social Setting*

In the situation in which the Mesopotamian economy found itself, it was difficult to escape from the regular agrarian risks imposed by weather and pests. Hoarding is therefore more, or at least something else, than the purposeless accumulation of unused capital: it is an absolute necessity for the stable existence of the institution and of the society in which it operates. We also used to have our strategic reserves. Accumulation of reserves is an essential element of (useful) capital formation. Proposing this point is, however, easier than delivering actual proof of an established policy, amazing though it may sound, at any rate concerning the ordinary agricultural products. If we are to discuss the question of investments it would be helpful if we could distinguish between an innate automatic inclination to hoard and a considered, purposeful accumulation of reserves. If this is already difficult, or rather impossible, the accumulation of capital with the intent to invest for the purpose of increasing profits becomes even more difficult to demonstrate.

Money as we know it did not exist. Markets had a limited reach, which means that money equivalents were not easily turned into freely usable liquid assets. The main money equivalents, with silver as the equivalent of equivalents, were the agricultural staple products: barley, dates and wool. Some of the money equivalents, notably barley, which also constituted the main defence against famine, cannot be hoarded for unlimited periods: last year's grain already looses part of its value after the new harvest and texts differentiate between new and old.

Hoarding precious metals is slightly better attested, but documented especially by the occasional use of the accumulated riches. That there is a scala of possibilities, is clear. The intentional scattering of tin, precious objects and textiles among "friendly monarchs" by Zimri-Lim not only happens to be known to us, but it also was notably well administered,[6] thus underlining ulterior motives. The disposal of the Ur treasures by Ibbi-Sin who sent them to Išbi-Irra is another manifest example.[7] Such an action entailed the

---

6 This type of administration constitutes the core of the Ebla archive and is well-represented in Mari and elsewhere, it is an essential aspect of the "palatial economy". It is difficult to separate "hoarding" and the exchange of goods as "gifts" and tribute which could be regarded as a form of "trade". The sending of gifts to "friendly" rulers on the occasion of a major conquest made by them, can, perhaps, be regarded as a kind of payment of an insurance premium.

7 UET 3 702.

risk of a charge of impiety, but it was not uncommon, as Assyrian propaganda against later Babylonian kings indicates. That hoards of metal were officially retrieved from graves is known from Mari, and the one-off purpose of the measure is noted in this case.[8] Our Egyptologist colleagues can tell better stories on this point.[9] The role of silver is investigated separately in this volume by Bongenaar and is not for me to discuss.

If capital formation has investment as its purpose, investing in security, in the benevolent attitude of higher powers, in irrigation ditches, oxen or people is always a choice determined by the ideology of the time. Much of the institutional expenditure concerned religion. But especially here, investment and expenditure are, for us, difficult to separate. We must not forget that religion, which plays a major part in both types of institution, is also the means by which the population is tied to the production process. The ideology is straightforward: the purpose of mankind is to relieve the gods from toil. Today much of our toil goes into social security which is based on the fiction of general solidarity. Without such fictions society cannot function and the accumulation of wealth, like it or not, looses much of its purpose. If we buy a house in order to live in it, do we spend our capital or do we invest it? If the Mesopotamian builds a house for his god and lavishes society's capital on it, does he spend or invest? The institutions operate within the society of their time, their actions reflect that fact, even when we are talking about "formation of capital".

3. *"Capital" and "Reserves": Further Considerations*

Spending and investing are, in principle, difficult to distinguish and in many respects, both now and in the past, merely a question of bookkeeping. This being so, can we make a practical attempt at differentiating between those assets required for the normal everyday production which keeps the institution operating, those "reserves" which were regarded as vital for continued existence and the "investments" (proper) intended to increase production? The Ancient Mesopotamians have provided us with the means for at least a qualified answer to this question, but perhaps it cannot be formulated as yet.

Assets are those items over which accounts had to be rendered by their managers. That is literally everything: land, people (= labour), plough animals, agricultural products, especially barley and (later in the South) dates, herds of cattle, sheep and goats as well as their products, especially wool, raw materials,[10] notably metals, for the crafts industries and their products, with, perhaps, a special place for silver (and gold) in that it was used as an equivalent of equivalents - and sometimes even for (real) payments. To regard these assets as "capital" is not misplaced in a Mesopotamian context, and not only because they appear summarised as sag.níg.ga.ra, "assets in hand", at the end of the first section of an Ur III balanced account, but because of the general practise of accounting for them.

---

8 Order given by Šamši-Adad: D. Charpin - J.-M. Durand, *NABU* 1989 no. 27. On the institutional fringe the appropriation of the estate of one official or person of rank and its transfer to another is a comparable phenomenon: chunks of wealth, assets, are shuffled around by those who have final say in institutional matters. For Mari this has been studied in a recent unpublished MA thesis by F. van Koppen (van Koppen 1997). In Egypt the transfer of the endowments of one mortuary temple to another is of a similar nature, cf. Haring 1997, 34-35.

9 Jansen-Winkeln 1995.

10 All grinding stones had to be imported in the South, all flint even, quite apart from metals.

But can we already separate the "investment" from the "reserves"? We could reason that the trappings needed for the cult and for the maintenance of status, which implies intentional occasional dispersal, were part of the "reserves", but from a social point of view they constitute essentials. Materials for the replacement of the tools[11] and the (very) essential buffer, which cushions the effects of bad harvests and the like, cannot be spent - that is invested -, either. Hoarding is essential but not easily identified. We can not balance institutional assets against requirements, but will contend that there is an arguable imbalance between the various types of asset available which provides us with an opportunity to obtain some insight in the degree of effectiveness of institutional economic decision making, which has a bearing on the question of investments.

A notable difficulty is caused by the very personal manner in which Ancient Mesopotamian accounting took place. Every manager is responsible for his specific resort. The outcome of the account for the preceding period was a fact, what was the (assessed) income was known and the outlays were specified, but in the end the "reserves" appear as the backlog of the person responsible, immaterial whether they were in store, that is available, were still due from underlings or had really disappeared.[12] Even though it must be accepted that occasional inventories are available for some types of asset, I have been unable to trace them in a meaningful manner for the more important money equivalents, which are the more obvious forms of liquid capital.[13] As yet I am unaware of a comprehensive balanced account of a third millennium ka.gur$_7$ and we cannot ever expect to consult the later, Neo-Babylonian, wax tablets. Yet it is unlikely that institutional managers would not have known how much barley was actually available in the silo and what that meant in relation to requirements. What is carried over from previous accounts is perhaps in some respects the equivalent of "reserves". But at least a part of what was still due from the person accountable had to be used to bridge the gap to the next harvest or constituted the real bad weather reserve: this reserve, the contents of the store room, is not identical with a surplus that can be invested.[14]

---

11 The regular recycling of many small agricultural tools and their recasting could suggest that the materials used for this type of tool is in many a sense a liquid or at any rate a multi-purpose asset. Recasting an adze or hoe with the direction of the blade changed by 90° turns it into a battle axe.

12 Stock taking is poorly documented, but is not unknown. Especially concerning personnel and animals there is much material. Herds were regularly inspected in all documented periods. Personnel is listed and rated regularly, with or without computation of the amount of food or wool and textile required, or the amount of food that has been made available is checked against the number of those entitled. We will see that occasional inventories of land available exist. But inventories of barley, dates, wool or silver in stock, to mention only the most important money equivalents, are unknown to me. For textiles Lagaš Ur III texts like HLb 84 (Barton I Pl. 48) and BM 19817 (CT 5 50), using the term níg.gál.la, could be mentioned, but perhaps only the first text represents real stocktaking, and the second deals with registration of work done or not done, in this case by the fuller. From Drehem we have a group of texts of which the colophon contains the phrase šu.šum.ma both for animals managed by named individuals and for precious object belonging to minor gods.

13 Some partial, very limited, insight is provided by the texts studied by T. Breckwoldt (Breckwoldt 1995-96, esp. 64-67) and K.R. Veenhof (Veenhof 1985, 285-306), but even here it is not storage as such which is being administered. The texts betray that "managers" were fully capable of manipulating the various techniques of measuring and assessing what was in store. The use of different measures for what comes in and for what goes out would complicate our task considerably, but only if the nature of the documentation available made such a differentiation feasible.

14 An Old Assyrian merchant would insist on immediate reinvestment of all available capital.

In parenthesis it should be added that institutional participation in trade is here regarded as a means of providing necessities, not as an attempt to profit from the participation. Especially the evidence from Neo-Babylonian Uruk suggests that institutional attempts to obtain the necessary *mēreštu* was on an *ad hoc* basis, or that needs could be satisfied by sending a person of authority to the capital with silver or with access to some money equivalent.[15] In short, I suppose that the gains were for the trading agent, the *tamkāru,* not for the institution, though it may have gained, or lost, on further exchange. No insights in institutional capital formation can be gained here.

4. *A Limited Answer?*

We cannot identify in an effective manner what constituted the surplus over basic institutional requirements and obligations. Capital formation in our context means a successful effort to enlarge the supply or to improve the effective use of each or any of the assets in such a way that the net result is, after deduction of costs, positive and available for investment. It must be stressed again, however, that this net result did not benefit the organisation, the "household" that produced it.

If the practical "facts" are difficult to assess, the reconstruction of "policies" will be even more difficult. In the available material they find expression only rarely, but if so, the evidence is of special importance. Nebukadnezzar will have discussed the building of his palace and he will have been confronted by the humble objections of the various administrators. Their complaints about insufficient resources compared to tasks imposed in this and similar cases will have resulted in pressure lower down the line, perhaps visible in the Sippar and Uruk records: policies are formulated at the highest level possible. We will not hear the discussions, but the signs of intervention by central authorities are visible.

This is therefore inevitably a disappointing story: perhaps more about possibilities than about palpable realities. We are not dealing with the equivalents of large trading companies, but rather with agricultural enterprises, where capital invested, stored or spent on wages or seed (an investment!) remains rather undifferentiated, is actually one and the same commodity.

II. *Mentalities*

A significant aspect of institutional management is the manner in which the institutions exploited what was, at any rate at first sight, their most important asset: land. The practical solutions preferred indicate directly how the various assets, that is "capital", were handled in relation to one another. That the institutions attempted to increase production is reasonably clear, but that this occurred under external pressure by central authorities is equally certain. As stated the Mesopotamian institutions are not autonomous entities but, in the end, the tools of an authority of which the workings can be imagined, and to a degree observed, but which is poorly documented.

---

15 For instance wool still on the sheep, see my remarks in *BiOr* 43 (1986), 19. Cf. also note 53, below.

The institutions were managed and staffed by a bureaucratic hierarchy of which the various Early Dynastic Lú-lists are perhaps the best early (written) witness.[16] The existence of a managerial layer which is capable of calculating the effects of various policies is an essential aid in assessing whether simple hoarding is replaced by (conscious) "capital formation", which presupposes both the will and the scope to invest. Translate: where assets are used in a considered manner to expand production. It is difficult to discuss "rationality of management" when attempting to assess the workings of Ancient Mesopotamian institutions. But we cannot claim complete rationality as our share either.

Mesopotamian institutions from the earliest period seem to have felt the need for the sound administration of their assets, without that, discussion of the subject in hand would be completely impossible. That elaborate bookkeeping was intended to prevent, or at any rate reduce, the risks of fraud by its own personnel seems obvious, but that the existence of such an administration might signify subordination to a higher outside authority should also be considered. There are indications that assessments of means and requirements are already present at the very inception of now understandable texts. The striking fact about such texts is that they could suggest a high degree of (purely mental) convertibility of one "commodity" into another: x barley is y labour or z *bur* of land ploughed and sown, with an additional role for silver, which in turn can be converted into (or perhaps rather expressed in terms of any) other commodity. It should be stressed that in this respect labour, land and silver, however little it may be liked by some, are already commodities in the third millennium BC. In the third millennium we could envisage a sufficiently trained bureaucrat calculating the value of his institution in barley, silver or man-days. Whether he would have had much practical use for such knowledge is another question. Yet we will gain notably in the understanding of our subject if we can distinguish texts belonging to the sphere of planning and speculation from those pertaining to everyday practice, even though they may look very similar at first sight. Even if such planning texts are branded "school texts", they betray a contemporary awareness of certain relationships governing institutional economics.

Perhaps we must refine somewhat: the practical meaning of the calculation suggested above is limited to bookkeeping, since realising these values on a "market" was only possible to an extremely limited extent.[17] The values are on principle what Powell, if I have understood him well, has called, "mode values",[18] which presupposes, if we are allowed to elaborate, the (notional) existence of a kind of system of "fixed" values between commodities in a local system. Differences in these fixed rates increase with distance, which makes long distance trade lucrative if transport is feasible. In practise the mainly notional fixed prices within a local system fluctuate according to the seasons[19] and more violently so in case of poor harvests or political upsets.[20] Much of the hoarding, which is here regarded as inseparable from "capital formation", is intended to mitigate the

---

16 *MSL* 12, 3-21.

17 The institution could, for instance, to a limited degree hire labour. Who the customers of the products disposed of by the Old Babylonian *Palastgeschäfte* were, remains to be studied.

18 Powell 1990, 77.

19 For the Old Babylonian period for barley cf. Farber 1978, 17-21.

20 Examples: the Nippur siege documents, K. Deller's collection of scarcity prices in Assyria (Deller 1964).

consequences of these fluctuations.[21] That a large proportion of the available capital could be tied up in this way stands to reason: ideally the product of one to one-and-a-half harvests should be kept in reserve if small-farmer's wisdom is applied. If, as is at least sometimes the case in Mesopotamia, this equals the value of the land used, it would represent a considerable "capital investment". The relative security of irrigation agriculture in the South and the availability of easy transport there makes, however, the necessity of the maintenance of reserves of this magnitude questionable. In the North the situation will have differed because of the greater uncertainty caused by dependence on rainfall and expensive transport.

In a context were bookkeeping and speculation about policies are routine matters for bureaucrats working in a system of administrative subordination, talking about *capital* and *investment* should be no problem, but the real question is whether the capacity to calculate is consciously and consistently applied to ensure optimal exploitation of available resources to increase the capital of the institution in order to have the wherewithal to invest. This is asking too much, but that there was at least an awareness of the under-use of certain assets, is, for me, indisputable. It can be made reasonably certain for Ur III Lagaš and it is a fact of life in the Neo-Babylonian period and in Zimri-Lim's Mari.

III. *Practical Evidence*

There can be little doubt that under normal circumstances Mesopotamian agriculture produced a surplus. The institutions knew how to compel, either through force or through other means, especially ideological pressure, the institutional agricultural producer to produce more than subsistence requirements and to part with (most of) that surplus.[22] Otherwise the graves of Ur, the palaces of Nineveh or the walls of Babylon would not be there: all are the result, in the end, of the creaming off of agricultural endeavour. The problem is to find the evidence and to provide the proof.

The institutions which are sufficiently documented for it now to be possible to formulate questions concerning their performance as regards the assets listed earlier, are not very numerous: Pre-Sargonic Lagaš, Ur III Lagaš and Umma, the Old Babylonian Mari palace, if we are lucky, Kassite Nippur potentially, but for the moment not, Neo-Babylonian Sippar and Uruk.

---

21 But primarily for insiders only. The (private) hoarder exacerbates the shortage and profits from it. Joseph in Egypt is an excellent example.

22 I do not believe that the entire Ancient Mesopotamian economy was in the hands of the institutions, but subsistence agriculture, possibly in tribal contexts, takes place at another level. (Pseudo) private agricultural undertakings of (high) officials as recently outlined for Mari by van Koppen (van Koppen 1997) are best regarded as off-shoots of institutional activities. The documented smaller private interests of "ordinary" townsmen, best known from the Old Babylonian and especially the Neo-Babylonian periods, are in fact activities of people who can in most cases be traced back to the margins of the institutions. But, on the other hand, it is not realistic to assume that Mesopotamian town dwellers in general were not directly involved in agricultural matters, certainly not in the smaller towns, that is practically all towns. Documentation is the result of intensification of contacts with authorities. If such contacts do not exist or were of limited meaning, there was no need for written documents.

There are of course others, like "Fara", but only if we accept that text groups found there in different localities are treated as one entity. Ebla is clearly a palace archive, but the published material, quite apart from the obvious problems, comes predominantly from the department of "diplomatic gifts and tributes", and does not cover the entire economy. Akkad period text groups are generally too small and fragmented to be helpful, even the texts from Tello. The same is valid for the Gudea period texts there. We need reasonably complete ledgers. Small, that is one or two entry texts, can have a bearing on our investigation only if we possess long files dealing with the same set of persons or administrative units.

Old Babylonian Larsa and Ur provide some material on the way institutions were run, but this is of little direct assistance. The system of the *Palastgeschäft*[23] illustrates both the inefficiency of the institutions, which had to part with a considerable share of the potential gains, which were diverted into the pockets of "agents", and their capacity to absorb the (notional) losses implied in changing the agricultural produce into silver. The impression is strengthened by material from Sippar. The silver earned by transactions in Sippar was transferred to the central administration in Babylon. The Neo-Assyrian palaces or the Aššur temple provide no suitable archival material, though there is perhaps some anecdotal evidence. The, so to say, extra-economic availability of corvé or prisoner labour in the sphere of the palace economy is the, perhaps, most notable fact. Persepolis is inaccessible to me, but does not seem to be particularly relevant. Anyhow, it can be repeated, the evidence from Old Babylonian Larsa and Ur, with that of the rent farm from Neo-Babylonian Uruk and Sippar suggests that the institutions were not the most effective bodies to optimise capital formation.

We can select observations from the material belonging to the major archives listed and suggest that features well illustrated in one instance may have a far more general application even if we are covering a period of 2500 years. The reasons for this belief can be found in the last paragraphs of this contribution: the history of the Ancient Mesopotamian economy can be seen as a succession of waves, the crests of which are caused by more or less successful exploitation of land, people, plough teams and animals as a unified system, using techniques which remain fundamentally unchanged.

IV. *Capital: The Asset "Land" as a Problem*

Ancient Mesopotamian society, at least from the Halaf period onwards, is a productive agrarian society. This can be stated with some confidence because differences in settlement size become visible and the gradual coming into existence of institutions and of towns indicates that agriculture produced a surplus. Administrative documents from all the periods for which they exist, make clear that the institutions were in possession of land, people, plough teams and herds. Did the institutions try to make optimal use of these assets and did they attempt to escape from constraints?

This is best investigated by looking at land: its use is the key to an assessment of institutional economic efficiency. For land in itself is not a problem in Ancient Mesopotamia, certainly not if the vital question of water is ignored. In the alluvium water is ultimately a question of the application of manpower and of avoiding tampering with

23 Kraus 1958, 75-105, cf. Kraus 1984, 215-235; Charpin 1982.

the system for political purposes. This needs no discussion here. The evidence for the surplus of available land as far as indicated by prices has been discussed recently in a contribution to the Leiden CNWS symposium entitled *Landless and Hungry*.[24] Here we can discuss other aspects of the same phenomenon.

We select our example from Ur III Lagaš. The existence of surplus land is confirmed in several different ways, each of which can be used as an indicator of the same phenomenon in other periods where documentation is less complete:

1. Land survey records list unused land.[25] The best preserved of these texts, Truro 1,[26] an unpublished duplicate of which exists in the British Museum, deals with land managed by the ensi of Lagaš, either directly, it would seem, or through three of the main "Temple-estates". Much of the 3230 *bur*, about 21000 ha of unused land listed is unsuitable as it is covered by brackish water (5350 ha), or has to be reclaimed from flooding (4250 ha) to mention only the two most important entries, but in third place comes 4050 ha of the best land, which is not used either. This text from Š 36 does not stand alone. Also virtually complete is BM 14615, published by Pettinato.[27] It dates from the same year, but covers only about 3050 ha, of which some 600 is of good quality, again about 20 per cent of the unused land. Preempting what is to come, exploitation of these two entries of good land would require at least 1350 men and an equal number of oxen if a system of fallow in alternate years is applied, that is an additional 340 teams of substandard size for the period in an organisation which was able to field some 420 (bigger) teams.[28] Though speculation about the deployment of 600 teams is known,[29] using all the already available suitable land would require an even greater investment, far beyond what was feasible. It should be noted that we have used only two texts from a series which includes more (fragmentary) texts: there was evidently much more land available.

2. The amount of land assigned to plough teams is too much per team. K. Maekawa has published a text which speculates about assigning 20 *bur*, 130 ha, to a team.[30] If half is regarded as fallow, we are still dealing with about 65 ha, which is rather a lot. But we must differentiate texts from the sphere of planning and theory from those of daily practise. The so-called round texts are of this class, most of them have been published by Pettinato[31] with additions by Maekawa,[32] who has established that these texts deal with pre-harvest assessment of the yield that was to be delivered by the head of the plough team responsible for cultivation, depending on the conditions of tenure.[33] The texts mention the size of the field concerned, which is probably identical with the area of land

24 Van Driel 1998b.

25 This is the type of inventory of "material in hand" we would like to have for more types of assets. That the land inventories discussed here as a group date from Š 36 suggests some special purpose.

26 Walker 1973, Tf. 17-18.

27 Pettinato 1970-71, 299-304.

28 This number derives from TuT 5.

29 K. Maekawa, *ASJ* 9 (1987), text 53.

30 K. Maekawa, *ASJ* 9 (1987), text 52 (111-112 and 122-123).

31 Pettinato 1969.

32 K. Maekawa, *ASJ* 4 (1982), texts 20-23.

33 Maekawa 1974, 16-40 discusses and tabulates the "round tablets" then available, supplemented by *ASJ* 4 (1982), 100-101.

initially sown and thereafter gives the size of different parcels in an order of diminishing yield. The last parcel in this list is generally stated to deliver no yield. The problem is whether this parcel has been included in the cultivation process or not, which understandably affects the size (and the average yield) of the field tilled by the team. My private inclination is to say yes, which means that the team was accountable for this parcel without yield.[34] Maekawa stresses the fact that for all practical purposes a plough team deals with from 6 to 7 *bur* of land, 39 to 45 ha, if a *bur* is put at 6.5 ha, which is fractionally more than it probably was.

A rapid look at a small sample consisting of three of these texts provides sufficient illustration of the practical situation. All are from AS 8,[35] they indicate that only three teams are responsible for the cultivation of over 10 *bur*, 65 ha, of which there is no yield from about 20 ha in one case and from about 13 in the two others. In the first text other pieces of land are smaller. From one of 39 ha there is no yield for 26 ha and from three similar ones there is no yield at all, but only the remark that the land is to be transferred to another plough team. In the second text only transfers are listed, the biggest parcel is about 40 ha, but several (four) are about 25 ha, including the parcels without yield. Those fields which seem to have lost their ploughmen are considerably smaller in size than the 6 to 7 *bur* fields which seems to be the practical, ordinary, size. This is what is found in the third text. There is a clear discrepancy between what the planners regard as desirable and what is actually feasible. The amount of land without yield increases rapidly if the size of a field worked by one team increases beyond a certain limit. This is well-illustrated by Pettinato's texts 25 and 26, though the second team of no. 25 managed to cope with an exceptional 15 *bur*, even after subtraction of the small parcel without yield. There seems also to exist an understandable tendency to transfer smaller fields, we may suppose, to bigger units. It seems clear that more land was assigned to teams than they could cope with, one more indication of a land surplus.[36]

3. The same phenomenon is indicated by a third fact: the variation in and the reduction of the amount of preparatory tilling. In assessing the workload it should be understood that the distance of the furrows is minimally 50 cms and that 60 or 75 cms are much more common on good land. In itself this lavish use of land, which has clear agronomic advantages as regards weeding, tillering and, probably, salinisation, is also a sign that land was in ample supply. Tilling, however, does not mean seeding alone. Texts from Umma give better information on this point than those from Tello, where information on the preparatory ploughing is less detailed.[37] In Umma the intensity of this preparatory work varied enormously, from two consecutive types of deep and cross ploughing and trice harrowing to a simple harrowing only on part of the same field by the same team. With the varying size of the plough team this makes assessment of the actual workload difficult. Though we can only speculate about possible sound agronomic reasons for the different treatment of land by the practical men in charge, there are still grounds for

34 On this question cf. Liverani 1990, 169.

35 Pettinato 1969, nos. 1-3.

36 The considerable difference in size of Ur III plough teams is, however, a problem. Cf. now, especially, K. Maekawa, *ASJ* 19 (1997), text no. 124.

37 A good example from Umma is YOS 4 210 (ŠS 4). There are of course more texts of the same type.

concluding that if land was assigned to an individual plough team, the intensity with which it worked its land could vary. This will always be the case, but it is primarily a sign that the teams had to cope with a workload that tended to be too heavy.

These three facts about institutional land use in Ur III Lagaš and Umma suggest that shortage of usable, prime quality land was not a problem and we may even conclude that water supply was, at least in theory not a problem either in view of the qualification "good" for the same land, and of the presence of a sizeable amount of other land with the qualification "to be drawn from the water" for other (unused) land. The problems incurred in exploiting land are to be explained by other factors: manpower and traction. This same type of problem can be found in later institutional contexts. Manpower is the real bottleneck.

V. *How to Tackle the Problem of the Surplus of Good Quality Land?*

As stated above, the institutions in Lagaš had too much good land, that is land with a water supply. Some of this institutional land was withdrawn from the institutions by central authorities, the zi.ga lugal, paralleled, perhaps, by the *gizzatu šarri* of later times. It was probably used to provide personnel belonging to the central organisations with suku-land, "maintenance land". But the organisation could also try to find outside farmers for the unused land, people who had spare personnel and oxen with which to exploit this surplus. The motive for accepting such a lease may have been easy access to water. In the Ur III period confirmation is perhaps to be found in the initial payment in silver required in these cases, the máš a.šà.ga, which is in some cases explicitly related to payment for water rights.[38] Though the income for the institution was restricted to a share in the harvest, sometimes after contributing (initially) the seed corn, this type of transaction constitutes a definite attempt at increasing income beyond the limits set by the assets directly available. Understandably the real limit is set by the asset which is in shortest supply.

That there were serious drawbacks to this method of leasing is obvious when it becomes clear that it is one of the ways in which insiders obtained preferential treatment. A explicit Neo-Babylonian case is YOS 6 67, but similar arrangements will be the case with other insider leases which occur at least from Pre-Sargonic times onwards.

What might be called "selective intensification" is another possibility. From third millennium Lagaš there is not much evidence about date cultures, but from Umma there is a whole range of texts listing the yield of individual palm trees. In view of the date of these texts, month VI, it may be assumed that these are detailed pre-harvest per tree assessments of what has to be delivered. In later periods, notably the Neo-Babylonian period, such assessments are always done per orchard, which probably indicates, if not increased routine, at least an increase in volume. In the Achaemenid period it took the assessment commission for the date gardens of Eanna two months to assess the various

---

38 Steinkeller 1981, esp. 119-120. The phenomenon indicates that silver circulated in society in general, as Bongenaar will argue. The subject of rent paid in products or in silver needs further elaboration.

gardens belonging to the institution. Assessing individual trees is probably a sign that this type of institutional culture was still in the development stage in Ur III Umma.

For the institution, introduction and expansion of date culture meant diversification of production. In the early archives, such as Ur III Lagaš and Umma, dates are very much a secondary product compared to barley. In the later archives of Neo-Babylonian Sippar and Uruk barley and dates are almost interchangeable and dates have become much more common.[39] Planting a date orchard means accepting a limited yield for some seven years from land closest to the river or canal, where one man with a shovel tends a date plantation, which is of course much smaller in area than a field tilled with a plough, but which does not require the investment, human and otherwise, resulting from employing a plough team.

In the Neo-Babylonian period we note a conscious attempt to expand date cultures along the various canals, not only in institutional contexts, but also by private individuals. The lessee contracted with the landowner to plant the garden, in lieu of payment of rent. Thus the lessee had the free use of it during the years, mostly seven, during which the trees did not bear fruit. It is, however, clear that in cases in which this rent-free period was increased to 10 years, as in YOS 6 33 (19 IX Nbn 3) from the Eanna archive in Uruk, that those in the right position could profit considerably from this type of contract. The lessee in this case is a slave of the *bēl piqitti* of Eanna, one of the royal supervisors of that institution, who grants the lease, and who is probably the real beneficiary.[40]

We must probably understand the process which turned the banks of canals and rivers in Southern Mesopotamia into a vast date plantation as a process of concentration of effort, requiring an initial investment of at least the loss of income during a number of years on some of the available land but which would ultimately provide increased production with reduced manpower, as well as eliminating the need for traction. Contracts insist that cultivation under the trees should be done by hand. Again the difficulty is to adstruct the statement with hard figures. Though we know the yield in a certain year for many a date plantation and of a few also the exact number of trees in a certain year, we cannot match the two sets of figures. Equal amounts of barley and dates are often (but not always) treated as equivalents. Date plantations are on aggregate much smaller than barley fields. Increased productivity from less land with more intensively used water and reduced man power requirements seems reasonable, but strictly spoken it remains a hypothesis. And it may imply more under-use of the less favourably situated land lower down the slope of the levee, which was probably also exposed to additional salinisation resulting from constant use of water higher up.

At present there is insufficient evidence to construct a comparable case regarding vineyards in Northern Mesopotamia, which were more than a purely Neo-Assyrian phenomenon.[41]

Other methods of expanding and diversifying agricultural production exist and require further investigation, although the evidence is very limited. Without an extensive horticultural sector, the Mesopotamians, with their reliance on barley and other cereals,

---

39 For instance in the case of wages and *maššartu* payments consisting of barley or dates in alternating months.

40 This is probably betrayed by the plural in line 17: "they will enjoy": not only the nominal lessee gains.

41 This and related issues are being studied by R. Jas.

would not have survived. This sector is poorly documented in institutional archives, other than, perhaps, the Pre-Sargonic Emi archive, where various horticultural products figure prominently and a reconstruction of their cultivation has been attempted.[42] Yet another type of agricultural diversification is suggested by institutional lease contracts with individuals not only regarding barley or cereals in general, but also other products like sesame (ŠE.GIŠ.Ì) and *saḫlû*. Sesame is a summer product with, therefore, special water requirements which limit possible cultivation. A contract like YOS 6 41 (11 II Nbn 3) therefore indicates an attempt at diversification.[43] It is notable that though the text is damaged, no time limit seems to have been set for the duration of the contract.[44]

VI. *Other Assets: Coping with Shortages of Manpower and Traction*

Especially in the Neo-Babylonian period the fact that manpower and plough teams constitute a bottleneck becomes explicit in the documents.[45] The inspections of plough teams which record the incompleteness of the teams are direct evidence, especially as in this period the size of the teams has become standardised: four men, four oxen, and additionally, two cows for keeping up the number of the animals.[46] This makes assessment much easier. In Lagaš and Umma Ur III teams are much bigger, but their composition is irregular.[47]

TCL 13 182 (13 IV Dar 2) has often been discussed as it is one of the prime texts for understanding the workings of institutional agriculture in Mesopotamia.[48] The property belonging to Eanna could not be exploited properly because there were not enough ploughmen and plough teams. Eanna even had trouble with finding an applicant for the "general-farm", although on principle such contracts can be expected to be favourable for the contractor. One of the tasks of these lessees was to find tenants (*errēšu*'s) who must possess the means for bringing unused land under the plough.

That this policy of introducing outside tenants had some positive results can for once be seen in TCL 12 227 (Nbn 3-7), from Eanna, although this text also illustrates how difficult it is to come to valid generalisations. The text summarises various types of agricultural income entering Eanna in the years Nbn 3-7.

In year 4 the income derived from the general farm of Šum-ukin and Kalba (lines 8 and 9) amounted to 15198 *kor* of barley, 1106 *kor* of emmer, 7715.5 *kor* of dates, and 350 *kor* of *kasû*. The tenants, that is the tenants not belonging to the personnel owned by

42 If I am well-informed in the unpublished dissertation by J. Marzahn.

43 It is striking that so little is known about the production of flax. In an institutional context Or 47-49, 324 is notable, which, with its clearly agricultural engar gu (I 28 and V 170) and its a.bala.gu (I 27) in a processing context could suggest that the production of flax and fabrication of textiles from it were managed by one specialised institutional department.

44 In the not directly institutional world of the (military) lease holders of the later OB period there is also a marked interest in the growing of sesame.

45 I regard this as matter of documentation, not as a phenomenon specific to the period.

46 Cf. my remarks in *BSA* 5 (1990), 224f.

47 The same is the case in Old Babylonian Mari, where the plough team obviously is the organisation on which all aspects of tillage are based, with additional man power requirements during the harvest (cf. van Koppen 1997).

48 Cf. primarily Cocquerillat 1968, 43-44.

the institution, delivered 3753 *kor* of barley, 247 of emmer, 71.5 of dates, and over 35 *kor* of sesame. It is clear that the institution kept the exploitation of the date plantations separate, and with the date plantations go the under-cultures. But for cereals the use of tenants increased the net income which could be spent by the institution by 25 per cent.[49] The risks of working with this type of material is illustrated, however, by the information given for year 5: the results as a whole drop by more than a third and the share delivered by the tenants decreases even more than that, to about 12.5 per cent. Dates, which stood at one per cent of the directly produced amount disappear completely. As the document is not completely filled in, the evidence from the other years covered cannot be used. Attracting outside tenants was nonetheless an alternative for the manpower shortage, but in good years more so than in bad.

That this was a constant feature can be concluded from the fact that tenants are already present in the Pre-Sargonic Emi texts and from the evidence from Mari discussed recently by F. van Koppen. In both North and South the lack of manpower constitutes the problem.[50] There are no clear signs of population pressure, which is understandable in an agrarian context where availability of land and water do not constitute a fundamental problem. Though there are instances of people transferring themselves or their children to the temple in periods of hunger, there are also signs, at least in the Neo-Babylonian period, that people avoided this irrevocable step, and preferred seeking refuge with an ordinary citizen, even if that implied, of course, a reduction in status.[51]

VII. *Animal Husbandry - an Aside*

That cattle, other than the plough teams, and sheep and goats - with the wool and hair produced - are an important asset, which with due care is self-perpetuating, needs no argument. That wool is the basic material for a textile industry which not only kept the Mesopotamians in clothing but also supplied the only important wholly home-produced export product is also self-evident.

In all periods the institutions inspected their herds and flocks at regular intervals and though quantifiable figures are rare, these texts form an important source. Globally, it appears that at Neo-Babylonian Sippar, the herds from the reign of Nabopolassar are small, but they were increasing rapidly.[52] In view of the capacity of flocks of sheep to recuperate losses in little time, not too much value should be attached to these as yet meagre sets of figures. Nevertheless what is available reflects a conscious policy: male animals are required for the cult of the gods, who, conveniently, prefer the rams surplus

49 The amount of land involved cannot be established.

50 During the meeting Prof. Renger remarked that the shortage of plough teams should also be understood in terms of the cost implied in the need to feed the oxen. Feeding of the oxen with barley is found in the texts, especially from Ur III Lagaš and Umma during the period when the actual seed ploughing took place, not for the rest of the year, though it seems certain that young animals ultimately destined for the plough teams were fed with barley for longer periods. As Prof. Powell suggested the feeding of the plough team with barley is explained by the relatively short period available for seeding. The rest of the year the animals had to fend for themselves, which, in my opinion, means that this type of costs is of relatively small importance, equal to half the amount of seed required for the area sown.

51 This question is discussed in van Driel 1998a, 174-178.

52 Cf. the table in *BSA* 7 (1993), 257.

to breeding requirements. Unless barren, all female animals are retained systematically in the herd. As the remuneration of the herdsman takes the form of a share in the young female lambs this clearly implies the existence of incentives.

In view of the importance of textiles it might seem reasonable to expect special wether flocks kept solely for wool. Direct traces of such a policy are not numerous, but they do exist.[53] The subject requires more study as there are obvious differences in composition between herds from the Ur III period and, for instance, their Neo-Babylonian counterparts. The number of male (or "male") animals compared to females in institutional Ur III herds is so striking that wool production can be the only reason. Separate herding is almost unavoidable and makes good sense.

Though there is no room and very little basis for a long discussion, the available numerical evidence on animal husbandry suggests policies directed at maximising this volatile asset. The lack of pressure on the land will have assisted this tendency. What happened when (in the Sassanian period) the situation changed and agricultural land use expanded to approach the maximum possible, remains obscure.

VIII. *Conclusion*

It is easy to pose questions and to formulate problems. Though the mere act of formulation may suggest an answer, it is difficult to provide adequate proof. The difficulty is caused, perhaps, not only by the way the documentation has reached us. Huge amounts of documents deal with products entering and leaving the institutions. That which accumulates, or to which a claim is laid, and that which is due, appears, and then only rarely, as the balance in the accounts of the people responsible for the various "departments". Documents providing an overall balance are rare and as yet indicative more of fluctuations than of tendencies.[54]

---

53 TCL 1 177 lines 1-3, the first herd. M. Stol, however, pointed out the related text CT 45 31 where the phenomenon does not re-occur.

54 Two examples from Ur III Lagaš illustrate the point. First the three-year barley account RTC 407: in the two cases calculations are possible, one shows a production of slightly over the 30 *kor* per *bur* "norm", in the other, the third year, only 18.5 *kor* is reached. BM 18060, Maekawa *ASJ* 3, no. 1, deals with totals for 10 years, but is not very straightforward. Average production as actually delivered over the 10 year period is about 22 *kor* per *bur*, considerably less than the "normative" 30. This can be understood, but the amount delivered (line 5) is not only less than what should have been delivered (line 3; an amount identical with expenditure, line 9 plus shortfall, line 11, assuming the correctness of a partial restorations of one number), but smaller than what was actually spent (line 9) which represents an average yield of 23.7 *kor* per *bur*. The function of the clearly estimated round sum of 60000 *kor* (in 10 years) in line 7 and of lines 13-25 (in total nearly 4700 *kor per annum* over 10 years, but, perhaps, rather to be regarded as a kind of final outcome) is not clear to me. If the níg.gál.la of line 15, 29500 odd *kor*, really represents the reserve in hand that would amount to less than half of what was actually delivered in an average year, and even less of what was actually spent. This may be of some importance for practical hoarding in the South, but the question remains at which moment in the accounting year this "reserve" was available.

With this type of material long(er) term developments cannot be made clear. If institutional administrators really worked with a yield norm of 30 *kor* per *bur* it is, however, clear that in most years, and in the long run always, they would have to cope with shortfalls. The early history of the *begrotingstekort*, the budgetary deficit, seems to go back far. That a policy of systematically over-estimating income would cause problems, and not only for investment, seems evident, especially

Otherwise capital formation, in the sense of an increase in invested productive capital, may make itself visible in an increased volume of what comes in and what goes out. Relevant documents are rare for the earlier periods, and almost non-existent for the later phases of history, as by then such accounts, as a rule, will have been written on the now lost wax-tablets. Documents dealing with successive years often show notable fluctuations, and general trends will only become recognisable when information on a number of years is available. For the moment this is asking too much. In Assyriology there is a strong argument for continuing what our classical colleagues disparagingly call "stamp collecting", for there is ample scope for the turning of the anecdotal into something substantial by further exploitation of the archival material.

I must end with an impression. Archaeology constitutes an essential element in the study of the Ancient Mesopotamian economy, whoever denies it does so at his or her peril. Adams' surveys of Southern Mesopotamia leave a lasting impression of a land swept by successive tidal waves of increasing agrarian productivity, which invariably recede when their power is spent. The natural environment imposes limits, which are drawn tighter by the human folly displayed by people like Hammurabi and Samsu-iluna. Our best information on capital formation is found in the speculations of Lagaš Ur III bureaucrats published by Maekawa and in the documents showing the Neo-Babylonian institutional managers in Uruk coping with the lack of balance regarding the assets they had to exploit for an ostensibly ever hungrier central administration.

The Lagaš Ur III example is perhaps fairly close to the crest of a wave which is to break on politically motivated destructiveness, in Uruk the wave is relatively young, it will not break before the end of the Sassanian period. The waves imply an ever more intensive use of assets: a virtually total exploitation of suitable land in parts of Southern Mesopotamia in the Sassanian period is suggested by Adams.[55] But it is exactly this maximum use of assets under the agrarian conditions prevailing which causes the wave to ebb away. This is insufficiently documented and under-investigated.

---

without the "money" as we know it. We must, perhaps, assume that the institutions had other sources of income.

55 Visualised in Adams 1981, 181.

UR-DUMUZIDA AND UR-DUN

Reflections on the Relationship between State-initiated Foreign Trade and Private Economic Activity in Mesopotamia towards the End of the Third Millennium BC*

HANS NEUMANN (HEIDELBERG)

Hardly any period of ancient Mesopotamian history has left us in numerical terms such an extensive range of sources as the period of the so-called Third Dynasty of Ur, at the end of the third millennium BC (2111-2003 BC). So far almost 40,000 texts from the Ur III period are known to scholars - mainly in copies or transliterations - with the material basis being constantly expanded by the publication of new texts. The overwhelming majority of the sources contain facts from the areas of state economy and administration. We have private legal documents in much smaller numbers; at present we have some 2,000 texts of this nature. They include the so-called court documents, which derive from the area of state judicial activity, but overwhelmingly concern legal transactions and legal disputes between private persons.

The texts which we so far know come almost exclusively from the southern Mesopotamian towns Girsu, Umma, Puzriš-Dagān, Ur and Nippur, where they have been brought to light by regular or illegal excavations. It is thought at present that there are still some 50,000-60,000 unpublished texts from Ur III, which are distributed among the various museums of the world.[1]

The very extent of the documentary material available - supplemented by a law code, royal and private inscriptions and a literary tradition which in part goes back to the Ur III period - makes it clear that investigations into the social and economic problems of Mesopotamia at the time of the Third Dynasty of Ur are especially promising (even if this should not blind us to the fact that because of the curt formulation in the administrative texts and the peculiarities of Sumerian administrative terminology understanding of the administrative and commercial proceedings and material circumstances underlying the documents is still often subject to certain limits). It is not, therefore, surprising in this context if certain themes of Mesopotamian commercial and social history of the late third millennium have been studied. This follows naturally on the one hand from the constantly changing position of the sources and on the other hand from the fact that there are different ways of looking at the material and various interpretive approaches. Both these -

---

* The present study reviews - and supplements - reflections that have already been produced elsewhere; on the relevant detailed comments and on the details (further references to the literature and in particular textual documentation) see in particular Neumann 1992a and 1993. - Abbreviations of dates: AS = Amar-Su'ena, IS = Ibbi-Sîn, Š = Šulgi, ŠS = Šū-Sîn. Abbreviations follow *PSD* and/or *CAD*. Archi-Pomponio-Bergamini Umma = A. Archi - F. Pomponio - G. Bergamini, *Testi cuneiformi neo-sumerici da Umma*, Torino 1995; Gomi-Yıldız Umma 4 = T. Gomi - F. Yıldız, *Die Umma-Texte aus den Archäologischen Museen zu Istanbul IV (Nr. 2301-3000)*, Bethesda 1993.

1 Englund 1990, 3 n. 23.

the problem of the sources and the different way of putting questions - also play a role in those studies which seek to describe foreign trade in Mesopotamia and the role and function of the merchants in the Neo-Sumerian period. In the last 20 years there have been studies on this by Englund, Limet, Neumann, Powell, Sigrist - Butz, Snell, Steinkeller, van de Mieroop, and Young.[2]

The dam-gàr

In addition to determining the commercial goods on the basis of philological analysis, to explaining the administrative procedures in the context of the accounting activity of the merchants and of issues about price setting and value measurement (most recently also Renger 1995 and Powell 1996) and those which relate to inter-regional commerce as a whole in that period, there is also the problem raised in the studies mentioned of how the social position and social function of the persons indicated in the texts as dam-gàr ("merchant"; Germ. "Kaufmann") or ga-eš$_8$ ("traveling merchant"; Germ. "Kauffahrer") are to be assessed. In essence there are two opinions about this. On the basis of the thesis that palace and temple had a commercial monopoly in third millennium Mesopotamia the role of the Neo-Sumerian dam-gàr as an independently and separately acting merchant is often denied. This is usually also expressed in the translations of the term dam-gàr, such as where one speaks of the dam-gàr/*tamkārum* as a "commercial agent" or "Tauschagenten".[3] In particular on the basis of the administrative texts from Girsu and Umma - in the latter case this concerns the so-called "balanced accounts" drawn up in connection with the activity of the respective dam-gàr (Snell 1982, 15-17; Neumann 1993, 72 n. 14) - but also in view of the corresponding texts from Ur - here related to the activity of the ga-eš$_8$ (Neumann 1979, 56-59; Waetzoldt 1984, 414f with n. 66) - one sees in the merchants of the Neo-Sumerian period mainly commercial agents depending on state commercial units and strictly controlled by the state administration (Renger 1989, 244).

According to the other opinion, the dam-gàr in the Ur III period was an independent merchant who traded on a profit-oriented basis and for whom the state was indeed an important client and a necessary protector but to which the merchant was not subject as a dependent commercial agent (Powell 1977, 27). Thus the Neo-Sumerian merchant comes close to the Old Babylonian *tamkārum*, in whom Kraus (1982, 29) saw "nicht primär 'a commercial agent' der Obrigkeit, sondern einen selbständigen Unternehmer", "der auch mit der Obrigkeit Geschäfte macht(e) oder machen (konnte)". In a similar style van de Mieroop (1986) described the position of the Neo-Sumerian dam-gàr, using the 40 texts of an archive of unclear origin, which relate to commercial activity of the merchant Tūram-ilī during a period of 10 years (ŠS 3 - IS 3), as his basis.

In view of the discussions which have in some cases been conducted from very single minded positions about the dam-gàr in the Ur III period, it must in general be remarked that in assessing the social structures of a society one must guard against the assumption of extreme opinions which hardly permitted differences on pain of being

2 Englund 1990, 13-55; Limet 1977; Neumann 1979, 1992a and 1993; Powell 1977; Sigrist - Butz 1986; Snell 1977, 1982, 1988 and 1991; Steinkeller 1986; van de Mieroop 1986; Young 1979.

3 Englund 1990, 17f with n. 60.

unable to do justice to the complexity of real social relations and the social and economic factors which conditioned them. It is certainly beyond doubt that the major economic powers were concentrated in the context of the palace and temple economy, which enabled the ruler and the institutions connected with him to put a large part of the profits created in the state commercial units into trade. This was the basis for the dominance of the state in the field of external commerce, which, however, should not be equated to a monopoly. Apart from the clearly demonstrated state initiated and controlled commerce, there was always private commercial and business activity. However, this also means that the merchants did not constitute a uniform social class. Even the position of the trader acting on instructions of state commercial units should be assessed differently, since there were both dam-gàr(-e)-ne as part of the personnel to be provided with rations and also independent merchants, who undertook commercial journeys on the basis of commissions from the state and its institutions. This makes it at the same time clear that the state economy on the one hand and private property and private commerce on the other were in closer interaction with one another even in the Ur III period than is usually supposed. In addition, it should be noticed that even the state commissions and commercial enterprises carried out with state funds very much left enough leeway for the accumulation of private wealth, which could even lead to criminal actions on the part of the merchants. In any case, there are examples that merchants were cited as fences or were taken into custody because of embezzled silver.[4]

The "Balanced Accounts"

Investigations of the commercial activity and social position of merchants in the period of the Third Dynasty of Ur are usually based on the cuneiform records from the provincial capital of Umma. The texts from the other provinces and towns of the Neo-Sumerian kingdom - especially from Ur, Nippur and Girsu - are used for purposes of comparison but often play only a subordinate part in the attempt to describe the activities of the Ur III merchant and his position in the context of Neo-Sumerian commercial organization. The concentration on Umma essentially derives from the specific fact of the sources passed down from this city, which particularly well document the commercial activity of merchants.

As already briefly mentioned, these texts are so-called "balanced accounts", which were produced by the state administration on the material performances of individual merchants in a specific period of time.[5] In the documents, the financial and material resources made available by the administration (sag̃-nì-gur$_{11}$-ra) are indicated as "debit" in the balance, against which the turnovers realized by the merchants, *i.e.* the "credit", are offset (šà-bi-ta ... zi-ga). In order to be able to compare the products and materials with one another in terms of value, the values of the goods are given in silver (kù-bi). The difference produced between debit and credit on the account, the "balance", could be positive (diri) or negative (lá-NI). Since the documents here under discussion are accounts of the performances of the merchants, a turnover which was lower in

4 Neumann 1992a, 85f notes 27f.

5 But see the criticism made by Englund (1990, 25 n. 90) of the entrenched concept of "balanced accounts".

comparison to the initial fund produced a negative balance, expressed by the lá-NI "negative amount" or "deficit". This then appeared as the "remainder" (si-ì-tum) of the (balanced) accounting period in the subsequent balanced account as an element of the debit. If the merchants had realized a turnover which in terms of value were above the funds made available, the balance was in this case positive and the "surplus" (diri) was entered in the account on the credit side.[6]

The dam-gàr accounts are not only of great importance for characterizing the activities of merchants, but include in particular important information on prices and value equivalencies in the Neo-Sumerian period. In addition, from the documents essential information can be taken to clarify book keeping practice in the context of state administrative activity. It is true that merchant accounts in the form here described come almost exclusively from Umma,[7] but a few examples from Girsu show that this type of accounting for the performance of merchants was also standard in the other provinces of the Neo-Sumerian state, although we should of course notice differences in the respective structure of the commercial organization.

Problems of Interpretation

Despite the progress which has now been achieved especially by Snell (1982) and Englund (1990, 13-55) in the understanding of the balanced accounts, it must be said that there are still a series of unanswered questions in connection with this group of sources. In particular, there are problems about the relationship as documented by the texts between the state administration and the merchants and the social and economic reality of the commerce of goods on which it was based. Here in the first place one should mention the problems about the accounting period, which on the evidence of the texts varied greatly. Snell (1982, 106) takes the view that the texts can be made to yield the impression "of a loosely semi-annual accounting", but this should by no means be considered to be a secure conclusion.[8] In principle one must also assume that "die Unregelmäßigkeit ... eine Folge unterschiedlichen Tauschvolumens gewesen (ist)".[9] However, the question then arises what conditioned the volume - quantitative and qualitative - of business, *i.e.* in what did the true commercial basis of the documented transactions between administration and merchants consist. Snell[10] assumes that the funds made available to the merchants (sağ-nì-gur$_{11}$-ra)[11] were connected with the commission to purchase for them the necessary raw materials and products and to pass these on to the administration. In this connection, he speaks of "standing orders" on the part of the administration, which made specifying the respective purchase orders in the accounts usually not necessary and at the same time made possible an uninterrupted supply of goods.

6 Englund 1990, 25-51.

7 See also now in this connection the note in the pisağ-dub-ba-label Grégoire 1996, pl. 22 Ashm. 1911-176, 11, relating to the supervision of (commercial) activity of merchants (gúrum-dam-gàr).

8 Neumann 1993, 73 n. 18.

9 Englund 1990, 48 n. 166.

10 1982, 55, 96-99 and 270-278.

11 On the definition of the term see Neumann 1979, 38 n. 164.

In contrast to this view, Steinkeller[12] takes the opposite line that the funds were made available by a so-called "tax office" and that the raw materials and products delivered by the merchants in reality involved procedures which were not in any direct mutual connection. He assumes that the merchants had adequate storage capacities and could at any time cover from their stocks the requirement of the administration for specific goods. The "tax office" had a "standing account" with the merchants, which was always filled up again at specific intervals by the administration. In return, the merchants supplied the various commercial areas of Umma with the required goods, which were covered by the equivalent of the fund amounts. Individual receipts were given for these transactions which according to the creditor-debtor principle remained in the relevant institution. The "balanced accounts" according to Steinkeller therefore constitute the counter-settlement of these receipts made for a specific period of time, which had the consequence of a positive or negative balance for the respective merchant.

We can agree with this opinion to the extent that the accounts are documents of a book-keeping unit which did indeed keep records of transactions of the merchants but in which it must not necessarily have been involved as an immediate partner itself. As Steinkeller emphasises, this applies in the first place to the relationship between the merchants and the consumer of the products, but a similar conclusion can also be drawn to some extent for the relationship between the provider of the fund amount and the merchant who received it on each occasion. Apart from the competent authority which was directly involved in this, represented in particular by a certain Lukala, it seems that other persons and administrative bodies also made payments to be settled by the merchants. Since products other than silver used to provide the funds (especially barley, wool, dates and fish) show only a narrow range of variation, the number of the relevant suppliers was always lower than that of the customers on the credit side of the accounts, and in addition there were so to speak potential client areas for the same product, which in the accounts are set out one after another. Even in the case of the provision of a fund, there must also have often been direct deliveries to the merchants, as can be recorded on the basis of individual receipts or the existing references in the "balanced accounts". The provision of funds must of course have been continually in order to ensure as a counterpart the supply of the individual commercial areas with raw materials and products by the merchants. Whether in this connection one can speak of a "standing account" of the administration with the merchants, is a moot point. In any case, one is struck by the different orders of magnitude on the debit side of the accounts. This suggests that the scale of the funds must have stood in relation to the volume of transactions of the merchants, documented on the credit side of the accounts. It is clear that the fund was also geared to the expected or required supplies on the part of the merchants, even if often no direct connection can be perceived between the debit entries and the specific entries on the credit side. The latter point cannot, however, be generalized, since specific notes in the debit section indicate that at least in part the funds were provided in a purpose-linked manner, that selected and essentially named goods were acquired in exchange for the relevant fund amount.[13] As a rule, the different commercial areas in Umma received the required raw materials and goods from the storehouses of the merchants, *i.e.* the commercial and business transactions of the merchants were overwhelmingly independent

12 Steinkeller 1986, 4ff.

13 Neumann 1993, 75 n. 32.

of the actual notification of requirement by the administration,[14] although of course here too we should note deviations from the rule. Since the texts of the commercial administration of Umma only provide information by exception on the administrative and commercial procedures at that time, no definitive clarity can be achieved on the relationships lying behind the bald book-keeping terminology, which of course also applies to the present question.

In connection with the merchant accounts, reference is usually made to the problem of price and price setting in Mesopotamia towards the end of the third millennium. It is true that on the basis of the texts the value equivalence applying at any time for a large number of raw materials, goods and products can be determined,[15] but it is difficult to explain satisfactorily the connection between these value statistics which were used for internal calculations, and the social and economic price setting factors. This is a highly complex problem, whose treatment must wait until there has been further commercial historical research, although in recent years there have been some programmatic pronouncements.[16] However, even questions of the Neo-Sumerian price structure itself, as it appears in the sources transmitted, have not been adequately treated, if one thinks about the problem of local price differences, say, or fluctuations in the price level of the same products due to quality considerations. In this regard, the "balanced accounts" of the merchants obviously offer the best conditions for the appropriate studies, but there is no getting round the fact in asking this sort of question that the cuneiform source material from that period must be considered in its totality.

The "balanced accounts" make it clear that in the context of the state commercial administration of Umma the commercial activity of the merchants was by no means of minor importance. The acquisition of raw materials and goods by the dam-gàr, whether in foreign trade or through purchases in the internal market, supplemented the material basis in the state controlled commercial units or made production possible in them in the first place, as in the case of the metal, wood and stone processing industries. At the same time the commercial activity was very useful for the acquisition of luxury goods. As far as can at present be seen from the sources, it seems that the number of merchants - at least those who were doing deals for the provincial administration - was not really so large.[17]

Umma: Ur-Dumuzida

Even if the contingencies of survival must of course be borne in mind, it is still obvious that in the context of the commercial and business activity of the provincial administration of Umma three merchants played a special role: Šeškala, Pada and Ur-Dumuzida. They are most often documented in the texts, and in particular Ur-Dumuzida is given an exalted function.[18] About his activity, which is to be sketched as an example in what follows, there are at present nine account texts, which in the words of Englund[19]

---

14 Steinkeller 1986, 5f.

15 Snell 1982, 115-207; Waetzoldt 1986, 331-335.

16 Renger 1986 and Powell 1990.

17 Neumann 1979, 25-27.

18 Neumann 1993.

19 Englund 1990, 48 n. 166.

describe him as a "sehr beschäftigte(n)" merchant. According to a seal (MVN 13 860) he was dam-gàr-^{d}Šára "merchant of the (god) Šara",[20] which may refer to his institutional field of operation. With regard to the sons of Ur-Dumuzida, it can be stated that they - in particular Ur-Šulpae, A'akala and Lugal-ursag - were also engaged in commercial activities to the order of the administration.[21] This shows that the profession of the father was also exercised by his sons, which may have been the norm and can also be documented for other areas.

As already indicated, Ur-Dumuzida was a merchant for whom commercial and business activity is documented on a not inconsiderable scale. The very period in which he acted as a dam-gàr is itself remarkable. It can be shown that Ur-Dumuzida was active for at least 32 years (Š 36 - IS 1).[22] From the entries on the debit side of the "balanced accounts" drawn up for Ur-Dumuzida it is evident that the commercial and trading volume to be achieved by this merchant could reach impressive orders of size. Only twice did the fund fall in value terms below five minas,[23] and twice it was almost 15 minas of silver.[24] As a rule, the fund of Ur-Dumuzida was made up of the account transfers of previous accounts (si-ì-tum) and the current deliveries to him, so that in two cases settlement chains can be documented.[25] The balance with a negative amount (lá-NI) for the merchant was the rule, but another text (TCL 5 5680) shows that the balance could also be positive, which was credited to the merchant in the next balanced account. A zero balance was produced by an account from the year AS 9 (YOS 18 123), so that neither a deficit nor a surplus had to be recorded.

The fund made available to Ur-Dumuzida on each occasion was not in any way different in its composition to that of other merchants in Umma. In addition to silver (kù-babbar) Ur-Dumuzida was given barley (še), wool (síg), dates (zú-lum), wheat (gig) and fish (ku_6) on sometimes considerable scales. This is also essentially in line with the picture which can be drawn from other texts, which also have the supply of fund amounts as their content but cannot be brought into a direct relationship to the entries in the debit section of the present "balanced accounts", which is to some extent due to the chances of transmission.[26]

In the context of his commercial and business activity, Ur-Dumuzida did not specialize in particular products. He supplied the different commercial areas of Umma with both domestic and imported goods. This is shown by the entries on the credit side of his "balanced accounts" as well as notes in the individual receipts which cover an

---

20 On the seal see also Mayr 1997, 483 no. 881. Šara was the chief god of Umma.

21 On the sons of Ur-Dumuzida see in particular Neumann 1993, 78 with notes 54-56. Another son is now documented by MVN 16 718, 4f. (Ur-^{d}A-šár), although his professional activity and social position cannot yet be determined.

22 Apart from the documents collected in Neumann 1993, 79 note 58 (supplement *ibid*, 86) now see also MVN 20 160, 4 (Š 47); MVN 16 1002, 3 (AS 3/V); Archi-Pomponio-Bergamini Umma no. 530, 2 (AS 5/VII); 651, 2 (AS 7/III); MVN 18 262 (= Molina 1996, 315f.) III 12' (ŠS 2/III); Gomi-Yıldız Umma 4 no. 2307, 3 (ŠS 2/IV); 2413, 4 (ŠS 2/IV); MVN 16 1099, 4 (ŠS 5/VI/11); Gomi-Yıldız Umma 4 no. 2579, 4 (ŠS 5); MVN 16 718, 5 (without date). The same Ur-Dumuzida also in MVN 18 467 (= Molina 1996, 391), 2 (ŠS 1/VIII)?

23 Chiera STA no. 22; YNER 8, pl. XVIIf no. 10.

24 AOAT 203, 216; YOS 18 123.

25 Chiera STA no. 22 and YOS 18 122; YNER 8, pl. XVf no. 9 and ibid pl. XVIIf no. 10.

26 See Neumann 1993, 81f and now also MVN 18 262 III 11'f (síg).

extremely wide range of raw materials and products, as were required to satisfy the needs of production and the demands for luxury goods in the commercial and administrative units. The goods to be acquired by Ur-Dumuzida were in particular gold (kù-sig$_{17}$), copper (urudu) and tin (nag̃g̃a [AN.NA]), as well as products which are described generally as resins, essences and oils. The latter were particular luxury goods, which were needed above all in the household of the provincial governor (énsi). It seems that Ur-Dumuzida in particular had adequate stored stocks of such products, which made it possible for him to supply the interested administrative and commercial areas on a continuous basis. In addition, the activity of Ur-Dumuzida in the context of the acquisition and provision of bitumen (ésir), wood, "alkali" (nag̃a-(si-è)), reed (gi), fruits and honey (làl) is recorded.[27]

As already mentioned, Ur-Dumuzida was dam-gàr-^{d}Šára, which perhaps does not only refer to his area of activity but could possibly also indicate a particular position of this merchant as against other merchants in Umma. It is also striking that according to the "balanced accounts" that we have the commercial and business volume of Ur-Dumuzida was sometimes much greater in value terms than that of other merchants. A similar impression can be gleaned from the texts in which several merchants are mentioned together in a comparable function. The products made available on each occasion and goods delivered vary in terms of quantity very significantly, however, at least with regard to their relation to the debit and credit of Ur-Dumuzida. Most usually, the business volume of the merchants Pada and Šeškala came closest to that of Ur-Dumuzida.[28] Of particular importance in this connection could be the text Sauren New York Library No. 335, since this possibly allows us to see a superior responsibility on the part of Ur-Dumuzida in relation to other merchants. To what extent one should already see here a reference to the existence of a professional organization of merchants in Umma must remain an open question. However, the "foreman of the merchants" (ugula-dam-gàr-ne) evidenced in another text indicates that we should assume some such arrangement in Umma (Nikolski II 447, 27). The role which Ur-Dumuzida may have played in the context of this organization can only be conjectured, but must not have been insignificant.

Evidence for the private commercial activities of Ur-Dumuzida is available, but is extremely scarce, so that no conclusions can be drawn even about the extent of the private transactions of Ur-Dumuzida. The extensive lack of relevant private contracts is due in the first place to the chances of transmission, but certain peculiarities of private book keeping should also be borne in mind. In principle, the basic assumption must be that the "Abgrenzung zwischen Staats- und Privathandel ... schwierig (ist) und nie genau möglich sein (wird)"[29]. In the case of Ur-Dumuzida, one may certainly suppose that his position can be assessed similarly to that of the merchants from Nippur for whom extensive private commercial activities are documented.

---

27 On the goods delivered by Ur-Dumuzida to the administration see in particular Neumann 1993, 83-85 and also now for *metals*: MVN 20 160; *oil*: Gomi-Yıldız Umma 4 no. 2307; *bitumen*: Archi-Pomponio-Bergamini Umma no. 651, Gomi-Yıldız Umma 4 no. 2413; *wood*: MVN 16 1099, Gomi-Yıldız Umma 4 no. 2579; "*alkali*": MVN 16 1002, Archi-Pomponio-Bergamini Umma no. 530.

28 Englund 1992, 82-87; Neumann 1993, 85 n. 118.

29 Waetzoldt 1984, 410.

Nippur: Ur-DUN

With regard to the private business activity of the Neo-Sumerian merchants in Nippur, up to the most recent period more than once reference has been made to the special position of Nippur in the context of the commercial organization of the Ur III state, which in fact because of the differing archives in the individual provincial capitals can hardly be right. Whereas the majority of the texts from the other locations of the Neo-Sumerian state of Ur, *i.e.* in particular from Girsu, Umma, Puzriš-Dagān and Ur, come from the area of the state administration, most of the documents excavated in Nippur are documents in private law, *i.e.* the majority of the Neo-Sumerian text transmission derives from the state archives of an integrated palace and temple economy, whereas the legal documents are mainly derived from private archives, and the majority of the Ur III Nippur texts belong to such private archives.[30] A more extensive complex of documents from the area of the temple administration of Nippur has now been published and analyzed by Zettler (1992). The material comes from the Inanna Temple and includes also private law documents relating to the transactions of the senior administrative personnel.[31]

The assets of the merchants as they can be seen from the Nippur documents and the role of the dam-gàr in credit transactions at that time has already been discussed many times in the literature and will not interest us here further as a general problem. However, so far the role of the merchants has not been much considered in the context of the inter-regional commercial traffic. Despite the unsatisfactory situation of the sources in this respect, however, certain conclusions can be drawn. The evidence that merchants from Nippur were integrated into the external trading activity of that time is particularly interesting because the private legal transactions of the merchants in the area of the inner city commercial life can and should no longer be assessed in isolation.

The basis for the reflections to be made in this connection is the activity of a certain Ur-DUN who according to the seal of his son was a merchant (dam-gàr) and whose activity probably stretched over 20 years to the year ŠS 8 (Neumann 1992a). In contrast to the other merchants from Nippur, we do not have any texts with regard to Ur-DUN which can be unambiguously allocated to the archives of this merchant. We are thus referred to the mentions of Ur-DUN in texts from other archives.

For example, there is the document Owen Nippur No. 302 which provides information in particular on the assets of the (subsequently deceased dam-gàr) Ur-DUN. According to this text, in which there is an inheritance dispute between the brother and the widow of Ur-DUN (Owen 1980), Ur-DUN inherited from his father Namḫani fields outside the city (uru-bar-ra), household utensils, property in the city (uru-šà-ga) and 17 male and 10 female slaves. This makes it clear that Ur-DUN must have been a very wealthy merchant. This is also basically shown by those documents which relate directly or indirectly to the commercial activity of Ur-DUN. Of particular interest in this connection is a document literarily transmitted in several copies, which has as its content a (public) announcement of loss of the seal of Ur-DUN.[32] Even if linguistically and indeed in terms of content this is a new creation of the Old Babylonian é-dub-ba-a, the reference to the historically documented Ur-DUN - and indeed it is a situation which can easily be

30 Neumann 1992b and van Driel 1994.

31 On this see above all van Driel 1993 and Sallaberger 1994.

32 Ali 1964, 113-116; Neumann 1992a, 97 n. 47.

imagined for him - shows that in the context of the commercial life and the local administrative hierarchy of Nippur he must have held a prominent position, so that the memory of it in the Old Babylonian period was still present either because of archives which had survived or because of an oral tradition.

The social position of Ur-DUN however, is not only to be ascribed to his commercial activity and to his relationships in the local area, important as they may have been. Ur-DUN was particularly connected with the royal house, to which a letter (YBC 5011) which is preserved in the literary tradition and so far in only one copy, seems to refer, which mentions the merchant Ur-DUN as the sender and probably was directed to king Šulgi.[33] Without going into details here about the authenticity of the event described in this text, mention should be made of the fact that the letter may not indeed be a primary source in the strict sense but because of the circumstances represented in it and the range of persons connected with them it seems nevertheless to reflect thoroughly real events more or less correctly. At least the text, which indeed not without reason mentions the very Ur-DUN as its author, refers to the inter-regional importance of the activity of this merchant in the Ur III period, which was also often apparently recognized later. Ur-DUN is shown in the letter mentioned as a merchant by royal commission in "the far-off mountain land", who has fallen out with measures of a high state authority taken against him (removal of the commercial goods by the representative of the king in Subir, Apillaša), which has finally led to the present letter of complaint. With regard to the specific role of Ur-DUN, it is interesting that he carried out commercial transactions by commission of the royal house, himself undertook the appropriate commercial journeys and did not have the deals concluded by commercial agents. It appears that he enjoyed the full confidence of the king, and one would not be wrong to suppose that in such enterprises commercial activity and diplomatic mission were combined. His relationship to the royal house may in essence have been the basis of the privileged position of Ur-DUN.

In the context of his activity as a merchant, Ur-DUN also collaborated with other merchants. His documented partners include Adda'a and Ur-Nusku. For the latter, an extensive and diverse commercial activity over 38 years can be established.[34] He is also mentioned as dam-gàr-10,[35] and so was something like a "chief merchant", with ten other merchants below him. The merchant Katar seems have been a predecessor of Ur-Nusku as dam-gàr-10 (FAOS 17 No. 7, 8f). In this function, they are both comparable with the ugula-dam-gàr(-ne) "foreman of the merchants", as is indeed documented for Umma (see above page 50) and Girsu (MVN VI 395 e. 1). It seems that in Nippur and other cities of the Ur III period there were professional merchants' organizations, to which reference is also made by the titles ḫa-za-núm-dam-gàr-ne "mayor of the merchants" in a document of unknown origin (Gomi-Sato British Museum No. 220, 14) and dub-sar-dam-gàr "clerk of the merchants" in a text from Girsu (Reisner Telloh No. 130, 17). However, these references in themselves tell us nothing about the level of organization of the merchants in the Ur III period. Of particular interest in this connection should be the text Owen Nippur No. 511, according to which Ur-Nusku carried out transactions with the already mentioned Adda'a, who at the time of writing the document was resident in Zimudar in

33 Michalowski 1976, 216-220.

34 Š 31 - IS 2; Neumann 1992b, 169 n. 49.

35 BE 3 15 + Owen Nippur no. 367, 4.

the Diyala Region. The communication was through a messenger (lú-kíĝ-gi$_4$-a) of Adda'a in the é-dam-gàr "merchant house",[36] which should perhaps be interpreted with Steinkeller[37] as "the headquarters of the Nippur guild". It would not be wrong to suppose that we are here dealing with a kind of organization such as is similarly described by Kraus (1982) for Ešnunna, Larsa and Babylon in the Old Babylonian period. However, the question arises here whether this organization was a state dominated or at least controlled system or rather an association to represent (private) commercial interests. With regard to the already mentioned merchant Tūram-ilī of unknown origin, who was also ugula-dam-gàr,[38] van de Mieroop[39] was disposed to make the latter assumption. This may also be true for Nippur which of course does not rule it out that the merchants conducted commercial transactions to state commission, to which the relevant texts refer.[40] That this type of commercial activity was of particular importance has already been stressed at the start.

In addition, there are a number of indications that the merchants also conducted privately initiated and financed transactions. In the case of loan transactions for which there is abundant evidence in Nippur at least in some cases it must be assumed that these were not consumer but investment loans. Also the earliest examples of *kasap tappûtim* transactions, which also come from Nippur, point in this direction.[41] The sworn declaration of a merchant which can be found in a loan document, to pay back the amount lent "if he gets back from his commercial journey (kaskal)",[42] may also be mentioned as evidence for a privately financed enterprise.

In conclusion, it should be stated once again that the comments here made on the Ur III merchant and his transactions should make it clear that our current picture of Ur III society and its economy requires a stronger differentiation, not least with regard to developments which are perceptible in the subsequent Old Babylonian period.

---

36 See also Civil 1990, 110.
37 Steinkeller 1986, 7.
38 *JCS* 38, 77 no. 37, 3.
39 Van de Mieroop 1986, 15.
40 Neumann 1992a, 90 n. 81.
41 Neumann 1992b, 174f.
42 Owen Nippur no. 322.

SILVER AND CREDIT IN OLD ASSYRIAN TRADE

KLAAS R. VEENHOF (LEIDEN)

1. *Introduction*

Silver played a vital role in Old Assyrian trade.[1] Its acquisition was the main goal of the traders whose caravans imported tin and woollen textiles into Anatolia in order to convert them, directly or indirectly, into silver[2] which was invariably shipped back to Assur. There, after the necessary payments had been made (expenses, taxes, debts, interest, dividend), much of what remained was again used for commercial purposes, either directly, by contributing to or equipping a new caravan, or indirectly, by investing it in a firm or issuing a loan to a trader. Silver, thus, was not only the goal of the trade, it was also its motor and lubricant which kept the system going. As generally accepted and easily shipped means of payment and as valuta of account it facilitated commercial transactions, also in indirect exchange and by book transfer. Most importantly, it played a key-role in all kind of credit transactions (commercial credit, straight loans, investments) which dominated the trading system. Much silver, moreover, entered Assyrian society, both on a public level, in the form of payments for facilities, taxes, fines and institutional profit, and in the private sphere, as dividend, interest, profit, commission, wages (for personnel), and as payment to those who supplied caravans with donkeys, harnesses, and food. Traders and their families, moreover, used it to buy (expensive) houses and the necessities of life, such as barley, oil, and wool.

Gold too was exported from Anatolia to Assur, though on a more modest scale, but it played a peculiar role. Gold which arrived in Assur[3] was normally converted into silver, which then was used for payments and purchases. It is never mentioned who bought the gold, but thanks to a letter by the ruler of the City to the colony in Kanish we know that there existed a law (inscribed on a stela) which prohibited the sale of gold to non-Assyrians (the text speaks of people, presumably traders, from Akkad, Amurru, and Subartu) on penalty of death.[4] On the other hand, gold was the preferred valuta in which standard investments or shares (called *šipkātum*) in a trader's "sack capital" (*naruqqum*)

---

1 Abbreviations of editions of Old Assyrian and other texts are those used in the *Chicago Assyrian Dictionary*, vol. 17 (Š/1). In addition: EL = G. Eisser - J. Lewy, *Die altassyrischen Rechtsurkunden vom Kültepe* I-II (*Mitteilungen der Vorderasiatisch-Aegyptischen Gesellschaft* 33 und 35/3; Leipzig 1928, 1930); I = K. Hecker - G. Kryszat - L. Matouš, *Kappadokische Keilschrifttafeln aus den Sammlungen der Karlsuniversität Prag* (Praha 1999); POAT = W.C. Gwaltney Jr., *The Pennsylvania Old Assyrian Texts* (*HUCA Supplements* 3; Cincinnati 1983); TPAK 1 = C. Michel - P. Garelli, *Tablettes paléo-assyriennes de Kültepe volume 1 (Kt 90/k)* (Paris 1997).

2 The texts use the expression *luqūtam ana kaspim ta'urum*, "to turn merchandise into silver".

3 In Anatolia one used the designation *ḫurāṣum ša ḫarrān ālim*, "gold for the journey to Assur", possibly meaning "gold to be shipped to Assur", perhaps in order to distinguish it from gold used locally. See for the role of gold, Veenhof 1972, 381f.

4 See for the text and its interpretation Veenhof 1995, 1733ff.

were rated. But it is clear that actual payments for obtaining such shares were made in silver.[5] Whoever may have acquired the gold which arrived in Assur (we may suspect institutional hoarding), its role in the actual trade must have been limited and we may ignore it here.

The following remarks do not deal with investments, the capital of the traders and firms, partnerships etc (key words: *naruqqum, šipkātum, ebuṭṭū, bulātum, ummeānum, tappūtum*, etc), which are discussed in the contribution to this volume by Dercksen. My focus is the role of silver in the actual trade and especially in commercial credit of various kinds, which means features such as loans, debts, advances, consigment, agency, and special arrangements for paying debts or their deferment. And this of course requires a serious look at the persons involved in such operations, especially the ubiquitous *tamkārum*, whose role still is a matter of disagreement.

Before doing so a few essential features of the trade, which condition the role of the silver and those who handle it, have to be mentioned.

a) The long-distance trade, carried out by regular donkey caravans and operating through a system of trading stations spread out over a large part of Anatolia, required considerable investments in transport, communications, local facilities, and personnel. It was feasable and profitable thanks to the differences between the exchange value of the goods traded in Assur and Anatolia. Silver, rich in supply in Anatolia, once shipped to Assur allowed the Assyrians to buy there tin and textiles, which in Anatolia could again be sold for two (tin) to four times (textiles) as much silver as they had cost in Assur.

b) The overland trade required caravan journeys of ca. six weeks between Assur and Kanish and was impossible during the ca. four months of the Anatolian winter. This made time precious and timing important. If purchases and sales could be carried out without delay two journeys and *vice versa* within one year might just be possible. Reduction of transaction time meant reduced costs and offered the possibility of additional profit. In achieving this silver as a highly valued, generally accepted, and easily transported type of money played a key role. This may also account for the high official ("according to the ruling of the *kārum*") rate of interest of 30 per cent per year (during the preceding Ur III period and in roughly contemporary Babylonia the annual rate of interest usually was only 20 per cent) and explains that silver was always in demand and constantly changed hands.

c) The continuous presence of Assyrian traders in Anatolia, in a network of ca. 30 trading stations and "colonies", substantially enlarged commercial possibilities. More and different markets could be reached, storage in reaction to seasonal fluctuations in demand and supply or to political disturbances became possible, and medium and long term credit (up to 12 months; *ana ūmē qurbūtim/patiūtim*) could be granted, both to Assyrian agents (*tamkārum*) and to local traders and palaces. Trade could also be carried out by indirect exchange (tin or textiles > copper > silver, or silver > wool > silver) over a wider area and between different markets, either for reasons of Anatolian supply or in order to increase profits.[6] But this development also entailed additional costs and risks and required new legal procedures and rules for the conversion of goods, the transfer of

---

5 See for *naruqqum*, Larsen 1977 and *RlA* 9 (1999) *s.v. naruqqum* (forthcoming). Collation of the one known *naruqqum*-contract Kay 313, preserved in the museum at Kayseri (Larsen 1977, 125 n. 16), has shown that the first line which is preserved contains the word *šipkātum*.

6 See for this type of exchange, in which copper played a prominent role, Dercksen 1996, 149f.

payments among a bigger number of participants, and periodic accounting. Giving credit frequently was unavoidable due to the market situation (local palaces usually did not pay cash) or was preferred in order to obtain better prices and to serve more markets by means of selling agents travelling around with merchandise given on credit (called *qīptum*). Credit sale, however, meant deferred payment and the possibility of problems with insolvent, overdue or unwilling debtors and agents, which explains the many references in letters to outstanding claims (*bābtum*) resulting from "leaving behind" (*ezābum*) merchandise.[7] Payments not infrequently had to be enforced from both Assyrians and local customers by the threat of fines (default interest) or by means of formal summonses and lawsuits. Anatolian palaces, rulers and dignitaries at times had to be induced by gifts and bribes to meet their obligations. All these complications, of course, added to the costs and resulted in more correspondence and more administration, as the archives show.

2. *Commercial Credit and Straight Loans*

In the framework of the trade commercial credit was granted in different situations and for various reasons. We meet it in connection with the purchase of merchandise in Assur, with its sale in Anatolia, and in a variety of situations in both areas, where need for credit arose. Commercial loans were granted both to people at the bottom of the commercial hierarchy and to rich merchants, not only in order to enable them to carry out more trade and to make more profit, but also because, to quote a phrase of Goitein (used to describe the situation during the early medieval trade in the Mediterranean), which fully applies to the Old Assyrian situation, "owing to the principle of having one's capital working all the time and other circumstances even well-to-do persons were not rarely short of cash".[8]

a. *Commercial Credit*

A first form of credit were interest-free advances to relatives and close business associates, to which the sources refer with phrases such as "I paid for you out of my own funds" (*ina raminia ašqulakkum*), "let your silver be withdrawn from your disposal for a few months" (*kaspum libbeʾelka*[9]), or when there is mention of "favours" (*gimillum*), usually granted in such conditions. These "favours" often consisted in making merchandise available at favourable conditions, buying it quickly at a good price, or sending the silver which the merchandise would yield to Assur as soon as possible, even before the sale was completed. Such "favours" apparently could imply specific agreements on quantities, prices and terms and we have texts which speak of "the rest of the favour" still due.[10] In (the second page of) a letter,[11] a trader offers his addressee to

---

7 See Veenhof 1972, 419ff. with n. 537, and Skaist 1994, 46ff., 186ff.

8 Goitein 1967, 252.

9 See for this expression Veenhof 1972, 409ff.

10 In the unpublished letter kt n/k 1654 (courtesy of S. Çeçen) we read: "Let him give (to P.) 70 minas of tin .... of the favour I owe to E. and let him (P.) give him (for it) 10 minas of silver, not later

send silver to pay for the investments he made for him, but adds: "Do me a favour (*scil.* by advancing the silver), and if you cannot advance it, charge me interest as brothers pay to each other". In KKS 29 the favour asked by a trader who calls himself "a man of favours", to stress the mutuality of the concept, consists of quickly buying tin and textiles and shipping the silver to Assur. The writer of KKS 12 mentions two alternatives, either paying interest for 2 1/2 months or granting (lit. "to become indebted for") a favour (*gimillam liḫḫiblam*). In KTS 22b a trader asks for help to carry out a quick sale of his *ḫusārum*-stone (lapis lazuli?), suggesting that the addressee might pay for it immediately, out of his own funds and he concludes with: "For the silver which you will send me from your own funds I will owe you a favour (*gimillam laḫḫiblakkum*)". Many such requests occur in the correspondence of business partners and close associates, *e.g.* that between Pūšu-kēn and Šalim-aḫum, where the latter in particular is always anxious to speed up transactions in order to obtain silver as soon as possible. In one of his letters[12] Šalim-aḫum writes: "If you agree, send me, as soon as you hear my letter, 13 1/3 minas of silver and I will make available twice as much (*šitta qātēn laddi*). Then I will make the purchases you will write me and send them to you (even) while the merchandise which belongs to us jointly is still on its way up (to Anatolia). When D. (the transporter, a son of the writer) arrives there, you can take your silver from the first sales you make and one can bring me my silver here (later)". This type of informal credit is quite common in early trade, also in the Geniza documents studied by Goitein, and we leave it with these general remarks.

For the sale of the merchandise in Anatolia various methods were used. Part of it was usually kept by the manager in Kanish (or elsewhere) who was the destination of the caravan, probably because he intended to sell some of it himself. Part was sold to the local palaces, usually at credit,[13] part was entrusted to employees of the firm, at times the transporters who had accompanied the caravan and who also had to sell their own textiles.[14] A substantial part usually was entrusted to selling agents (called *tamkārum*), who must have sold it elsewhere in Anatolia, but since their sales apparently were mostly cash, we have very little evidence on their activities. This last option meant, as the texts say, that lots of merchandise (frequently including transport donkeys) were "given to" (*tadānum ana*), "laid/given upon" (*nadā'um/tadānum iṣṣēr*) or "entrusted to" (*qiāpum* with double accusative) such agents; the different terms at times are used in one and the

than in spring. Approach him (E.) in connection with the rest of the favour he is entitled to and say: 'Do not force the gentleman to pay directly from the (the yield of) his *naruqqum*-capital. Let him send you favours (plural!) from the City (of Assur), so that he may do you a favour'". Apparently E. is asked to be kind enough to supply him with merchandise from Assur, which he can sell in Anatolia, so that he will be able to pay the favour due to E. with the silver he had earned. This becomes clear from the related letter kt n/k 1346:18ff., where we also learn that the size of the original favour was 30 minas of silver.

11 The Burton-letter, published by R.D. Biggs in E. Leichty *et al.* (eds.), *A Scientific Humanist. Studies in Memory of Abraham Sachs* (Philadelphia 1988), 33ff.

12 Published by D.O. Edzard and K. Hecker in *MDOG* 102 (1970), 86f.

13 See for the behaviour of the local Anatolian palaces as buyer of merchandise, Dercksen 1996, 165ff. and my observations on the type of debt-note called *iṣurtum* in Veenhof 1995b, especially 321ff.

14 Textiles they usually bought in Assur with the silver of the interest-free loan (normally 25 to 30 shekels of silver, called *be'ūlātum*), which was made available to them there in remuneration of their work with the caravan; see Veenhof 1972, 86f., with notes 130f.

same document.[15] The various options are nicely described in Aššur-iddin's letter POAT 5, which deals with the sale of a load of tin and textiles which has arrived in Kanish. The writer first cancels an earlier instruction to "give" the load to I. (apparently an employee and transporter of the firm), because "he has (already) 'taken' much tin from his (previous) transport" (line 29 speaks of "20 minas of earlier silver owed by him"). The better textiles and the tin now must be handed over or sent to A. (one of the addressees of the letter and hence also an employee or partner of the writer), who has to ship them to "wherever any silver can be earned for me". If A. has already left on a trip, the merchandise has to entrusted to ("laid upon") a reliable agent for a specified credit term (*ana ūmē*) and a few months longer do not matter, if only the agent is reliable![16]

The merchandise such agents received hence could be called *qīptum*, which implies, as is the case in Old Babylonian,[17] that they were middlemen who sold the goods to the real customers and had to pay back in due time to their owners who had granted them credit. As was the case with Old Babylonian *qīptum*-loans, no interest was charged, but the due date of the credit was fixed and the price agreed upon obviously depended to some extent on the length of the credit term. Such credit transactions yielded promissory notes, the most frequent type of Old Assyrian contract, which simply state that a particular person has a debt claim on (*iṣṣēr ... išû*) another person for a sum of silver to be paid not later than a particular date, on penalty of default interest, among Assyrians usually a rate of 30 per cent per year. Occasionally such contracts mention a guarantor, rarely a pledge (see below).[18] Contrary to Rosen, I am convinced that the bulk of these contracts does reflect commercial credit, but this is not so easy to prove because the documents almost never state the reason and background of such debt claims. Among the few exceptions are EL 88, a debt-note for "51 shekels of silver, price of three *kutānum*-textiles", and ICK 1 102, a quittance for "two minas of silver, price of two donkeys and two *kutānum*-textiles".[19] When the debt claims recorded are large amounts of silver or copper a commercial background has to be assumed. But many of the contracts which record relatively small debts of up to one mina of silver, may also reflect credit sale of merchandise, in particular textiles. In the trade documented by the Cairo Geniza it was as true as in Old Assyrian times, to quote again Goitein,[20] that "the wholesale textile merchants often sold single pieces too. The reason for this was the relatively high value of each piece" (good textiles were sold in Anatolia for prices ranging from 10 to 45 shekels of silver apiece, usually 20 to 30 shekels). Of course, various other commercial transactions and liabilities could also result in such promissory notes, which were also drawn up in consequence of settlements of accounts to record remaining debt claims.[21]

---

15 *E.g.* in kt n/k 528 (courtesy of C. Günbattı), which summarizes various such transactions with the words: "In all we entrusted (*niqīp*) two talents minus one mina of silver".

16 The letter has a virtual duplicate in BIN 4 53 and also links up with CCT 4 2b, both of which help to improve its reading and understanding as offered in POAT.

17 See Skaist 1994, 41ff., for Old Babylonian ŠU.LÁ = *qīptum*.

18 See for such contracts EL 12-103, where they figure as *Verpflichtungsscheine*, and Rosen 1977, who edited such contracts published after 1935.

19 It is no accident that these two contracts are the only ones dealing with the sale of imported goods to figure in Kienast 1984.

20 Goitein 1967, 150.

21 Old Assyrian promissory notes almost never use the so-called ŠU BA.AN.TI / *ilqe*-formula, which usually identifies the claim as resulting from a straight loan. The standard formula "creditor has a claim

Proof that the bare facts mentioned in such contracts do reflect commercial credit granted to selling agents may be derived from some letters, called "caravan accounts, group 2" in Larsen 1967, of which the letter BIN 4 61 (Larsen type 3:11) is a good example. It tells us that upon arrival of a caravan with tin and textiles some merchandise was "given" to those working for the sender (lines 42ff.), some was sold to the local palace (44ff.), and some was entrusted to the caravan-leader as interest bearing-loan (49-69). The bulk, however, was entrusted (*illibbi* PN *tadin*) to two persons acting as selling agents, who were to pay for it fixed sums of silver (in all 68 minas) after 45, 47, and 50 weeks (lines 26-42a). Promissory notes for similar amounts of silver and similar credit terms are not rare and the letter quoted explicitly states that the credit agreement resulted in written contracts, whose dates (month III) are mentioned in the caravan account. Many more letters refer to such claims recorded in "valid deeds" (*ṭuppum ḫarmum*), sealed by the debtor, with a fixed due date, but actual contracts which mention more facts than the name of creditor and debtor, the amount of silver to be paid and the due date are rare. An exception, already quoted in Larsen 1967, 162f., is ICK 1 162: "31 minas of tin (and) six *kutānum*-textiles, (part of) our trust (*ša qīptini*), N. has carried to Ḫattum. He shall not yield tin or textiles (to somebody).[22] For this merchandise he will pay eight minas and 10 shekels of silver within 37 weeks, (reckoned) from the week of Š. and D. (sealed by two witnesses)".

The persons who were granted such commercial credit were not working for a fee or a share in the profit, as a Babylonian commercial agent (*šamallāʾum*[23]) might, nor was interest charged for the credit received (as could be the case in Old Babylonian, see the Laws of Hammurabi, paragraph 100). They were only liable for paying the amount of silver stated in the promissory note at the due date mentioned. They would sell the goods during the term granted at the best possible prices and what they earned over the amount due was their own profit, from which they had to live and to cover their expenses. The at times long credit terms must have allowed them to do more than just sell their merchandise and I assume that in the mean time they may have used the silver acquired for additional transactions in the hope of maximalizing their earnings before their due dates[24] (see also below, the remarks on the impact of default interest).

---

of .... on debtor" (*iṣṣēr ... išû*), which does not reveal the background of the transaction, may refer to a straight loan, to commercial credit (*qīptum*), to claims resulting from partial payments and settlements of accounts, and to taxes, fees, and profits still due. The very frequent description of amounts of silver (or merchandise) as *ina libbi* PN, "(still) owed by PN", is equally vague and may refer to all kind of transactions and liabilities. Only interest free loans supplied to personnel contracted to serve as transporters are clearly recognizable, because the loan is designated as *beʾūlātum*, "working capital" (lit. "put at their free disposal", *ana beʾālim*) and their recipient is said "to be held by the silver (received)" (*išti kaspim uktāl*, an expression also used of personal pledges). See for *beʾūlātum*, Kienast 1989 and Veenhof 1994.

22 Assyrian *waššurum*, "to release, to yield", which means credit sale which results in an outstanding claim (*bābtum*) and deferred payment.

23 The term occurs in Old Assyrian, but is rare; see *CAD* Š/1, 291, la.

24 Something similar must have been the case with some Old Babylonian trading agents in Larsa. In TCL 10 125, an agent (in Ešnunna?) receives a consignment of silver for delivery in Larsa, within six or eight months, and in TCL 10 20 the term for delivery of the silver in Susa is five months (see for the texts Leemans 1960, chapter 3). These agents may not have received cash silver, but rather merchandise for which they had to weigh out in due time, in the cities mentioned, silver, presumably less than what they could have earned by selling their goods.

The use of these selling agents allowed merchants to supply more customers and markets and saved them the time and trouble of acting themselves as travelling salesmen in deals with local inhabitants and institutions and to face problems such as deferred payments, payment in other valuta than silver or gold (copper, wool), and various risks and delays due to political or military problems, season (no trade during harvest time), or climate (no trade during winter). In return for fixed and guaranteed sums of silver they must have sacrificed part of the profit and accepted delays in the recovery of the silver. We note that letters frequently raise the issue of the conditions of credit granted, notably the alternatives of cash sale (*ana itaṭlim*), short-term (*ana ūmē qurbūtim*) or long-term (*ana ūmē patiūtim*) credit. "Let your report reach me concerning my merchandise, whether you have entrusted it to an agent for a particular period, or whether you have sold it cash" (kt 87/k 347:11ff., courtesy of K. Hecker). Medium and long-term credit must have allowed better prices. In BIN 4 61, those for the terms of almost one year (45-50 weeks) were one shekel of silver for seven shekels of tin and 30 shekels of silver per textile, which is very favourable. The selling agent of the contract ICK 1 162, quoted in the previous paragraph, would have been able to pay the silver due, if he managed to sell his tin at a rate of one shekel of silver for six shekels of tin (yield: five minas and 10 shekels) and his textiles at 30 shekels apiece (yield: three minas). Hence an even higher price for the tin, notwithstanding the fact that he had about three months less time to realize his sales. The mere existence of this contract shows that such conditions could be met and that there still must have been a margin allowing the agent to earn something for himself. Unfortunately, we are mostly unable to relate such prices to the realities of supply and demand (time, place, specific conditions) and the relations between those granting credit (*e.g.* the anonymous "we" in ICK 1 162) and the selling agents. But there is no doubt that "market factors" were at work, as the letter TC 3 49 shows, where cash sale was impossible and "silver was difficult to obtain/expensive" (*kaspū dannū*). The selling agent eventually found agreed to a credit term of four weeks and it does not surprise that the prices were rather low, in particular that of only 13 1/2 shekels of silver per *kutānum*-textile, which is 55 per cent less than the price in BIN 4 61 and ICK 1 162. But, as will be seen below, there were also cases where indebted and defaulting agents had to accept hard conditions in order to survive.

Equally important must have been at what time of the year credit was granted, because it mattered much whether payment could be expected well before the winter, so that the silver could be sent to Assur in time and people there could arrange to have the next caravan ready for departure in early spring, as soon as "the roads became open". In BIN 4 61, the contracts with the selling agents were drawn up in the third month, that is in early spring, which left them lots of time for selling their goods. The remainder of the merchandise was "given" to an employee of the firm only in the eleventh month, shortly before the winter, and he had to pay only one shekel of silver for eight shekels of tin and 20 shekels of silver per *kutānum*-textile, hence resp. 15 and 33 per cent less, but he was charged interest.

Cash sale, which made it possible to ship the silver to Assur "with the next caravan", in order to equip a new caravan or to pay debts whose "interest is mounting", was of course the most attractive option and at times friends were asked the "favour" (*gimillum*) of paying cash for merchandise from their own funds (see above). Not rare are instructions of the type "They must sell tin and textiles cash, not grant credit, nor yield them. They shall not yield tin and textiles until the silver arrives".[25] We find them in several letters sent by Šalim-aḫum to Pūšu-kēn, but cash sale frequently was impossible. What was meant by "to yield"[26] is not very clear, because it is a general term for giving up possession of something, also used for giving back debt-notes after the debt has been paid. It presumably means real credit sale, not to agents but to customers who will pay later, hence a transaction also described as "leaving behind" (*ezābum*) merchandise, which creates "outstanding claims" (*bābtum*), a frequent topic of Old Assyrian business letters.[27] Other, more careful and patient traders insist on the quality of the selling agent who should be "reliable as you yourself",[28] so that there will be no reason for fear. In such cases they even are ready to grant longer credit,[29] but there were other options too. The writer of the letter POAT 22, Imdīlum, asks his correspondent to sell tin and textiles cash, but "if this is impossible, let my tin remain under seal", hence be kept in store for the time being. At times a compromise was inevitable, as in the unpublished letter kt n/k 524:44ff. (courtesy of C. Günbattı): "Of all the merchandise which has been cleared you must entrust (*nadā'um iṣṣēr*) half at long-term and half at short-term credit to reliable selling agents with fixed terms. Do not attach too much importance to a few months, if only your agents are reliable!". Frequent emphasis on the reliability of the agent is rooted in the experience that *tamkārums* regularly exceed their terms and delay payments, when they get into financial problems or may prove to be "unwise" (*lā tašīmtum*). This creates serious problems for the merchant in question, who has to meet his own due dates for satisfying financiers and authorities in Assur, as we learn from Pūšu-kēn's letter BIN 4 32, discussed in Dercksen's contribution.[30] How merchants tried to deal with defaulting agents will be discussed in paragraph 4.

b. *Straight Loans*

There are dozens of references which show that all kind of traders were able to "obtain silver at interest" (*kaspam ana ṣibtim laqā'um*) in Assur. Frequently this happened "at a merchant's house" (*bēt tamkārim*), at times in considerable quantities, ranging from a few to 30 minas of silver. This shows that there was a lot of silver available in the city and that its owners apparently were ready to use it not only for (long-term) investments in the capital (*naruqqum*) of a trader, but also to extend straight loans at interest to businessmen in need of money. The silver borrowed frequently served to acquire or increase funds necessary for buying merchandise for export to Anatolia. Some examples are: TC 3 26:7: "We borrowed silver in accordance with your instruction and now we will buy textiles"; BIN 6 117:15ff.: "When we bought tin we borrowed four

25 *Ana itaṭlim liddinū lā iqippū lā uššurū adi kaspum errubu annakam u ṣubātī lā uššurū*; variant: *lā uṣṣiū*, "they (the goods) shall not leave (before ...)".

26 *Waššurum*, see above n. 22.

27 See for these terms the literature quoted in n. 7.

28 *Lū kēn kīma qaqqidika.*

29 "Do not attach too much value to a few months" (*warḫam ištên u šina lā tušēqarā* or *tabe'elā*), cf. Veenhof 1972, 443f.

30 Lines 17ff.: "Among the selling agents on whom I depend there are two or three unwise ones, so that I have lost much silver, but it is not expedient to reveal their names to you".

minas of silver at interest; let the interest on the silver not get (too) much!"; TC 1 28:10f.: "Š. and M. brought us 8 1/2 minas of silver and in accordance with your instruction we (also) borrowed silver at a merchant's house and made purchases for you"; TC 2 11:19ff.: "Since tin was expensive, we did not call at a merchant's house and did not buy it, we only sent you what we bought with your own silver"; TC 3 73:28ff.: "(For) the tin I sent him I had borrowed silver at a merchant's house; the interest is mounting, I am worried"; TC 3 36:30ff.: "Your wrote me: 'I will send you the eight minas of silver later'. Since the caravan [is delayed?], we borrowed 7 1/2 minas [+ x shekels] of silver as equivalent of the (delayed) eight minas of silver"; AnOr 6 2 rev. 5'ff.: "We borrowed five minas (of silver) at a merchant's house and we (ourselves) added six minas of silver. We paid it for (buying) the textiles for wrapping which E. had brought for you, until the silver shipped by Ḫ. had arrived".

All examples mention the borrowing of silver and the question arises whether loans granted or credit received "at a merchant's house" could not also consist of merchandise (hence tin and textiles), perhaps rated in and in due time to be paid in silver. In the the unpublished text kt m/k 92:14f. (courtesy of K. Hecker), which uses the designation *qīptum*, we read: "We fully paid in silver (*kaspam nušabbi*) for all *qīptum*-loans we contracted at a/various merchant's house(s)",[31] but their is no proof that *qīptum* here refers to merchandise. CCT 4 32b:15 states: "For the merchandise (*luqūtum*) which we contracted (as a loan; verb *šasāʾum*) at a merchant's house, you only sent us the capital sum (*šīmat kaspim*); because we also had to add interest and had to refine the silver (you sent), the merchant still has a claim on us of one mina and 22 1/3 shekels of silver and he retained our promissory note. (To pay it) we borrowed the silver at interest and interest accrues since the eleventh month". Here the loan or credit received could be the merchandise mentioned, but it certainly is not impossible to understand the words "the merchandise which we contracted (as loan)" as an abbreviation of "the merchandise for (the purchase of which) we contracted (a loan)". Without better proof the question has to remain open.

Loans were also taken out to meet financial liabilities, both debts to the City-office (for which people were dunned by the *līmum*-official, who could seal the house of a debtor and eventually even sell it) and to private creditors. I offer just a few illustrative examples. According to kt n/k 515 and related texts,[32] D. who was guarantor for M., "called at a merchant's house to borrow eight minas of silver and paid it for your debt to the City-office". In TPAK 1 26:17ff., *bērum*-officials (inspectors?) in Assur seized a family's house for debts to the City, whereupon "we called at a merchant's house for 75 shekels of silver, your share, and paid it to the *bērū*, who brought it to the City-office". Private debts are a reason for borrowing money, *e.g.* in BIN 6 74: 6-15, where I. writes to E.: "You wrote me as follows: 'Let your report reach me about how much silver you took at interest [9] and inform me.' As soon as I heard this tablet I wrote you in my letter [12] 'For the 30 minas of silver which you owe me I borrowed refined silver at an interest of 5/6 shekel (per mina per month)'". This also happens in ATHE 28:17-25: "In addition to the 18 minas of silver which you brought me, I borrowed for you 13 minas of refined silver at an interest of 20 per cent per year. They sealed our contract and then we paid 31

---

31 The verb is in the iterative Gtn-stem and *bēt tamkārim*, with the regens in the construct state, may also be a plural.

32 See the analysis in Veenhof 1995, 1723f.

minas of refined silver, your debt to P.". In a letter in the Trinity Museum of Archaeology (San Antonio; unpublished), the addressee is asked to collect a claim which P. has on E. and he is ordered: "If he (= E.) refuses to settle the silver account and does not yield the merchandise, borrow eight minas of silver at interest and let P. establish his claim on it".

Silver and at times copper were also borrowed for the purchase of usually expensive houses in Assur.[33] The writer of the letter VS 26 8 tells the addressee: "We borrowed at interest the silver which we owe to A. and paid him. We also borrowed six talents of copper, being the price of the house. Send silver lest the interest becomes a problem for you (*imarraṣakkum*)" (lines 9-18). And in TTC 6:12ff., a letter addressed to Pūšu-kēn, we read: "Ša. and Šu., without (consulting) us, bought the house for you for 16 minas of silver and now they have written to you: 'We borrowed the silver at interest'. But we did not borrow any silver at interest for you, Ša. paid 10 minas of silver as price for the house out of his own money".[34]

Borrowing silver for such purposes apparently was an established practice and one never reads that this was difficult or impossible. Silver was available and its owners were ready to extend loans, not only friendly advances or soft, interest-free loans to relatives and close associates, on whose help one might rely "when one had to be saved" (*ana ūm eṭārim*), but also business loans at the attractive rate of interest of 30 per cent per year, at times also cheaper. We have references both to people taking out such loans and to those granting them and to how they recorded them in valid debt-notes. The writer of kt n/k 486 (unpublished, courtesy C. Günbattı) gives the following instruction: "As for the 30 minas of silver I wrote you about, let E. give 20 minas of silver and you yourself give 10 minas, send it to me (in Assur) and take the interest from me when I arrive". In AKT 3 64:7-12, a debt of more than 11 minas of silver had to be paid to I. The debtors sent one mina of gold and two minas of silver and add: "As for the remainder, borrow at interest whatever you need and pay the debt we owe to I.". The writer of TC 3 31 asks his addressees "to deposit silver as his share at the *kārum*-office and to take it from the silver you have obtained from my outstanding claims. If you have not obtained it from [my] outstanding claims, borrow it at interest" (lines 29-33). Some texts show that traders used the possibility of lending out silver which would not be used for making purchases in the near future, in order to make it productive.[35] BIN 6 25:15ff. "You wrote me: 'B. has paid us silver and it lies idle here (*nadi*)'. The silver must not lie idle (*lā nadi*)! If I. needs it, let him take it, but if not, lend it out (*tadānum*) at interest!" Very instructive is Šū-Suen's letter VS 26 69:

> E. brought 20 minas of silver under your seals and the son of K. brought you 10 minas. Was it my instruction to have the silver sent in order to let it lie idle? Please, my brothers, if one needs silver in the *kārum*-office, unpack the silver and loan it at

---

33 See also Michel 1996, 295f.

34 See for this letter C. Michel, *RA* 80 (1986), 110f. The letter written by Ša. and Šu. must have been very similar to TC 2 11, where Aššur-bānī and Ša. inform Pūšu-kēn about their purchase of the house in question for 16 minas of silver.

35 Silver not used, not invested in the trade for making purchases and profit, could be said "to be(come) hungry", see Veenhof 1987, 62ff.

interest. If you cannot give it to the *kārum*-office, loan it at interest to a trader reliable as you yourselves, who need not be feared![36]

Another example is VS 26 67:7ff.: "You wrote me as follows: 'We acquired the silver of A., but since the terms of your selling agents were almost due (*ūmū tamkārīka qurbū*), we loaned it at interest, thinking: we will send all the silver (later) with Š.' Payment by my agents, however, has been delayed (*ūmū tamkārīa ana warkišunu ittūrūnim*), therefore send the silver of A. with K. and do not (wait until you can also) send the silver of my agents." In the letter I 637, in reaction to a request to buy tin in order to earn ("make") silver, the writer answers: "There is no tin for sale here, but there is silver for sale and you must send as much silver as can be put out at interest" (*ana ṣibtim alākum*). Revealing is the text of the last will *RA* 60 (1966), 143:26ff., where two ladies receive as their share in an inheritance the usufruct of a capital of five minas of silver (which eventually will be divided between two brothers), which is put out at interest: "From the remainder (of the assets) they will put out at interest five minas of silver and she and her mother will have its usufruct (*ekkalā*)". In TC 3 29:10ff. a trader, being asked for silver, answers: "the silver has been put out at interest, I need its interest".

All this suggests that there was indeed a constant circulation of silver in Assur and in this flow we can distinguish various "streams". In the *first* place the vast amounts of silver which arrive from Anatolia, the bulk of which was regularly used by "Kanish traders" to buy merchandise for caravans leaving for Anatolia. Most of this silver was paid to the "houses" of merchants, and presumably also to the "City-office" (*bēt ālim*), which acted as a kind of wholesale dealers. The latter in turn must have used a large part of this silver to buy tin and textiles from the traders (from Elam (?) and Babylonia) who imported these goods into Assur. This is the *second* stream, which left Assur. In the *third* place there was the stream of silver made available to those who traded on Anatolia, either as long-term investment (*naruqqum, ebuṭṭū*, etc) or by granting credit and straight loans to those in need of cash. The first and third streams to a considerable extent must have consisted of the same silver, earned by "Kanish traders" and reinvested in the trade by Assur-based merchants. We have to assume that investments, commercial credit, and short-term loans of some size - apart from what moved between close relatives and business partners - were granted by persons grown rich from the trade. This group of people probably comprised men of means who had always stayed in Assur and successful, presumably older merchants who had returned there from Anatolia and may have become wholesale dealers who granted credit and used their capital also as financiers and money-lenders. Both may have functioned as a kind of merchant-bankers, who could supply the silver needed by the traders. If this is correct, we may perhaps distinguish two kinds of merchants. On the one hand those directly involved in the actual trade on Anatolia, frequently on the move or staying abroad and constantly in need of silver for their transactions and hence pressing their debtors and selling agents for prompt payment. On the other hand those, presumably older and richer, who lived in Assur as wholesale dealers, investors, and merchant-bankers. They enjoyed the 30 per cent interest received on credit and loans and hence perhaps were more patient with their debtors as long as the latter did not default on interest, while they could supplement their earnings as money-lenders by the dividends and profits which their investments yielded.

36 See the edition of this letter in Michel 1991, 230f. no. 169; I take lines 6f. as an ironical question.

The references to borrowing silver (and occasionally also copper), including those which add "at a merchant's house", however, are not restricted to Assur. The same happened in Anatolia, especially in Kanish, as the following examples show. In EL 254 the representatives of the debtor Š. authorize the son of his creditor "to borrow silver at a merchant's house at interest", promising that they would pay him back capital plus interest from the assets of the debtor. According to TPAK 1 6:8ff., "We called at a merchant's house for two talents of copper and paid it to our father's creditor", and also in kt e/k 67 somebody "borrows copper at interest" in order to be able to pay the instalment of his debt to his creditor. In I 612 the writer states: "I borrowed 8 1/4 shekels of silver at a merchant's house and paid it to the Anatolian for our mother's debt". TC 3 67:10ff. mentions that the trader Enlil-bānī "had been booked in a merchant's house as guarantor for K.", who must have borrowed silver there, and kt m/k 122:24ff. (courtesy of K. Hecker) mentions "silver for settling accounts, at a rate of three shekels per mina, at a merchant's house, paid in the name of K.". Other examples of silver borrowed in Anatolia are TC 2 39:21ff. (3 1/2 minas) and BIN 6 33 (10 minas), while the writer of CCT 4 8b:16ff., who intends "to sell tin before there is too much tin here" (which will affect the price), "will borrow tin for a value of 10 minas of silver at a merchant's house". We also have about a dozen debt-notes, which authorize the creditor "to enter a merchant's house and to borrow silver at interest for (at the expense of) the debtor" if the latter fails to pay back in time (published examples: EL 87 and 185; ICK 2 95 and 147; AKT 1 34; TPAK 1 169), most of which seem to refer to transactions in Anatolia. Finally it should be mentioned here that the expression "to enter a merchant's house in order to borrow (take) silver (at interest)" has a perfect parallel on the Anatolian scene, where the word "merchant" (which in Anatolia may also have the meaning "Assyrian trader") is replaced by "native Anatolian" (*nuʾāʾum*).[37] It shows that for people in need of cash also Anatolian merchants or money-lenders were available. The only published occurrence is in AKT 2 53:20-24: "Make Š. pay the silver and if he refuses to pay, say to him: 'I will borrow it at interest in the house of an Anatolian'".

c. *Borrowing at a bēt tamkārim*

In many cases loans are referred to simply by the words "to borrow (take) silver at interest" (*kaspam ana ṣibtim laqāʾum*), without any indication of where and from whom the silver was borrowed. But more frequently (in a few dozen cases) it is stated that silver is borrowed "at a merchant's house" (*bēt tamkārim*; henceforth *b.t.*). The majority are in letters, which give instructions about or report on such loans, but there are also about 10 occurrences in promissory notes, which stipulate that, if the debtor defaults the creditor will "take" the silver due "at a merchant's house". While promissory notes are always formulated objectively, in the third person ("the creditor has a claim of x silver on the debtor"), the clause authorizing the creditor to borrow is always in the first person singular. We meet it in various formulations:

---

37 Kt f/k 101:22f. distinguishes a person's debtors in *nuʾāʾū* and *tamkārū*. In the divorce settlement kt n/k 1414:7ff. (Sever 1992) the divorced wife is allowed "to go either to a *nuʾāʾum* or to a *tamkārum*, whatever she prefers", and the letter kt k/k 47:9ff. asks for the purchase of two slave boys (*ṣuḫārū*), "either of *tamkārums* or of citizens of Kanish".

1) "I will enter and take (the) silver at a merchant's house" (*errabma b.t. kaspam alaqqe*),
   EL 87:11ff.;185:12ff.; kt a/k 604:10f.;
2) "I will enter and take silver in a merchant's house" (*errabma ina b.t. kaspam alaqqe*),
   I 475:17ff.;
3) "I will enter a merchant's house and take silver" (*ana b.t. errabma kaspam alaqqe*),
   ICK 2 147:19'ff. (*nerrabma*, with two creditors, who borrow "the silver and the interest on it"); TPAK 1 169:7'f. (in a letter);
4) "I will take silver at a merchant's house" (*kaspam b.t. alaqqe*, without *errab),*
   AKT 1 34:15ff.; ICK 2 95:8f.

Interest is mentioned in various ways. I 475 writes "I will take silver at interest" (*ana ṣibtim*), followed by "and he shall compensate (*malluʾum*) the interest". TPAK 1 169:10'f. adds "and you will be responsible to me for (*ana .... tazzazzam*) the silver and the interest on it". Some contracts do not speak only of "taking silver", but state that the loan is *ana bitiqtim*, "(to make up) for what is missing" (AKT 1 34:15f.; EL 185:13f.; kt a/k 604:11f.), or add that "he (the debtor) shall compensate what is missing" (*bitiqtam šūtma umalla*; AKT 1 34:18f.; kt a/k 604:14f.; ICK 2 95:10, with plural *bitqātim*). In some cases we have *alaqqešum* (EL 87:13; AKT 1 34:17; kt a/k 604:13; in letters also *alaqqeʾakkum*), where the pronominal dative suffix refers to the debtor "for whom/at whose expense" the silver is borrowed.

The occurrences in promissory notes are the only ones where the verb "to enter" is used to describe the action of the creditor;[38] it never occurs in letters. I would link this with the fact that it is only in these contracts that the creditor speaks in the first person ("I will enter and take ...") and assume that they reveal the full wording (*verba solemnia*) of a formulaic expression by means of which the creditor publicly states his right to indemnify himself at the expense of the defaulting debtor. Letters and other non-legal documents omit the formulaic "I will enter and", without changing the meaning.

There are actually two variants when the expression is used without the verb "to enter". One uses the verb "to take/to borrow" (*laqāʾum*), the other the verb "to call (at)" (*šasāʾum, e.g.* CCT 4 32b:4f.; KTS 9a:5; TC 1 28:7; TC 2 11:20; TPAK 1 6:11f.; 26:17f.; *CAD* Š/3, 159f., 6 translates: "to ask a creditor for, to contract for a loan"). The use of the latter verb perhaps indicates a public and formal act, since borrowing at the expense of somebody else cannot be done privately, but requires witnesses and probably evidence of the claim on which the action is based. Compare also the Old Babylonian expression *bīt (*in Old Babylonian Susa also *bāb*) PN *šasûm*, "to call at a person's house/gate to demand (something from him)", which also has a formal ring.[39] But *laqāʾum* and *šasāʾum* are used as synonyms in our expression, as the alternation between the two in EL 309, tablet and case (both with personal dative suffix) shows.

---

38 Earlier (see *e.g.* EL 87 with commentary) the debtor was considered to be the subject of the verb "to enter" and the clause was interpreted as stating that he would "enter the house of the creditor (*tamkārum*)", presumably in antichretic debt bondage. The occurrence of the plural *nerrab*, "we will enter", in ICK 2 147:19', followed by *kaspam nilaqqe*, "we will borrow the silver", shows that it actually was the creditor who took out the loan.

39 See the discussion in Kraus 1984, 301f.

Equally remarkable in the expression is the regular mention of "the house" of the merchant as the place where one borrows silver, also in the dozens of occurrences which omit the verb "to enter". This mention of "the house of the merchant" as the place where one borrows is also (but rarely) attested in Old Babylonian. In ARMT 13 17 rev. 2', it occurs together with the verb "to enter", when a heavily fined man states "I will en[ter] the house of a merchant and will borrow [silver]".[40] In AbB 9 64:10f. a man intends "to borrow (take) silver in a merchant's house" in order to buy an ox (cf. AbB 13 53:13). But one may also omit "the house" and use simply (*kaspam*) *itti tamkārim leqûm* (AbB 12 88:25, for buying barley; perhaps also AbB 13 4:7), which parallels in Old Assyrian *kaspam išti tamkārim laqā*ʾ*um* (CCT 4 49a:17f.), which is very rare. The use of *erābum* in the full expression shows that *bētum* is a physical entity, not "firm, household", but "house". The substantial loans we are dealing with were not negotiated on the market, but in a merchant's office and the expression evokes the picture of a person in need of silver calling at and entering a merchant-banker's office, where the latter works, keeps his bullion (in a strongroom or safe) and draws up and keeps his records.

How we understand *bēt tamkārim* depends on the interpretation of *tamkārum*. Garelli described him as a kind of merchant-banker, whose role or perhaps duty it was to facilitate commercial transactions of other merchants by granting credit and also by taking care of the sale of merchandise on the basis of his knowledge of the market. The many debt-notes with *tamkārum* as creditor would reflect his role as *intermédiaire agréé*, because they would allow merchants who granted credit to travelling traders to transfer their claims to such a *tamkārum*, who then could pay off their debts or carry out purchases for them.[41] In a later study he draws the picture of the well-known merchant Pūšu-kēn as such a *tamkārum*.[42] In his first analysis he also quotes TC 1 28:6f., where he translates *kaspam bēt tamkārim laqā*ʾ*um* with "prélever de l'argent dans la maison du *tamkārum*" (in this letter for making purchases in Assur) and this indicates that in his opinion it was indeed the house of such an intermediary where one usually borrowed silver. Garelli's use of the article ("du *tamkārum*"), while probably not to indicate that there was only one such figure, nevertheless suggests a specific function held by a few persons generally known and recognized as such, which hence could remain anonymous.

It is difficult to find conclusive evidence for this view and in my opinion none of the texts discussed by Garelli supports it. We certainly know that not all people designated as *tamkārum* had the same status, job, or background. The term is frequently used to designate the selling agents who acquired merchandise on credit, at times it is the designation of important managers or *tractatores*, presumably the heads of the Anatolian branches of the firms and prominent ("big") members of Kanish (probably also known as "*dātum*-payers" or "men with an account" in the *kārum*-office), at times it designates the owners of silver or merchandise who wish to remain anonymous. The noun, in my opinion, is less a professional designation than a term indicating a person's activity or function in a particular context.[43] This ambiguity makes it difficult to prove and risky to

40 See the improved rendering of this text in *MARI* 1 (1982), 149f.

41 Garelli 1963, 237f.

42 Garelli 1977.

43 See the remarks in Veenhof 1997, 351-364 on the use of the term, the role of the *tamkārum*, and his frequent anonymity. [But I have to add now that a recently deciphered text, kt 92/k 206:11 and 30,

assume that the *tamkārums* in whose houses one could borrow silver represented a special class, with a specific function. A translation "a merchant's house" hence is fully acceptable. It implies that there were several (perhaps many) merchants who were ready and perhaps in the habit of loaning silver. And in fact, such "houses" do not occur only in Assur, but also in Anatolia. Moreover, that Assyrians, as pointed out above (3b, end), could "borrow silver at a native's house" (*bēt nuʾāʾim*), indicates that rich Anatolian merchants were ready to loan silver in a similar way, and there is no evidence that the Anatolian kingdoms too had special *intermédiares agréés* to facilitate the trade. Just as in the trade documented by the Geniza material, succesful merchants not only regularly granted commercial credit in natura, but could also supply straight loans for commercial purposes.

Perhaps we may go one step further and suggest that wealthy merchants who did not (no longer?) travel used their capital more and more for financing the trade, either as investors, or by granting commercial credit (especially if they were also owners of warehouses), or by straight loans, satisfied with the dividends, profits, fees and interest they were entitled to (usually 30 per cent per year, but 20 per cent in ATHE 28:20 and 16 2/3 per cent in BIN 6 74:14). They were willing and able to provide cash silver, at times as short-term loan, when traders were temporarily short of funds or wanted to carry out purchases or to leave on a caravan journey before the silver due from Anatolia had arrived. Just as there were other merchants who, when the silver from Anatolia could not yet be used for the trade, tried to put it out at interest, because they hated to see it "lie idle" (see above, 2b). Such practices help to explain that a list of a dead merchant's assets mentions not only "silver under seals which he has left behind, silver of his which he has deposited somewhere, and tablets of his with oustanding claims", but also "silver which he has loaned at interest to somebody (*lū kaspam ana ṣibtim ana mamman iddin*), either in Ḫattum or in Burušḫattum".[44] The rare Old Babylonian references to (houses of) merchants where one may borrow silver (for making purchases) must reflect a similar situation. There is no reason to assume, with W.F. Leemans, a more public or at least communal character of such a *bīt tamkārim*.[45]

3. *Special Arrangements*

Besides straight silver loans to traders and credit granted to selling agents (which resulted in debt-notes simply mentioning a silver debt), there were various other forms of commercial credit, whereby silver or merchandise were entrusted to relatives and business associates on special conditions. As an example I quote KTH 24 (= EL 109, analysed in Larsen 1967, 24), which concerns a certain Dadāja (= D.):

> The 15 minas of refined silver, excise added and transport fee paid for, which $S._1$ made D. bring to the City, to the address of P., E., and I., for making purchases - the

mentions a year-eponym identified not only by the name of his father but also by the designation *tamkārum*: "Abu-šalim, *tamkārum*, son of Iliānum".]

44 P. Garelli, *RA* 59 (1965), 152 no. 23: 45ff.

45 In his *The Old Babylonian Merchant* (SD 3, Leiden 1950), 89f., where he refers for his interpretation to the meaning of *bēt tamkārim* in Old Assyrian!

silver from here (Kanish) and the merchandise from there (Assur) will cross the country in the name of *tamkārum*. When the merchandise will come up from the City, if he wants (it), D. can take the merchandise and pay 22 1/2 minas of silver. If he does not want (it), *tamkārum* will take the merchandise and he will hand over to D. the tablet which $A._1$, $A._2$., and L. have sealed. Witnessed by $S._2$, $A._3$, and $A._1$.

This is neither a straight loan nor credit granted to a selling agent, nor a standard partnership (which implies sharing profit and losses). D. also seems to be more than a normal transporter (*kaṣṣārum*) - who works within the framework of a service contract and brings silver to Assur and merchandise back to Kanish - since he has the option of buying the merchandise upon arrival in Kanish. Moreover, the last clause shows that there was a previous contract (recording a liability of his), which will be "yielded" (*waššurum*) to him if he does not take the merchandise but leaves it to *tamkārum*. The latter must be identified with $S._1$, the owner of the silver, in whose name and at whose cost silver and merchandise are shipped, but who wants to remain anonymous. As the discussion by Larsen shows (1967, 24 with 179f.), it is not easy to discover what is behind this contract. The most likely solution, in my opinion, is that D. is "used" by $S._1$ to get a lot of merchandise from Assur to Kanish, because D. owes him a debt (recorded in the tablet he eventually will get back). The "value" of the work to be done by D. is fixed at 7 1/2 minas of silver and if he yields the goods brought from Assur to his creditor, his debt to the same amount (cf. the debt recorded in two documents edited in Larsen 1967, 22f.) will be cancelled. The alternative is to pay 22 1/2 minas of silver (the silver given him plus the added value once the goods are in Kanish) to his creditor and to keep the merchandise. He is assumed to be able to sell them in Anatolia with a profit of even more than 50 per cent, which will allow him to pay his creditor (he would have signed a promissory note for the 22 1/2 minas of silver, or perhaps more depending the length of his credit term) and also to earn something for himself.

Was this a normal arrangement or something special? The limited number of such agreements suggests the latter and the fact that the conditions laid down for D. are not unfavourable, is indicative of a form of help rather than an ultimatum by his creditor.

From time to time Old Assyrian traders of course did run into financial problems, due to losses during caravan trips, political unrest in Anatolia (resulting in the breaking down of communications, *sukurtum*), delayed payments (by agents and by local palaces), defaulting debtors, or actions (such as smuggling) which earned them at times heavy fines (in Assur) or imprisonment and payment of ransom (in Anatolia). All these misfortunes could result in mounting debts and interest, but it remains a guess how frequent and serious such problems were, since most of our evidence bears on individual cases reported in letters which are difficult to date. The well-known trader Pūšu-kēn obviously ran into serious financial problems in his earlier years, as described in the famous letter BIN 4 32.[46] And when he had died, his daughter wrote, in a letter in Prague (I 680), that "the complete fortune of our father has been spent" (*emūq abini kulušu ittagmar*), even though that clearly was too pessimistic an assessment, since Pūšu-kēn's children do inherit shares in the various investments he had made.

Mutual help among partners and relatives, supplemented by straight loans, could help to overcome temporary cash problems, as pointed out above. When problems got

46 See Garelli 1963, 233f., and Dercksen elsewhere in this volume.

very serious special measures might be taken, because the commercial debts usually were so big that the traditional Mesopotamian security devices such as pledging, selling property, and debt slavery must have been utterly insufficient; only the forced sale of expensive houses in Assur might have helped. Since nobody would really profit from a bankruptcy, it may have been up to the creditors to try to solve such crises, in particular if the person in problems was a relative, a close business associate, or employee, whose ruin would have both economic and social effects (for traders their "reputation", *šumu*, was very important, and "coming to shame in the city-gate" was dreadful). The obvious solution was to offer the debtor a chance to recover (*balāṭum*) by granting him a special loan or credit while exploiting the only asset he still had to offer, his energy and skill. The person (boss, creditor, guarantor, etc.) who helped the debtor of course wanted to make sure that the loan given or the merchandise entrusted to the debtor would not be seized by other creditors and would be put to good use in Assur, through the purchase of merchandise which could be sold in Anatolia with a nice profit. In some cases, it seems, the debtor was not even granted a loan, but is simply exploited as transporter or agent for his creditor, so that his condition was not unlike that of an person working for his creditor as antichretic pledge.

A first example of such a special arrangement concerns Kukkulānum (henceforth K.) in his relation with Enlil-bānī (henceforth E.), as described in EL 108 (published as VS 26 102), TC 3 67, and CCT 3 27a. All three texts were edited and discussed in Larsen 1967, 8ff., as his "standard texts" (the contract type 1:1, and the letters type 2:1 and type 3:1), on the assumption that all three indeed refer to the same transaction. K. travels to Assur with 30 minas of silver, entrusted to him for transport (type 1:1:5), secured by his own and E.'s seals (type 2:1:6f.), but also called "E.'s silver" (type 1:1:7). E. had formally established his claim on or title to this silver ("E.'s hand has been laid on it", *qātam šakānum ina*, type 2:1:13f.), and the same has to be done in Assur by E.'s representatives (the addressees of the letter type 2:1) with the merchandise bought there, publicly (type 1:2:26f. specifies "in the city-gate"). In Assur the purchase of tin and textiles has to be closely supervised by E.'s representatives, who have to assist K. (type 2:1:15f.), so that the purchase is one which guarantees profit, allows him "to recover" (*šīmum ša balāṭišu*, a term typical for such situations).[47] E. advised them to use half of the silver for buying tin and half for buying textiles, apparently in order to spread the risk (type 2:1:17f.).[48] When the caravan with tin and textiles arrives in Kanish, E. will take the merchandise (type 1:1:13ff.; one of the alternatives mentioned in EL 109, quoted above). The special arrangement which allows E. to control every stage of the transaction and to secure a profitable purchase, must be explained from the fact that E. "has been inscribed here (in Kanish) in a merchant's house as K.'s guarantor" (type 2:1:10ff.; *qātāt* K. *allipit*). Apparently K. had been forced to borrow a substantial amount of silver from a merchant-banker and E. had been ready to guarantee for him, which implies a fairly close relationship between the two. E. may have been the head of the firm for which K. was working and/or E. already may have had a debt claim on K. (in type 3:1:35, K. calls E. *tamkārum*). As guarantor E. would have to pay for K. if he defaulted,[49] hence E.'s

47 See for this terminology, Veenhof 1987, 56ff.

48 For unknown reasons much more silver is used for buying tin, even though it was expensive, than for textiles.

49 As will be shown below, the distinction between a guarantor and a co-debtor was not very big.

concern to use the loan optimally, also for his own benefit. The "caravan account" (text type 3:1, sent from Assur) reveals that K. brings back an amount of textiles and tin, which could be sold in Anatolia for at least 50 to 60 minas of silver, presumably more than enough to pay back the loan from the merchant-banker.

However, if the contract type 1:1 bears on this same transaction, E. would have taken the merchandise upon arrival in Kanish and then it remains unclear what benefit K. would have derived from his caravan journey. If the 30 minas of silver really was the amount borrowed by K. from a merchant-banker, it is strange that E. fully controls the transaction and is entitled to take the merchandise upon arrival in Kanish. In my view, the only solution which explains all the facts is that E., as guarantor, already had been forced to pay for K. and that the amount of 30 minas of silver was actually made available to K. by E. in order to allow him to recover. Type 1:1 then shows that K. was only "used" as transporter in order to allow E. to make profit from selling merchandise brought from Assur by K. How K. would have had to pay his own debts (which had forced him to take out the loan) remains unclear. He did not have the favourable option offered Dadāja in EL 109.

Since the interpretation of the relationship between E. and K. is difficult and hypothetical, I offer a few other examples of "special arrangements". The second is POAT 2, which records an arrangement between I. and his creditor A. It reads:

> [1] A. will give to I. 10 minas of refined silver for one year. I. will add the excise and transport fee, and [7] for the silver which A. will give to I. a debt-note of I. for an amount of 29 minas of silver will be drawn up, [11] stating that the silver will travel twice to the City and that A. (then) will take his 29 minas of silver. [15] If there is more, I. will take it, if there is too little, I. will supplement it. [18] From month IV, eponymy-year of PN. [20] The valid debt-notes in Kanish, Durḫumid, or Kunanamid, or those in the possession of D. - all these earlier bonds recording debts of I. are herewith cancelled. (Before three witnesses).

The last lines show that this agreement (still to be carried out, since all verbs are in the future tense) results from a settlement of accounts between A. and I. Its purpose is to enable I., by means of to caravan trip to Assur, to earn an amount of silver which has to be paid to A., apparently his creditor, enough to pay for his old debts and to return the new loan of 10 minas. This makes it highly likely that this new loan was granted for this very purpose and the rather harsh conditions - almost tripling the amount borrowed by two trips Kanish-Assur and *vice versa* within one year,[50] - suggest that I. was in serious problems and had little choice. The operations would be successful if I. managed to realize a net profit of ca. 75 per cent per trip,[51] which means a gross profit of ca. 100 per cent, minus travel expenses of ca. 10 per cent per trip, exit and import fees, dead capital invested in donkeys and loans to personnel, etc. Note that I. does not have to hand over to A. the merchandise brought from Assur (as K. has to E. in the previous case and as is one of the options of Dadāja in EL 109), but simply an amount of silver. This means that he is supposed to sell himself the merchandise brought twice from Assur, and that all

---

50 EL 109, analysed above, starts from a profit of only 50 per cent per trip.

51 The curious amount of 29 minas may reflect the amount of the previous debts plus interest or be equal to three times the loan minus certain fees and costs.

within one year. The agreement is dated to the fourth month, which means early spring, so that I. would have had at least eight months available, ca. six months for travelling twice to Assur and back (ca. six weeks per trip), plus two months for selling the loads in Anatolia. This may have allowed him to succeed, but it is a tight schedule and the agreement is realistic enough to consider both a deficit and a surplus.

There are a few other texts which inform us about the possibilities of multiplying a sum of silver by caravan trips Assur-Kanish and *vice versa*. In the unpublished contract Cole 1, a person who receives 31 3/4 minas of silver agrees to pay back 42 1/3 minas or 50 per cent more to his creditor "after the merchandise has come up from the City and has been converted into silver". EL 216 assumes that a trader who is given 30 minas of silver is able to pay back the double (*i.e.* one talent) if "the silver travels twice to the City".[52] These arrangements are much more realistic and favourable than the one of POAT 2, which can only be compared with ICK 2 262, where one-third mina has to become one mina "when he comes up from the City", but here the amount of silver is very small indeed.

My third example is in BIN 4 224, a letter written by Iddin-Suen (I.) to the creditors (*bēl kaspim*) of Aššur-bēl-malkim (A.), which deals with the debts of the latter. It reads:

> [7] 30 minas of silver A. owes to you (plur.) and he also owes me 30 minas of silver, for which I have his valid bond. According to your proposal, you would make available (*nadāʾum*, "deposit") the capital put at his disposal (*būlātišu)* and the silver which you yourselves hold back (*kaʾulum*), [14] and send that silver to the City, so that goods bought would come up (to Anatolia) and you then could satisfy yourselves (*tuštabbā*) with your silver and I would take what remains. [19] A. is now bringing you 11 minas of silver under my seal and you must (now) give back his capital which you hold back. Seal all this silver together and send it to Š. and your representatives (in Assur), [25] and let A., assisted by your representatives, carry out a purchase which is profitable for him (*šīmam ša balāṭišu*) and let the merchandise come up and be converted into silver and then satisfy yourselves with your silver and I will take what remains.[34] If you do not put this silver and his capital which you hold back under seal and send it to the City, you must divide with me (what is available) on the basis of our respective claims in silver (*ana baʾabāt kaspini*).

Without entering into the details of this complicated arrangement, we can state that A. was a debtor both of I. and of a group of creditors. Both had agreed to make capital available to A., which would allow him to make a caravan trip to Assur and back, in the

---

52 Travelling twice to the City is also mentioned in ATHE 64:18ff. but without exact figures. I also mention the contract published recently as AKT 3 28, where an anonymous creditor (*tamkārum*) "gives" to the scribe A. the huge amount of 92 minas of silver, to be shipped to Assur for making purchases. The creditor is entitled to take the merchandise which A. will bring up from Assur, if he likes it. If not, A. has to pay him the double, "[three talents and] four minas of silver". The second alternative implies that A. would be able to make a net profit of at least 100 per cent on the sale of the merchandise in Anatolia. Damage of the text (line 22) robs us of information on the amount of time granted him to achieve this, but the contract is dated to the eighth month, which may have left him just enough time to ship the merchandise to Anatolia before the winter. The fact that A., if his creditor decides to take the merchandise, was left with empty hands and apparently without reward for his caravan trip, may indicate that A. as a defaulting debtor was "exploited" by his creditor, as was Kukkulānum in EL 108.

hope that the proceeds of this trip would allow them to get back their silver. I. is rather modest in proposing that they would first take their claim, whereas he would be satisfied with what remains. The amount of silver to be made available to A. by the creditors apparently is a capital to which A. is somehow entitled without owning it, "capital put at his disposal" (*būlātišu*), but which they (because he is a defaulting debtor?) "hold back", *i.e.* thus far have not made available to him (lines 12f. mention "his capital *and* the silver which you hold back", line 21 has "his capital which you hold back"). The last line of the letter, which is a plea to the creditors to live up to their earlier promise, states that if this arrangement cannot be carried out, the creditor and the writer will have to divide A.'s assets in proportion to their claims and to be satified with what is now available.

This document is interesting because it shows that different creditors cooperated to reach an agreement on supplying a defaulting debtor with a loan, a special arrangement for granting commercial credit, which aims at recovering their capital.

4. *Collection and Payment of Debts*

A system based on regular commercial credit and deferred payments, supplemented by straight loans, could only thrive if financial liabilities were taken seriously (the "ethics" of the trade), could be enforced, and if there existed good procedures for collecting payments. This was particularly urgent in a system of overland trade, based on at times complicated contractual (which is not identical to written) relationships, where those involved could not always be personally present on due dates at places agreed, while at the same time the caravan system required good timing.

Collection of payments due in general seems to have worked fairly well, otherwise the trade could not have been so successful. On the other hand, in many letters and judicial records (of private summonses and formal trials) collecting payments, dunning overdue or defaulting debtors, and solving disagreements on such liabilities are important and frequent issues. The imperatives "seize him and make him pay" (*ṣabassuma šašqilšu*) abound in the correspondence and concern in particular the many, at times elusive selling agents (called *tamkārum*), who had acquired lots of merchandise on credit (for which they sealed promissory notes rated in silver) and regularly exceeded their terms (*ūmē šētuqum*). The occasional insistence on "reliable ones, trustworthy as you yourself, for which you don't have to be afraid" and the existence of many memorandums listing overdue commercial debts from various years, also point to problems. Some may have been due to special circumstances - *e.g.* interruption of commercial trafic (*sukurtum*, "blockade"; political turmoil) or the sudden death of an active trader, which always meant delays and complications - but they are not the main causes of financial problems of merchants.

It is difficult to estimate how serious and frequent such payment problems were. The written sources which mention them in many cases owe their existence to them and transactions finished smoothly do not leave such written traces. The briskness of the trade and the large number of participants must have meant many hundreds of individual transactions each year, so that a few dozen problem cases should not surprise us. More serious difficulties, moreover, could easily result in small files (of up to 10 documents) of letters and records, all dealing with one particular case, which may yield a somewhat biased picture. The number of surviving promissory notes reflecting loans or credit granted to selling agents and other business associates - perhaps around 300 - cannot simply be interpreted as evidence of unfinished transactions and unpaid debts. Normally returned and "killed" upon payment, such bonds might also be preserved, since without the sealed envelope (which turned them into a "valid deed", *ṭuppum ḫarmum*) they lacked legal force.[53] The numbers of records of old debts found in the regularly excavated archives (as far as we can see at present) is not alarmingly big. Moreover, however much traders strove for written evidence of financial liabilities, there were always also oral transactions, conducted before witnesses and among close relatives or associates, which might have caused part of the problems reflected in the documentation, especially if a trader died and claims could only be honoured if "proved by witnesses" (*ina šībēšu ikūan*), as stipulated in Old Assyrian law.

Financial claims were protected by various means, including those known from slightly earlier (Ur III period) and contemporary Babylonia, such as (default) interest or fines, surety by collatoral, and guarantors. But the Old Assyrians also developed new devices for easily and quickly collecting payments due.

a. *Interest and Default Interest*

The "official" rate of interest, between Assyrians normally 30 per cent per year (occasionally lower, *e.g.* between friends, or higher for loans contracted by bad debtors), "in accordance with the ruling of the *kārum*", was rather high compared with Babylonia (20 per cent per year). Many documents mention high amounts of silver due as interest, which must be the result of debts left unpaid for many years, other complain about or warn of "interest which mounts" (*imaʾid*) or "becomes a problem" (*imarraṣ*). There are not a few cases where debtors at first only can pay back part of a debt or only the capital sum (*šīmtum*), at times in instalments, and only get their promissory note back later, after the final instalment (*tašbītum*) or the interest has been paid. The rather high rate of interest (which I would like to explain from the commercial value of the silver in the overland trade) may have had a dual effect. On the one hand it offered the creditor an attractive compensation if the debtor defaulted, the same one wealthy merchants received on straight silver loans. This may explain why some promissory notes do not stipulate a due date and why we meet many overdue debts listed in memorandums. Merchant-bankers, active as financiers and granting credit or loans, apparently were ready to settle for this interest. But this probably was much less the case with active traders, who needed the silver for their commercial activities, which aimed at much higher profits, though at the expense of more investments, work, trouble, and risks. On the other hand, a debtor or selling agent should not be too afraid of this rate of interest when he defaulted. The frequently rather long credit terms (many between 6 and 12 months) granted to selling agents must have allowed them not only to sell the merchandise acquired on credit with profit, but also to use the silver earned in the mean time for additional transactions in order to increase their profit, before they had to pay back their creditors. Such additional profit may have balanced default interest and could explain the occurrence of many delayed payments and old debts.

53 See for this issue also Veenhof 1987, 46ff. and Michel 1995, 19ff.

b. *Pledges*

Protection of claims by pledges (*šapartum, erubbātum*) was not widespread. Most occurrences (household goods, slaves, houses) are in loans to native Anatolians (which are regularly charged higher interest), but they are much less common with commercial loans or credit granted to Assyrians.[54] They do occur, a few times also for substantial debts, possibly in cases where payment already had been deferred or loans were novated and the creditor required added surety, but not frequently enough to warrant C. Michel's statement, that "houses frequently served as surety for the creditor".[55] According to the letter KTS 2 9, a claim of 49 pounds of silver is secured by a pledge (*erubbātum*) of two (usually expensive) houses in Assur.[56] Gold serves as a pledge in CCT 4 29b // BIN 4 4 // AnOr 6 19, where a claim of 25 pounds of silver is protected by a pledge of 10 pounds of gold and a guarantor has to provide additional surety, which is remarkable since the value of the gold (usually eight times the value of silver, hence equal to ca. 80 pounds of silver) is already the multiple of the the claim. In kt 87/k 119 (courtesy K. Hecker) nearly one mina of gold serves as a pledge (*šapartum*) for a debt. Pledges also occur for small commercial debts. In VS 26 60:14ff., an amount of tin was given (offered?) as pledge for a debt of nearly one talent of copper (value ca. half a mina of silver), and in KTS 13b:28 an unspecified amount of tin secured a debt of only 15 shekels of silver.

Noteworthy is the fact that at times also promissory notes served as pledges. In the Neukirch-tablet lines 5ff., there is mention of "a valid bond for 20 minas of wool[!], being P.'s debt, [10] pledged to the creditor (*erubbāt tamkārim*), which A. is bringing you".[57] In VS 26 1, A. reports:

> I owed K. 24 talents and 10 minas of good copper and my representatives have satisfied K. in Ullama with that copper, obtained my debt-note and left it in deposit (*ana nabšêm*) with I. Today I. refused to yield my tablet, saying 'They deposited it with me as pledge', although it was not as pledge that they deposited it!

EL 320:14ff. and CCT 3 42b:6ff. show that a pledged tablet (bond) might be used to recover money owed to the one who had obtained it. In the former the documents pledged (called *iṣurātum*) most likely recorded liabilities of an Anatolian palace to pay copper to the *kārum*, which the *kārum* for whatever reason had ceded to B. The latter in turn had left them behind for (or ceded them to) I. and now wants to know whether I. had used them to collect copper in B.'s name.[58] In the second text too, the possibility is considered that the creditor has used the records pledged to collect silver.[59] This shows that pledged bonds could be more than hypothecary pledges, since their owner might use them to

---

54 An example is EL 169, where household utensils serve as pledge for half a mina of silver due as interest. See for an earlier survey, with emphasis on the legal aspects, Kienast 1975-76.

55 Michel 1996, 298.

56 Lines 6-9: A tablet of 49 minas of silver *ša* A.$_1$, the *gubabtum* priestess, his sister, and A.$_2$, his brother *ša šina bētān erubbātunni*; see for this letter Michel 1995, 25f. Note also TPAK 1 194, where a house is pledged for a debt of a little more than two minas of silver.

57 Quoted EL I, 231 note d.

58 See for this document my remarks in Veenhof 1995b, 325.

59 "Today I hear that he has deposited the bond as pledge. Inform me how much silver he has collected where (from the person with whom) he has deposited the bond" (lines 5-10).

collect the assets they embodied.[60] He might do this either for himself or in the name of the original creditor, in order to balance the money collected in this way with the debts due to him from their original owner. A creditor quite naturally felt cheated when, as was the case in kt r/k 17:6-9, he received as security tablets which were no longer valid (*ṭuppū ukkušūtim*). How and under which condition pledged tablets could be converted into money is a difficult question and I may refer to my observations in Veenhof 1997, 356ff. I also call attention to the arrangement worked out in EL 104, where A. leaves/cedes (*ezābum*) to I. two bonds with debt claims on B. and U. for in all to 7 1/2 minas of silver. I. pays him their value ("equivalent", *meḫrātum*) in silver, 7 1/2 minas of silver, and henceforth B. and U. are debtors of I., liable for the payment of interest, which A., their original creditor guarantees.

c. *Guarantors*

Guarantors are more frequent in commercial debt-notes of Assyrians than pledges, but by no means a standard feature. I have noted ca. 15 cases, usually a simple mention at the end of the contract: "PN is guarantor" (*qātātum*).[61] Also persons designated as *šazzuztum*, a general term meaning "representative" (lit. the person who is made to "stand in" for somebody, who is designated and empowered to act for him),[62] hence frequently "agent", can act as guarantors. In the letter AKT 3 83:8-16, E. writes "The one mina and half a shekel of silver, which A. owes to the *kārum* and for which I am 'stand-in' (*šazzuztu anākuma*), I indeed paid that silver out of my own funds". While references to guarantors in contracts are usually short and laconic ("PN is guarantor"), we know more about them from letters and judicial records, when debtors were asked or forced to supply them[63] or problems arose about the settlement of accounts between debtors and guarantors. In a number of cases the guarantor (*bēl qātātim*) is made responsible for the presence of the debtor at the time and place of payment (*Gestellungsbürgschaft*). Such contracts speak of the guarantor's duty of "bringing the man (usually a debtor, who is about to leave on a business trip) back".[64] More frequent are cases where being a guarantor implied the liability of paying for the defaulting debtor. In such cases the guarantor's right of regress on the debtor is at stake, together with the question of the

---

60 This is probably also the case in the Neukirch-tablet (see note 57), since the writer goes on say that the wool (recorded as debt in the pledged debt-note) should be given to a trader for transport.

61 See for references EL II, 123ff. and *CAD* Q, 170, 3a; see also CTMMA 1 84:16f.; KKS 13 (debt of 10 minas of silver); *JCS* 14 (1960), 1 no. 1:1-4; *ibidem*, 10 no. 5:5-10.

62 The noun occurs together with the verb "to stand", both in the basic stem (*šazzuzti* PN *izzaz)* and with the causative stem (*šazzuztam ušazzaz*); see for references *CAD* Š/2, 245f. Note that in the two connected documents mentioned below, in footnote 65, the one states that the son-in-law "stands in for the debt" (*ana ḫubullim izzaz*) of his father-in-law, while the other designates him as "guarantor" (*qātātum*).

63 The expression is *ana ša qātātim tadānum*, with personal accusative object. *E.g.* KTS 38c:12: "If they refuse to pay, hold them by the hem of their garments and make them provide guarantors until I arrive" (*a-ša qātātim adi allakanni itaddinā̆šunu*). From the point of view of the guarantor the action can be described as "let oneself be booked/inscribed as somebody's guarantor" (*qātāt* PN *litaptum/nalputum*, with the verb both in the reflexive Gt- and in the N-stem).

64 In Akkadian *awīlam taʾurum*; see for references P. Garelli, in *Studies Erica Reiner* (AOS 67, Connecticut 1987), 111f. and VS 26 37.

whereabouts of the debt-note, which the original creditor should hand over to the guarantor who paid him instead of the debtor.[65] Regress by the guarantor on the debtor could be the substance of a verdict by the City, which could authorize him (especially if he had been forced to take out a loan in order to be able to meet his liability) to charge the debtor "interest and interest on interest", due to the guarantor as new creditor and to the merchant who had provided the loan. He may also be authorized "to look for (*šeʾāʾum*) silver of the debtor, wherever it proves to be/turns up".[66]

In Kanish, as we have seen above (§ 2d), Enlil-bānī "had been booked as guarantor of Kukkulānum (*qātāt* K. *nalputum*) in "a merchant's house" (TC 3 67:10), where K. must have taken out a loan of 30 pounds of silver in order to meet his cash problems. This supports the idea that in most (?) cases guarantors were only asked for if a debtor was (already) in financial problems, which can also explain the not infrequent combination of a guarantor and a pledge (TC 3 232; BIN 4 4 and parallel texts, see above under b, "Pledges"). In CCT 5 8a, Aḫaḫa reminds her brothers (sons of Pūšu-kēn) of their liability, since "they had been booked as guarantors for their (by now dead) father for an amount of 30 pounds of silver". Several times we meet persons "booked as guarantor" for debts owed by somebody to the City-office in Assur, which the *līmum*-official is collecting.[67] In EL 332, a man is guarantor for the debt of a business partner of no less than 50 minas of silver.

Being guarantor, as wisdom texts stress, is risky because of the inescapable obligation of paying for the debtor, even if a loan has to be contracted for that purpose. The writer of BIN 6 27:16ff. even fears that it might turn him into a (debt)slave (*ana wardūtim erābum*), which explains why usually only relatives or close business associates were ready to act as such, *e.g.* the sons of Pūšu-kēn for their father in CCT 5 8a, a sister and a son as guarantors in EL 215:4 and 227:33, 45, and Enlil-bānī for his employee(?) Kukkulānum. Guarantors also tried to protect themselves against the risks they took. The unpublished contract kt 92/k 173 stipulates that, if A.'s debt of 11 minas of silver, for which B. and C. have been recorded as his guarantors, "is collected at the expense of B. and C., A.'s house in Assur is a pledge for the silver". The obligation of subsidiary payment and the already existing close association between guarantor and debtor may explain why in the same transactions persons can be designated both as guarantor and as co-debtor,[68] an association which can also be formalized by the clause of subsidiary liability for the debt, literally "the silver is contractually bound on the person ('head') of the one who is solvent and present".[69] But this did not mean that debtor and guarantor were identical and exchangeable. The contract kt 91/135 explicitly states, after mentioning that S. is D.'s guarantor and that there is subsidiary liability for the debt, "S.

65 See *e.g.* EL 325-326, BIN 6 215; *JCS* 14, 10 no. 5. A nice example, involving a man and his son-in-law, is to be found in two interrelated documents excavated in 1991, published in my article 'Two Marriage Documents From Kültepe', *Archivum Anatolicum* 3 (Emin Bilgiç Memorial Volume, Ankara 1998), 357ff.

66 One may use the verb *bašāʾum*, "to be", or *buārum*, "to turn up, to prove to be". See Veenhof 1995a, 1723ff. for a well documented case.

67 See the case discussed in Veenhof 1995a, 1723f.

68 See for examples EL 331 // 332 and the remarks in EL II, 124 and Veenhof 1983-84, 20 n. 19. Additional examples are kt 91/k 131 and 135.

69 *Kaspum ina qaqqad šalmišunu u kēnišunu rakis*; examples are BIN 6 238; kt k/k 44:44f.; and kt 87/k 293:30. The reservation still made in EL II, 124 hence is not necessary.

did not receive anything, D. shall pay it". D. hence is the original debtor, who received the tin owed and accordingly has to weigh it out, while S.'s liability is subsidiary.[70] Plurality of guarantors is not rare and if one of them pays accounts have to be settled with the others and later with the debtor, which may create complications resulting in records.

As an example of the complications caused by guarantee, which also shows how small the differences between the status of guarantor, co-debtor, and partner were and how flexible Old Assyrian traders could be, I quote from the letter TC 3 110. It was written by Ennam-Aššur to Aššur-ennam and concerns copper borrowed by the former (D. = debtor) from the son of A. (C. = creditor) whereby Aššur-ennam acted as guarantor (G.) D. states:

> We (D. and G.) borrowed one talent of copper from C., whereby you acted as G. Later you came back on the transaction, saying: "I will give you a tablet with my seal for the copper and the interests (plural!) on it, stating that the debt is our debt and not that of you (alone)". In the presence of two sons of financiers (acting as witnesses) you gave (were to give?) me that tablet with your seal, but you changed your mind and (*tassiḫirma u*) wrote a tablet for one talent of copper, stating that I (D.) would enjoy half of the profit and would be responsible for half of the losses. I (D. speaks again) have satisfied you with the copper and you gave me my tablet. I asked you also for the (original) tablet of C., with my seals, and you said: "What does it concern you?" A tablet with my seals to which you are not entitled you shall not keep! You have been satisfied with the copper, therefore give the tablet of C. with my seals to my father. Do not keep it!

The final lines imply that G., by paying for D. to C., had obtained the original promissory note of D., which the latter wants back now that he has fully paid G. Having paid for D., G. had become his creditor and was entitled to get the copper back from him, but he decided to make himself co-debtor, which means that D. only owes him half a talent of copper. The purpose must have been to maintain some kind of relationship with D., by creating a common fund, which could be used for commercial purposes, even though D.'s share consisted only of the copper granted him as credit by G. The next step of G. was to define their relationship more clearly as a ḳind of (unequal) partnership, in which profits and losses would be shared. D.'s contribution, at least as long as he had not paid back G., most probably would be to manage the capital and do the actual trading (just like the manager or tractator of a *naruqqum*-enterprise, to whom similar stripulations on profits and losses applied), while G., as financier, would be rewarded with his share in the profits and probably also with interest on the capital which he had advanced to D. Moreover, D., when successful could use his share in the profits to pay back his creditor G., which in fact might well be the main reason why the latter opted for a partnership.

d. *Measures against Defaulting Debtors*

Defaulting debtors were warned, privately summoned (before witnesses, which could yield a valid record of the summons), or sued in a formal trial, especially if the

---

70 *S. mimma lā ilqe D. išaqqalšu.*

summons failed. Another possibility was to seize property, frequently slaves, of the debtor as security or pledge, for which one uses the verb *katāʾum*.[71] An example is TC 3 60:10ff.:

> When you lived in Kanish and S. was living in your presence, you failed to seize him and make him pay the silver. Now you are running around in the countryside (Anatolia) over a distance of 10 double hours (in order to seize him). Does he not have a slave-girl and a slave in Kanish? Take his slave-girl and his slave as surety and (so) obtain the silver!

Another measure was to seal a debtor's house, thus denying him access to his property (merchandise) and archives, a measure which probably had to be authorized by the judicial authorities. "The City has passed the following verdict: A. shall take x silver from whatever B. owns. He (A.) has indeed sealed our house once and twice" (YBC 13089:8-11, unpublished). The next step could be the sale of the debtor's property, as described in the letter AKT 3 87:35-59:

> Ḫ. and S., by order of the City, have to pay (to the writer of this letter) 22 minas of silver from whatever they own. [38] They are jointly liable for this silver. Here [40] Ḫ. has not given me anything! Seize him and make him pay the 22 minas of silver! If he refuses to pay, [43] in accordance with the verdict of the City, sell all he owns for silver and take the silver! (...) [49] I paid three minas and half a shekel of silver to the Anatolian in the name of A., [51] in the sixth month, during the eponymy of [52] Kapatia. By virtue of a verdict of the City I am entitled to take from all he owns, from the stock (in the *kārum*), while calling for 20 per cent (interest), the silver [54] and the interest on it (to be reckoned) from the day I paid the silver. [56] Make him pay the silver and the interest on it. (If not) [57] I have a tablet of the City, sell all he owns and give him notice!

The same measure was applied in Assur by officials of the City to people indebted to the City-office. They could confiscate merchandise, take and sell household goods (especially valuable bronze objects) and even sell the house itself. In TPAK 1 26, it is reported that *bērum*-officials ("inspectors"?) of the City, because of fiscal debts to the City-office, seize a family's house in order to force its four members to pay each 75 shekels of silver (in all five pounds) and even threaten to sell it, whereupon the writer of the letter takes out a loan with a merchant to pay the debt. In TPAK 1 46, we read (rather differently from the editors, who misunderstood parts of this letter): "Our father's stocks (*išittum*) and houses have been entrusted (*paqqudā*; to the creditor or a guarantor?) for silver". Because it was not sufficient, the writer's own house, together with the household goods (*utuptum*!) of him and his wife were sold. From this document we also gather that such sales of houses by defaulting debtors at times (in periods of economic crisis?) were considered a social problem and that measures were taken to counter them. After the lines quoted we read to our surprise: "Aššur has now taken mercy on his city: a

---

71 With as internal object *kutuʾātum*, see for references *CAD* K *s.v.*

man whose house has been sold can again enter it when he pays half of its price, and for the rest (of the price) terms in three (annual?) instalments haven been set".[72]

e. *Collection of Payment for Creditors*

The Old Assyrian merchants used and developed a few additional procedures to help the creditor get back his silver without delay, irrespective of where creditor or debtor stayed. Many debts were collected by representatives, partners (it was one of the possibilities granted by a formal partnership, as we learn from its dissolution as recorded in ATHE 24), and employees. In the absence of the original promissory note (which might be deposited elsewhere and which one did not like to send overland) this could be achieved by means of copies made available to a partner, agent, or employee who was asked to collect the silver, at times with a written authorization. It was apparently assumed that the debtor, confronted with the exact data on his debt and with the names of the witnesses to the transaction, would not refuse to meet his liability, also because he incurred the risk of having to pay default interest. When paying in such situations, he would normally receive a formal quittance (a *ṭuppum ša šabāʾē*, "a tablet of satisfaction", sealed by the one who received the payment), which in due time he could exchange for the original bond,[73] whereupon both tablets could be cancelled ("die").

f. *Payment Contracts*

At times, however, a debtor would refuse to pay, because he wanted to be shown the original debt-note, because he had already paid (elsewhere or to somebody else), because he contested the claim as such, or for other reasons. To prevent a deadlock one could then "take a contract against" (*tarkistam laqāʾum ana*) the party which refused to comply, either the debtor who refused to pay or the creditor who pressed his disputed claim. Such a contract basically consisted of a formal promise, before witnesses and usually recorded in a tablet sealed by the one making the promise, of an extra payment if the refusal or claim in due time could be formally refuted by testimony or written evidence. The fine usually was paying two or three times the amount disputed or twice the normal amount of interest for the unpaid debt. A clear example is EL 182 (published as VS 26 98): "R., representing Z., seized five shekels of silver of S. Should he (Z.) not have a claim on S., then R. shall pay 10 shekels of silver to S.; witnessed by P. and I.". Persons confronted with the choice between paying or giving up their claim and signing such a contract, of course would give in unless they were very sure of being right and able to prove it. In TC 3 263, S. claims 13 pounds of copper from A., who however tells him that a certain Q. had already paid back for him to I. (apparently a friend or agent of S). "If Q. confirms him (A.'s statement), S. will pay the triple (*šušalšum*) to A., without resorting to legal trial or fight". The writer of the letter CCT 4 5b requests: "Seize P. and make him pay the gold, it is mine. (...) I have here his valid promissory note. If he protests, take a contract

---

72 Read in lines 22f. *Aššur ennān ālišu ilteqe awīlum ša* .... Elsewhere I will offer a full analysis of this text and the unique legal measure it describes.

73 See for evidence Veenhof 1983-84, 13f.

against him and make him pay the gold". According to *RA* 59 (1965), 31f. no. 11:11ff., Q. owes to P. one pound of silver and P. tries to enforce his claim, even though the silver already would have been collected for P. by A. and I. "If Q. produces A. and I. (as witnesses), P. will pay to Q. as capital sum (*šīmtum*; this term may have been chosen to leave the matter of additional interest open) two minas of silver". In TC 3 251, where a creditor seizes silver from D., we read: "Should D. prove not to owe him silver, he will add three shekels of silver per mina per month since (...)" (no doubt apart from the obligation to return the capital), which means twice the normal rate of interest of 30 per cent per year).

Such contracts by their heavy sanction prevented unfounded demands and refusals, hence delay of payment and so contributed to the circulation of silver. They could build on a stipulation already attested during the preceding Ur III period, that debtors who failed to pay in time, at times after a summons followed by a promise, would pay double.[74] The Old Assyrian traders adapted this device, which during the Ur III period only protected the interests of the creditor and used it to solve payment problems in the interests of both creditors and debtors. A later adaptation is found in the Laws of Hammurabi, paragraphs 106-108, where the trading agent who denies his liability has to pay three times the capital, but the financier and creditor who denies payment by the agent, six times, an (idealistic?) attempt to balance justice with the goal of protecting the weaker party.

g. *Borrowing by Creditors*

A last device to help the creditor was a clause in the promissory note which authorized him, if the debtor defaulted, "to borrow for him" (*laqā'um* with personal dative suffix) the sum owed "at a merchant's house", where "for him" means for the debtor and at his expense. See for full data and an analysis above, under 2c. It was an efficient and fast method of self-help, which could avoid the problems and loss of time which the use of pledges, guarantors, summonses, and lawsuits would entail. The occasional use of the verb "to call" (*šasā'um*), instead of "to take/borrow" (*laqā'um*), suggests a formal, public act, as one would expect when one takes out a loan at the expense of somebody else. There is no evidence that the debtor had to repay the merchant-moneylender, the loan plus the interest to be paid on it remained the liability of the creditor, but he would charge it to his debtor, in addition to the interest he was anyhow entitled to since payment was overdue. This explains the clause "and he (the debtor) shall supplement the interest". The promise, in EL 309, that the creditor is allowed "to borrow silver at a merchant's house at an interest of three shekels per mina per month" (which is twice the normal rate), perhaps refers to the double interest due to the creditor or is a fine for a broken promise (see for this feature above, under 4f). The solution was similar to the one offered to guarantors who had to take out a loan in order to be able to pay for a debtor (see above, 4c). The presence of the "*bēt tamkārim* clause" in the debt-note itself allowed creditors to act quickly on the basis of a contractual right, without having to resort to "lawsuit and fight" (*balum dīnim balum ṣaltim išaqqal*, TC 3 263:24). If it is no accident that the amounts of silver owed in such cases are not very big,

---

74 See H. Limet, *OrNS* 38 (1976), 520-32 and Neumann 1992b, 171f.

the device will have been introduced to avoid time-consuming and expensive procedures when only minor debts were at stake.

5. *Promissory Notes to tamkārum and "Bearer Cheques"*

A last device to be mentioned here are promissory notes which do not mention the creditor by name, but refer to him as *tamkārum*, "the merchant/creditor". In a few cases such notes at the end add the phrase "the bearer of this tablet is *tamkārum*" (*wābil ṭuppim šūt tamkārum*). This clause suggests the possibility of a transfer of debt-notes and of ceding claims, which would make it a precursor of later "bearer cheques". It is a very interesting procedure for facilitating the flow of money and especially the collection of debts, when creditor and/or debtor were in different places (which must have happened frequently in a community of overland traders) or perhaps even before the due date. I have recently discussed it and instead of repeating my conclusions I refer the reader to this publication.[75] I may add that in general the size of the debts owed to "the merchant/creditor", and especially those of the rather few debt-notes mentioning that "the bearer of the tablet is the creditor", again are not very big, which is confirmed by two new examples. In kt 92/k 202 the debt is (only) 12 minas of copper (equivalent to seven or eight shekels of silver) and in TPAK 1 120a (which uses the phrase "who holds the tablet", *mukaʾil ṭuppim*) half a mina of silver, owed by two debtors.[76] This suggests that this device may have been developed in the interest of creditors, for easily collecting small debts or settling accounts by transferring bonds instead of cash money (see the remarks on EL 104 at the end of paragraph 4b).

75 Veenhof 1997, 351ff.

76 The contract was drawn up to state that henceforth only one of the debtors was liable for it; when it was claimed from the other he had to "clear" him (read *ú-ba-áb*[!]*-šu* in line 22).

ON THE FINANCING OF OLD ASSYRIAN MERCHANTS

J.G. DERCKSEN (LEIDEN)

This paper deals with the main forms of financing Old Assyrian trade during the 19th century BC and not with its organisation which will be treated elsewhere.[1] Since the forms of credit during this period will be discussed by K.R. Veenhof (see the preceding paper), I will treat the borrowing of capital or money sparingly. A few important texts will serve as a point of departure. According to P. Garelli, finance rested on three main institutions: the *naruqqum*-partnership provided to "starting" entrepreneurs; the temple-loans called *ikribū*; and credit referred to as *beʾūlātum* (*bûlātum*).[2]

I. *The Sources: BIN 4 32 and RA 88 Brieux*

1. *BIN 4 32*

The first text which deserves a closer examination is BIN 4 32. P. Garelli discussed it extensively (1963, 234) and also M.T. Larsen (Larsen 1977, 130, 133, 143). The key-words in there are *ummiānum*, *tamkārum*, *bûlātum*, and *maškattum*. The writer, Pūšu-kēn, experienced financial problems and had asked his creditors to allow him more time to fulfill his obligations. During the term granted to him, he would "go" (*alākum*), that is to say, be active as a merchant and collect as much of the capital entrusted to him as possible. The text runs in translation as follows:

> 1-3 Speak to the *ummiānu*'s, Šū-Ḫubur, and my representatives, thus (said) Pūšu-kēn: 4-9 I requested a term of three years from the god (= the City Assembly?), saying: "I shall go to recover my *bûlātum*, and I shall put it, be it a little or a lot, before (my financiers)." 9-10 Šū-Ḫubur promised me a term of five years, and you yourselves agreed to that. 12-17 I shall apply to him and say: "I cannot wait for five years. I will go the length of the term I requested from the god and recover my *bûlātum*." 17-20 Two or three of my *tamkāru*'s, on whom I am dependent, were foolish so that I was deprived of a lot of silver. 21-22 This is not the right moment to disclose their names to you. 23-28 I thought however: "As soon as they go the *tamkārum*-retailer will release to them every shekel of silver (he owes them) and then they will bring to me as much as they can." By Aššur and by your (pl.) god! I have been deprived of some two talents of silver. That is enough! 28-31 My dear lords, if you please, consider how many *nisḫātum* can be levied at the house of my *ummiānu*(*m*/'s); 31-35 draw up a certified document stating that my *maškattum* will

[1] I wish to thank The Netherlands Organization for Scientific Research (NWO) for enabling me to write this paper as part of its project *The Economy of Ancient Mesopotamia*.

[2] Garelli 1977, 103. See J.G. Dercksen, *Archivum Anatolicum* 3 (Ankara 1998), 75-100 on *ikribū*.

go for three years and that the silver can not be claimed (by another). 36-37 Write me something friendly which my servant can communicate to me. 37-38 I shall collect some silver of my *bûlātum* (already) at harvest time (and send it to you).

2. *Tamkārum and ummiānum*

In his analysis of the Old Assyrian commercial system[3] Garelli stated that the word *tamkārum* in the texts from Kültepe denotes a functionary whose task it is to facilitate trade. He does so by acting as a banker: *i.e.* through borrowing money and providing credit to the merchants. He also acts as a trader who takes it upon him to sell merchandise. This function is reflected in the expression "a trustworthy *tamkārum*" (*tamkārum kēnum*). The origin of his capital is uncertain, but it most likely resulted from his own commercial activities. As a banker he automatically became a creditor and as such he is seen in the documentation dealing with the division of the property of deceased merchants.

The word *ummiānum*, Garelli continues, is not a functionary's title; it denotes financiers (*bailleurs de fonds*) who, because of their wealth and influence, almost monopolize the supply of credit (silver, copper), or "control the money market". They are apparently only found in the capital Assur. Their agent is called the "son of the *ummiānum*" (*mēr ummiānim*) whose task it is to travel through Anatolia and keep them in contact with the merchants active there. This interpretation found wide acceptance. In one of the latest publications of Kültepe texts the expression is still translated "der Angestellte des Geldgebers" (AKT 3 92).

Garelli's interpretations of *tamkārum* and *mēr ummiānim* were not embraced universally. The word *tamkārum* can in all texts be rendered in its basic meaning "merchant." But from this simple word several specific meanings derived, which in most cases are only understandable through the context: "licensed merchant", "(Assyrian) creditor", "retail-seller", and "debtor".[4] There are no indications that a *tamkārum*, for instance those merchants acting as moneylender, ever held an official position as such.

The investor in a *naruqqum*-partnership was also called *ummiānum* and in general it can be said that every merchant dependent on the capital of others had one or more *ummiānum*. Their number is rarely specified and their identity remains often unknown. A welcome exception forms the text kt a/k 534 (unpublished Ankara), written by eight individuals in Assur who are the *ummiānu*'s of the deceased Aššur-taklāku. They communicated to their representatives in Kanish about the progress made in settling the affairs of the dead man. We not only find *ummiānu*'s in Assur, but also in Anatolia, often in connection with the inspection of the possessions of a deceased merchant to whom they had entrusted money. This is the case in *e.g.* VS 26 116, where the *ummiānu*'s of the late Šū-Suen enter his house together with his heirs and three witnesses. A number of times it is possible to identify a person as the *ummiānum* of a certain merchant because he is mentioned with this title. L. Matouš (Matouš 1969) has discussed the dossier concerning the aftermath of the death of Puzur-Aššur. From a comparison of his text B2:17-21 (page 169) with TC 3 270:24-30, it is clear that Busāsu is identical to Puzur-Aššur's *ummiānum*, who is coming from Waḫšušana, and who, until that moment, also continued

---

3 Garelli 1963, 235ff.

4 See K.R. Veenhof, *AoF* 15 (1988), 248 and my remarks in *BiOr* 39 (1992), 794-795.

the partnership with Puzur-Aššur which dated back to the time of his deceased father Pūšu-kēn.

The presence of *ummiānu*'s in Anatolia is much greater once it is realized that the expression "son of an *ummiānum*" does not refer to an employee but often to an *ummiānum* himself. The word "son" can here denote both a member of this class and, at times, literally the son of such a member. In AKT 3 92 (lines 20-21) someone looking for witnesses asked "10 or 15 *mer*ʾ*e ummiānī*" to testify for him. Their status made them suitable to convey valuable cargo to Assur.

The conclusion here is that *ummiānum* refers to anyone investing money in a merchant's business. Apart from acting as financier, they could be actively engaged in the Anatolian trade as well, as for example Busāsu did. Those residing in Assur belonged, by their wealth and status as financier, to the class of well-to-do Assyrians.

3. *Bûlātum*

P. Garelli refrained from translating *bûlātum* in BIN 4 32 lines 16 and 37, but in his commentary equated it with *be*ʾ*ūlātum*, "capital d'exploitation" (1967, 249). J. Lewy had done so before (EL, 127 note a). The term *be*ʾ*ūlātum* occurs in documents related to the caravan trade and denotes a sum of money given to an employee with which he can conduct trade and make a profit.[5] This amount is usually a fraction of a mina of silver and rarely exceeds it.

The *bûlātum* in BIN 4 32, as well as in several other texts, is found in a different context where it refers to a more substantial investment or loan. It is there never written *be*ʾ*ūlātum*.[6] Larsen, for whom *bûlātum* equals *be*ʾ*ūlātum*, remarked that it refers to the investments administered by Pūšu-kēn, that is to say, his *naruqqum*-contract.[7] We find for instance in TC 2 36:4-5: "We grabbed Iddin-abum and he declared: 'I will collect my *b.* and place it before my creditors (*tamkārum*)'." Compare further the "10 talents of copper (which) Aššur-nādā possesses in Kunanamit as *b.* (pl.)" (CCT 2 23:35-37); "winter has come upon us and the *b.* I was expecting became an outstanding claim" (CCT 3 7a:8-13); "he is bringing you 10 minas of silver, his *b.*" (CCT 4 33b:15-16). An amount of 90 minas of silver as someone's *bûlātu* occurs in RA 81 55:2'-3'. *Bûlātum* in these texts denotes either the capital managed by another person or the goods bought with it. It is provided to a merchant by his financier(s). Such a financier can speak of "my *b.*" when referring to the capital he had invested.

The rare writing *bu*ʾ*ūlātu* for *be*ʾ*ūlātu* occurs on the tablet of BIN 4 211 (= EL 163), while the text on the case has the "normal" writing. This makes a distinction between both spellings difficult. It bears also on the interpretation of the word, consistently written *bûlātu*, in the dossier concerning the financial problems of Aššur-bēl-malkim (texts: BIN 4 224 (discussed in Veenhof's contribution, § 3); CCT 2 27; CCT 3 10; kt 91/k 471; RA 81 2). Assets forming part of the *bûlātu* of this trader are being held back as security

5 See Veenhof 1994, 183-184.

6 W. von Soden, GAG § 16i, assumes that *bûlātum* is the contracted form of *be*ʾ*ūlātum*, while K. Hecker, GKT § 19e, leaves open the possibility that it derives from *bu*ʾ*ūlātum*.

7 Larsen 1976, 130.

(*ka^ʾulum*)[8] by several of his creditors who are apparently dissatisfied with his financial position. According to CCT 2 27 and RA 81 2[9] these are Iddin-Suen, Ḫināya, and other partners. They only seem to be willing to release these assets when other merchants extend loans to him, thereby spreading the risk and allowing him to earn money. This "fund-raising" is left to Iddin-Suen who is to ask colleagues for silver *ana beʾālim* for Aššur-bēl-malkim. This phrase is connected with putting a working capital (*beʾūlātum*) at someone's disposal,[10] usually of a *kaṣṣārum*, but Aššur-bēl-malkim does not appear to be a *kaṣṣārum* and it refers to a more substantial investment or loan in this dossier than a mere "working capital". In other words, there is an argument in favour of equating *bûlātu* with *beʾūlātum*, for which the traditional meaning "working capital" is insufficient. A better translation would be "assets someone may have at his disposal". These texts indicate that such *beʾūlātum*-loans could also be given by several persons to the same individual. Perhaps linked with the taking of securities is kt 91/k 471 which mentions the seizure (*ṣabātum*) by Ḫināya of claims (*bābtum*) Aššur-bēl-malkim had on two other persons. See for the proposed solution CCT 3 10:31-41, where Aššur-bēl-awātim writes to Iddin-Suen:

> As you promised us here to do, if you are (still) our brother, ask silver *ana beʾālim* from colleague(s) and friend(s) for Aššur-bēl-malkim and send the sealed silver to us. Then we will return his *bûlātu* to him and send him to the City. If you do not ask (silver) for him *ana beʾālim* his *bûlātu* will be no more.

I interprete *bûlātu* as the goods in the possession of a merchant which he obtained with the money of others. The word covers a different portion of the trader's funds than *šalṭum* which occurs a number of times in the tablet published in RA 88 (see below).

4. *Šalṭum*

The assets freely available to a trader could be called *šalṭum*, *i.e.* "ready goods," "uncommitted goods," or "cash on hand" (*CAD* Š/1, 270). The verb *šalāṭum* can have the meaning "to cash in", especially with *bābtum* as its object, the not yet received proceeds from a sale or outstanding claims.[11] See for example the unpublished letter kt 91/k 490 (courtesy of K.R. Veenhof), lines 5-9: "When I left, I cashed in (*ašluṭ*) the copper from my *bābtum* and entrusted (it) to you, saying: Take the copper out (of the house or town) and send 3 1/2 talents to A." Extremely informative in this context is the text which C. Michel published in RA 88 (1994), 121ff. Here some of the Anatolian assets of the

---

8 See for the use of this verb without *šapartum* as its object B. Kienast, *WO* 8 (1975-76), 220.

9 Read in RA 81 2 line 39: *le-ri-sú*[!]*-ma*; line 40: *li-iṭ*[!]*-ru-da-šu.*

10 See B. Kienast, *JCS* 41 (1989), 91; Veenhof 1994, 183 "... vielmehr als ein kleines Betriebskapital zu verstehen, das dem *kaṣṣārum* zu Beginn seines Dienstes zur freien Verfügung (*ana beʾālim* (...) gestellt wurde."

11 RA 60 (1966) 133 Thierry, reads in lines 50-51: "They are both liable for the debt towards the god Suen and for my debt-notes in Anatolia. Their preferential shares (*eliātu*) are ... (*ša-lu-ṭá*)." A possible translation is "freely available", but the exact relationship between this and the preceding clause is unclear to me.

deceased merchant Ḫurāṣānum are listed which totalled *c.* 148 minas of silver. This text, in the possession of M. Brieux, can be translated as follows:

> 1-5 Speak to the *ummiānu*('s) of Ḫurāṣānum and to his representatives, thus (said) Pūšu-kēn, Aššur-imittī, and Dān-Aššur. 6-11 The moment Ḫurāṣānum died, his creditors (*tamkārū*) entered (his house) and sealed (his) strong-room. This is the reason we did not write to you when he died. 12-15 We thought: "Let his creditors settle the accounts. Then we shall write them our detailed report." 16-19 His creditors have remitted the (default) interest and have been fully paid with the silver due to them. They "devoured" (*ēkulū*) both tablets and debtors and have been fully satisfied. 20-22 The silver, whether out of reach (*rūqum*), disputed (*nukurrāʾū*), or lost by fraud (*sarartušu*) amounts to about one talent.
> (...)
> 31-39 Regarding the 40 talents of copper which he booked to his *šalṭum* at the palace in Waḫšušana: no copper will leave there. His brothers know this, they themselves informed us that no copper will leave the palace.
> 40-42 As to the 12 minas of silver belonging to Innāya which he booked in his *šalṭum*, (it belongs) to Innāya.
> 42-45 Here, after he had "slipped in" (*iḫlupu*) the 12 minas of silver, he has compensated for (it by paying) three minas of go[ld?] as "interest".
> 46-51 As to the 12 minas of silver from the son of Suen-nādā, he booked (it) h[ere] in his *šalṭum* and then gave (it) to Ennu-Bēlum, (who) booked him for three minas of gold in his (= E.'s) *naruqqum*.
> 51-52 Regarding the 40 minas of silver which he gave to his brother Ikūppīa, this silver belongs to his (the brother's) *naruqqum*. 53 We have heard that he booked it there to his *šalṭum*.
> 53-54 Silver, (another amount of) 40 minas, (was added) to a *naruqqum* as well.
> 54-55 The 40 talents of copper from the palace at Waḫšušana are not available.

The expression *ana šalṭīšu lapātum* occurs in lines 33 and 53 and is used with the preposition *ina* in lines 41 and 48 without apparent difference in meaning. The verb *lapātum* "to book" implies the actual registration of the amount concerned on a special tablet recording the total amount of Ḫurāṣānum's *šalṭum*. This suggests a form of bookkeeping. S.D. Goitein, in his study of commercial life as reflected in the Medieval Geniza documents from Cairo, makes the remark that those traders did not use ledgers and that there are no remnants of systematic bookkeeping.[12] What we do find there are accounts in many forms which resemble the situation of the Old Assyrian traders. A possible tablet recording assets (*šalṭu*'s) might be CCT 5 43, edited in Michel 1991 as no. 197 (with collations). Ḫurāṣānum had prematurely added his claim on the copper in lines 31ff. to his *šalṭum*, which constituted a financial dilemma as it became almost certain that no copper would be handed over. The amounts of twelve minas of silver are divisible by four and equal a *naruqqum*-share of three minas of gold which we find in line 50. In fact, Ḫurāṣānum twice booked an amount to his own *šalṭum* which he subsequently invested in another's *naruqqum*; *i.e.* that of Ennu-Bēlum and of Ikūppīa. It is noteworthy to find that the capital invested in a *naruqqum*, by definition not easy to withdraw therefrom, can

12 Goitein 1967, 206.

be considered *šalṭum*. Two examples will suffice to demonstrate that the two were considered to be different. In CCT 2 45b, silver had to be recovered from a debtor named Zupa: "Either from Zupa's *naruqqum* or from *šalṭum*-items he owes (me)" (lines 9-11: *lū ša naruq Zupa lū šalṭātua ša libbi Zupa*). The combination occurs also in CCT 6 22b:11-13: "either from silver from my *šalṭum* or from my *naruqqum*." Also the text recording the capital of Elamma (kt 91/k 482) distinguishes between what forms his *naruqqum* (lines 1-21), and his *šalṭum*. The latter consists of barley, slaves, his share in the inheritance from his father, and *kursinnu*-assets which is summarized in line 30: "All this constitutes my *šalṭum*" (*mì-ma a-nim ša-al-ṭí*). The conclusion is that *šalṭum* means the assets which a trader possessed. It must be distinguished from his *naruqqum*-capital which he could only manage but did not own.

Three types of financial loss are mentioned: *rūqum* "out of reach", which already occurred in BIN 4 32 lines 20 and 27 from the verb *ruāqum*; *nukurrāʾū* "disputed"; and *sarartum* "(lost because of) fraud". The difference between these terms needs further investigation elsewhere.

5. *Maškattum*

The word *maškattum* is often the object of a verb expressing a movement, *e.g.* to carry away (*radāʾum* Š), to bring (*wabālum*), or to send (*wabālum* Š). A *maškattum* "goes" as in BIN 4 32: hence the word in most texts refers in practice to a transport of merchandise or money. An example of this usage can be found in O 3918: "He gave me 20 minas of silver to make purchases in the City. However, he wrote from Kanish to his representatives in Tegarama who took the *maškattum* I was bringing to the City away from me and brought the silver to him in Kanish."[13]

Merchandise designated as *maškattum* is mentioned in RA 59 26: "(As for) my *maškattum* transported by you (*ša šēpīka*), they sold the tin at a ratio of 7:1 and the textiles at half a mina each and brought me the silver." Compare also BIN 4, 47:18-21 concerning a debt of 7 1/2 talents of tin: "half you can take out of my first *maškattum* and half from the second". The first shipment of tin coming up to Anatolia contained four half-packs with five talents which were sealed by the debtor and addressed to his representatives and "the merchant". They were to be given to the creditor. In fact "half and half" here means two-thirds and one-third. In TC 3 13:15-16, *maškattum* refers to an amount of merchandise (*têrtum*) as well:

> I personally brought both your and my goods (*têrtum*), which had to be transported, into the city. I will sell the copper at any price and whatever silver I shall obtain, as well as the gold which Il-wēdāku borrowed here, I will bring with me, the silver, as much as your and my *maškattum* (originally was/amounts to).

In the letter quoted at the beginning of this paper, BIN 4 32, *maškattum* denotes either the transport itself or the proceeds therefrom which Pūšu-kēn owed to his financiers. Note that the funds themselves, with which he was able to conduct trade, are referred to as *bûlātum* in line 6.

---

13 Lines 13-21. The text has been published by K.R. Veenhof in *Akkadica* 18 (1980), 31ff.

Current interpretations of *maškattum* are "*account*" (*CAD* M/1, 375 and *AHw* 627a: "Konto (*šakānum* = anlegen)") and "*deposit*" (*CAD* M/1, 375). "Deposit" means here "something placed for safekeeping" and not "something given as a pledge or security".

K.R. Veenhof discussed this word in the publication of the Brussels text O 3918 and concluded that the exact meaning remained elusive. His tentative translation was "invested capital" ("geïnvesteerd kapitaal").[14] Subsequently (*JESHO* 28 (1985), 113) he considered it a loan protected by special securities. He explained the *maškattum* as the consequence of the action *qātam ina* (goods/money) *šakānum*, "to lay claim to (goods/money)". If a creditor had physically seized ("laid his hand on") goods or capital, the loan was called a *maškattum*. A passage from BIN 4 32:31-35 could be used to prove that a *maškattum* could not be seized by a third party because a claim had been laid on it. A confirmation of this view may be found in the affair surrounding the death of Puzur-Aššur as discussed by L. Matouš (1969). Of interest is the action taken by Busāsu. He demanded from Enna-Suen all the silver, gold, and debt-notes which Puzur-Aššur's *ummiānu*'s and *tamkāru*'s had entrusted to him. Busāsu wanted to use this capital and entrusted it to Aššur-šamšī who was to take it to Assur, make purchases and return with the merchandise. Busāsu earmarked the capital as belonging to a "*tamkārum*". The creditors and children of Puzur-Aššur, however, seized this opportunity to demand the merchandise bought with it by claiming that their father Puzur-Aššur was the *tamkārum*. Busāsu told Il-wēdāku in TC 3 270 how he laid claim (literally "his hand") on the money of the deceased:

> I grabbed Enna-Suen and he released to me all the silver, gold and tablets which Puzur-Aššur's financiers and creditors had entrusted to him. I entrusted the silver to Aššur-šamšī and marked (it) with the name of the *merchant*. I laid my hand on the silver. The merchandise was bought at my father's house and my representatives laid their hands (on it) at the city gate. Later on the attorney and children of Puzur-Aššur came to me and said: "The silver left our father's strongroom: our father is the *merchant*". This is why I sent my representatives to (the town of) Ṣupana where they entrusted it to Kulumāya.[15]

In the parallel text I 633, Matouš's text D1, Busāsu does not mention the claim he laid on the goods but instead uses the word *maškattum* to refer to the capital and the goods bought with it: "Aššur-šamšī brought my *maškattum*, the silver sealed by me, to my representatives. He was to bring the textiles and the tin sealed by my representatives to me; (but) you have taken away my *maškattum*."[16] A comparison of these two texts

---

14 *Akkadica* 18 (1980), 18.

15 TC 3 270: [26] *En-na-Sú-en*$_6$ *aṣ-ba-at-ma* [27] *lu* KÙ.BABBAR *lu* KÙ.GI *lu ṭup-pí* [28] *ša um-mì-a-nu ù tám-kà-ru* [29] *Puzur*$_4$*-A-šur ip-qí-du-šu-ni* [30] *ú-šé-ra-ma* KÙ.BABBAR *a-na A-šur*-UTU-*ši* [31] *áp-qí-id-ma šu-mì tám-kà-ri-im* [32] *ú-dí-ma i-na* KÙ.BABBAR *qá-tí áš-ku-ma* [33] *ší-ma-am* (mistake for *ší-mu-um*) É *a-bi-a i-ší-ma-ma* [34] *ba-áb a-bu-lim ša ki-ma i-a-tí* [35] *qá-sú-nu iš-ku-nu i-na* [36] *wa-ar-ki-tim-ma ra-bi-ṣú-um* [37] *ú me-er-ú Puzur*$_4$*-A-šur i-li-ku-nim-ma* [38] *um-ma šu-nu-ma* KÙ.BABBAR *i-na ma-ṣa-ar-tim* [39] *ša a-bi-ni ú-ṣa-am um-ma* [40] *ra-bi-ṣú-ma ú me-er-ú Puzur*$_4$*-A-šur-ma* [41] *a-bu-ni tám-kà-ru-um a-ší-a-tí* [42] *a-Ṣú-pá-na ša ki-ma i-a-tí* [43] *áš-pu-ur-ma lu-qú-tám a-na Ku-lu-ma-a* [44] *ip-qí-du.*

16 I 633: [4'] ... *ma-áš-kà-tí* KÙ.B *ku-nu-ki-a* [5'] *A-šur*-^{d}U[TU-š]*i a-ṣé-er ša ki-ma i-a-tí* [6'] *ub-lu-ma* TÚG.ḪI.A *ù* AN.NA *ku-nu-ki* [7'] *ša ki-ma i-a-tí A-šur*-^{d}UTU-*ši a-na* [8'] *ṣé-ri-a i-ra-dí-a-ni ma-áš-kà-tí* [9'] *tù-uš-ta-ar-dí.*

suggests that a *maškattum* is literally "something on which the hand has been laid" as a public token of claiming ownership. The texts demonstrate furthermore that this public action made the capital and the goods a shipment which could be called a *maškattum.*

The translation "deposit" does not fit in the examples cited above. It is too narrow and presupposes that the goods or capital are kept at one place while in reality they can move from one place to another. It is true that they were entrusted to an individual, but largely for the purpose of transport. The meaning "to send merchandise or capital through a third party" for *maškattam šakānum* instead of "to make a deposit" as in the *CAD* fits better in most contexts.

II. *Qīptum, naruqqum, and ebuṭṭum*

In a letter to his father Aššur-iddin, Aššur-nādā writes that Aššur-šamšī was bringing "20 minas of silver from my *qīptum*, my *naruqqum*, and my *ebuṭṭum*".[17] This sentence contains three other key-words used in the Assyrian financial terminology which I now wish to explore.

1. *Qīptum*

The *CAD* defines *qīptum* as: "an amount of silver entrusted to an agent for buying goods to be sold on consignment, or the consigned goods themselves, on which interest is not charged until a particular (usually unspecified) period has elapsed." The second part of this definition relates to what Larsen calls "the *qīptum*-procedure" whereby goods are entrusted on credit to a retail agent in Anatolia.[18] However, the word is also used for a credit of a different type, whereby the House of the City in Assur may act as creditor. The silver used to buy merchandise can be re-used for the same purpose after the proceeds become available. In other words, it is a special kind of loan provided by a moneylender or merchant. The amount of such a *qīptum* could even exceed 30 minas of silver according to TC 1 29:35-36.

2. *Naruqqum*

Partnerships existed in many forms from short-time cooperations to long-term *naruqqum*-contracts. One example of a service partnership in which an Assyrian trader "hires" an Anatolian to perform work for him is ICK 1 83 (case is ICK 2 60). This contract was partially formulated on the basis of a normal loan (*iṣṣēr išū*) and partly as a *beʾūlātum*-contract (*uktaʾal* and the clause about the debtor's possible disappearance).[19] The merchant Iddin-Ištar had a claim of 4 1/2 minas of *liti*-silver on Aluluwa who had

---

17 SÉ 147, republished by M. Jursa and K. Radner in *AfO* 42/43 (1995-96), 99: [3] 20 *ma-na* KÙ.BABBAR [4] *lu ša qí-ip-tí-a* [5] *lu na-ru-qí-a* [6] *lu i-na e-bu-ṭí-a* [7] *A-šùr-*^{d}UTU*-ši* [8] *na-áš-a-kum.*

18 Larsen 1976, 104. The *qīptum* as an interest-free loan in merchandise has been discussed by K.R. Veenhof in his contribution, see there the section *Commercial Credit.*

19 See also Kienast 1989, 95.

agreed to repay the amount by working for the merchant. It was stipulated that the creditor would take two-thirds and the debtor one-third of the total profit (*takšītum*) they should realize. The debtor could, by Iddin-Ištar's explicit consent only, hire himself out to someone else. The background may be that Aluluwa had an outstanding debt towards Iddin-Ištar which he could only repay in this way. Both persons occur in ICK 2 12 where Iddin-Ištar has a claim of one mina of silver on Aluluwa. This seems to be a normal loan.

A partnership constituted for a specific purpose is reflected for instance in the text ICK 1 1, last edited in Michel 1991 as no. 125. Four persons, one of whom contributed the silver, formed a *tappā'uttum* with the aim of purchasing *aši'um*-iron. The key-word in texts referring to partnership funds is *ša bari*, "(capital) belonging to the common fund of". Real partnership contracts are rare in Old Assyrian texts.

The richest documentation on partnerships concerns the so-called *naruqqum*-contracts. This institution formed the subject of a detailed study by M.T. Larsen (Larsen 1977), who built on the interpretation presented by Landsberger. At the time only a single *naruqqum*-contract was available for study: Kayseri 313. Larsen describes how the trade of those Assyrians operating in Anatolia was financed by means of the *naruqqum*-contract which was therefore of crucial importance. He assumed it was established at the capital Assur and under supervision by the city authorities who also kept the document containing a merchant's *naruqqum*. One indication for this seems to be the fact that the *laputtā'um*-official acted as the first witness.
In the contract a number of proper names connected with an amount of gold represented the investors with their investments. The last investor in this text was the same man who was entrusted with this capital. The text continues in Larsen's translation:

> In all: 30 minas of gold, the *naruqqum* of Amur-Ištar. Reckoned from the eponymate (of) Susaja he will conduct trade for twelve years. Of the profit he will enjoy (lit. "eat") one-third. He will be responsible (lit. "stand") for one-third. He who receives his money back before the completion of his term must take the silver at the exchange-rate 4:1 for gold and silver. He will not receive any of the profit.

Larsen dates the contract to the first half of Pūšu-kēn's generation at Kanish. The person receiving the capital, the so-called tractator, might have been the son of Amur-ili. As we have only one contract, it remains uncertain how far it is representative for all other *naruqqum*-contracts. We must reckon with the existence of individual stipulations. The investor is called *ummiānum*. The word *šamallā'um* could be used for the tractator but was probably used for persons not managing a *naruqqum* as well. The tractator was usually a merchant travelling with the caravans or living in Anatolia. However, the wealthier merchants at Assur could have had a *naruqqum* as well. The same trader might have had "sack capital" and at the same time be the investor to other merchants. The whole *naruqqum* capital was handed over to the tractator when the contract was drawn up. Additions to the original capital could be made later. Creditors might even agree to convert a debt into a share (*ḫubullum ana naruqqīšu illak*). The *naruqqum* manager conducted trade (*makārum*) with the capital as well as administered the funds. The tractator had to send the proceeds to the house of his financiers in Assur where a *nisḫātum* was levied on this silver of *c.* four per cent after which they would purchase goods for him. This meant regular business activities for them. The word *be'ūlātum* (*bûlātu*) as used by Pūšu-kēn in the letter to his *ummiānu*'s (BIN 4 32, see above) which can be understood as "goods or money over which someone is allowed to 'rule' under certain conditions", refers here to his *naruqqum*-capital. The discussion about a term in this letter might refer to an extension of the period stipulated in his contract but the clearence mentioned in it does not mean the end of it. The *naruqqum* might exist during, or even beyond, the lifetime of its tractator. There are examples in which investments are inherited by a trader's children: for instance in the case of Pūšu-kēn. The shares could be transferred or sold. Texts Dalley 6 and 8 (= EL 327 and 328) even demonstrate that father and son could manage the same *naruqqum*.

Kayseri 313 contains stipulations regarding two-thirds of the profit. The terms used were *nēmulum*, the net profit on a commercial operation, and *šalšātum*, one-third of the net profit. The profit was determined during periodic accountings which probably took place at the end of each individual caravan transaction. It is also possible that the accountings took place during regular intervals. If the document was written for the investors stipulating the duties of the tractator, some of his rights might not necessarily be mentioned. An investor lost his right to a share in the profit if he withdrew his share before the end of the term. The clause that the tractator was responsible for one-third of the profit seems to have been a guarantee for the investor that there would always be at least one-third of the profit to divide. In Landsberger's reconstruction of events, an accounting took place at the end of each transaction: the tractator received one-third of the profit; one-third which he had guaranteed was reinvested in the *naruqqum*, and the last one-third (not mentioned in the contract) might have been reserved to compensate eventual losses. Larsen assumes that the last one-third was reinvested as well. The tractator would then be responsible for only half of the reinvested profit which would give him more freedom of action and allow him to recover from possible losses. He could take his share in the profit out of the common fund. The investors receiving the same amount (together) had to wait till the end of the term. The sum remaining of the last one-third probably went to the investors.

It is difficult to trace this accounting in the texts simply because the terminology is used for other forms of commercial transactions as well. Texts in which the words *šalšātum* and *mišit ellitim* "the fund of the company" occur side by side probably refer to the division of profit, which might have been reinvested in the company as in the case of the *mišit ellitim*. The verb *šapākum*, on the other hand, could denote individual investments in a *naruqqum*; but it is unclear whether the word *šipkātum* "accumulations", refers to the computed profit guaranteed by the tractator. The word *munūtum* "something counted" denotes any kind of computed profit and might refer to dividends from a *naruqqum*-investment. The verb *elāʾum* in the Š-stem is used for "realizing a profit". The *šēlūʾutum* might further denote prematurely withdrawn investments.

Larsen stresses that the exchange rate of 4:1 for gold and silver in connection with the premature withdrawel of a share was limited to the *naruqqum*-contracts. However, the current exchange rates in Assur, which were comparable to those in Anatolia, were higher than 4:1. But in all probability the shares were not paid in gold but in silver, and the exchange rate of 4:1 used for an investment was an artificial one as well. This meant that when dissolving the partnership the investor realized a profit of one hundred per cent at a normal rate of 8:1 on the capital invested.

Since the publication of the article by Larsen, the number of texts with references to *naruqqum*-contracts has increased. One text from Elamma's archive summarizes the contents of his *naruqqum*-contract in addition to other funds at his disposal. The document is kt 91/k 482 and will be published by K.R. Veenhof. According to the contract the tractator was to present an account after the term of 10 years (*ana* 10 *šanātim nikkassī iddan*).

Larsen's interpretation of the term *šēlū'utum* was accepted by the *CAD* rendering it "profit, dividends" (Š/2, 276). The three attestations of the word (CCT 4 49b:8; ICK 1 177:29; TC 3 84:34) all refer to a payment which might be connected with a *naruqqum*. One passage from text CCT 4 49b can either be explained as an interim accounting or as the final accounting:

> D. came here and presented an account, and A. son of I. gave us (the) *šēlū'utum*. The silver, both that from D. as well as that from A., my "counts" and your "counts", I will give D. for (his) *naruqqum*. One mina 25 shekels of silver fell to your share, both from that of D. as from that of <A.>.

The question is whether the phrase "to give an account" means the final account at the end of the term, and whether "to give an account" can be equated with "to give *šēlū'utum*". Regardless, the result would have been the same: a disbursement of silver which in view of the small amount concerned can only be taken as some sort of profit sharing. If "to give *šēlū'utum*" took place before the end of the contract, to which the passage from TC 3 84 points as well, this term would indeed denote an "interim dividend" as suggested by Larsen. In his view an investor could "impose" the *šalšātum* on the tractator in case the latter was unable to meet his obligations resulting in the end of the contract.[20] The texts used to corroborate this view concern the *naruqqum* of Ikūnum and his inability to make payments to his investors. Note that the verb *elā'um* Š can only mean a withdrawal of investments in the conflict between Iddin-Ištar and the family of Zuzu (Kay 275:12 and JCS 41 no. 3:10).

The financiers were of course well aware how much the value of a trader's *naruqqum* was. The phrase "I will collect my *naruqqum* and go to the City" (KTS 2 45:10-12) demonstrates that this merchant in any case knew how much money belonged to it. He must have kept a record of this investment, otherwise it would have been impossible to present an account of the way he had managed the *naruqqum* to his *ummiānu*'s. The documentary evidence, unfortunately, contains only few texts which enable us to trace the *naruqqum* money and goods, an obscurity shared with that of *ikribū* funds.

While there are numerous references to transports of silver or gold to one's *ummiānu*'s in Assur, the instances where such a transport is qualified by the addition "belonging to the *naruqqum*" are rare. Did the unqualified amounts originate from a *naruqqum* in which the *ummiānu*'s had invested? And if so, did such a shipment constitute the complete proceeds of a caravan financed with *naruqqum* money or only a part of it? One of the texts containing a qualification is BIN 6 175 where the first entry has "eight minas of silver belonging to my *naruqqum*". The second is CCT 4 10a, a letter sent by Aššur-nādā to his father Aššur-iddin in which he announces that six minas of refined silver belonging to the latter's *naruqqum* was being brought to him. Aššur-iddin asked his son, according to TC 1 18, to send him 40 minas of silver for his *naruqqum*

20 Larsen 1977, 139.

apparently because he had to present his financiers money which they could use for purchasing goods for him. His son was to take this silver out of his own assets and from the money of Aššur-iddin's *naruqqum*. In the document accompanying the silver he should write that half of it belonged to his father's *naruqqum* and half belonged to the "merchant", that is the son. Šalim-aḫum wrote to his son Dān-Aššur that he should hand over silver from his *naruqqum* to his brother in order to bring it to Assur (AKT 3 67).

The word *naruqqum* was used both for the capital invested by several persons as recorded in the contract as well as for every individual investment. The Old Assyrian texts contain numerous references to additions made for various reasons to an existing *naruqqum*-contract. It remains unclear, however, whether those instances where a merchant was provided with a *naruqqum* always meant an increase in the original amount or a possible increase in the number of his investors. Moreover, there are a number of texts where *naruqqum* is neither a joint investment made by several people nor an addition to such a contract already in existence. For example EL 157 (Sayce 1):

> 1-3 I. gave four minas of refined silver to E. 4-9 Within four years from the *ḫamuštum* of A. and B. he will pay eight minas of silver. (9-12 Month and eponym) 12-14 [As much silver] as he took, he did because of his *naruqqum*. 15-18 I. will take the same amount (as E.) from the profits which E. will realize. 18-20 The *naruqqum* will enter I.'s house. (21-23 before two witnesses).

Compare also the contract kt c/k 451,[21] which apparently deals with an exclusive obligation towards a single investor. The translation of this text is (C. = Aššur-bēl-šaduʾe, the creditor in Assur; D. = Uṣur-ša-Aššur, the debtor):

> 1-6 C. will give 200 *kutānum*-textiles of normal quality to D.'s representatives in the City and the textiles will cross the land at D.'s risk and cost.
> 6-12 The textiles will go to Kanish where C.'s representatives will draw up D.'s debt-note for 50 minas of silver with a term of 50 weeks and (after payment) the silver will be booked to his *naruqqum*; it cannot be withdrawn.
> 12-18 If, at the end of his term, (D.) has not brought the silver nor placed it before C., he will add 135 grains of silver per mina per month as default interest.
> 18-20 The *naruqqum* will enter C.'s house.
> 20-25 Should C. break the contract by withdrawing D.'s silver, C. will pay 10 minas of refined silver to D.
> 26-33 Should D. break the contract by saying: "Take your silver, I will not carry your *naruqqum*", D. will pay 15 minas of refined silver to C.
> (33-36 before three witnesses).

In both contracts the *naruqqum*-investment concerns only the debtor and the creditor. No other investors in the *naruqqum* seem to exist. The expression "the *naruqqum* will enter PN (= the creditor)'s house" (*naruqqum ana bēt* PN *errab*) points in this direction as well. It means that the proceeds obtained by selling the merchandise bought with money invested in a *naruqqum* have to go to the investor or *ummiānum* who had

21 Published by A. Uzunalimoğlu in *Anadolu Medeniyetleri Müzesi 1989 Yıllığı* (Ankara 1990), 50. Read in line 23: *e-té-ṭé-er*.

provided the capital. At his house or office (in the House of the City?) the *nisḫātum* was levied and, we may expect, the money was used to buy new goods for the tractator. The house is identified as that of "my/our father" (BIN 6 199:10'; CCT 2 44b:7), "our house" (Adana 237D:11)[22] or simply the "house of PN" as in EL 157 and kt c/k 451.

The debtor was obliged to pay 50 minas of silver (that is 15 shekels per textile) within a specified period. He may have been able to realize a better yield in Kanish, in which case he apparently kept the rest of the proceeds. The booking of "silver" to his *naruqqum* follows immediately on the clause mentioning the term for repaying the 50 minas and concerns the same money. His *naruqqum* is therefore booked at 50 minas for an unspecified term. Apart from the phrase "(silver) *ana naruqqīšu lapātum*" the addition of an investment to an existing *naruqqum* can also be expressed by "(silver) *ana naruqqīšu illak*". The profit for the creditor is of course dependent on the price he had paid in Assur. If this had been five shekels apiece, his profit would amount to 200 per cent. He probably provided the debtor with such an opportunity in order to enable him to repay a debt which he could not return otherwise. By doing this the creditor saved his debtor from bankruptcy and was able make a profit without great risk or costs.

3. *The ebuṭṭum*

The current interpretation of *ebuṭṭum*[23] is that of a special type of loan (*CAD* E, 20). The *CAD* adds in the discussion section:

> The *ebuṭṭu* loan, in contrast to the *ḫubullu* loan, carried no interest, was not safeguarded by witnesses and contracts (no witnessed contract concerning an *ebuṭṭu*-loan is known) and was without term (...). In contrast to loans *ana šiʾamāti*, "for the purchase of merchandise," the use of money given as *ebuṭṭu* appears to have been at the discretion of the borrower. Presumably it was a loan transacted among merchants who trusted each other implicitly and served commercial purposes, which, however, cannot be defined more closely. (...)

The *c*. 30 references to *ebuṭṭum* show the important role it must have played within trade. Some texts mention it as one of several modes of finance. In SÉ 147 it is mentioned together with *qīptum* and *naruqqum* and it occurs as an alternative to *naruqqum* in *e.g.* kt a/k 394 and kt n/k 460.[24] Compare also RA 59 23:52-54: "Whether he (made) *naruqqum*-investments or gave *ebuṭṭu*'s to anybody."[25] The tractator "accepts" or "takes" (*laqāʾum*) an *ebuṭṭum* (kt n/k 460) or "carries" one (*našāʾum*, kt a/k 1056), just like a *naruqqum*. As with the *naruqqum*, every individual investment is called *ebuṭṭum* as well. The plural is also used at times and denotes goods given as *ebuṭṭum*, or the various deposits.

---

22 Published by V. Donbaz in *AfO* 31 (1984), 23ff.

23 J. Lewy, EL I, 302 note d., rendered it "Treugut". Von Soden rendered it "interest-free loan" (*AHw* 184b: "zinsfreies Darlehen"). The spelling with *ṭ* is based on the Hebrew word *ᶜabōṭ* "security".

24 See Veenhof 1995a, 1725.

25 A text dealing with the legacy of Šū-Anim. Lines 52-54: [52]... *lu ší-ip-kà-tim* [53] *lu e-bu-ṭí . a-na ma-ma-an* [54] *i-dí-in*.

The value of the *ebuṭṭum* is usually expressed in silver (never in gold) and ranges from 3 (ICK 1 7) to 22 1/2 minas (KTS 2 7). In other cases the *ebuṭṭum* consists of merchandise, as in BIN 6 141 or VS 26 49. According to CCT 3 30 it was possible to keep an *ebuṭṭum* for 20 years by postponing its repayment.

The expression "to book an amount as *ebuṭṭum* on someone's *ebuṭṭum*-tablet with his *ummiānu*'s in Assur" suggests that *ebuṭṭum* can partly be compared to the *naruqqum*-institution and denotes a specific kind of investment which a merchant could obtain from others. Additions to the original *ebuṭṭum* were, like the *naruqqum*, booked on a special tablet. The individual handing over of silver or goods as an *ebuṭṭum* was recorded on a separate tablet naming also the witnesses. There is at present no text available which records the individual investments of several persons into a merchant's *ebuṭṭum*-capital as is found in the *naruqqum*-contract texts. The specific clauses connected with the possession of an *ebuṭṭum* remain therefore unknown. However, one text (unpublished kt n/k 1841) records, however, an *ebuṭṭum*-investment: two persons, one of which preferred to remain unknown and is referred to only as the "merchant", provided 10 minas of silver. The text is dated but does not mention a term. It contains the clause that the debtor has to bring "the silver and its *miqtum*", which suggests that there was some kind of profit-sharing after ending the *ebuṭṭum*. This text, in fact, invalides the definition given by the *CAD*, for it is a contract drawn up in the presence of witnesses.

In addition there is the letter TC 1 28 (cf. Garelli 1963, 246), which contains the following passage:

> Concerning the merchant about whom you wrote as follows: "I want to add (or: let him add?) 1 1/2 mina of silver to (*ana*) my *tadmiqtum*," he refused to add (it). We borrowed 1 1/2 mina and credited the merchant for 3 minas of silver with the *ummiānu*'s on the tablet concerning the *ebuṭṭu*-deposits. All *ummiānu*'s gave him each four minas (of silver). If you please, add there to him one mina of silver. Send the 1 1/2 mina which we borrowed with the first person leaving (for Assur) so we can pay it back.[26]

The background to this letter and its interpretation are unclear to me, but it illustrates how an additional amount could be added the one's *ebuṭṭum*. The *tadmiqtum*-credit at times amounted to considerable sums of silver; is it in some way connected with the *ebuṭṭum*? The *ebuṭṭum* is clearly a type of investment provided to a merchant to increase his assets. In return he paid part of the profits to the investor.

Only a number of financial key-words could be discussed in this article. Yet, the ones I have discussed show that the capital with which a trader was working consisted of his own assets and of funds put at his disposal by other merchants and financiers. The

26 TC 1 28: [19] ... *a-šu-mì* [20] *ša* DAM.GÀR *ša ta-áš-pu-ra-ni* [21] *um-ma a-ta-ma* KÙ.BABBAR 1* (collation by M.T. Larsen) 1/2 *ma-na* [22] *a-na ta-ad-mì-iq-tí-a* [23] *lu-ra-dí-am ra-du-am ú-lá i-mu-a* [24] 1 1/2 *ma-na ni-iḫ-bu-ul-ma* [25] 3 *ma-na* KÙ.BABBAR *iš-tí um-mì-a-ni* [26] *i-na ša e-bu-ṭí i-na ṭup-pí-im* [27] *šu-mì* DAM.GÀR *ni-il*$_5$*-pu-ut ku-lu* [28] *um-mì-a-ni* 4 *ma-na*.TA *i-dí-nu-šum* [29] *šu-ma li-bi-kà a-ta a-ma-kam* [30] 1 *ma-na* KÙ.BABBAR *ṣí-ib-šum* [31] 1 1/2 *ma-na ša ni-iḫ-bu-lu iš-tí* [32] *pá-né-e-ma šé-bi-lam lu nu-ta-er*.

first were his *šalṭu*, the other his *bûlātu*. That which he could dispose of, the *bûlātu*, consisted in turn of short-term and long-term investments, among which the most important are the *naruqqum* and *ebuṭṭum* partnerships. Further research is needed to refine this picture and establish the proportions between own and borrowed capital. It should also attempt to delineate the problems of the value of a merchant's capital.

TRADERS IN THE NEO-ASSYRIAN PERIOD*

KAREN RADNER (HELSINKI)

In contrast to many other periods of the history of the Ancient Near East, trade in the Neo-Assyrian period has been but little studied.[1] Whereas there are several papers devoted to the royal trade agent, the *tamkāru* = DAM.GÀR, namely by M. Elat, the study of private trade has just begun with the discovery of the importance of the so-called EN KASKAL documents by K. Deller. Evidence that could be interpreted as referring to peddling trade has not been collected so far.

A. L. Oppenheim concluded his important article 'Trade in the Ancient Near East' sketching the directions into which research should move. The first subject he suggested was the geography of trade, the second the language of the merchant. The third topic was "the social position of those engaged in trade on all economic levels."[2]

In this paper I will present the sources for those who are associated with trade (or might be thought to be) and try to outline their position in society.

1. *The Royal Trade Agent*: *tamkāru* = DAM.GÀR

The Neo-Assyrian *tamkāru*[3] is a royal agent. Legitimated by the king and equipped with quasi-diplomatic status[4] he travels near and far to provide the king with the items needed to run state matters smoothly.

---

* For the preparation of this paper, I was able to use my own files as well as the database of the Corpus of Neo-Assyrian Texts. The former have been employed for collecting the material for the second part of this study and as a basis for its first part, the latter for supplementing the data for the first part and for collecting the attestations for the third part of this study. For generously allowing me access to the Corpus of Neo-Assyrian Texts I wish to thank Prof. Dr. S. Parpola. For the permission to work with the Assur texts kept in the Vorderasiatisches Museum, Berlin, I am indebted to Dr. E. Klengel, former Director, and Prof. Dr. J. Renger, Chairman of the Assur Committee of the Deutsche Orient-Gesellschaft. Many thanks are due to Dr. V. Donbaz for sharing his transliterations of the Assur texts kept in the Istanbul Arkeoloji Müzeleri. I was able to collate parts of these texts with the help of the excavation photographs in the VAM. I wish to thank Dr. R. Jas, Leiden, for his critical remarks and suggestions and Dr. G. van Driel for his comments on the EN KASKAL texts.

1 Compare the remarks of Fales (1984, 207).

2 Oppenheim 1970, 22f.

3 See Deller 1987, 1 n. 1 for the proposal to read the logogram (LÚ.)DAM.GÀR as *tankāru* in Neo-Assyrian, but compare the writing LÚ*.*tam-qar* in ADD 229 = SAA 6 111 r. 4. The title *rab tamkārē* is attested in two texts (ADD 860 ii 20 and ND 2684 r. 9, see already Elat 1987, 253). However, the difference between this professional title and the simple *tamkāru* cannot be reconstructed from these references. Its existence would imply a hierarchic organization of the trade agents.

Sources mentioning the *tamkāru* (not listed are the legal documents used for the prosopographical part): **A. Letters: 1. Assyrian letters from the Kouyunjik correspondence:** ABL 186 (Ubru-Nabû to Esarhaddon); ABL 196 = SAA 1 33 (Sennacherib to Sargon II); ABL 233+ = SAA 1 116 (Aššūr-bāni from Kalhu to Sargon II); ABL 234 = SAA 1 117 (Aššūr-bāni from Kalhu to Sargon II); ABL 310 =

The *tamkāru* is associated with the armed forces[5] and may himself command military personnel. The *tamkāru* Addî[6] is closely connected with Kakkullānu, *rab kiṣri* of the crown prince whose dossier of legal documents has been unearthed as part of the royal archives in Nineveh. A distinctive group of persons appears as witnesses on behalf of Kakkullānu, most of them having high military functions. Addî is very likely to be part of the army and of high rank as well. This is evident in the case of Aramiš-šar-ilāni. This *tamkāru* from Carchemish had at least fifty soldiers and twelve horses under his command.[7] Since collecting and transporting the tribute for the Assyrian king is an important part of the duties of the *tamkāru*'s, close cooperation with the army is necessary. A bitter comparison of the Old Testament prophet Nahum bears witness to this: he describes the traders, garrisons, and scribes of Assyria as ever hungry locusts.[8]

SAA 5 202 (Šarru-ēmuranni to Sargon II); ABL 529 = SAA 5 224 (Adad-issēʾa to Sargon II); ABL 532 (Iddin-Aššūr to the king); ABL 992 (Issi-Šamaš-balāṭu to Esarhaddon); ABL 1058 = SAA 5 218 ([...] to Sargon II); ABL 1273 = SAA 5 149 ([...] to Sargon II); ABL 1371 ([...] to Esarhaddon); ABL 1442 = SAA 1 159 (Šulmānu-[...] to Sargon II); CT 53 10 = SAA 1 179 (Bēl-iqbi of Ṣūpat to Sargon II); CT 53 16 (Issi-Šamaš-balāṭu to Esarhaddon); CT 53 59 = SAA 5 150 (Atanḫa-Šamaš to Sargon II); CT 53 307 = SAA 1 37 (Sennacherib to Sargon II); CT 53 874 = SAA 5 143 (Šulmu-bēli to Sargon II); CT 53 344 = SAA 1 242 ([...] to Sargon II); K 992 = Jas 1990, 5 (to Esarhaddon, no introduction formula). **2. Babylonian letters from the Kouyunjik correspondence:** ABL 458 (Bēl-ibni from the Sealand to Ashurbanipal); ABL 702 = SAA 10 169 (too fragmentary to assign); ABL 968 (Šumu-iddin to Esarhaddon); ABL 1317 (too fragmentary to assign); ABL 1404 (Nergal-ibni from Sippar to Ashurbanipal); CT 54 447 (a Babylonian to Sargon II); CT 54 502 (a Gambulean to Ashurbanipal); CT 54 510 = SAA 10 164 (Nabû-iqbi from Kutha to the king); CT 54 546 (too fragmentary to assign). **3. A private letter from Assur:** KAV 197 (the oilpressers of Assur to Irmulu). **B. Administrative texts: 1. From Nineveh:** ADD 812 = SAA 11 26; ADD 815+ = SAA 7 30; ADD 822 = SAA 7 39; ADD 993 = SAA 7 118. **2. From Kalhu:** ND 2497; ND 2458; ND 2728+; CTN 2 126.

Literature on *tamkāru*: The most important study is Elat 1987, 233-254. Other relevant works are Deller 1987, 1-29; Elat 1978, 20-34; Elat 1979, 527-546; Elat 1991, 21-35, and the short, but important remarks of Postgate 1979, 205-207. An article by M. Elat with the title 'Assyrian Imperialism and International Trade' has been announced to appear in *Assur* 5 and has been quoted occasionally, see Deller 1987, 2 n. 8 and Elat 1991, 22 notes 8 and 23. However, to my knowledge this article has never been published.

4 The diplomatic competence of the *tamkāru*'s is doubted in a letter from the crown prince Sennacherib to his father Sargon II, ABL 196 = SAA 1 33. The emissaries of Kumuhhu question the authority of the *tamkāru*'s to select the king's tribute. The king himself must decide whether their claims are legitimate or not. It seems that there was nobody in the provincial administration, not even the crown prince Sennacherib, who could decide the matter:

> The emissaries of Kumuhhu have come, bringing tribute and with it seven teams of mules. ... They also brought *red* wool (SÍG.MEŠ LUM.LUM). The *tamkāru*'s told me that they have selected seven talents from it but that the men from Kumuhhu did not agree but said: "Who do you think you are? You are not to make the selection. Let them take it over (to Assyria) and let the king's female weavers make a selection over there." The king, my lord, should write me to whom they are supposed to give it.

5 See also Elat 1987, 251-253.

6 The references for the *tamkāru*'s mentioned in the following can be found in the prosopographical section.

7 ABL 186.

8 See Elat 1987, 248f on the Nahum passage and 245ff for a discussion of some of the letters from Kouyunjik mentioning *tamkāru*'s in connection with tribute (ABL 196 = SAA 1 33; ABL 458 = de Vaan 1995, 257-259).

Tamkāru's may be part of the household of a member of the king's family or a high official. Thus, Suḫarāmû belongs to the house of the crown prince. Zizî is part of the entourage of the queen. Sabirî seems to be a member of the household of the governor of Kalhu.[9] Also, the *rab tamkārē* Sēᵓ-gabbar is part of the staff of a governor, probably from Kalhu. However, most of the titles of *tamkāru*'s are not further specified and they are probably subordinates of the king himself.

In my opinion, the position of the Neo-Assyrian *tamkāru*'s may be compared to the likes of Francis Drake, Christopher Columbus, or Hernando Cortez employed more than two millennia later by the kings and queens of Britain and Spain. Both these men and the Neo-Assyrian *tamkāru*'s are equipped with military and diplomatic competences by the ruler of a world empire: using these in war and peace, they travel along well-known routes, reestablish almost forgotten ones[10] and discover new ones, their ultimate goal being to get what their monarch needs to rule the country: slaves,[11] horses,[12] metals,[13] and luxury goods of any kind.

Through their position the *tamkāru*'s - like their "successors" in medieval Britain and Spain - could gain vast influence. We know of one Salmānu-[...][14] who is quite probably a *tamkāru* although this is not explicitely stated in the one letter that is known to us. He not only received gifts of honor[15] from king Sargon II, possibly for his merits as *tamkāru*, but also lent the enormous sum of 570 minas of silver for the building of Dūr-Šarrukēn to the king. He wrote a letter[16] to the king urging him in rather frank language to pay back this debt:

> To the king, [my] lord, your slave Salmānu-[...]. Well-being to the king, [my] lord! The king, my lord, told [me]: "Until the work at Dūr-Šarrukēn is completed nobody will pay back your debts (*ḫa-bul-li-k*[*a*])!" The credit (*ni-is-ḫu*) for (that part) of Dūr-Šarrukēn that has (already) been built they have pa[id back] to the (other) *tamkāru*'s, but nobody has [remembered] me! 570 minas of silver with [my seal] and due this year have not been repaid as yet. When the king, my lord, bestowed gold and pre[cious stones] onto me I told the king, my lord, that my father was much indebted to Ḫar[...], Ḫuziri and [...]. After my father('s death) I paid half of [his debts], but now their sons [are telling me]: "Pay us the debts that [your] father owes to our fathers!" As soon as Dūr-Šarrukēn has been [completely] bu[ilt], the king, my lord, [will ...] to the house [...] and pay back the debts to [...]. The king, my lord, may ask Šar[ru-ēmuranni]: half of [his work ass]ignment in Dūr-Šarrukēn [is completed].

9 See Elat 1987, 253.

10 In the case of the Neo-Assyrian empire, the most important example is the desert route to Egypt.

11 See Radner 1997, 227ff.

12 See especially ABL 259 = SAA 5 224; ND 2458 = *Iraq* 23 pl. 15; and CTN 2 126. *Tamkār sīsē* "trade agent for horses" is a title of its own, see ᵐ*i-gi-li-i* LÚ.DAM.GÀR ANŠE.KUR URU.*kal-ḫa-a-a* ADD 806 = SAA 11 222 r. 9f and ᵐ*na-din-ia* LÚ*.DAM.GÀR ANŠE.KUR.R[A.MEŠ] ADD 261 = SAA 6 86 r. 9.

13 One of the three Neo-Assyrian standards for silver is the mina of the *tamkāru*.

14 See Radner 1998, 34f on the realization of the divine name Salmānu (formerly read Šulmānu).

15 For this interpretation of ABL 1442:16f compare the evidence assembled by Postgate 1993, 235-237.

16 ABL 1442 = SAA 1 159. On another interpretation of this letter, differing from mine in some respects, see Deller 1987, 16ff.

This letter is interesting for a variety of reasons, most important in the present context that *tamkāru*'s could be extremely wealthy, could gain personal access to the king - a truly remarkable position![17] - and could feel safe enough to use pressure on the king. Therefore, some of the *tamkāru*'s obviously belonged to the most influential circles in the Assyrian empire. It is not surprising that later, in the Neo-Babylonian Empire at the time of Nebuchadnezzar, *rab tangārē šarri* was the title of one of the king's top officials.[18]

For obvious reasons, the *tamkāru* had to stay away from his home quite often. The above-mentioned Aramiš-šar-ilāni from Carchemish is only one of the *tamkāru*'s whose provenance is known to us. Lāmur-Marduk, operating in Kalhu, is from Nineveh. Dadūsu and Igilî, both active in Nineveh, are from the cities of Kalzi and Kalhu respectively. Nabû-rība is also from Kalhu. Šarî is from the city of Kannuʾ. The hometown of Ammīni-ilu operating in Babylonia is the oasis Tema in the Arabian desert. Ramānû, who is active in Nineveh, is a man from Kišqa (URU.*kiš-qa-a-a*). Sukki-Aia, selling slaves in Nineveh, is from the country of Kumuhhu, classical Commagene.

Especially because of a passage in the Book of Ezekiel,[19] but also because of a letter from Tiglath-pileser III's delegate Qurdi-Aššūr-lāmur to his king,[20] the importance of the Phoenician merchants for international trade is well known. Without doubt, the Assyrians had to rely on them entirely for the maritime trade.[21] However, the Phoenicians clearly did not have a monopoly on trade in the Neo-Assyrian empire,[22] especially since Assyrian imports did not focus on oversea destinations. There is no proof that the control over the overland trading routes to Babylonia,[23] Anatolia,[24] Arabia,[25] Egypt, Iran,[26] and the countries further east and north was in the hands of Phoenician traders. Quite on the contrary, it is obvious that other West-Semitic people as *e.g.* the Philistines,[27] the Arabian

---

17 The contact of the Assyrian king with his subjects seems to have been extremely limited, compare ABL 1091 with the case of a man who, when insisting to speak to the king in person, was led to him veiled. On this letter see Parpola 1980, 171ff; see especially 176 n. 12 on the fact that ordinary people were not allowed to see the king.

18 See Oppenheim 1964, 94 with n. 18 and Elat 1987, 254.

19 See Liverani 1991, 65-79 for a recent commentary on Ezek. 27 and an interpretation of the trade network of Tyre.

20 NL 12 = *Iraq* 17 pl. 30, see Postgate 1974, 390f. For a commentary on this text see Elat 1978, 27 and Postgate 1979, 206.

21 Elat 1991, 24ff.

22 However, quite frequently international trade is described as being more or less exclusively in the hands of the Phoenicians, see *e.g.* Oppenheim 1967, 253f and, more recently, Snell 1993, 223.

23 On the trade with Babylonia see Cole 1996, 64ff.

24 Trading activities in Kumuhhu and Harrān are documented in ADD 812 = SAA 11 26.

25 A good example for the trade with Arabia and its restrictions is CT 53 10 = SAA 1 179, a letter of Bēl-iqbi of Ṣūpat to Sargon II: "As to what the king, my lord, wrote to me: 'You have made Ḫuzaza into a *tamkāru*'s town! The people have been selling iron for money to the Arabs! Who are the *tamkāru*'s who have been selling there?'" On this letter and illegal iron sales see also Cole 1996, 65f.

26 ABL 1273 = SAA 5 149, a letter from an unknown official to Sargon II, shows that *tamkāru*'s were active in northern Iran (rather than in Eastern Anatolia as I stated in Radner 1997, 228. Thanks are due to A. Fuchs for pointing this out to me). Reporting on the disastrous situation in the city of Ḫargu the writer finished his letter by quoting some people who came to seek his help: "They said: "[...]. We are to be sold for money. We know our *tamkāru*'s (better: the *tamkāru*'s? LÚ.DAM.GÀR-*ni* could stand for a plural form *tamkārāni*)."

27 Elat 1978, 30ff on the role of the Philistines in the trade with Egypt.

nomads,[28] and people from Anatolia[29] were deeply involved in trade. The role of the Assyrians themselves should not be underestimated. Above, *tamkāru*'s from Nineveh, Kalhu, and Kalzi in the heartland of Assyria have been mentioned. If one chooses to go by their names, men like Šulmu-šarri, Ululāyu, and Ubru-Sebetti are probably Assyrians, too. The *tamkāru* with the rather foreign sounding and certainly non-Semitic name Mauau is quite possibly a native of one of the many countries north and east of Assyria proper.

To conclude: it can hardly be argued that a certain ethnic group dominated the trade in the Neo-Assyrian empire. It seems that persons from all over the empire and beyond could act as *tamkāru*'s, the most important criterion for their engagement probably being whether the king trusted their loyalty and their abilities to fulfill their task. It seems only sensible that the king preferred to keep a close eye on his *tamkāru*'s and several letters from the royal correspondence refer to their surveillance.[30]

K. Deller[31] has drawn attention to the interesting fact that surprisingly often the *tamkāru*'s remain anonymous in the texts. The best example for this is, in my opinion, a legal document from Nineveh.[32] A heavily indebted man, Mannu-kī-Inurta, is kept in debt-slavery by his creditor together with his family. This creditor is a nameless *tamkāru*. Another man, Ṣalmu-šarri-iqbi, pays the debt to the *tamkāru* and thus frees the family who has to serve him in turn. It is highly unusual that the name of the creditor is not

---

28 See, for now, Oppenheim 1970, 17 on the role of the nomads and semi-nomads. Above, Ammīni-ilu from the North-Arabian city of Tema has already been mentioned.

29 The *tamkāru* Sukki-Aia from Kumuhhu has already been mentioned above. His father bears a good Anatolian name, ^{m}*par-nu-u-a-ri*, see Zadok 1994 *sub* 8.

30 Thus we read in ABL 1058 = SAA 5 218, a letter by an unknown author to Sargon II: "As for the *tamkāru* Bēl-aḫḫē about whom the king, my lord, wrote: I shall secretly send word that they bring him to me, and I shall (then) send him t[o the king, my lord]." The answers of Aššūr-bāni from Kalhu to the king's inquiry about one *tamkāru* respectively several *tamkāru*'s in ABL 233+ = SAA 1 116 and ABL 234 = SAA 1 117 are unfortunately not preserved.

31 Deller (1987, 2 with n. 6) quotes Garelli (1977, 101) for a similar situation in the Old Assyrian period.

32 ADD 85 = ARU 656:

^{1} [NA$_4$.KIŠIB] ^{m}*man-nu-ki-i-*^{d}MA[Š] ^{2} [x MA.NA KÙ].BABBAR *ḫa-bu-li-š*[*u*] ^{3} [^{md}NU-M]AN-*iq-bi a-na* LÚ.DAM.GÀ[R] ^{4} *i*[*d-di*]*n* ^{m}*man-nu-ki-i-*^{d}MAŠ MÍ.4*.DINGIR.KI-MAN-*ra*[*t*] ^{5} MÍ-*šú* DUMU.MÍ-*su*

(Unused seal space, showing that the text is a later copy of the original sealed tablet, see Radner 1997, 40ff.)

---

^{6} PAB 3 ZI.MEŠ TA* IGI LÚ.DAM.GÀR *ip-ta-ṭar* ^{7} [*k*]*u-um ru-bé-e šá* KÙ.BABBAR *a-na* ^{md}NU-MAN-*iq-bi* ^{8} [*i-p*]*a-lu-ḫu-šú lu-u* LÚ.GAR-*nu-šú* $^{lo.\ e.\ 9}$ [*lu-u ḫa-za-nu* UR]U$^{?!}$-*šú ša* KÙ.BABBAR $^{r.\ 1}$ [*a-di ru-bé-e a-na*] ^{md}NU-MAN-DUG$_4$.GA $^{r.\ 2}$ [*id-din-u-ni* UN.MEŠ *ú*]-*še-ṣa* ($^{r.\ 2b\text{-}7}$ date (eponym not preserved) and list of witnesses)

> [Seal] of Mannu-kī-Inurta. [x minas of sil]ver, his (= Mannu-kī-Inurta's) debt, [Ṣalmu-ša]rri-iqbi gave to the *tamkāru*. (Thus) he freed Mannu-kī-Inurta, Arbail-šarrat, his wife, (and) his daughter, together three individuals, from the *tamkāru*. Instead of the interest of the silver they will serve Ṣalmu-šarri-iqbi. (Whoever it is), either his (= Mannu-kī-Inurta's) governor [or the mayor of] his (= Mannu-kī-Inurta's) [to]wn, who [gives] the silver [with the interest to] Ṣalmu-šarri-iqbi will redeem [the people].

For the restoration of line 9 compare the similar text ADD 77 = ARU 133:8.

mentioned at all. However, the situation is parallelled in a *dēnu* document that settles a lawsuit concerning a very similar matter. The creditor there is the eunuch of the king whose name is not mentioned, either. Although this title could be held by several persons at a time,[33] the title of the chief eunuch of the king could only be held by one person. In the case that the person in question was the king's chief eunuch, there could be no doubt about the identity of the creditor. Is it possible that the situation was somewhat similar for the *tamkāru*'s?

Whereas one might easily imagine that there was one person who was *the tamkāru* in the sense of the king's chief *tamkāru* of his time, thus recognizable by mentioning only his title, there can be no doubt that otherwise a number of *tamkāru*'s were operating simultaneously. This is evident from studying the prosopography. Even though the number of references not naming the *tamkāru* in question is high, there are 67 *tamkāru*'s whose names are known.[34] Not surprisingly, most of the names are obtained from the witness lists of legal documents where anonymity was impossible by definition.

The prosopography of the tamkāru's:

1. Abdî: ^{m}*ab-di-i* ⸢LÚ.DAM⸣.GÀR ND 5550 = SAA 12 96 r. 22 as witness (Biq).[35]
2. Adda-ḫāri: ^{m}10-*ḫa-ri* LÚ*.DAM.GÀR O 3706 r. 11 as witness (693).[36]
3. Adda-rapâ: ^{m}10-*ra*-⸢*pa*⸣-*a* LÚ*.DAM.GÀR ADD 197 = NALK 104:1 as seller (Bšn).
4. Addî: ^{m}*i-di-i* DAM.GÀR ADD 344 = ARU 364 r. 2' as witness (date lost).
   ^{m}*i-di-i* LÚ*.DAM.GÀR ADD 623 = NALK 128 l. e. 1 as witness (Sšu palace scribe).
   ^{m}*i-di-i* LÚ.DAM.GÀR ADD 318 = NALK 125 r. 10 as witness (Sšu palace scribe).
   ^{m}*a-di-i* LÚ.DAM.GÀR ADD 312 = NALK 131 r. 13 as witness (date lost).
   ^{m}*i-di-i* LÚ*.DAM.GÀR ADD 308 = NALK 120 r. 13 as witness (Ṣši).
   ^{m}*a-di-i* LÚ.DAM.GÀR ADD 414 = NALK 127 r. 33 as witness (Sšu the replacement).
5. Aḫī-aḫu-īdi: [^{m}]*a-ḫi-aḫ-i-di* ⸢DAM.GÀR⸣ ND 3427 = *Iraq* 15 141:1 as seller (Ddi).
6. Aḫi-qāmu: ^{m}⸢PAP⸣-*i-qa-m*[*u* LÚ*].DAM.GÀR ADD 251 = SAA 6 246 r. 1' as witness (date lost).
7. Ammīni-ilu: ^{m}*am-mì-ni*-DINGIR LÚ.⸢DAM.GÀR⸣ LÚ.*te-ma-a-a* ABL 1404:4 in a letter (reign of Ashurbanipal).

---

33 Cf. a purchase document for a garden from Assur, VAT 9763 (quoted by Weidner 1966, 69) in which eight royal eunuchs act as witnesses.

34 M. Elat has announced the publication of a study dealing with the prosopography of the Neo-Assyrian *tamkāru*'s. However, to my knowledge the work has never been published, see note 3. Elsewhere, he writes that "I also treated all the personal names of the *tamkāru* known from documents of this period, 54 in all. It is evident from them that Aramean names formed a considerable portion (22 or 23) but not the majority, and this probably correctly reflects the percentage of Arameans among the population of the major Assyrian cities in general" (Elat 1991, 23). Since the study of the prosopography of the *tamkāru*'s is vital in the present context and since Elat's work announced since 1987 is still unavailable I decided to collect the data myself. It seems that the enterprise was worthwhile since I was able to identify some new *tamkāru*'s. Elat's statement about the relation between West-Semitic and Akkadian names still holds true. [M. Elat's article has now been published in S.M. Maul (ed.), *Festschrift für Rykle Borger* (Groningen 1998), 39-57. - Ed.]

35 The abbreviations used for the Post-Canonical eponyms are those given in Millard 1994, 128.

36 Unpublished tablet in the Musées Royaux d'Art et d'Histoire, Brussels, from Ma^{c}allānāte.

8. Aramiš-šar-ilāni: ^{md}*a-ra-miš*-MAN-DINGIR.MEŠ ... LÚ.DAM.GÀR URU.*gar-ga-mes-a-a* ABL 186:11, r. 8 in a letter to the king (reign of Esarhaddon).
9. Aplāyu: ^{m}A-*ia* LÚ.DAM.GÀR ADD 711 = NALK 124 r. 10' as witness (Nšu palace scribe).
10. Atār-ḫām: ^{m}*a-tar-ḫa-am* LÚ.DAM.GÀR CT 53 59 = SAA 5 150:4, r. 6' mentioned in a letter (reign of Sargon II).
11. Baᵓal-qāmu: ^{m}*ba-ᵓa-la-qa-mu* LÚ.DAM.GÀR ND 2306 = *Iraq* 16 pl. vi r. 10 as witness (687).
12. Bēl-aḫḫē: ^{m}EN-PAB.MEŠ LÚ*.DAM.GÀR ABL 1058 = SAA 5 218 r. 9 in a letter (reign of Sargon II).
13. Bēl-nūrī: ^{m}EN-ZÁLAG LÚ*.*tam-qar* ADD 229 = SAA 6 111 r. 4 as witness (680).
14. Bir-Šamaš: ^{m}*bir*-^{d}*šá-maš* LÚ.DAM.GÀR ADD 281 = SAA 6 134 r. 10' as witness (694).
15. Dadūsu: ^{m}*da-du-su* LÚ.DAM.GÀR URU.*kàl-zi-a-a* ADD 50 = NALK 388:7 as witness (Mka).
16. Diddî: ^{m}*di-di-i* LÚ.DAM.GÀR ADD 349 = NALK 118 r. 21 as witness (Ṣši).
17. Erība-ilāni: ^{m}SU-DINGIR.MEŠ-*ni* LÚ*.⌜DAM⌝.GÀR ADD 328 = SAA 6 124:7 buys a house (698).
18. Ḫadasâ: ^{m}*ḫa-da-sa-a* LÚ*.DAM.GÀR ADD 281 = SAA 6 134 r. 9' as witness (694).
19. Ḫaldi-rēmanni: ^{md}*ḫal-di-rém-a-ni* LÚ*.DAM.GÀR ADD 261 = SAA 6 86 r. 10 as witness (date lost).
20. Ḫallî: ^{m}*ḫal-li-*[*i* LÚ*].DAM.GÀR ADD 312 = NALK 131 r. 14 as witness (date lost).
21. Ḫarrada: ^{m}*ḫar-ra-da* LÚ.DAM.GÀR ND 2306 = *Iraq* 16 pl. vi r. 11 as witness (687).
22. Igilî: ^{m}*i-gi-li-i* LÚ.DAM.GÀR ANŠE.KUR URU.*kal-ḫa-a-a* ADD 806 = SAA 11 222 r. 9f (not dated).
23. Ilti-bāštī: ^{m}*il-ti*-TÉŠ LÚ*.DAM.GÀR ADD 387 r. 5' as witness (653).
24. Ilu-iddina: ^{m}DINGIR-SUM-*na* LÚ.DAM.GÀR VAT 9685 = *SAAB* 9 77 r. 12 as witness (date lost).
25. [Ilu]-immē: [^{m}DINGIR]-*im-me* DAM.GÀR ADD 214 = NALK 217 r. 12 as witness (Upq).
26. Il-maᵓādi: ^{m}DINGIR-*ma-ᵓa-di* LÚ*.DAM.GÀR O 3680 r. 14 as witness (687).[37]
27. Inurta-erība: ^{md}MAŠ-SU LÚ.DAM.GÀR ND 5550 = SAA 12 96 r. 23 as witness (Biq).
28. Inurta-malak: ^{m}MAŠ-*ma-lak-ka* LÚ.DAM.GÀR DeZ 10461 = SH 88/8977 IV/200 r. 12 as witness (Bld).[38]
29. Issār-dūrī: ^{m}15-BÀD LÚ*.DAM.GÀR ADD 1248 r. 6' as witness (date lost).
30. Issār-paia$^{?}$: ^{md}15-*pa*$^{?}$-*ia*$^{?}$ LÚ.DAM.GÀR ADD 160 = NALK 205 r. 8 as witness (MšA).
31. Kurillāyu: ^{m}*kur*-DINGIR-*a-a* DAM.GÀR ADD 4 = NALK 147 r. 3 as witness (Šdn).[39]
32. Kakkānu: ^{m}*ka-ka-a-nu* ... DAM.GÀ[R].ME[Š] MADD 2 = SAA 6 133 r. 12 as witness (694).
33. Lāmur-Marduk: ^{m}IGI-^{d}ŠÚ LÚ.DAM.GÀR DUMU URU.*ni-nu-a* CTN 3 7 r. 5 as witness (Slu).
34. Maliktu: ^{m}*ma-lik-tú* LÚ*.DAM.GÀR ADD 233 = NALK 146 r. 14 as witness (659).

---

37 See note 36.

38 Unpublished tablet from Tell Sheikh Hamad, kept in the National Museum of Deir ez-Zor.

39 On the name see Lipinski 1997, 90-92.

35. Mauau: ... ^{m}*ma-u-a-u* DAM.GÀ[R].ME[Š] MADD 2 = SAA 6 133 r. 12 as witness (694).
36. Nabuzâ: [^{m}*n*]*a-bu-za-a*ʾ LÚ*.DAM.GÀR ADD 1152 = SAA 6 105 l. e. 2 as witness (690).
37. Nabû-erība: ^{md}PA-SU URU.*kal-ḫa-a-a* ABL 529 = SAA 5 224 r. 12f mentioned as a horse trader in a letter to the king (reign of Sargon II).
38. Nabû-šumu-iddina: ^{md}AG-MU-AŠ LÚ*.DAM.GÀR CTN 2 96 r. 2 as witness (691).
39. Nabûʾa: ^{md}PA-*u-a* LÚ.DAM.GÀR ND 5463 = SAA 11 95 r. 9 as witness (655).
40. Nādināya (or Nādin-Aia): ^{m}*na-din-ia* LÚ*.DAM.GÀR ANŠE.KUR.R[A.MEŠ] ADD 261 = SAA 6 86 r. 9 as witness (date lost).
41. Palḫu-šēzib: ^{m}*pal-ḫu-še-zib* LÚ*.DAM.GÀR ADD 276 = SAA 6 192 r. 10 as witness (682).
42. Qar-rāpiʾ: ^{m}*qar-ra-pi-i*ʾ LÚ*.DAM.[GÀR] Gezer 1 r. 10' = *JEOL* 27 (1981/82) 81 as witness (652).
43. Raḫīmi-šarru I: ^{m}*ri-ḫi-me*-MAN LÚ.DAM.GÀR ADD 237 = SAA 6 319 r. 11 as witness (665).
44. Raḫīmi-šarru II: ^{m}*ra-ḫi-me*-MAN L[Ú*.D]AM.GÀR Šariza 146 = *SAAB* 2 (1988) 12ff no. 4 r. 4' as witness (Mšu).
45. Ramānû: [^{m}*r*]*a-ma-nu-u* LÚ*.DAM.GÀR URU.*kiš-qa-a-a* ADD 357 = NALK 71 r. 10 as witness (date lost).
46. Raʾuzu: ^{m}*ra*-[ʾ]*u-zu* LÚ*.DAM.G[ÀR] CTN 2 53 r. 8' as witness (778).
47. Rēmanni-ilu: ^{m}*rém-a-ni*-DINGIR LÚ.DAM.GÀR ADD 197 = NALK 104 r. 4' as witness (Bšn).
48. Sabirî: ^{m}*sa-bi-ri* ⌜LÚ⌝.DAM.GÀR CTN 2 93: 9 as *bēl ḫabulli* (793).[40]
49. Sēʾ-gabbar: ^{m}*se-ga-bar*-[*ri*] LÚ.GAL DAM.GÀR.MEŠ ND 2684 r. 9 in an administrative text (probably reign of Sargon II).
50. Suḫarāmû: ^{m}*su-ḫa-ra-mu-u* LÚ*.DAM.GÀR *ša* DUMU MAN ADD 330 = SAA 6 220 r. 14 as witness (676).
51. Sukki-Aia: ^{m}TE-*a-a* A ^{m}*par-nu-u-a-ri* LÚ.DAM.GÀR KUR.*ku-mu-ḫa-a-u* TIM 11 2:2 as seller (Agt).
52. Ṣalmūte: ^{m}*ṣal-mu-te* LÚ.DAM.GÀR ADD 318 = NALK 125 r. 12 as witness (Sšu palace scribe).
53. Ṣilli-Aia: ^{m}*ṣil-la-a-a* LÚ*.DAM.GÀR ADD 200 = SAA 6 309 r. 9 as witness (667). ^{m}*ṣil*-[*la-a-a* LÚ*.DAM.GÀR] ADD 297 = SAA 6 348 r. 7 as witness (date lost). [^{m}*ṣil*?-*l*]*a*?-*a-a* LÚ*.DAM.G[ÀR] ADD 1248 r. 9' as witness (date lost).
54. Šamaš-nammir: ^{md}*šá-m*[*aš*]-*nam-mir* LÚ.DAM.GÀR ADD 392 = SAA 6 13 r. 5' as witness (710).
55. Šarî: ^{m}*ša-ri-i* URU.*kan-nu-u*ʾ-*a-a* ABL 529 = SAA 5 224: 7 mentioned as a horse trader in a letter to the king (reign of Sargon II).
56. Šimanu: ^{m}*ši-ma-nu* LÚ*.DAM.[GÀR] ADD 266 = SAA 6 297 r. 10' as witness (671).
57. Šulmu-šarri: ^{m}DI-*mu*-MAN DAM.GÀR BM 103389 = *AfO* 32 (1985) 38ff. r. 11 as witness (Sšu of Ḫindānu).
58. Šumma-ilāni: ^{m}*šum-ma*-DINGIR LÚ.DAM.GÀR ADD 326 = SAA 6 42 r. 12 as witness (692).

---

40 See Jas 1996, 76 n. 74 on *bēl ḫabulli*.

59. Ubru-Sebetti: ^{m}SUḪUŠ-^{d}7.BI LÚ.DAM.GÀR ADD 364 = SAA 6 204 r. 12' as witness (679).
    ^{m}SUḪ[U]Š-^{d}7.BI LÚ.DA[M.GÀR] ADD 860 r. i 5 in an administrative list (not dated).
60. Ululāyu: ^{m}ITU.KIN-*a-a* LÚ*.DAM.G[ÀR] ADD 1248 r. 8' as witness (date lost).
61. Zizî: ^{m}*zi-zi-i* LÚ.DAM.GÀR ADD 285 = SAA 6 166 r. 2' as witness (686).
    [^{m}*zi*$^{?}$-*zi*$^{?}$]-*i* LÚ*.DAM.[GÀR *ša*] É MÍ É.GAL ADD 262 = SAA 6 140 r. 11 as witness (date lost).
62. [...]a^{ʾ}: ... [^{m}x-x-x]x-*a*^{ʾ} ... [3 LÚ.DA]M.GÀR.MEŠ CT 53 59 = SAA 5 150 r. 2' mentioned in a letter (reign of Sargon II).
63. [...]am: ... ... [^{m}x-x-x]-*am* [3 LÚ.DA]M.GÀR.MEŠ CT 53 59 = SAA 5 150 r. 3' mentioned in a letter (reign of Sargon II).
64. [...]-iddina: [^{m}x-x]-AŠ LÚ*.DAM.GÀR ADD 256 = SAA 6 239 r. 5' as witness (676).
65. [...]iṣāyu: [^{m}x]-*i-ṣa-a-a* DAM.GÀR ADB 14 = SAA 11 208:1' as a land owner in the Harrān area (not dated, reign of Sargon II).
66. [...]mea: [^{m}x]-*me-a* LÚ*.[D]AM.GÀR ADD 472 = NALK 174 r. 14 as witness (668).
67. [...]-mutaqqin: [^{m}x-x]-LAL LÚ*.DAM.GÀR ADD 632 = SAA 6 285 r. 5' as witness (date lost).

Name lost:
[...] LÚ*.DAM.G[ÀR] CTN 2 79 r. 1' as witness (783).
[...] ... ... [3 LÚ.DA]M.GÀR.MEŠ CT 53 59 = SAA 5 150 r. 2' mentioned in a letter to the king (reign of Sargon II).
[... LÚ*].DAM.GÀR ADD 179 = SAA 6 127 r. 2' as witness (697).
[... LÚ].DAM.GÀR TIM 11 2 r. 12-16 five *tamkāru*'s as witnesses (Agt).
[... LÚ].DAM.GÀR ADD 417 = NALK 207 r. 8 as witness (date lost).
[...] LÚ.DAM.[GÀR] CTN 2 73 r. 6 as witness (date lost).

2. *The Private Entrepreneur*: **bēl ḫarrāni* = EN KASKAL

K. Deller was the first to draw attention to a group of loan documents which feature the term EN KASKAL.[41] This logogram - probably realized as *bēl ḫarrāni* in Neo-Assyrian[42] - is to the present knowledge exclusively used in debt-notes from Assur.[43] Deller interpreted these documents as dealing with the financing of trade ventures. The term EN KASKAL documents will be used to refer to this group of texts.

---

41 Deller 1984, 240-247, 250f (new edition of Scheil 3).

42 A syllabic writing of EN KASKAL is hitherto unattested. Although *ḫūlu*, not *ḫarrānu* is the normal Neo-Assyrian realization of the logogram KASKAL (see Radner 1997, 277f n. 1559 and note especially the gloss *ḫu-u-li* for KASKAL in ABL 406 = SAA 10 70:15) the clause [...] *ḫarrāni saḫḫurtušu mimma lā usaḫḫar* in two royal grants where *ḫarrānu* is written syllabically (see Kataja - Whiting 1995, xxviii) seems to indicate that KASKAL is to be realized as *ḫarrānu* in the meaning "trading expedition". Therefore, I prefer to use *bēl ḫarrāni*, not *bēl ḫūli* as has been suggested by Postgate (1995, 403).

43 The term EN KASKAL^{II} is mentioned in two Neo-Babylonian letters from the Kouyunjik correspondence, ABL 214:5 and CT 54 507 r. 9. Since it is not clear whether these attestations are connected with the EN KASKAL texts from Assur they are left out of the present discussion. It seems much more likely to link them to the Neo-Babylonian *ḫarrānu* documents, see note 55. - K. Deller (1984, 242 n. 56) drew attention to a possible attestation of EN KASKAL in ABL 523:4: LÚ*$^{!}$.EN$^{!}$ KASKAL$^{!}$. However, according to a collation by S. Parpola the text has *i-nak-kil* instead.

Before discussing them I will present all texts presently known to me. Though the larger part of the texts (18 out of 20) are silver debt-notes, there is also one copper debt-note (text 2) and one barley debt-note (text 9) containing the term EN KASKAL. The references cover more than a century: the earliest known text is dated in the year 717 BC (text 1) while the latest is dated in the eponymy of Pāšî, almost certainly either the last eponym at Assur before its fall in 614 or the one immediately appointed afterwards (text 12).[44]

	Date	Reference	Text type	Spelling
1	717	A 1913 = N 12 (3)	silver loan	3 EN KASKAL.MEŠ
2	694	VAT 10024 = N 3 (31)	copper loan	6 EN KASKAL
3	685	VAT 20365 = N 9 (66)	silver loan	not mentioned
4	650	VAT 9699 = *SAAB* 9 98	silver loan	[3] ŠEŠ EN KASKAL.ME
5	649	MAH 16602 = *JSS* 28 155	silver loan	not mentioned
6	Bēl-aḫu-uṣur	VAT 20362 = *SAAB* 5 64	silver loan	3 EN KASKAL
7	Bēl-iqbi	A 1905 = Ass. 13424	silver loan	2 EN KASKAL
8	Daddî	VAT 15457 = N 33 (23)	silver loan	2 EN KASKAL.MEŠ
9	Nabû-šarru-uṣur	VAT 20345 = *SAAB* 5 2	barley loan	2 EN KASKAL
10	Nabû-šarru-uṣur palace scribe	VAT 9144 = *SAAB* 9 121	silver loan	4 1/2 EN KASKAL
11	Nabû-tappûtu-alik	Scheil 3 = *RA* 24 115 = *BaM* 15 240ff	silver loan	3 EN KASKAL.MEŠ
12	Pāšî	VAT 9606 = *SAAB* 9 115[45]	silver loan	3 EN KASKAL
13	Sîn-šarru-uṣur	A 1889 = N 31 (49)	silver loan	not mentioned
14	Šarru-mītu-uballiṭ[46]	Assur 23 = *Al-Rāfidān* 17 no. 21	silver loan	not mentioned
15	Šamaš-šarru-ibni	Assur 18 = *Al-Rāfidān* 17 no. 17	silver loan	2 EN KASKAL.ME
16	Upāqa-ana-Arbail	Assur 25 = *Al-Rāfidān* 17 no. 23	silver loan	3 EN KASKAL.ME
17	Zababa-erība	VAT 9707 = *SAAB* 9 87	silver loan	2 EN KASKAL^{II}.MEŠ
18	(unreadable)	VAT 8647 = N 33 (31)	silver loan	3 EN KASKAL
19	[...]	A 1871 = N 31 (21)	silver loan	3 [EN KASKAL.MEŠ]
20	[...]	A 2630 = N 10 (16)	silver loan	[5] EN KASKAL.MEŠ

1 (A 1913 = N 12 (3)):

1 NA$_4$.KIŠIB 3 EN KASKAL
2 24 GÍN KÙ.BABBAR
3 *ša* ^{md}EN-*a-su-*[*ru*]
4 *ina* IGI 2 ^{m}*ki-ṣir-aš-š*[*ur*]
5 *ina* IGI ^{md}EN-*a-su-*[*ru*]
6 [P]AP 3 EN KASKAL.[MEŠ]
7 *a-na pu-u-ḫi it-*[*ta-ṣu*]
8 *a-na* 4-*tú-šú* GAL

44 R. M. Whiting, personal communication.

45 Not VAT 9609, see Deller - Fales - Jakob-Rost 1995, 101 n. 134.

46 Because of the Aramaic spelling *srm*[*t*]*blṭ* in a text from Tell Sheikh Hamad (see Röllig 1997, 373 n. 30) it is clear that this eponym's name is Šarru-mītu-uballiṭ, not Šamaš-mītu-uballiṭ.

inner tablet:
1 24 GÍN KÙ.BABBAR
2 ša mdEN-*a-su-r*[*u*]
3 2 m*ki-ṣir-aš-šur*
4 1 mdEN-*a-su-ru*
5 [P]AP 3 EN KASKAL.⸢MEŠ⸣
6 *a*-[*na*] *pu-u-ḫi it-ta-*⸢*ṣu*⸣
7 *a-na* 4-*ut-ti-šú* [GAL]

2 (VAT 10024 = N 3 (31)):
1 4-*me* 10 MA.NA URUDU
2 *ša* m*ṭu-da-a-a*
3 3 md*na-na-a-tak-lak*
4 1 m*ṭu-da-a-a*
5 1 m*bu-sa-su*
6 1 m*maš-il-šu*
7 PAP 6 EN KASKAL.MEŠ
a-na pu-u-ḫi 8 *i-ta-ṣu*

3 (VAT 20365 = N 9 (66)):
1 11 GÍN.MEŠ KÙ.BABBAR
2 *ša* mLUGAL-IGI.LAL-*a-ni*
3 *ina* IGI m :
4 *ina* IGI m[x-x]-U.GUR
5 *ina* IGI m*aš-šur*-KI-*ia*
6 [*ina*] IGI mEN-SU

4 (VAT 9699 = *SAAB* 9 98):
1 59 GÍN.MEŠ KÙ.BABBAR
2 *ša* m*man-nu-ki*-PAP.MEŠ
3 *ina* IGI mdPA-PAP.MEŠ-*bal-liṭ*
4 *ina* IGI m*man-nu-ki*-PAP.MEŠ
5 ⸢*ina* IGI m*l*⸣*im-ṭu-ri-mu-u-tú*
6 [PAP 3] ⸢ŠEŠ?⸣ EN KASKAL.ME
7 *a-na* mdPA-PAP.MEŠ-*bal-liṭ*
8 *i-du-nu* m*man-nu-ki*-PAP.<MEŠ>
9 ⸢*a-di*⸣ *ru-bé-e* ⸢SUM⸣

5 (MAH 16602 = *JSS* 28 155):
1 30 MA.NA 11 1/2 GÍN KÙ.BABBAR
2 SAG.MEŠ *ša* 15 *šá* URU.*arba-ìl*
3 *ša* m*na-nu-u-ni*
4 *pa-an* m*na-nu-u-ni*
5 : m*qa-a-a*
6 : m15-I
(7-8 date)
9 [*ana*] 4-*tú-šú* [GAL]-*bi*

6 (VAT 20362 = *SAAB* 5 64):

1 NA$_4$.KIŠIB 3 EN KASKAL
2 6 MA.NA KÙ.BABBAR *ina* 1 MA.NA-*šú* 3 *ša* ^{d}15 *šá arba-ìl*
4 *ša* ^{m}DILI-*le-šir*
5 *ina* IGI ^{m}*aš-šur*-TI-*su-e* 6 A ^{m}*aš-šur*-DI-IGI.LAL
7 *ina* IGI ^{m}*aš-šur*-SU 8 A ^{m}*kak-kul-a-ni*
9 *ina* IGI ^{m}*aš-šur*-AD-GIŠ
10 PAP 3 EN KASKAL
a-na pu$^{!}$*-ḫi*$^{!}$ 11 *it-ta-ṣu ana* 6-*su-šú* GAL (12-17 ...)
18 DUG.ŠAB GEŠTIN *ina* UGU-*ḫi* SUM-*nu*
l. e. 1 *ša kar-me-u-ni* 2 SUM-*an*

7 (A 1905 = Ass. 13424):

1 1/2 MA.NA 1 GÍN KÙ.BABBAR 2 *šá* 15 *šá arba-ìl*
3 *šá* ^{m}ZU-*šá*-[*maš*]
4 *ina* IGI ^{m} :
5 *ina* IGI ^{m}*mu*-LAL-*aš-šur*
6 PAP IGI 2 EN [KASKAL]
7 KÙ.BABBAR *là i*-⌜GAL⌝

8 (VAT 15457 = N 33 (23)):[47]

1 NA$_4$.KIŠIB 2 EN KASKAL.MEŠ
2 6 GÍN KÙ.BABBAR
3 *ša* ^{m}*mu*-SIG-*aš-šur*
4 *ina* IGI ^{m}30-*bal-liṭ-su* 5 A ^{m}*aš-šur-ḫu-sa-a-ni*
6 *ina* IGI ^{md}PA-TI-AŠ 7 A ^{md}PA-NUMUN-AŠ
8 *ana* 4-*ut-ti-šú* GAL-*bi*

9 (VAT 20345 = *SAAB* 5 2):

1 6-BÁN 5 *qa* ŠE.PAD.MEŠ
2 *ša* ^{m}*da-da-ḫi*
3 *ina* IGI ^{m}ITU.KIN-*a-a*
4 6-BÁN 5 *qa* ŠE.PAD.MEŠ
5 *ša* ^{m}*da-da-ḫi*
6 *ina* IGI ^{m}U.GUR-PAB-*ir*
7 PAP 2 EN KASKAL
8 *a-na pu-ḫi* 9 *i-ta-ṣu*
10 ^{m}IT[U.KI]N-*a-a* 11 EN Š[U^{II}.M]EŠ
12 *ina ad-ri* SAG.DU-*šá* 13 SUM-*an*
šúm-mu la i-din 14 *a-na mit-ḫar* GAL-*bi*

10 (VAT 9144 = *SAAB* 9 121):

1 6 GÍN KÙ.BABBAR 2 *šá* 15 *šá arba-ìl*
3 *šá* ^{m}*mu*-DI-*aš-šur*
4 ^{md}PA-MAN-PAB.MEŠ-*šú*

---

47 The inner tablet does not mention EN KASKAL.

5 ^{m}*aš-šur*-LAL-*a-ni*
6 3 4-*tú*.MEŠ ^{m}UŠ-*tú-aš-šur*
7 3 4-*tú*.MEŠ ^{m}GIN-*i*
8 PAP 4 1/2 EN KASKAL
9 *ana pu-u-ḫi it-*<*ta*>*-ṣu*
(10-12 date)
13 *ana* 8-*tú-šú* GAL-*bi*

11 (Scheil 3 = *RA* 24 115 = *BaM* 15 240ff):
1 NA$_4$.KIŠIB 3 EN KASKAL.MEŠ
2 1/2 MA.NA KÙ.BABBAR SIG
3 *šá* ^{m}*aš-šur*-MU-GIN
4 *ina* IGI 2 ^{md}U.GUR-SUM-*na*
5 *ina* IGI ^{m}*ki-ṣir*-^{d}PA
6 *ana pu-u-ḫi* ÍL-*ši*
7 *ana* 4-*tú-šú* GAL-*bi*
8 ^{md}PA-PAB-*ir* EN ŠU^{II}.MEŠ 9 *šá* KÙ.BABBAR
6-*šú* KUŠ.E.SIR 10 *i-du-nu*

12 (VAT 9606 = *SAAB* 9 115):
1 NA$_4$.KIŠIB 3 EN KASKAL
2 [x+] 8 GÍN KÙ.BABBAR
3 *ša* ^{m}*aš-šur*-MU-GIN
4 *ina* IGI ^{m}*aš-šur*-MU-GIN
5 *ina* IGI ^{m}MU-LAL-*aš-šur*
6 *ina* IGI ^{m}ÌR-*a-a*
7 *ana* 5-*si-šú* GAL-*bi*

13 (A 1889 = N 31 (49)):
1 6 GÍN.MEŠ KÙ.BABBAR
2 *ša* ^{m}ÌR-*aš-šur*
3 *ina* IGI ^{m} : :
4 *ina* IGI ^{m}*la-u-uḫ-a-me-ḫi*
5 ITU.KIN SUM-*an*
6 *šum-ma là* SUM-*nu* 7 *a-na* 4-*tu-šú* 8 *i-rab-bi*

14 (Assur 23 = *Al-Rāfidān* 17 no. 21):
1 9* GÍN KÙ.BABBAR
2 *ša* ^{m}15-SU
3 *ina* IGI ^{m} : :
4 *ina* IGI ^{m}*aš-šur*-KUR-LAL
5 *ana* 8-*tú-šú* GAL

15 (Assur 18 = *Al-Rāfidān* 17 no. 17):
1 NA$_4$.KIŠIB 2 EN KASKAL.ME
2 8 GÍN KÙ.BABBAR
3 *ša* ^{m}*aš-šur-kal-la-ni*

4 *ša* ^{m}*man-nu-ki*-DINGIR
5 *ša* ^{m}DINGIR-*a-e-diš*
6 *ina* IGI ^{m}*ab-di-mu-nu*
7 *ina* IGI ^{m}*ia*-PAB-*nu*
8 *ina* IGI 2 EN KASKAL.ME
9 *ana* 5-*tú-šú* GAL-*bi*
10 *šá kar-mu-ni* KÙ.BABBAR SUM-*ni*

16 (Assur 25 = *Al-Rāfidān* 17 no. 23):
1 NA$_4$.KIŠIB 3 EN KASKAL.ME
2 4 1/2 MA 2 1/2 GÍN KÙ.BABBAR 3 SAG.ME *šá* 15 *šá arba-ìl*
4 *šá* ^{m}*aš-šur-mu*-DI$^{?!}$ (copy: IGI NU)
5 *ina* IGI ^{m}*aš-šur*-KUR-LAL
6 *ina* IGI ^{m}ÌR-*aš-šur*
7 *ina* IGI ^{md}PA-*šam-gur*
8 *a-na* 8-*tú-šú* GAL-*bi*

17 (VAT 9707 = *SAAB* 9 87):
1 NA$_4$.KIŠIB 2 EN KASKAL^{II}.MEŠ
2 70 GÍN.MEŠ KÙ.BABBAR 16 *ša* 15 *šá arba-ìl*
3 *ša* ^{m}*aš-šur-bé-sún*
4 *ina* IGI ^{m}*aš-šur-bé-sún*
5 *ina* IGI ^{m}*aš-šur-mu*-SIG
6 KÙ.BABBAR *ana* 6-*si-šú* GAL

18 (VAT 8647 = N 33 (31)):
1 24 GÍN.MEŠ KÙ.BABBAR
2 *ša* ^{m}*mu-na-bit-tú*
3 2 ^{m}KA.TAR-15
4 1 ^{m}PAB-SU
5 PAP 3 EN KASKAL
6 *ana pu-u-ḫi i-ta-ṣu*

19 (A 1871 = N 31 (21)):
1 [x M]A 2 GÍN KÙ.BABBAR
2 *ša* ^{m}ÌR-*aš-šur*
3 *ina* IGI ^{m}*la-tu-*[*ra-man-ni-aš*]-*šur*
4 *ina* IGI ^{m}[x-x-x-x]
5 *ina* IGI ^{m}[x-x-x-x]
6 PAP 3 [EN KASKAL.MEŠ]
11 *a-na* 4-[*tú-šú* GAL]

20 (A 2630 = N 10 (16)):
1 1/2 MA.NA 2 G[ÍN KÙ.BABBAR]
2 [*šá* ^{m}x]-⸢x-x-x⸣
3 [^{m}]*ia-qi-ri*
4 [^{m}]*kan-dàl-a-nu*

5 ^{m}*aš-šur*-A-PAB
6 ^{m}*mu-še-zib-aš-šur*
7 [^{m}*m*]*u-tak-kil-aš-šur*
8 [PAP 5] EN KASKAL.MEŠ
ina pu-u-ḫi 9 *i-ta-ṣu*
ana 4-*tu-šú* GAL-[*bi*]

Note that interest is only to be paid in 11 out of 20 cases. In text 7, it is explicitly stated that the debt sum bears no interest. Even though the usual interest of 25 per cent is asked for in six cases, the interest rate is surprisingly often lower: it is set at 20 per cent in text 15, at 16.6 cent in text 17, and at 12.5 per cent in texts 10, 14, and 16.

The outstanding features of the EN KASKAL documents are that there are always two or more debtors and that the creditor can be, and indeed quite frequently is, one of these. As is proved by VAT 15457 (text 8) where EN KASKAL is mentioned on the envelope, but not in the inner tablet, EN KASKAL is not an integral part of the formulary. Therefore, all inner tablets which show the features described above are included in the present study even if they do not mention EN KASKAL.

Two different types of EN KASKAL documents can be distinguished:

Type 1: *Documents with limited partnership*:
1a: The creditor lends money to several debtors (texts 6, 8, 9, 11, 16, 18, probably 19, 20).
1b: Several creditors lend money to several debtors (text 15).

Type 2: *Documents with full partnership*:
The creditor is at the same time one of several debtors (texts 1-5, 7, 10, 12-14, 17).[48]

Whenever the term EN KASKAL is mentioned, it is in combination with a numeral. In most cases this is simply the number of debtors. However, sometimes the numeral exceeds the number of debtors (texts 1, 2, 11, 18). In those documents, the name of the debtor is also preceded by a numeral.[49] If this numeral were to be "1" it can be dropped (texts 1, 10, 11). When added the overall sum always matches the numeral preceding EN KASKAL. VAT 9144 (text 10) is a special case.[50] Here, the numeral preceding EN KASKAL is 4 1/2. There are five debtors, two of whom are marked with the numeral 3/4 while the other three are not marked at all, thus adding up to the expected sum of 4 1/2. This case leaves no doubt that the numerals cannot refer to the debtors themselves. EN KASKAL cannot possibly be a title of the debtors.[51]

---

48 Contrary to Deller (1984, 243) the creditor is not necessarily the first of the debtors, see texts 1, 2, and 4.

49 Note that "*ina pān*", an integral part of the loan documents of the conventional type, can be dropped, see texts 1 (only in the inner tablet), 2, 10, 18, and 20.

50 Compare Deller - Fales - Jakob-Rost 1995, 109.

51 Deller (1984, 244) proposed on the grounds of ND 2335 to equate the logogram KASKAL with *maškuru* and to translate EN KASKAL as "Transportunternehmer mit *maškuru*-Booten". However, I prefer Neumann's interpretation of ND 2335 (Neumann 1997, 288-290). See Ponchia 1990, 53 on the connection between ND 2335 and ND 2338.

Therefore, the numerals must give the number of shares of the debt sum held by the individual debtors. A. L. Oppenheim has shown that in the Neo-Babylonian period, to finance commercial activities, partnerships were formed, each partner holding a certain share called *mēreštu* in Neo-Babylonian.[52] When in 1974 H. Lanz studied the so-called *ḫarrānu* documents[53] which constitute such partnerships, he dealt with 114 texts covering the period from the reign of Ashurbanipal to that of Xerxes.[54] He distinguished two types of *ḫarrānu* documents: 1. "Begründungsurkunden mit einseitiger Kapitalbeteiligung" with the basic formulary *x kaspu ša* creditor *ina muḫḫi* debtor *ana ḫarrāni*,[55] 2. "Begründungsurkunden mit zweiseitiger Kapitalbeteiligung" with the basic formulary *x kaspu ša* PN_1 *u x kaspu ša* PN_2 *itti aḫâmeš ana ḫarrāni iškunū*.[56] As has been shown above the same types can be discerned in the Neo-Assyrian EN KASKAL documents.[57]

The Neo-Babylonian documents make it clear that trade was not the only reason for setting up a partnership. Any kind of business could be financed like this. Thus, it is reasonable to consider this possibility also for the Neo-Assyrian evidence. Even though there is presently no proof for this (mainly due to the concise phrasing of the documents), the comparatively small sums that are sometimes the subject of the EN KASKAL documents seem to indicate that not all partnerships focused on trade enterprises.

Finally, I propose to translate x EN KASKAL.MEŠ as "holder of x shares of a business enterprise". The debtors' names are arranged according to the number of shares they hold. Whoever holds most is mentioned first. By splitting the sum used for financing a business enterprise, especially an overland trade venture, among several persons, the risk for the individual is lessened - the same is of course true for the profits. If the enterprise is successful those who took more risk, *i.e.* more shares, get more of the profits, if it fails the losses are distributed accordingly.[58]

The following table shows who was involved in setting up business enterprises and how much capital the individual financiers bring into the business. The sums can be extremely modest, from one sheqel onwards, but also quite high (more than 1 1/2 minas of silver in text 16). Names in bold letters are persons acting both as creditor and debtor.

1:	creditor:	**Bēl-asūru**:	24 sheqels of silver
	3 EN KASKAL:	2 shares: Kiṣir-Aššūr:	16 sheqels of silver
		1 share: **Bēl-asūru**:	8 sheqels of silver

52 Oppenheim 1967, 239.

53 *Ḫarrānu* is always written with the logogram $KASKAL^{II}$.

54 Lanz 1976, 1-3.

55 Lanz 1976, 7f.

56 Lanz 1976, 49.

57 Already Deller (1984, 250) drew attention to the similiarities between the EN KASKAL and the *ḫarrānu* documents.

58 Typically for Neo-Assyrian legal texts, the EN KASKAL documents are extremely concise and therefore fail to give any information on this. Although the Neo-Babylonian *ḫarrānu* documents are also phrased in very terse terms they occasionally mention clauses that elucidate further details of the transaction, see Lanz 1976, 18-47 and 55-66.

2:	creditor:	**Ṭudāya**:	410 minas of copper
	6 EN KASKAL:	3 shares: Nanaya-taklak:	205 minas of copper
		1 share: **Ṭudāya**:	68 1/3 minas of copper
		1 share: Busāsu:	68 1/3 minas of copper
		1 share: Inurta-ilšu:	68 1/3 minas of copper
3:	creditor:	**Šarru-ēmuranni**:	11 sheqels of silver
	(4 EN KASKAL):	(1 share:) **Šarru-ēmuranni**:	2 3/4 sheqels of silver
		(1 share:) [...]-Nergal:	2 3/4 sheqels of silver
		(1 share:) Aššūr-issēʾa:	2 3/4 sheqels of silver
		(1 share:) Bēl-erība:	2 3/4 sheqels of silver
4:	creditor:	**Mannu-kī-aḫḫē**:	59 sheqels of silver
	3 EN KASKAL:	1 share: Nabû-aḫḫē-balliṭ:	19 2/3 sheqels of silver
		1 share: **Mannu-kī-aḫḫē**:	19 2/3 sheqels of silver
		1 share: Limṭu-rimūtu:	19 2/3 sheqels of silver
5:	creditor:	**Nanūnî**:	191 1/2 sheqels of silver
	(3 EN KASKAL):	(1 share:) **Nanūnî**:	63 5/6 sheqels of silver
		(1 share:) Qāya:	63 5/6 sheqels of silver
		(1 share:) Issār-naʾid:	63 5/6 sheqels of silver
6:	creditor:	Ēdu-lēšir:	6 minas of silver
	3 EN KASKAL:	(1 share:) Aššūr-balāssu-iqbi:	2 sheqels of silver
		(1 share:) Aššūr-erība:	2 sheqels of silver
		(1 share:) Aššūr-abu-lēšir	2 sheqels of silver
7:	creditor:	**Lēʾi-Šamaš**:	31 sheqels of silver
	2 EN KASKAL:	(1 share:) **Lēʾi-Šamaš**:	15 1/2 sheqels of silver
		(1 share:) Mutaqqin-Aššūr:	15 1/2 sheqels of silver
8:	creditor:	Mudammiq-Aššūr:	6 sheqels of silver
	2 EN KASKAL:	(1 share:) Sîn-ballissu:	3 sheqels of silver
		(1 share:) Nabû-balāṭu-iddina:	3 sheqels of silver
9:	creditor:	Dada-aḫḫē:	Twice 6 *sū* 5 *qa* of barley
	2 EN KASKAL:	1 share: Ululāya:	6 *sū* 5 *qa* of barley
		1 share: Nergal-nāṣir:	6 *sū* 5 *qa* of barley
10:	creditor:	**Mušallim-Aššūr**:	6 sheqels of silver
	4 1/2 EN KASKAL:	1 share: **Mušallim-Aššūr**:	1 1/3 sheqels of silver
		1 share: Nabû-šar-aḫḫēšu:	1 1/3 sheqels of silver
		1 share: Aššūr-taqqinanni:	1 1/3 sheqels of silver
		3/4 shares: Tardītu-Aššūr:	1 sheqel of silver
		3/4 shares: Kēnî:	1 sheqel of silver
11:	creditor:	Aššūr-šumu-ukēn:	1/2 mina of good silver
	3 EN KASKAL:	2 shares: Nergal-iddina:	20 sheqels of silver
		1 share: Kiṣir-Nabû:	10 sheqels of silver
12:	creditor:	**Aššūr-šumu-ukēn**:	[x+]8 sheqels of silver
	3 EN KASKAL:	(1 share:) **Aššūr-šumu-ukēn**	
		(1 share:) Mutaqqin-Aššūr	
		(1 share:) Urdāya (or Urdu-Aia)	

13:	creditor:	**Urdu-Aššūr**:	6 sheqels of silver
	(2 EN KASKAL):	(1 share:) **Urdu-Aššūr**:	3 sheqels of silver
		(1 share:) Lauḫameḫi:	3 sheqels of silver
14:	creditor:	**Issār-erība**:	9 sheqels of silver
	(2 EN KASKAL):	(1 share:) **Issār-erība**:	4 1/2 sheqels of silver
		(1 share:) Aššūr-mātu-taqqin	4 1/2 sheqels of silver
15:	creditors:	Aššūr-kallanni	together 8 sheqels of silver
		Mannu-kī-ilī	
		Ila-ediš	
	2 EN KASKAL:	(1 share:) Abdi-Munu:	4 sheqels of silver
		(1 share:) Ia-aḫūnu:	4 sheqels of silver
16:	creditor:	Aššūr-mušallim:	272 1/2 sheqels of silver
	3 EN KASKAL:	(1 share:) Aššūr-mātu-taqqin:	90 5/6 sheqels of silver
		(1 share:) Urdu-Issār:	90 5/6 sheqels of silver
		(1 share:) Nabû-šamgur:	90 5/6 sheqels of silver
17:	creditor:	**Aššūr-bēssunu**:	70 sheqels of silver
	2 EN KASKAL:	(1 share:) **Aššūr-bēssunu**:	35 sheqels of silver
		(1 share:) Aššūr-mudammiq:	35 sheqels of silver
18:	creditor:	Munnabittu:	24 sheqels of silver
	3 EN KASKAL:	2 shares: Dilīl-Issār:	16 sheqels of silver
		1 share: Aḫu-erība:	8 sheqels of silver
19:	creditor:	Urdu-Aššūr:	[...] minas and 2 sheqels of silver
	3 EN KASKAL:	Lā-turammanni-Aššūr	
		[...]	
		[...]	
20:	creditor:	[...]:	32 sheqels of silver
	5 EN KASKAL:	(1 share:) Iaqīrî:	6 2/5 sheqels of silver
		(1 share:) Kandalānu:	6 2/5 sheqels of silver
		(1 share:) Aššūr-aplu-uṣur:	6 2/5 sheqels of silver
		(1 share:) Mušēzib-Aššūr:	6 2/5 sheqels of silver
		(1 share:) Mutakkil-Aššūr:	6 2/5 sheqels of silver

The number of persons engaged in EN KASKAL enterprises illustrates clearly that the phenomenon is not restricted to a few persons but that a large number of Assur residents are involved. Why at present this kind of business is only attested in Assur, but there so frequently, must remain a matter of speculation for the time being. The special status of Assur and its inhabitants may be a decisive factor. However, another reason may be the fact that the archives found in Assur are the only true private archives unearthed so far.

Outside of these documents the term EN KASKAL is mentioned in the receipt VAT 14453:[59] "a male donkey together with its bundles" is qualified as *ša* EN KASKAL.M[EŠ]. The document VAT 14450[60] from the archive of the *ḫundurāyu*'s surely belongs into the

59 VAT 14453 = *SAAB* 5 12 (dated 675 BC).

60 VAT 14450 = *SAAB* 5 17 (eponymy of Daddî).

context of these private trade ventures. The text records an agreement between Mudammiq-Aššūr and Sākip-Aššūr. Even though the text is not entirely clear, the *qīptu ša šaddê lū karānu lū ṣarpu* is certainly to be understood as "merchandise from the mountains, be it wine, be it silver".

J.N. Postgate[61] has already linked the EN KASKAL texts to administrative documents such as VAT 20354.[62] Like VAT 14450, this text refers to wine and silver, specified as *ša ina* KUR-*ú*. Those commodities are written down to a number of persons. Later in the text certain sums are set aside for donkeys and four *maškuru*-boats. Some texts of an Assur archive unearthed in 1990 make still clearer reference to trading expeditions.[63] The texts are lists similar to VAT 20345 naming different persons together with sums. Several are headed with the remark "first voyage of PN",[64] "second voyage of PN",[65] or "third voyage of PN",[66] thus leaving no doubt that these documents are balance sheets for trading expeditions (KASKAL). Because of the many different individuals mentioned in these balance sheets they are probably the persons who received parts of the merchandise brought back from an expedition.

A deep involvement in overland trade is also portrayed by the letters found in this archive. They show that people from Assur equipped caravans to go to the mountain region using both the river and the land route. That trading is the main concern in these letters is already clear from the greeting formula which features the clauses *šulmu alaktu libbaka lū ṭābka* "The caravan is well. Your heart may rejoice!"[67] The letters As 51, 63, and 67,[68] written by Aššūr-mātu-taqqin[69] and/or Nabû-taqqinanni, travelling abroad, to Dūrī-Aššūr and/or Ṭāb-šar-Papaḫi, staying in Assur, mention wine, clothes (*kubšu* "cap") and silver, transported with *maškuru*-boats and donkeys. Similar to the post-scriptum of Scheil 3 (text 10), shoes are asked for in As 67 l.e. 1f. J. N. Postgate[70] has already stressed the importance of suitable footwear to those engaged in much walking. Traders certainly fall under this category.

We can surely identify all those persons active in trading in Assur with those liable to the payment of "taxes for using harbours, crossings, and gates on land or water" (*miksē kārē nēbirē abullē ina šaddê u ḫirītī*)[71] as well as the taxes on the conclusion of trading expeditions[72] mentioned in several royal grants of Ashurbanipal and Aššūr-etel-ilāni.

---

61 Postgate 1995, 103.

62 VAT 20354 = *SAAB* 5 27.

63 As 9*, 10-12, 18-21, 24, 29, 32, 33, 64-66, see Hecker 1991, 112. Thanks to the generosity of K. Hecker, his copies of most of these texts are at my disposal.

64 *E.g.* As 20:1: KASKAL IGI ^{m}*mu-še-zib-aš-šur*.

65 *E.g.* As 29:1: KASKAL 2-*u* ^{m}*mu-še-zib-aš-šur*.

66 *E.g.* As 108 r. 3: KASKAL 3-*u*.

67 As 51:3; As 51:4f; As 67:5f.

68 See Hecker 1991, 112.

69 For details see my entry on Aššūr-mātu-taqqin in *The Prosopography of the Neo-Assyrian Empire* 1/I (1998).

70 Postgate 1995, 403.

71 People presented to different persons by the kings Ashurbanipal and Aššūr-etel-ilāni are exempted from those dues in SAA 12 25 r. 3; SAA 12 26 r. 3; SAA 12 32 r. 1; SAA 12 35 r. 23; SAA 12 36 r. 29'; SAA 12 39 r. 7'; and SAA 12 40 r. 3', see Kataja - Whiting 1995, xxviii and Postgate 1979, 205f.

72 SAA 12 35 r. 27 and SAA 12 40 r. 8', see Kataja - Whiting 1995, xxviiif.

3. *On the Existence of Peddling Trade: An Evaluation of the ša X-šu Professions*

If only comparatively little is known about the long-distance trade in the Neo-Assyrian period virtually nothing is known about the retail trade. So far, it has not even been proved whether this form of trade existed at all or only came into being in the Neo-Babylonian period.[73]

While it has been widely accepted that the Neo-Babylonian professional titles formed according to the pattern *ša X-šu* (X = commodity), literally "the one of commodity X" are to be interpreted as "peddler of commodity X",[74] Landsberger, when studying those titles, explicitly refused to assign the same meaning to the Neo-Assyrian titles formed by using this pattern.[75]

However, no general interpretation of these Neo-Assyrian professional titles has been forwarded so far. Also, the attestations have never been collected in a systematic way.[76] Therefore, an evaluation of the material seems to be necessary, especially since the proof of the existence of specialized peddling trade in the Neo-Assyrian period would be crucial for the understanding of the concept of trade.

The dictionaries use various translations for the different professions, like "peddler of X", "producer of X", or "X worker". The reason for this lack of consistency is easily traced back to the fact that most of the attestations are found in a context that gives few or no hints on the exact nature of the profession. Typically, the individuals bearing the titles are listed in administrative documents or in legal texts, usually as witnesses.

Since the contextual information given in the individual texts is too scanty to throw a light on what exactly these professionals are doing I will study all of the *ša X-šu* professions together as a group. This method is justified since other professional titles formed according to the same pattern can be interpreted and translated as uniform groups. The best examples are the titles *rab X* "chief X" (X = profession, *e.g.* cook, eunuch, goldsmith) and *ša muḫḫi X* "overseer of X" (X = institution, *e.g.* city, palace, part of the palace, household).

---

73 See Oppenheim 1970, 21 and 1967, 244 for an interpretation of the Neo-Babylonian evidence.

74 Landsberger 1967, 186f, Oppenheim 1967, 244. See also the bibliographical references quoted by Kinnier Wilson 1972, 86 n. 86.

75 Landsberger (1967, 186 n. 1) quotes three Neo-Assyrian professions: "Dagegen NA *ša būlišu CAD* B 316 'an official concerned with cattle', *ša gaṣṣātēšu* G 54 'Sammler (nicht 'Verkäufer') von Brennholz'; *ša ginēšu* ADD 328, 19 'Hirte der Opferschale'." Only the title *ša gaṣṣātēšu* is relevant for our context. As *AHw* 864 and Kwasman (1988, 85) have shown, it is *ša pūlīšu*, an official dealing with *pūlu* "limestone", not with *būlu* "cattle" – a term not at all attested in Neo-Assyrian, see Radner 1997, 270 with n. 1488. The attestation for ^{md}PA-PAB *ša gi-né-šú š*[*a* x x] in ADD 328 = SAA 6 124 r. 4 (698) does not belong to the *ša* X-*šu* group, but to the title *ša gīnê*, on which see Menzel 1981, 273. The -*šu ša* is used probably due to Aramaic influence, compare the frequently used PN_1 *māršu ša* PN_2. - Oppenheim (1950, 278 and 1970, 21), however, does not seem to have made a distinction between the Neo-Babylonian and Neo-Assyrian titles, obviously followed by Saggs (1984, 173).

76 The most exhaustive study so far are the remarks of Kinnier Wilson (1972, 85f).

The following list contains all the *ša X-šu* professions attested so far.

1. *ša akussīšu* (*akussu* - a kind of soup)[77]

ša–a-ku-si-šú CTN 3 87 r. 43 in an administrative text from Kalhu (not dated, no firm dating criteria available).[78]

LÚ*.*ša–a-ku-si-šú* CTN 3 87:22 in an administrative text from Kalhu (not dated, no firm dating criteria available).

2. *ša billīšu* (*billu* - a variety of beer)[79]

LÚ*.*ša–[b]il-li-šú* CTN 3 87 r. 43 in an administrative text from Kalhu (not dated, no firm dating criteria available).

LÚ*.*šá–b[i]l?-li-šú* CTN 3 87:23 in an administrative text from Kalhu (not dated, no firm dating criteria available).

[LÚ*.*ša–bi*]*l-li-šú* *BaM* 24 239+ = SAA 12 83 r. 13 listed as part of the professionals transferred from Assur to Kalhu (reign of Ashurnasirpal II).

m*lu-ša-kin* LÚ.*šá–pi-li-šu* ND 3463 r. 20 as a witness in a legal document from Kalhu (eponymate of Aššūr-garūa-nēre, reign of Ashurbanipal).

3. *ša dūdīšu* (*dūdu* "kettle")[80]

m*sin-qi-aš-šur šá-du-di-šú* As 19:5 in a list of persons involved in a trade venture (not dated, reign of Ashurbanipal or later).

m*sin-qi-aš-šur šá-du-di-šú* As 29:4 in a list of persons involved in a trade venture (not dated, reign of Ashurbanipal or later).

4. *ša endīšu* (*endu* - an aromatic substance)[81]

m[...] LÚ.*ša–*GIŠ.*en-di-šú* ADD 640 = NALK 424 r. 12 as witness in a legal document (641 BC).

LÚ.*šá–*⌜*en*⌝*-di-šú* PKTA 36-38 = Menzel 1981 no. 22 ii 6 in a ritual for the Aššūr temple.

LÚ.*šá–*⌜*en-di*?!⌝*-šú* CTN 3 87:24 in an administrative text from Kalhu (not dated, no firm dating criteria available).

---

77 *AHw* 30.

78 See Dalley - Postgate 1984, 149.

79 While Dalley - Postgate (1984, 146f) use the unspecific translation "the official in charge of the *billu* mixture", Kataja - Whiting (1995, 96, 143) tentatively use the translation "alloy-worker". *CAD* B, 228f and *AHw* 126 give two meanings for this commodity *sub billu* A resp. *billu* I, an alloy or melt used in metallurgy and glass-making and a type of beer, well attested in Middle Assyrian and Nuzi texts. In Middle Babylonian and Neo-Babylonian sources a plant *b/pillu*, used for medical treatment, is attested, cf. *CAD* B, 229 *sub billu* C and *AHw* 863 *sub pillû*. Since the Neo-Assyrian profession *ša billīšu* is associated with cooks, confectioners, other providers of foodstuff as well as a multitude of edible commodities in CTN 3 87 the interpretation of *billu* as "alloy" or "herbal drug" seems to be excluded here. I therefore favour the interpretation as a kind of beer in the professional title which also would agree with the fact that the profession, if restored correctly, is listed just before the gardener and the vegetable farmer in the appointment of Nergal-apil-kumūʾā. Also K.V. Kinnier Wilson (1972, 86) connected *ša billīšu* with *billu* "a kind of beer", but favoured the interpretation as "barley water".

80 *CAD* D, 170.

81 See Menzel 1981, 271 and Deller 1983, 174 n. 24.

5. *ša erêšu* (*erû* "copper")
^{m}ÌR-[x *š*]*a*–URUDU.MEŠ-*šú* TIM 11 13 r. 2 as *urkiʾu* in a legal document from Ninūa (eponymy of Bēl-iqbi, after reign of Ashurbanipal).

6. *ša gabêšu* (*gabû* "alum")
LÚ*.*ša*–NA$_4$.*ga-bi-e-<šú>* *BaM* 24 239+ = SAA 12 83 r. 15 listed as part of the professionals transferred from Assur to Kalhu (reign of Ashurnasirpal II).

7. *ša gaṣṣātēšu* (*gaṣṣutu* "firewood")[82]
LÚ*.*šá*–GIŠ.*ga-*[*ṣa*]*-te-šú* *MSL* 12 238 r. 232 in the LÚ-list.
[LÚ*.*šá–ga*]*-ṣa-te-šú* *BaM* 24 239+ = SAA 12 83 r. 9 in a list of professionals transferred from Assur to Kalhu (reign of Ashurnasirpal II).
[^{md}PA-PAB-AŠ] LÚ.*šá*–GIŠ.*gaṣ-ṣa-te-šú* ND 5463 = SAA 12 95 r. 15 as witness in a legal document from Kalhu, related to the Nabû temple (655 BC).
^{md}PA-PAB-AŠ LÚ.*šá–ga-*[*ṣa*]*-te-šú* ND 5550 = SAA 12 96 r. 21 as witness in a legal document from Kalhu, related to the Nabû temple (616 BC).
LÚ.*šá–ga-ṣa-te*$^{!}$*-šú* PKTA 36-38 = Menzel 1981 no. 22 r. i 20 in a ritual for the Aššūr temple.
LÚ.*šá–g*[*a-ṣa-te-šú*] PKTA 36-38 = Menzel 1981 no. 22 ii 4 in a ritual for the Aššūr temple.

8. *ša ḫalluptīšu* (*ḫalluptu* "harness")[83]
šá–ḫal-lu-up-ti-šú-nu ADD 953 = SAA 7 115 r. i 8 in an administrative document from Ninūa (not dated, seventh century BC).
lú*.*ša–ḫal-lu-up-ti-*⸢*šú*⸣*-nu* *BaM* 24 239+ = SAA 12 83 r. 14 listed as part of the professionals transferred from Assur to Kalhu (reign of Ashurnasirpal II).

9. *ša ḫusinnīšu* (*ḫusinnu* - meaning unknown)
[^{md}P]A-TI-*su*-DÙG.GA LÚ.*šá–ḫu-si-ni-šú* ADD 284 + K 20900 = NALK 295 + unpubl. r. 7 as a witness in a legal document from Ninūa (668 BC).
[^{md}PA-TI]-*su*-DÙG.GA LÚ*.*šá–ḫu-si-ni-šu* ADD 537 = NALK 296 r. 6 as a witness in a legal document from Ninūa (date lost, reign of Ashurbanipal).
ša–ḫu-si$^{!}$ (text: *pa*)*-ni-šú* ADD 953 = SAA 7 115 r. ii 11 in an administrative document from Ninūa (not dated, seventh century BC).[84]

---

82 See Menzel 1981, 272.

83 Against Fales - Postgate (1992, 123, 225) who translate "clothing-dealer". Deller - Millard (1993, 223, 231) suggested the interpretation as "Hersteller von Panzern (für Pferd und Reiter)", accordingly Kataja - Whiting (1995, 96, 143) translated "armourer". This interpretation seems to be grounded on the fact that the profession is listed after the donkey driver and the horse trainer in the appointment of Nergal-apil-kumūʾa. *Ḫalluptu* is otherwise attested in connection with horses, especially of the chariotry, cf. *AHw* 312 and *CAD* Ḫ, 46. *CAD*'s suggestion to limit the interpretation of *ḫalluptu* to "harness" seems to point into the right direction.

84 In the edition in SAA 7 the reading *ša–ḫu-pa-ni-šú* is maintained. *Ḫupānu* is tentatively translated as "basket" (no reasons are given for this). See already *CAD* Ḫ, 238 *sub ḫupānu* for the assumption that the attestations in ADD 537 and ADD 953 refer to the same profession. Since *ḫusinnu* is attested in still another text the presumed writing mistake must be in ADD 953, the correct lemma being thus *ša ḫussinīšu*.

10. *ša kitturrīšu* (*kiturru* "footstool")[85]

LÚ.*šá*–GIŠ.*kit-tur-ri-šú* PKTA 36-38 = Menzel 1981 no. 22 r. i 18 in a ritual for the Aššūr temple.

[LÚ.*šá*–G]IŠ.*kit-*⸢*tur-ri*!⸣*-šú* PKTA 36-38 = Menzel 1981 no. 22 r. ii 1 in a ritual for the Aššūr temple.

11. *ša kubšīšu* (*kubšu* "cap")[86]

[^{m}*sa*]*m-si-id-ri* LÚ*.*šá*–⸢U.SAG!⸣.[MEŠ-*šú*] ADB 4 = SAA 11 213 iii 2 in the Harrān census (reign of Sargon II).

LÚ*.*šá*–U.SAG.MEŠ-[*šú*] ABL 1224 r. 11 in a letter to the king (reign of Sargon II).

LÚ*.*šá*–U.SAG.MEŠ-*šú-nu* ABL 1224 r. 12 in a letter to the king (reign of Sargon II).

^{m}*u-ṣa-*[...] LÚ.*šá*–U.SAG.MEŠ-*šú* ADD 247 = SAA 6 342:4 is sold as a slave (date lost, reign of Esarhaddon).

^{m}*da-di-ia šá*–U.SAG.MEŠ-*šú* As 19:12 in a list of persons involved in a trade venture (not dated, reign of Ashurbanipal or later).

^{m}*da-di-ia šá*–U.SAG.MEŠ-*šú* As 29:15 in a list of persons involved in a trade venture (not dated, reign of Ashurbanipal or later).

^{md}15-BÀD-⸢*qa*⸣*-li* LÚ*.*šá*–U.SAG.MEŠ-*šú* ADD 619 = NALK 69:8 is part of a gift consisting of a house in Ninūa and several slaves from a father to his daughter (eponymate of Marduk-šarru-uṣur, after reign of Ashurbanipal).

LÚ.*šá*–U.SAG.MEŠ-⸢*šú*⸣ *ZA* 73 5:2 in an administrative text (not dated).

12. *ša kurrīšu* (*kurru* "tanning fluid")[87]

šá–kur-ri-šu ADD 953 = SAA 7 115 r. i 3 in an administrative text from Ninūa, receiving wool from the treasurer (not dated).

13. *ša midlīšu* (*midlu* "salted meat")[88]

LÚ*.*šá–me-di-li-šú* CTN 3 87:19 in an administrative text from Kalhu (not dated, no firm dating criteria available).

14. *ša mutqītīšu* (*mutqītu* "sweet cake")[89]

LÚ*.*šá–mut-qi-ti-šú* ADD 26 = SAA 6 262:4 in a legal document from Ninūa (680 BC).

15. *ša parzillīšu* (*parzillu* "iron")

^{m}[*s*]*a-*⸢x⸣*-nu-u ša*–AN.BAR-*šú* ND 2440 r. ii 7 in an administrative text from Kalhu (not dated, reign of Tiglath-pileser III or Sargon II).

[*š*]*a*–AN.BAR-*šú-nu* ND 2440 r. ii 9 in an administrative text from Kalhu (not dated, reign of Tiglath-pileser III or Sargon II).

---

85 See Menzel 1981, 274f; for *kiturru* "stool" see Deller - Finkel 1984, 87f.

86 *CAD* K, 485f.

87 For *kurru* "tanning fluid" see Deller 1985, 327-330 and Deller 1991.

88 For *midlu* "salted meat" see Deller 1983, 169-175.

89 *CAD* M/2, 301.

16. *ša pūlīšu* (*pūlu* "limestone")[90]

^{md}PA-*rém-a-ni ša*–NA$_4$.*pu-li-šú* ADD 152 = NALK 73 r. 8 as witness in a legal document from Ninūa (658 BC).

^{m}*ki-ṣir*-^{d}15 LÚ*.*šá–pu-li-šú*$^!$ ADD 1076 = SAA 7 47 ii 2 in an administrative text from Ninūa (not dated, seventh century BC).

17. *ša sāgātēšu* (*sāgātu* maybe "belt")[91]

^{m}*ku-za-a* LÚ*.*šá–sa-ga-te-šú*$^!$ ABL 167 = SAA 1 128:17 is a person reported missing in a letter to the king (reign of Sargon II).

18. *ša seqqurrātēšu* (*seqqurtu* maybe "*zikkurat*-shaped cake")[92]

LÚ*.*šá–se-e-qu-r*[*a*$^?$-*te-šú*] CTN 3 87 r. 2 in an administrative text from Kalhu (not dated, no firm dating criteria available).

19. *ša ṣallīšu* (*ṣallu* "leather")

LÚ.*ṣal-li-šú-nu* ADD 953 = SAA 7 115 r. i 5 in an administrative text from Ninūa, receiving wool from the treasurer (not dated).

20. *ša zizibīšu* (*zizibu* "milk")[93]

ša–zi-zi-bi-⸢*šú*⸣ CTN 3 89 14 in an administrative text from Kalhu (probably reign of Sargon II).

LÚ*.*šá*–GA-⸢*šú*⸣-*nu* NWL 35 ii 22 in an administrative text from Kalhu (probably reign of Sargon II).

LÚ*.*šá*–GA-*šú* *BaM* 24 239+ = SAA 12 83 r. 10 listed as part of the professionals transferred from Assur to Kalhu (reign of Ashurnasirpal II).

So far, twenty different professional titles of the type *ša X-šu* are known. However, we can expect that there are a number of other, as yet unknown professions of this type since many of the attested ones occur in only one source. It may be pointed out that neither salt (*ṭabtu*) nor honey (*dišpu*), two commodities that would be especially suited for the peddling trade, are attested in the present context.

Primarily due to a tablet from Kalhu, CTN 3 87, a large number of professions dealing with food are known: *ša akussīšu*, *ša billīšu*, *ša midlīšu*, *ša mutqītīšu*, *ša seqqurrātēšu*, *ša zizibīšu*. Many other professions deal with different manufactured goods most of which are intended for daily use: *ša dūdīšu*, *ša ḫalluptīšu*, *ša kubšīšu*, *ša kurrīšu*, *ša sāgātēšu*, *ša ṣallīšu*, probably also *ša ḫusinnīšu*. The only notable exception is *ša ḫalluptīšu*, provided that the interpretation of *ḫalluptu* as "harness" is correct. Especially interesting are those professions that deal with metals (*ša erêšu*, *ša parzillīšu*) and stones (*ša gabêšu*, *ša pūlīšu*). Three professions are attested in the context of temples and deal with things needed for cultic ceremonies: *ša endīšu*, *ša gaṣṣātēšu*, *ša kitturrīšu*.

---

90 For *pūlu* "limestone" see *AHw* 864 *sub pīlu* I, *pulu*, *pēlu* and Kwasman 1988, 85.

91 *CAD* S, 28, *AHw* 1003 *sub sāgu* I.

92 See Dalley - Postgate 1984, 147.

93 *CAD* Š/3, 153.

The sources show clearly that most of the persons bearing these titles are part of the palace or temple staff. This certainly does not indicate that they are independant professionals working for their own financial profit. The evidence is especially clear in the case of two *ša kubšīšu* professionals. Issār-dūr-qalli is presented by a father to his daughter as part of a gift consisting of a house and various persons. He is obviously a slave. Another *ša kubšīšu*, Samsi-idrī, is mentioned as a dependent person in the Harrān census. The contextual evidence shows that the *ša X-šu* professionals are subordinate members of households, in most cases of the palace or temples. They are clearly not independent entrepreneurs and there is no explicit evidence whatsoever that they are engaged in buying and selling. The interpretation as peddlers seems therefore to be completely out of the question.

How then are we to understand the function of these professionals? A possibility would be that they are engaged in the production of the X commodities. In the case of some of the attested professions there are obvious overlaps with well-known professional titles, such as *nappāḫ parzilli* "ironsmith" versus *ša parzillīšu*, *nappāḫ erê* "coppersmith" versus *ša erêšu* or *nuḫatimmu* "cook", *āpiu* "baker", or *karkadinnu* "confectioner" versus the various *ša X-šu* professions dealing with foodstuffs. Kinnier Wilson interpreted those professions as "cook-boys",[94] probably having in mind the assistants of the cooks. It is easy to imagine that the enormous task of cooking for the palace with its hundreds of inhabitants was divided so that certain dishes were prepared by specialized employees. So far, there is no evidence for these professionals outside of the palace household. The case of *ša zizibīšu* is a special one. He might well be the one milking the cattle and could be involved in processing dairy products such as cheese, ghee, and yoghurt. The *ša kubšīšu*, the *ša dūdīšu*, and the *ša ḫalluptīšu* might be manufacturing hats, kettles, and harnesses, therefore being respectively specialized tailors or smiths. It is totally unclear whether the professions dealing with metals and stones are concerned with the procurement or with the processing of these raw materials. They are certainly not responsible for the safekeeping since this is part of the treasurer's job. In the case of the three professions related to the temple, the *ša kitturrīšu* seems to be responsible for the ceremonial footstool itself, certainly not for its production, while the *ša endīšu* and the *ša gaṣṣātēšu* might respectively provide the aromatics or the firewood used in the temple.

Whereas it is clear that an interpretation as peddlers for the *ša X-šu* professions is out of the question the exact nature of these occupations still remains unclear. The titles obviously define the subject of the professional's activities without restricting its range exclusively to collecting, processing or manufacturing of the commodity in question. Furthermore, the contextual evidence indicates that the professionals are in subordinate and dependent positions, mainly as part of the palace or the temple household. Therefore, a translation as "X man", however clumsy, seems to be the best solution for the time being, *i.e. ša akussīšu* "soup man", *ša billīšu* "beer man", *ša dūdīšu* "kettle man", *ša endīšu* "aromatics man", *ša erêšu* "bronze man", *ša gabêšu* "alum man", *ša gaṣṣātēšu* "firewood man", *ša ḫalluptīšu* "harness man", *ša ḫusinnīšu* "... man", *ša kitturrīšu* "footstool man", *ša kubšīšu* "cap man", *ša kurrīšu* "tanning fluid man", *ša midlīšu* "salted meat man", *ša mutqītīšu* "sweet cake man", *ša parzillīšu* "iron man", *ša pūlīšu* "limestone man", *ša sāgātēšu* "belt (?) man", *ša seqqurrātēšu* "*zikkurat*-shaped cake man", *ša ṣallīšu* "leather man", and *ša zizibīšu* "milk man".

94 Kinnier Wilson 1972, 85f.

To conclude: the existence of these professions cannot be used as proof for peddling trade in the Neo-Assyrian period. Therefore, the attestations cannot elucidate the question whether peddling trade existed and if so, how important its role for the economy was.

MONEY IN THE NEO-ASSYRIAN EMPIRE

KAREN RADNER (HELSINKI)

Even though there seems to be no lack of literature on money in the Neo-Assyrian period this is primarely due to the famous lion-shaped weights from Kalhu[1] and the fact that a passage in Sennacherib's inscriptions has controversially been interpreted as evidence for the existence of coinage in the Neo-Assyrian period.[2] Other, perhaps more important, features have not, or only in a cursory fashion, been studied so far.[3]

---

1 See most recently Mitchell 1990, 129-138 (catalogue) and Fales 1995, 33-55 (on the Aramaic inscriptions of the lion weights); photographs: Kwasman - Parpola 1991, xxivf and cover.

2 In a connection with his innovative method of casting huge metal sculptures, Sennacherib compares their manufacture to the casting of objects (weighing) half a shekel each: *ki-i pi-ti-iq* 1/2 GÍN.TA.ÀM [19] *ú-šak-li-la nab-ni-su-un* (see Frahm 1997, T 12 vii 189f). It is clear that this is intended to illustrate how simple and effective the new method is. Lipinski (1979, 565), Saggs (1984, 171), Engel (1987, 62), Parise (1987, 37f) and Dalley (1988, 104) refuse to assign any further implications to this passage, whereas the interpretation that Sennacherib had half shekel pieces cast as coins is maintained by *e.g.* Oppenheim (1970, 32f n. 55) and, tentatively, Snell (1995, 1491). The smallest amount of copper attested in the legal documents is half a mina of copper: CTN 2 90 (803): 52 1/2 minas of (copper or bronze); CTN 2 17 (783): two minas two shekels of silver and 2 1/2 minas of copper; ND 701 = *BaM* 24 259 no. 15 (744): 3 1/2 minas of copper; CTN 2 104 (738): 18 1/2 minas of copper; CTN 2 96 (737): 217 1/2 minas of copper; ND 679 = *BaM* 24 251 no. 7 (eponymy of Paqaha): 2 1/2 minas of copper; ND 2313 = *Iraq* 16 39 (date lost): one mina of silver and half a mina of copper. Half a shekel (ca. 4 g) of copper then obviously is a very modest sum and if we interpret the passage as evidence for the casting of copper coins we would be facing a matter altogether different from the roughly contemporary Lydian electrum coins (see the photograph in Snell 1995, 1494 fig. 3, and cf. Karwiese 1995, *passim*) which represented objects of extremely high value. Even though there is no physical evidence for the usage of coins in the Neo-Assyrian Empire (see Calmeyer - Naster 1995, 404 and Renger 1995, 307-309), S. Parpola convinced me not to dismiss the idea that coins were in use during the Neo-Assyrian period too easily. To have a standardized form for a sum like half a shekel of copper could be convenient in daily small-scale business which would only be delayed by the weighing process naturally employed for all dealings involving larger sums. If we interpret the passage as referring to the manufacture of copper pieces used as currency the very fact that Sennacherib claims to be involved in their production would indicate that they were made with his authorization and would be recognized as such. Thus, they might well be described as coins in the proper sense even if Sennacherib does not state whether he had them stamped or not. However, as mentioned above, no Neo-Assyrian coin, be it made out of copper or any other material, has been found so far and differently from coins made out of precious metals like silver, gold and electrum, copper coins are attested only much later. Though it would be rather unlikely that the hypothetical Neo-Assyrian copper coins had survived other than as part of a hoard (since copper could be used for virtually everything, coins not used as currency would have been melted and used as working material), the question whether copper coins were in use in the Neo-Assyrian period or not cannot be decided as long as no further evidence, archaeological or philological, has been found.

3 However, while this paper was written an article by F. M. Fales (1996, 11-53) has been published which deals with some of the aspects intended to cover in the present work. For these, namely the study of the term *maḫīru* and the so-called *Getreidekursangaben*, the reader is referred to the article by Fales. I only give my attestation lists which are more complete than Fales's in Appendix 4.

In this paper I will use the legal texts[4] and letters of the Neo-Assyrian period as the primary sources to investigate Neo-Assyrian "money". Besides my own files covering all published and many hitherto unpublished[5] legal documents of the period I was able make use of the Corpus of Neo-Assyrian Texts, the database of the State Archives of Assyria Project.[6]

1. *Metals used as Money: Silver, Copper, and Bronze*

In the Neo-Assyrian period, three metals are used as money: copper (URUDU = *erû*), bronze (ZABAR (UD.KA.BAR) = *siparru*),[7] and silver (KÙ.BABBAR = *ṣarpu*[8]). However, there is no proof that, using M. Powell's terminology, copper and bronze are only "low-range money" whereas silver is the "high-range money".[9] All metals can be used for both very high and very modest sums. That copper is not just used as small change is best observed in those instances when a price is made up by both silver and copper. According to a document from Imgur-Illil, modern Balawat,[10] "two minas of silver according to (the mina of) the king" and "one talent (in) mina(s) of copper" are taken on loan. According to a text found at Nineveh,[11] 4-*tú* KÙ.BABBAR 47 MA.NA URUDU.MEŠ "a quarter (mina) of silver and 47 minas of copper" are taken on loan. In a text from Kalhu,[12] the price of a cultivated field is given as "two minas and two shekels

---

4 When quoting Post-Canonical eponym dates I use the abbreviations given in Millard 1994, 128.

5 I am especially grateful to Dr. E. Klengel, former Director of the VAM Berlin, Dir. Dr. V. Donbaz, IAM Istanbul, and Prof. Dr. J. Renger, Chairman of the Assur Committee of the Deutsche Orient-Gesellschaft, for their kind permission to study the Assur texts.

6 I wish to thank Prof. Dr. S. Parpola for his generous permission to use the Corpus of Neo-Assyrian Texts database as well as Dr. R.M. Whiting for his ever patient help. I am indebted to Dr. R. Jas, Leiden, for his careful reading of the manuscript and his critical remarks.

7 It has been suggested that also the logogram ZABAR (UD.KA.BAR) may designate copper at this time when referring to the raw material, see Zaccagnini 1971, 123-144 and Postgate 1973, 25, approvingly. However, as Fales (1996, 18 n. 17) points out, there is a misapprehension of Zaccagnini's views from Postgate's side resulting in mistakenly quoting him for the "suggestion that both 'copper' (URUDU) and 'bronze' (ZABAR) may be used for bronze." It is true that in the royal inscriptions bronze is mentioned almost to the exclusion of copper but then, this need not reflect economic reality, see Walker 1988, 111f. In the legal and administrative texts URUDU and ZABAR are clearly different commodities, compare *e.g.* the inventory list of the dowry given to Abdi-Aširti's daughter in ND 2307 = FNALD 14:22: after a bed of bronze a footstool of copper is listed. Bronze is attested as currency over a period of 48 years (835-788 BC) and in texts from all sites where tablets dating from that period have been unearthed (Tell Billa, Nineveh [ADD 467 = NALDK 75, date lost], Nimrud). Therefore it is impossible in my opinion to explain away the attestations for copper as currency as a "local scribal habit ... leading to an indifferent use of the logograms URUDU and ZABAR in legal documents" as Fales (1996, 18) does who then suggests to interpret all the attestations as referring to copper. I prefer to keep the terms strictly separate when dealing with legal and administrative texts. However I would suggest that indeed copper is meant when Sargon II is speaking of bronze in connection with buying and selling (see the references in notes 18 and 19).

8 Not *kaspu*, see Deller 1987, 3.

9 Powell 1996, 224-242.

10 BT 127 (dated 692) = *Iraq* 25 pl. xxvi.

11 ADD 1246 = SAA 6 29 (dated 710).

12 CTN 2 17 (dated 783).

of silver, two and a half minas of copper".[13] Obviously the sum was composed of whatever metal supplies were at hand. However, copper is clearly perceived as being inferior to silver and is thus always mentioned in the second place, a situation paralleled in administrative lists and inventories.

As has long been known,[14] copper is the metal most often used during the eighth century whereas silver is almost exclusively the metal used in the seventh century. Nevertheless, silver serves as a currency as early as 783 BC and copper is still in use in the second half of the seventh century. It is interesting to note that bronze is widely used as currency before and during the reign of Adad-nērārī III - who got 3,000 talents of bronze as tribute from Damascus[15] - and not at all attested afterwards. That bronze becomes less popular is also reflected by the fact that references to this metal, which is prominently listed in the records of booty and tribute of the Assyrian kings in the 10th-8th centuries, are increasingly less common in the later inscriptions.[16]

Recently, G. Müller has linked the change from copper and bronze to silver as the metal used as currency to the successful campaigns of Sargon II resulting in the capture of immense quantities of silver, most notably from Carchemish.[17] The data gathered from the legal documents in Appendix 1 strengthen Müller's hypothesis. Indeed it is during Sargon's reign that silver replaces copper as the most frequently used metal. Sargon claims that the exchange value (*maḫīru*) of silver equalled the value of "bronze" in 712.[18] Even though this is an exaggeration this statement reflects the enormous influx of silver into Assyria: it is this very year that seems to mark the change from copper to silver as the most commonly used currency metal. During Sargon's reign copper and silver are used alternatively as is best illustrated by a passage in his inscriptions: "I returned the price of the fields of that city (= Magganūba, site of the later Dūr-Šarrukēn) according to the tablets of the purchase in silver and in 'bronze' to the owners".[19] During the reigns of Sargon's successors, copper falls more and more out of use but is still attested occasionally until the end of the Assyrian empire.

---

13 The price in CTN 2 18 (781) is too broken to be used as evidence: "16? minas of silver and [...] copper".

14 See *e.g.* Postgate 1973, 25.

15 RIMA 3 A.0.104.8:18.

16 Walker (1987, 112ff) lists the quantities of metal brought into Assyria as booty and tribute.

17 Müller 1997, 120; Postgate 1979, 18 tentatively linked the shift away from copper to silver to Sargon's successful campaign to the Taurus with its rich ore mines.

18 Ann 232-234 = Fuchs 1994, 130f.

19 Zyl. 51 = Fuchs 1994, 40: *ka-sap* A.ŠÀ.MEŠ URU *šá-a-šú ki-i pi-i ṭup-pa-a-te ša-a-a-ma-nu-te* KÙ.BABBAR *ú* ZABAR.MEŠ *a-na* EN.MEŠ *ú-tir-ma*. Note the close similarity to the widely used penalty clause regulating that whoever will break the contract *kaspu ana ešrāte ana bēlīšu utêr* "will return the price tenfold to its owner." Occasionally the price is to be paid *threefold*, see MADD 6 = SAA 6 194 (dated 681), VAT 9582 (dated 649) and BM 103389 = *AfO* 32 39ff (eponymy of Sîn-šarru-uṣur) and most of the texts from Dūr-Katlimmu; *twelvefold*, see ADD 473 = SAA 6 100 (dated 698), ADD 474+ = SAA 6 101 (date lost) and ADD 436 = SAA 6 102 (date lost); *twentyfold*, see Assur 2 = *Al-Rāfidān* 17 no. 2 (eponymy of Ṣalmu-šarru-iqbi); or *hundredfold*, see ADD 350 = SAA 6 32 (dated 707) and VAT 9750 (date lost).

2. *Metal Standards*

Different weight standards are applied for the different metals. So far, three standards for silver, one for copper and two for gold are known. Moreover, there are heavy (*dannu*) and light (*qallu*) norms in use for all these metals.[20] Two light minas weighing ca. 500 g are one heavy mina (ca. 1 kg).

Silver Standards

There are three weight standards used for silver: the king's mina, the mina of Carchemish, and the merchant's mina.[21] That it is indeed the weight that is referred to whenever *ṣarpu ina manê ša šarri/tamkāri/Gargamis* is mentioned is clear from a text from Assur where 1/2 MA.NA KÙ.BABBAR *ina* KI.LAL 3 *ša* LÚ*.DAM.GÀR "half a mina of silver according to the weight of the merchant" is used.[22]

In Appendix 2, all available attestations for the different silver standards in the legal texts have been collected. With 101 known attestations, the mina of Carchemish is clearly the most popular one. The king's mina is known from 35 texts and the *tamkāru*'s mina is attested in ten texts.

The earliest attestation for the king's mina is dated to the reign of Tiglath-pileser III. The standard is well in use until the end of Ashurbanipal's reign: the latest known attestation is dated in the eponymy of Aššūr-gārūa-nēre. However, this standard is already attested on weights inscribed with the name of Shalmaneser V. The Aramaic standard *zy ʾrqʾ* "mina of the country", attested on the same weights, seems to be identical with the mina of the king.[23]

Lion weights with inscriptions mentioning standards:[24]

	1 d *dannu*	2 d *dannu*	3 d *dannu*	4 d *dannu*	5 d *dannu*	6 d *dannu*
ʾrqʾ	Š5[25]	Š5	Š5	Š5		
mlk	Š5	Š5	Š5	Š5	Š5	Š5
šarru	[26]	Š5	Š5	Š5	Š5	Š5

20 See most recently Powell 1989-90, 515f and Fales 1996, 12-15.

21 The supposed attestation of a "mina of Arbail" in ND 3440 = *Iraq* 15 143 (652) is in my opinion best explained as 1 1/2 MA.NA KÙ.BABBAR *ša* 15! (tablet: KÙ.BABBAR) *ša arba-ìl*. The supposed attestation of an "Assyrian mina" in a fragmentary administrative text from Nineveh, ADD 1075 = SAA 7 48:5, is highly doubtful. The edition reads [x] GÍN *ina* 1 [MA] *aš-šur-[a-a]*. However, in view of the fact that this standard is not attested anywhere else, the restoration [x] GÍN *ina* m[x]-*aš-šur* [x x (x)] is far more likely.

22 VAT 9367 = *SAAB* 5 37 (date lost).

23 See Fales 1996, 15f.

24 Using the information provided by Fales (1995, 35-47). Š5 = Shalmaneser V, TP3 = Tiglath-pileser III, Sg = Sargon II. *Dannu* and *qallu* indicate whether the weights are based on the heavy or the light mina, see Fales 1995, 51.

25 The dating is inferred, see Fales 1995, 48 n. 31.

26 This weight bears only an Aramaic inscription.

	7 d	8 q	9 q	11 d	12 d	15 q
	dannu	*qallu*	*qallu*	*dannu*	*dannu*	*qallu*
ʾrqʾ	Š5			Š5		27
mlk		Š5	Sg			
šarru	Š5		Sg	Š5	Š5	TP3

The mina of Carchemish (if restored correctly)[28] is already attested in 747 in the reign of Aššūr-nērārī V but it is only during and after the reign of Sargon II that this standard is widely used. Müller (1997, 120) sees a connection between the enormous booty Sargon II brought from Carchemish to Assyria (2,100 talents of silver) and the growing popularity of the mina of Carchemish. I share this opinion. The mina of Carchemish is used until the end of the Assyrian empire.

The mina of the *tamkāru* also seems to be introduced during Sargon's reign. There are no known attestations after the reign of Esarhaddon.

Even though there is still no clarity on the exact implications of the different standards, the terms used seem to indicate a connection with the sources of silver. The king's mina could refer to the royal treasury, the merchant's mina to the overland trade and the mina of Carchemish to the booty and tribute taken from Western kingdoms as the origin of the silver.

Copper Standards

One standard is attested for copper,[29] the mina of the mountain: in a sale text found at Nineveh,[30] the price of two estates is given as 20 MA.NA URUDU.MEŠ 11' [*ina*] MA.NA-*e ša* KUR-*e*. It has been suggested that the same standard is attested as Aramaic (*zy*) *ʾrqʾ* "(of) the land" on some weights inscribed with the name of Shalmaneser V.[31] The writing *ša* KUR-*e* which normally would stand for *ša šaddê* "of the mountain" has then to be explained either as an error[32] or a representation for an Aramaic reading.[33] The need to harmonize the attestations for (*zy*) *ʾrqʾ* and *ša* KUR-*e* was created by the presumed inscription 2 MA.NA *šá* KUR on a weight bearing the name of Tiglath-pileser III. However, a recent collation by Fales has shown that the inscription reads 2 MA.NA *šá* LUGAL instead.[34] Since other evidence indicates that the standard of the country (*zy ʾrqʾ*)

27 This weight bears only an Akkadian inscription.

28 ADD 412 = SAA 6 17:13: *ina* 1 MA.NA ša U[RU.*gar-ga-mis*]. Probably *ina* 1 MA.NA *ša* LU[GAL] is to be restored. However, both readings are possible.

29 Note also the copper-*sūtu* used for measuring capacities and areas: CTN 2 17 (783); ADD 127 = SAA 6 46 (681); ADD 95 = SAA 6 276 (675); ND 5460 = *Iraq* 19 pl. xxx (667); ND 5451 = *Iraq* 19 pl. xxx (665); ND 5453 = *Iraq* 19 pl. xxx (662); ND 5468 = *Iraq* 19 pl. xxxii (652); CTN 3 13 (Mušallim-Aššūr).

30 ADD 376 = SAA 6 176 (date lost).

31 Powell 1989-90, 515.

32 Kwasman - Parpola 1991, 144.

33 Powell 1989-90, 515.

34 Fales 1995, 47.

corresponds to the standard of the king (Aram. *zy mlk* and Akk. *ša šarri*)[35] - a standard used exclusively for silver! - I see no reason why one should not translate the passage in ADD 376 as "twenty minas of copper according to the mina of the mountain".

The same standard is probably attested in another text from Nineveh as the price of several slaves: ⌜50 URUDU⌝.MEŠ *ina* 1 ⌜MA⌝.NA-*e* 6' [*ša* KUR-*e*].[36]

Gold Standards

Even though gold is not used as a currency in the Neo-Assyrian period, the standards used for gold will be discussed for the sake of completeness.

There are two known standards, the mina of Babylon and the mina of agate. In a letter to Sargon II, the treasurer Ṭāb-šār-Aššūr is reporting on some gold that he weighed: 1/2 MA.NA *ina ša* KÁ.DINGIR.KI *šú-u* "It is half a mina according to (the mina) of Babylon".[37] In a letter of a goldsmith from Assur to Ashurbanipal,[38] 23 MA.NA KÙ.GI *ina ša* BABBAR.DIL *a-du še-lu-a-ti* "23 minas of gold according to (the mina) of agate together with the votive gifts" are mentioned.[39] In another letter from the same goldsmith, 33 MA.NA KÙ.GI *a-du še-lu-a-te ina* BABBAR.DIL "33 minas of gold together with the votive gifts according to (the mina of) agate" are mentioned.[40] The agate mina is also mentioned in an administrative document from the reign of Sargon II listing gold quantities: 3 MA BABBAR.DIL "3 minas (according to the mina of) agate".[41]

3. *Metal Qualities and Methods of Refinement*

Beginning in the reign of Ashurbanipal, three adjectives are used to specify the quality of silver in the legal texts: *danqu* "good", *masiu* "washed", and *qaliu* "burnt". *Ṣarpu danqu* "good silver" is attested in two texts from Assur[42] and another two from Kalhu.[43] Attestations for *ṣarpu masiu* "washed silver" are found in three texts from Assur[44] and two texts from Kalhu.[45] *Ṣarpu qaliu* "burnt silver" is attested in three texts

---

35 Fales (1995, 53f) suggests an explanation for the parallel usage of these different terms.

36 ADD 265 = NALDK 113 (date lost).

37 ABL 180 = SAA 1 51:9.

38 ABL 1194:4'. For a new edition of the text see now SAA 13 28. Dating: the chief goldsmith Sîn-naʾid is mentioned in r. 4.

39 Probably also in ABL 1194:7f: GÚ.UN 19 MA.NA KÙ.GI *ina* MA!.NA! (text: URU.MA) 8 *ša* NA_4.BABBAR.DIL *ša ina* É NÍG.GA *ša* d30 *a-du še-lu-a-ti*. The meaning of *šēlûāte*, obviously the plural form of *šēlûtu*, in this context is not entirely clear: see for now *CAD* Š/3, 264 *sub šūlûtu*.

40 ABL 997:9, see SAA 13 29 for a new edition of the text.

41 ADD 676 = SAA 7 79 r. 11. Interpreted as "3 minas of agate" in the edition.

42 *RA* 24 114 no. 3 (eponymy of Nabû-tappûtu-alik) and *ZA* 73 251 no. 8 (eponymy of Aššūr-mātu-taqqin).

43 CTN 3 60 (eponymy of Nabû-tappûtu-alik) and ND 3432 (eponymy of Sîn-šarru-uṣur).

44 VAT 8641 (eponymy of Iqbi-ilāni), VAT 8663 (eponymy of Nabû-šar-aḫḫēšu) and VAT 15464 (eponymy of Šamaš-mītu-uballiṭ).

45 CTN 3 37 (eponymy of Aššūr-gārūa-nēre) and ND 2338 (eponymy of Nabû-šarru-uṣur palace scribe).

from Assur.[46] No text is known so far to mention good, washed, or burnt silver according to the mina of the king, the merchant, or Carchemish.

Masû "to wash"[47] and *qalû* "to burn"[48] are methods to refine silver. Another practice used is *ṣarāpu* "to fire".[49] The exact implications and differences of these methods are unknown to us. However, washing is the method most frequently attested. Not only silver, but also copper can be treated in this way.[50] This is proved by a letter from the Mannean frontier: "The copper which the servants of the magnates have washed"[51] is at the disposal of a subordinate of the treasurer. In a private letter from the goldsmiths' archive in Assur, "the house they wash silver in"[52] is mentioned. Judging from two letters from the royal correspondence, the washing, burning, and firing of silver are alternative techniques. In a letter to Ashurbanipal an official from Assur reports: "This silver I wrote to the king my lord about is of the income. It is neither burnt nor washed."[53] All these procedures naturally result in a diminishing of the metal: "After I have washed and/or fired (the silver) I will inform the king, my lord, about the decrease of the silver."[54] The firing of silver is also attested in a judicial document from the goldsmiths' archive in Assur: "Zērutî will pay back the silver they have fired."[55]

Even though the usage of adjectives specifying the quality of the metal used as currency is only attested after 658 there are many earlier references to washed silver. Silver thus qualified is frequently mentioned in the penalty clauses, mostly together with heated gold (*ḫurāṣu sakru*).[56] Note that *sakāru* "to heat" is a refining method exclusively used for gold.[57] *Ṣâdu* D is another technique only used for the refinement of gold.[58]

Appendix 3 is a table listing all attestations for penalty clauses which stipulate that whoever breaks the contract has to pay certain sums of washed silver and/or heated gold, usually to a god.[59] In one instance the payment of red gold is required.[60] Although the earliest attestation for washed silver is dated into the year 778, examples of this type of penalty clause are especially numerous in the second half of the seventh century. As has been stated earlier, gold was not used as currency in the Neo-Assyrian period. That the payment of gold is nevertheless stipulated in the penalty clauses is due to the fact that these clauses, as most other Neo-Assyrian penalty clauses, are part of the Middle-

---

46 A 2521 (658), CT 33 19 (eponymy of Aššūr-gārūa-nēre) and A 1916 (eponymy of Kanūnāyu).

47 *CAD* M/2, 30 and 32f.

48 *CAD* Q, 68 and 71.

49 *CAD* Ṣ, 102f.

50 See Dercksen 1996, 34-39 for the qualifications used for copper in the Old Assyrian period.

51 ABL 867 = SAA 5 257 r. 6: URUDU.MEŠ [7] *ša* ÌR.MEŠ *ša* LÚ*.GAL.MEŠ *i-ma-su-ni*.

52 VAT 8644 = KAV 115:32: É KÙ.BABBAR *i-ma-su-u-ni*.

53 ABL 1194 r. 8-9: KÙ.BABBAR *an-ni-u ša a-na* LUGAL *be-lí-ía* [9] *áš-pur-an-ni ša ir-bi šu-ú la qa-li la ma-si*.

54 CT 53 922 r. 7'-9': *ki-ma an-te-se ú-ṣa-[ri-pi]* [8'] LÁ-*e ša* KÙ.BABBAR *a-na* LUG[AL EN-*ia*] [9'] *ú-ša-áš-ma*, see Deller - Mayer 1984, 85.

55 VAT 8656:6-8: KÙ.BABBAR *ṣa-ar-pu-u-ni* [7] [m]NUMUN-*ú-ti-i* [8] *ú-šal-lam*, see Jas 1996, 36 no. 19.

56 *CAD* S, 81 and 213f.

57 See the attestations in *CAD* S, 214 *s.v. sekēru* B.

58 See the attestations in *CAD* Ṣ, 59 *s.v. ṣâdu* B 2.

59 If not stated otherwise "washed" stands for LUḪ(-*u/ú*) and "heated" for *sak-ru*.

60 On red gold see H. Waetzoldt, 'Rotes Gold?', *OA* 24 (1985), 1-16, and Reiter 1997, 36ff.

Babylonian legal tradition:[61] as is well known, gold was the monetary standard in the Kassite period.

4. *Handling of Precious Metals: Weighing and Sealing*

There can be no doubt that the quantities of metal mentioned in legal documents are actually passed on from one person to another.

Even though we cannot assume that sale transactions in the Neo-Assyrian period are always cash sales (*Barkäufe*), the price seems to have been paid *ad hoc* in most cases. The weighing and handing over of silver is explicitly attested in a judicial settlement from Assur in connection with the release of two persons from debt slavery: 30 GÍN.MEŠ KÙ.BABBAR *ša* ḪA.LA-*šú* ^{m}DÙG.GA-EN 8 *iḫ-ti-ia-aṭ a-na* ^{m}*bi-šá-a*ᵓ *i-ti-din* 9 MÍ.*a-pi-i*ᵓ NIN-*su* ^{m}*pa-ši-i* DUMU NIN-*šú* 10 TA ŠU^{II} ^{m}*bi-šá-a*ᵓ *ip-ta-ṭar-ra*. "Ṭāb-Bēl weighed 30 shekels of silver of his share and gave (it) to Bišaᵓ. He released his sister Apiᵓ (and) his nephew Pāšî from the hands of Bišaᵓ."[62]

The situation is more complex in the case of the obligation texts. Postgate proposed that only those texts that mention the clause *ina pūḫi našû* are true loans whereas all other texts are to be interpreted as debt-notes.[63] The problem needs further study. However, it is clear that the sum involved is actually changing hands when it is described in a rather awkward way that can only result from the process of weighing:[64]

ADD 37 = SAA 6 273: 5 MA.NA 6 GÍN LÁ (KÙ.BABBAR) *šá gar-*[*g*]*a-mis* "Five minas lacking six shekels (of silver) according to the (mina) of Carchemish" - debt-note (without *ina pūḫi*-clause) from Nineveh (676).
VAT 20338 = *SAAB* 5 18: 1 MA.NA 2 GÍN LÁ KÙ.BABBAR *ina* MA-*e* KUR.*gar-ga-mis* "One mina lacking two shekels of silver according to the mina of Carchemish" - receipt from Assur (eponymy of Aššūr-gārua-nēre).
CTN 3 38: 1/2 GÍN LÁ *a-na* 1/2 MA.NA KÙ.BABBAR "Half a shekel is lacking to half a mina of silver" - debt-note (with *ina pūḫi*-clause) from Kalhu (eponymy of Sîn-ālik-pāni).
VAT 9778 = Ass. 2282f: 1 1/2 GÍN LÁ *a-na* 1 MA.NA KÙ.BABBAR "One and a half shekel is lacking to a mina of silver" - sale of a slave girl from Assur (date lost).

In this context reference needs to be made to two texts from the vicinity of Nabula in the area of modern Girnavaz. In the land sales Gir 84/84 and Gir 86/23[65] some witnesses are qualified as *bēl ḫiᵓāṭi ša ṣarpi*:

---

61 See Radner 1997, 190f and 306 on two other Neo-Assyrian penalty clauses which clearly developed from Middle-Babylonian forerunners.

62 VAT 20374 = Ass. 11489c (eponymy of Kanūnāyu).

63 Postgate 1976, 37.

64 Compare ABL 1194:16f: 5 GÚ.UN.TA.AN 12 MA.NA LÁ KÙ.BABBAR 17 KI.LAL-*šú-nu*.

65 Published in Donbaz 1988, 7-9 (copy: 20f): Gir 84/84 (date lost) and 11f (copy: 23): Gir 86/23 (date lost).

Gir 84/84:14-19: IGI ^{m}*man-nu-ka*-DINGIR A ^{m}*ka-bar*-DINGIR ^{15} EN *ḫi-a-ṭi ša* 30 GÍN KÙ.BABBAR ^{16} IGI ^{md}PA-SUM-PAP.MEŠ EN *ḫi-a-ṭi* ^{17} *ša* 1/2 MA.NA 8 GÍN KÙ.BABBAR ^{18} IGI ^{m}EN-I EN *ḫi-a-ṭi* ^{19} *ša* 12 GÍN KÙ.BABBAR PAP 1 MA.NA 20 GÍN.
Gir 86/23:24f: IGI ^{m}*man-nu-ki-arba-ìl* A ^{m}*ab-da-a* ^{25} EN *ḫi-a-ṭi ša* KÙ.BABBAR. The following four witnesses are qualified as ^{30} PAP 4 EN *na-ši-e ša* KÙ.BABBAR.[66]

The function of a "master of the weighing of the silver" is obviously the supervision of the weighing process. The term *bēl ḫiʾāṭi ša ṣarpi* is up to now only attested in the texts from Girnavaz but it is realistic to assume that it is normally part of the witnesses' responsibility to make sure that the weighing is conducted properly.

The weighing of silver is also mentioned in some texts from Assur connected with the financing of private trade enterprises. In VAT 8648:9 from the goldsmiths' archive a list of silver sums and their owners is concluded: ⸢1/2⸣ MA 3 GÍN *ḫe-ṭu* "Half a mina (and) three shekels are weighed." This is, however, only a part of the total of the sums listed. In As 20 r. 9 and As 24 r. 13 from the archive unearthed by the Munich expedition to Assur in 1990 similar statements are made.[67]

The metals changed hands in the form of conveniently sized ingots which were cut into smaller pieces when needed. Several large caches of silver ingots and cut silver pieces have been discovered only recently in seventh century Ekron (Tel Miqne).[68] Other examples of silver ingots have been found in Samʾal (Zinjirli) and Nūš-i Ǧān.[69] To my knowledge, no copper or bronze ingots from the Neo-Assyrian period have been discovered so far.[70] However, this is not much of a surprise since the scarcity of metals in Assyria resulted in the reuse and recycling of metal objects throughout its history. Note in this context that only very few bronze weapons from the Neo-Assyrian period are known and that these often show clear signs of mending and reuse whereas numerous bronze weapons from contemporary Urarṭu, an area with rich metal sources, have been preserved.[71]

Large ingots being weighed with scales are depicted twice on Neo-Assyrian monuments. The first, a scene on a fragmentary obelisk from Kalhu attributed to Ashurnasirpal II, shows two Assyrian officials, one bearded, one beardless, who are engaged in weighing two stacks of ingots with a large scale after a city was captured and sacked by Assyrian forces (fig. 1).[72] The second illustration is found on the famous relief series from the palace of Sargon II in Dūr-Šarrukēn depicting the sack of Muṣaṣir. Two beardless officials are weighing a round ingot with a large scale which is technically

66 The term is also attested in VAT 20404 = *SAAB* 9 114 r. 21f: ^{m}*dan-nu*-U.GUR ^{m}*kun-di*-⸢x⸣ ^{22} EN KÙ.BABBAR *na-še-i*.

67 Thanks are due to Prof. Dr. K. Hecker who generously allowed me to use his copies of these texts.

68 Gitin 1997, 93f and 101 fig. 19f.

69 See Calmeyer - Naster 1995, 404 with literature, also Snell 1995, 1489f.

70 But compare the Mycenaen-style copper ingot from Middle-Babylonian Dūr-Kurigalzu, see Brinkman 1987, 35f. Ingots like this were used all over the Mediterranean in the Middle Bronze Age, compare *e.g.* the examples found in a ship-wreck off Cape Gelidonya (Southern Turkey), see Snell 1995, 1490 fig. 2. See note 2 for the possible allusion to the casting of copper coins in Sennacherib's inscriptions.

71 See Born - Seidl 1995, 9.

72 BM 11800: Gadd 1936, pl. 6, see Pritchard 1954, 119 fig. 350a.

advanced compared to the Ashurnasirpal one.[73] The surrounding scenes show Assyrian soldiers carrying away metal booty such as cauldrons and shields and destroying a statue, possibly to remove its metal parts (fig. 2).[74] Note that the ingots are round, just like the ones found in Samʾal.[75]

It seems that it is not only by chance or due to the fact that large scales would be difficult to handle alone that two persons are depicted weighing in both cases. Also the texts show that weighing precious metals is a task that needs the presence of more than one high official. An official named Urdu-Nabû[76] reports to the king that he, the treasurer, and the palace scribe weighed gold which was then put into the *bēt qātē* of the *rab danibāte*[77] and sealed. A letter from Harrān to the queen mother, probably Naqiʾa,[78] reports on the production of her statue. The author of the letter, the deputy of the governor, the second scribe of the treasurer, the temple scribe, and the priests of the temples of Harrān, together with the chariot driver Šarru-lū-dāri, have weighed the metal. A letter from Šarru-ēmuranni, governor of Māzamua, to Sargon II,[79] gives an account of how he, together with other unnamed persons, entered the treasury to get 420 talents of copper which were then weighed. Dated to the reign of Ashurbanipal are two letters from an unknown official from Assur closely related to the goldsmiths' guild who reports to the king on the progress made at the work on valuable objects for the temples of Assur. These letters refer to silver and gold that "we weighed".[80] Another letter from the sphere of the goldsmiths of Assur contains the order to weigh silver sealed with the seal of "the god who has saved me" and have it delivered.[81] However, an official named Nabû-bāni-aḫḫē does not have sufficient authority to weigh gold that is needed for the production of a statue. He therefore urges the king to send somebody to do so.[82]

The ultimate responsibility for the weighing of precious metals rests with the treasurer (*masennu*).[83] He seems to be the only official who can supervise the weighing procedure entirely on his own authority.[84] An administrative text from the reign of

73 See Hrouda 1965, 73.

74 The original slab was lost in the Tigris, only Flandin's drawing survived: Botta - Flandin 1849-50, pl. 142f, see Albenda 1986, pl. 133. For a description of the booty from Muṣaṣir see W. Mayer, 'Sargons Feldzug gegen Urartu', *MDOG* 115 (1983), 105-110.

75 For a photograph of a silver ingot inscribed with the name of Bar-rakib king of Samʾal see Kwasman - Parpola 1991, xxxiii.

76 ABL 114; see SAA 13 61 for a new edition. Menzel-Wortmann 1986, 224 assumes that Urdu-Nabû is a priest, maybe from the temple of Issār of Arbail. That he is indeed a priest is clear from ABL 177 r. 7' where his title is mentioned by Iddin-Aia, priest of Inurta of Kalhu. However, it is far more likely that Urdu-Nabû is likewise a priest in Kalhu, and not in Arbela.

77 Menzel-Wortmann 1986, 213-227 discusses the evidence for this official.

78 CT 53 921; see SAA 13 186 for an edition.

79 ABL 319 + CT 53 225 = SAA 5 206.

80 ABL 997:8, ABL 1194:2'; see now SAA 13 28 and 29.

81 VAT 15545 9 - r. 4: *u-ma-a* [1] *ṣib-te* KÙ.BABBAR *ša* NA_4.KIŠIB [2] *ša* DINGIR *ša-e-ṭir-an-ni* [3] *ḫe-e-ṭe a-na* mdPA-*re-ṣu-u-a* [4] *di-ni lu-bi-la* "Now weigh the silver stock with the seal of 'the god who has saved me' and give them to Nabû-rēṣūwa. He may bring it (to me)." The text belongs to the goldsmiths' archive (N 33).

82 ABL 531; see now SAA 13 127.

83 On this official see R. Mattila's forthcoming Ph.D. thesis *The Assyrian Magnates* (to be published in the SAAS series).

84 ABL 180 = SAA 1 51:8: *aḫ-ti-aṭ*.

Sargon II[85] lists quantities of gold which the governor of Kalhu sent and which are weighed. It is not surprising to find the treasurer involved. Although his name is not mentioned it is certainly Ṭāb-šār-Aššūr who is at work here. Also, two letters from Ṭāb-šār-Aššūr to Sargon II mention the weighing of gold.[86] All these texts refer to the manufacture of statues and other cult objects destined for the temples in Assur. Another fragmentary letter dealing with the weighing of copper belongs probably to the correspondence of Ṭāb-šār-Aššūr as well.[87]

It is important to note that the precious metals are sealed after they are weighed.[88] Obviously, the metals would be in the shape of ingots by then. It is not clear, however, whether the ingot itself was sealed or just its wrapping. It seems possible that whenever reference is made to a metal according to a certain standard we are dealing with such sealed ingots.

4. *Legal Documents used as "Money"*

As I have shown elsewhere, legal documents can be used as "money" in the Neo-Assyrian period.[89] Documents may serve as payment[90] and can form part of an inheritance share.[91]

5. *Money Sources of the Neo-Assyrian Empire*

Assyria proper is a country without metal sources of her own. As a consequence all metals used in Assyria must have been imported from elsewhere at one point in history.[92]

Fortunately, the Neo-Assyrian Empire was not founded on virgin soil but succeeded the economically successful Middle-Assyrian empire. We may therefore safely assume that the Neo-Assyrian kings inherited a treasury well stocked with gold, silver, copper, and bronze from their precedessors.

To come into the possession of metal, the Neo-Assyrian kings made use of all the traditional methods that had already been successfully employed for several millennia by then. They gained metal (1) through military force, resulting in the delivery of booty and tribute, as well as the expansion of the empire in order to include the sources of raw materials, (2) through diplomacy, resulting in the exchange of gifts and (3) through trade.

---

85 ADD 676 = SAA 7 79, dated 711 BC.

86 ABL 180 = SAA 1 51; ABL 1459 = SAA 1 52.

87 CT 53 628 = SAA 5 287.

88 ABL 114 r. 2; ABL 180:12; ABL 997:7; ABL 1194 r. 4; VAT 15545 r. 1f.

89 Radner 1997, 72-74.

90 ADD 419 = SAA 6 339; VAT 19495; VAT 9825; TIM 11 22; SU 51/44 = *AnSt* 7 139.

91 VAT 9330.

92 See Postgate (1979, 199f) on the possiblility that Sargon II undertook silver mining activities in the Taurus, Muhly (1973, *passim*) on sources of copper and tin, Dercksen (1996, 4-28) on sources of copper, Dalley (1988, 97-109) on sources for bronze and Maxwell-Hyslop (1974, 139-154) and Pleiner - Bjorkman (1974, 291-296) on sources of iron; compare also Liverani 1992, 160f.

Clearly, the Neo-Assyrian kings preferred to rely mainly on the first method.[93] Though we have evidence for the exchange of gifts between the king of Assyria and other rulers, it is not very exhaustive compared to other periods.[94] In contrast to this, the evidence for trade in the Neo-Assyrian period, both conducted by state agents and private entrepreneurs, is far less scanty than generally assumed.[95]

Whatever was acquired through one of these methods - private trade enterprises are of course excepted - was the property of the king. However, once in the possession of the Assyrian crown these goods started to circulate within the empire[96] since cities, temples, and officials received their share.[97] This practice is best illustrated by a letter of Sennacherib to his father Sargon II giving a detailed list of items to different members of the palace. Note that it is always silver that is the commodity to be mentioned in the first place.[98] Part of the commodities distributed came back into the crown's property by way of taxation,[99] and it is also through taxes that the king benefitted from private trade.[100]

---

93 The literature on booty and tribute in the Neo-Assyrian period is ample: Most important are the recent monograph of J. Bär (1996) and the contributions by Elat (1982, 244-251), Jankowska (1969, 253-276), Martin (1939) and Walker (1988, 111-118).

94 On gifts in the Neo-Assyrian Empire see, for now, Postgate 1994, 235-245 and Zaccagnini 1989, 193-215. A detailed study is needed.

95 Trade in the Neo-Assyrian Period is discussed in my other article in this volume.

96 The role of the temple in the distribution of money is somewhat overstated by Lipinski (1979, 565-588). The qualification of silver and copper in loans as *rešāti* of Issār of Arbail and Adad needs to be studied together with the evidence for *rēšāti*, *iškāru*, *ginû*, or *aṣudu* attested for a wide range of deities as well as members of the royal family and even the Royal Mausoleum. These references indicate that the sum thus described is intended for these gods, persons and institutions, not that their source is to be sought there. As a matter of fact, the temple is totally dependent on the king's plans and wishes in what concerns precious metals.

97 See Radner 1997, 226 on the distribution of capitives of war.

98 ABL 568 = SAA 1 34.

99 On taxation in the Neo-Assyrian Empire see the contributions by Garelli (1979, 7-18) and Hurowitz (1986, 289-294) and, most important, the monograph by Postgate (1974).

100 Postgate 1979, 205f.

Appendix 1: Metals used as currency according to the legal documents

Text	Metal used as currency	Year
CTN 2 100	bronze	835
Bi. 68 = *JCS* 7 169 no. 68	bronze	830
CTN 2 2	bronze	817
CTN 2 21	copper	803 - Adad-nērārī III
CTN 2 90	(copper or bronze)	803
CTN 2 14	copper	802
ND 673 = *BaM* 24 no. 3 pl. 60	bronze	800
CTN 2 101	bronze	798
CTN 2 91	bronze	797
CTN 2 92	bronze	795
ND 680 = *BaM* 24 no. 8 pl. 72ff	copper	794
CTN 2 93	bronze	793
CTN 2 3	copper	791
CTN 2 15	bronze	791
ND 684 = *BaM* 24 no. 9 pl. 75ff	copper	790
ND 685 = *BaM* 24 no. 10 pl. 78ff	bronze	790
ND 678 = *BaM* 24 no. 6 pl. 67ff	copper	788
ND 711 = *BaM* 24 no. 19 pl. 107ff	copper	788
ND 704 = *BaM* 24 no. 16 pl. 96ff	bronze	788
CTN 2 94	bronze	788
CTN 2 103	bronze	788
CTN 2 17	silver and copper	783
ND 679 = *BaM* 24 no. 7 pl. 70f.	copper	Paqaha (or later king?)
CTN 2 18	silver and copper	781
CTN 2 19	copper	779
CTN 2 20	[copper]	779
ND 675 = *BaM* 24 no. 4 pl. 61ff	copper	779
CTN 2 4	copper	769
CTN 2 22	copper	756
CTN 2 5	[copper]	754
CTN 2 23	copper	754
ADD 412 = SAA 6 17	silver - mina of Carchemish	747
ND 693 = *BaM* 24 no. 13 pl. 87ff	copper	746 - Tiglath-pileser III
CTN 2 24	copper	746
CTN 2 25	copper	744
ND 699 = *BaM* 24 no. 14 pl. 90ff	copper	744
ND 701 = *BaM* 24 no. 15 pl. 93ff	copper	744
ND 708 = *BaM* 24 no. 18 pl. 103ff	copper	744
CTN 2 26	copper	743
CTN 2 27	copper	743
ADD 61 = NALDK 70	copper	742
ND 677 = *BaM* 24 no. 5 pl. 64ff	copper	742
CTN 2 95	copper	740
CTN 2 106	silver - king's mina	738
CTN 2 98	copper	738
CTN 2 104	copper	738
CTN 2 107	silver - king's mina	737
ADD 320 = SAA 6 2	copper	737
CTN 2 96	copper	737
ND 686 = *BaM* 24 no. 11 pl. 81ff	copper	736

CTN 2 6	copper	735
BT 106 = *Iraq* 25 pl. xx	copper	734
ADD 90 = SAA 6 21	copper	734
ADD 415 = SAA 6 19	copper	734
ADD 1176+1236 = SAA 6 22	copper	729
CTN 2 108	copper	728
VAT 19872	silver	727
ADD 1156 = SAA 6 23	silver	727
CTN 2 29	copper	727
VAT 9764	copper	723
VAT 10022	copper	722 - Sargon II
CTN 2 249	copper	718
ADD 1195 = NALDK 353	silver	713
ADD 248 = SAA 6 6	copper	713
ADD 5 = SAA 6 26	silver - mina of Carchemish	711
ADD 1246 = SAA 6 29	silver and copper	710
BT 101 = *Iraq* 25 pl. xix	silver - merchant's mina	710
ADD 234 = SAA 6 34	silver - mina of Carchemish	709
TCL 9 58 = SAA 6 31	silver	709
ADD 350 = SAA 6 32	copper	707
ADD 365 = SAA 6 113	silver	702 - Sennacherib
ADD 1180 = SAA 6 115	silver - king's mina	702
ADD 112 = SAA 6 35	silver	700
ADD 294 = SAA 6 116	silver	700
ADD 176+323 = SAA 6 61	copper	700
ADD 328 = SAA 6 124	silver	699
ADD 1167 = SAA 6 119	silver - mina of Carchemish	699
ADD 198 = SAA 6 118	silver	698
ADD 475+510 = SAA 6 121	silver	698
ADD 468 = SAA 6 123	copper	698
ADD 1179+1233 = SAA 6 125	copper	698
VAT 9359 = *SAAB* 9 73	copper	698
VAT 9829	copper	698
VAT 19509	copper	698
ADD 179 = SAA 6 127	silver	697
ADD 381 = SAA 6 126	silver	697
BT 114 = *Iraq* 25 pl. xxii	silver - king's mina	697
BT 113 = *Iraq* 25 pl. xxi	copper	697
ADD 241 = SAA 6 130	silver - king's mina	696
ÉPHÉ 353	silver	695
ADD 34 = SAA 6 36	silver	695
ADD 244 = SAA 6 96	silver - merchant's mina	695?
ADD 31 = SAA 6 63	copper	695
ADD 58 = SAA 6 81	silver - mina of Carchemish	694
ADD 201 = SAA 6 103	silver - mina of Carchemish	694
ADD 427 = SAA 6 37	silver	694
BT 115 = *Iraq* 25 pl. xxiii	silver - king's mina, light	694
ADD 162 = SAA 6 83	copper	694
VAT 10024	copper	694
ADD 32 = SAA 6 139	silver	693
ADD 66 = SAA 6 97	silver - merchant's mina (?)	693
ADD 243 = SAA 6 138	silver - king's mina	693
ADD 240 = SAA 6 41	silver - mina of Carchemish	693
ADD 29 = SAA 6 64	copper	693
ADD 1177 = SAA 6 137	copper	693

ADD 238 // 239 = SAA 6 40 // 39	silver - mina of Carchemish	693 or 688
VAT 8925 = *SAAB* 9 137	silver	693 or 688
ADD 69 = SAA 6 146	silver	692
ADD 189 = SAA 6 144	silver	692
BT 119 = *Iraq* 25 pl. xxii	silver	692
BT 125 = *Iraq* 25 pl. xxv	silver	692
ADD 33 = SAA 6 143	silver - king's mina	692
ADD 242 = SAA 6 85	silver - king's mina	692
ADD 324 = SAA 6 142	silver - king's mina	692
ADD 326 = SAA 6 42	silver - king's mina	692
ADD 440 = SAA 6 65	silver - king's mina	692
BT 127 = *Iraq* 25 pl. xxvi	silver - king's mina; copper	692
VAT 9697 = *SAAB* 9 101	silver - mina of Carchemish	691 or 686
ADD 55 = SAA 6 104	silver - mina of Carchemish	690
VAT 8766/8767 = *SAAB* 9 122	copper	690
BT 100 = *Iraq* 25 pl. xix	copper	689
ADD 17 = SAA 6 150	silver	688
BT 126 = *Iraq* 25 pl. xxiv	copper	688
ADD 100 = SAA 6 156	silver	687
ADD 317 = SAA 6 88	silver	687
ADD 335 = SAA 6 154	silver	687
ADD 624 = SAA 6 160	silver	687
BT 105 = *Iraq* 25 pl. xix	silver	687
ADD 125 = SAA 6 158	silver - mina of Carchemish	687
ADD 43 = SAA 6 157	copper	687
ADD 218 = SAA 6 152	copper	687
ADD 456 = SAA 6 155	copper	687
ADD 232 = SAA 6 89	silver	686
ADD 374 = SAA 6 161	silver	686
VAT 9352	[silver]	686
BT 102 = *Iraq* 25 pl. xx	silver	686
BT 124 = *Iraq* 25 pl. xxii	silver - king's mina	686
ADD 9 = SAA 6 167	silver - king's mina	686
ADD 28 = SAA 6 107	silver - mina of Carchemish	686
BT 123 = *Iraq* 25 pl. xxii	copper	686
ADD 36 = SAA 6 175	silver	685
ADD 1170+1235 = SAA 6 174	silver	685
ADD 1190/1191 = SAA 6 170/171	copper	685
BT 140 = *Iraq* 25 pl. xxvi	copper	685
ADD 19/20 = SAA 6 43/44	silver	684
ND 2340 = *Iraq* 16 46	silver	684
BT 139 = *Iraq* 25 pl. xxv	silver	684
ADD 230 = SAA 6 177	silver - mina of Carchemish	684
S.U. 51/43A = *AnSt* 7 139	silver - mina of Carchemish	684
ADD 255 = SAA 6 59	copper	684
ADD 155 = SAA 6 178	silver	683
ADD 278 = SAA 6 109	silver	683
ADD 47 = SAA 6 183	silver - mina of Carchemish	683
ADD 51 = SAA 6 108	silver - mina of Carchemish	683
ADD 447 = SAA 6 90	silver - mina of Carchemish	683
ADD 463 = SAA 6 186	copper	683
ADD 21 = SAA 6 189	silver	682
ADD 215 = SAA 6 98	silver	682
BT 103 = *Iraq* 25 pl. xx	silver	682
BT 108 = *Iraq* 25 pl. xxi	silver	682

BT 128 = *Iraq* 25 pl. xxvi	silver	682	
ADD 222 = SAA 6 45	silver - mina of Carchemish	682	
ADD 89 = SAA 6 180	silver - king's mina	682	
ND 2080 = *Iraq* 16 pl. v	silver - king's mina	682	
ADD 679 = SAA 6 190	copper	682	
BT 136 = *Iraq* 25 pl. xxiv	copper	682	
ADD 30 = SAA 6 47	silver	681	
ADD 213 = SAA 6 197	silver	681	
VAT 20368 = *SAAB* 5 7	silver	681	
ADD 59 = SAA 6 91	silver - mina of Carchemish	681	
ADD 231 = SAA 6 110	silver - mina of Carchemish	681	
ADD 279 = SAA 6 196	silver - mina of Carchemish	681	
PSBA 30 111ff	copper	681	
ADD 73/74 = SAA 6 260/259	silver	680	- Esarhaddon
ADD 113 = SAA 6 221	silver	680	
ADD 212/226 = SAA 6 48/49	silver	680	
ADD 229 = SAA 6 111	silver	680	
ADD 360 = SAA 6 201	silver	680	
ADD 3/26 = SAA 6 263/262	silver - mina of Carchemish	680	
ADD 359 = SAA 6 202	silver - mina of Carchemish	680	
ADD 1194 = SAA 6 257	silver - mina of Carchemish	680	
ADD 114 = NALDK 79	silver	679	
ADD 364 = SAA 6 204	silver	679	
ADD 1154 = SAA 6 268	silver	679	
Assur 7 = *Al-Rāfidān* 17 no. 6	silver	679	
ADD 83/84 = SAA 6 223/224	silver - mina of Carchemish	679	
ADD 462 = SAA 6 269	silver [- mina of Carchemish]	679	
ADD 161 = SAA 6 265	copper	679	
ADD 18 = SAA 6 208	silver	678	
ADD 630 = SAA 6 271	silver	678	
ÉPHÉ 151	silver	678	
ADD 72 = SAA 6 272	silver	677	
RA 24 116 no. 5 = *BaM* 15 247ff	silver	677	
ADD 11 = SAA 6 240	silver	676	
ADD 629 = SAA 6 226	silver	676	
ADD 37 = SAA 6 273	silver - mina of Carchemish	676	
ADD 175 = SAA 6 274	silver - mina of Carchemish	676	
ADD 256 = SAA 6 239	silver - mina of Carchemish	676	
ADD 330 = SAA 6 210	silver - mina of Carchemish	676	
VAT 19506	silver - mina of Carchemish	676	
ADD 40 = SAA 6 214	copper	676	
ADD 186 = SAA 6 227	silver	675	
ADD 1158 = SAA 6 229	silver	675	
VAT 9694 = *SAAB* 9 95	silver	675	
VAT 14453 = *SAAB* 5 12	silver	675	
ADD 1196 = SAA 6 275	silver - mina of Carchemish	675	
ADD 70 = SAA 6 252	silver	674	
ADD 383 = SAA 6 278	silver	674	
ADD 8 = SAA 6 216	silver	673	
ADD 178 = SAA 6 244	silver	672	
ADD 425 = SAA 6 283	silver	672	
ND 2333 = *Iraq* 16 44	silver	672	
BM 30190	silver	672	
VAT 19504	silver	672	
ADD 15 = SAA 6 234	silver - mina of Carchemish	672	

ADD 64 = SAA 6 245	silver - mina of Carchemish	672
ADD 41 = SAA 6 235	silver - mina of Carchemish	671
ADD 257 = SAA 6 284	silver - mina of Carchemish	671
ADD 42 = SAA 6 291	silver	670
ADD 44 = SAA 6 237	silver	670
ADD 99 = SAA 6 236	silver	670
ADD 625 = SAA 6 287	silver	670
ADD 796+499 = SAA 6 286	silver	670
ADD 172 = SAA 6 301	silver - king's mina	670
ADD 181/199 = SAA 6 289/290	copper	670
ADD 103/104 = SAA 6 293/292	silver	669 - Ashurbanipal
VAT 8955 = *SAAB* 9 123	silver	669
ADD 183+188/187 = SAA 6 305/306	silver - mina of Carchemish	669
BM 73164 = A.H. 82-9-18, 13175	silver - mina of Carchemish	669
ADD 310 = NALDK 149	silver - mina of Garsamesi(!)	669
ADD 284+ = NALDK 295	silver	668
ADD 472 = NALDK 174	silver	668
VAT 14428 = *SAAB* 5 30	silver	668
TCL 9 61	silver	668
ADD 184 = NALDK 6	silver - king's mina (?)	668
ADD 65 = SAA 6 307	silver - mina of Carchemish	668
ADD 208 = NALDK 402	silver - mina of Carchemish	668
ADD 190 = NALDK 412	silver - mina of [...]	668
ADD 200 = SAA 6 309	silver	667
ADD 315 = NALDK 400	silver	667
ADD 1186/1187 = NALDK 85	silver	667
ADD 27 = NALDK 213	silver - mina of Carchemish	667
ADD 60 = SAA 6 317	silver	666
ADD 258/801 = SAA 6 313/312	silver - mina of Carchemish	666
ADD 331 = SAA 6 311	silver - mina of Carchemish	666
ADD 420/421 = SAA 6 315/316	silver - mina of Carchemish	666
ADD 237 = SAA 6 319	silver	665
VAT 9357	silver	665
ADD 35 = SAA 6 318	silver - mina of Carchemish	665
ND 3424 = *Iraq* 15 140	silver - mina of Carchemish	665
ND 2329 = *Iraq* 16 43	silver	664
VAT 8280	silver	664
ADD 115/116 = SAA 6 323/324	silver - mina of Carchemish	664
VAT 8270	silver	663
ND 2315 = *Iraq* 16 40	silver	663
ADD 586 = NALDK 82	silver	661
ADD 782 = *RT* 20 205 no. 4	silver	661
VAT 8643 + VAT 20782	silver	661
VAT 9683 = *SAAB* 9 99	silver	660
ADD 444/445 = SAA 6 329/330	silver - mina of Carchemish	660
ADD 233 = NALDK 146	silver	659
VAT 20394 = *SAAB* 9 Appendix 2	silver	659
TIM 11 18	silver - king's mina	659
ADD 1241 = NALDK 195	silver - mina of Carchemish	659
MADD 16	silver	659 and 658
ND 2081 = *Iraq* 16 33	silver	658
ND 2336 = *Iraq* 16 45	silver	658
ND 2337 = *Iraq* 16 pl. ix	silver	658
TCL 9 66	silver	658
ADD 48/49 = NALDK 40	silver - mina of Carchemish	658

VAT 8936 = *SAAB* 9 129	silver - mina of Carchemish	658
VAT 9400 = *SAAB* 5 38	silver	657
VAT 20352 = *SAAB* 5 29	silver	657
VAT 20359 = *SAAB* 5 55	silver	657
BT 109 = *Iraq* 25 pl. xxvi	silver	657
ND 2328 = *Iraq* 16 43	silver	656
ND 2330 = *Iraq* 16 43	silver	656
TIM 11 17	silver	655
ND 2342 = *Iraq* 16 pl. ix	silver	655
VAT 20822	silver	655
ADD 1198 = NALDK 390	silver	654
VAT 8651	silver	654
VAT 14451 = *SAAB* 5 1	silver	653
BM 103206 = *ZA* 73 252 no. 9	silver	653
CTN 3 63	silver	653
ADD 86 = NALDK 401	silver	652
ADD 7 = ARU 284	silver	650
ADD 206 = NALDK 406	silver	650
ADD 1245 = NALDK 203	silver	650
CTN 3 10	silver	650
ND 2305 = *Iraq* 16 36f.	silver	650
ND 3430 = *Iraq* 15 142	silver	650
ND 3437 = *Iraq* 15 142	silver	650
VAT 9330 = *SAAB* 9 71	silver	650
VAT 9699 =*SAAB* 9 98	silver	650
TCL 9 62	silver	650
FS Garelli (1991) 358 no. 1	silver	650
ND 3435 = *Iraq* 15 142	silver - mina of Carchemish	650
ADD 1199	silver	649
VAT 9582	silver	649
VAT 20380 = *SAAB* 9 118	silver	649
ND 3426 = *Iraq* 15 pl. xii	silver - mina of Carchemish	649
ADD 197 = NALDK 104	silver	648
MAH 16602 = *JSS* 28 155	silver	648
MAH 20613 = *RA* 22 147ff	silver	648
TH III 1160 = *AfO Bh.* 6 pl. 22	silver	648
ADD 622 = NALDK 105	silver	Adad-rēmanni (Adr)
Gir. 84/84 = *SAAB* 2 20f	silver	Adr
VAT 8232	silver - mina of [...]	Adr
Assur 4 = *Al-Rāfidān* 17 no. 4	silver - mina of Carchemish	Adr
ND 3451 = *Iraq* 15 144	silver	Adr
ND 2079 = *Iraq* 16 pl. v	silver	Adr
Assur 22 = *Al-Rāfidān* 17 no. 20	silver	Adr
VAT 19496	silver	Adr
ADD 38/39 = NALDK 81	silver	Adr
RA 24 112, no. 2 = *BaM* 15 226ff	silver	Adr
ADD 98 = NALDK 172	silver	Aššūr-gārūa-nēre (Agn)
ADD 340 = ARU 361	silver	Agn
CTN 3 37	washed silver	Agn
VAT 20351	silver	Agn
VAT 20378 = *SAAB* 5 9	silver	Agn
VAT 20379 = *SAAB* 9 107	silver	Agn
CT 33 19 = FNALD 26	burnt silver	Agn
Ass. 95721 = *SAAB* 5 39	silver - mina of Carchemish	Agn
A 2692 = *BaM* 18 223	silver - king's mina	Agn

ADD 16 = NALDK 233	silver	Aššūr-gimillī-tirri (Agt)
TIM 11 2	silver	Agt
CTN 2 219	silver	Agt
CTN 3 34	silver	Agt
ND 2082 = *Iraq* 16 34	silver	Agt
ND 2343 = *Iraq* 16 47	silver	Agt
ND 2078 = *Iraq* 16 33	silver	Agt
VAT 9703 = *SAAB* 9 90	silver	Agt
VAT 9865 = *SAAB* 9 Appendix 1	silver	Agt
VAT 20338 = *SAAB* 5 18	silver - mina of Carchemish	Agt
VAT 20761	silver	Agt
Assur 30 = *Al-Rāfidān* 17 no. 11	silver	Agt
ADD 23 = NALDK 138	silver	Aššūr-mātu-taqqin (Amt)
ADD 46 = NALDK 140	silver	Amt
ADD 80 = NALDK 141	silver	Amt
ADD 307 = NALDK 214	silver	Amt
ADD 361 = NALDK 121	silver	Amt
ADD 621 = NALDK 126	silver	Amt
BM 139950 = NALDK App. I	silver	Amt
ND 3453 = *Iraq* 15 144	silver	Amt
ND 3457 = *Iraq* 15 pl. xiii	silver	Amt
ND 3461 = *Iraq* 15 145	silver	Amt
VAT 8656	silver	Amt
ZA 73 251 no. 8	good silver	Amt
ADD 45 = NALDK 290	silver	Adad-nādin-aḫi
ADD 327 = NALDK 122	silver	Aššūr-rēmanni (Ašr)
MADD 17	silver	Ašr
CTN 3 48	silver	Ašr
VAT 5387 = VS 1 91	silver	Ašr
VAT 5393 = VS 1 94	silver	Ašr
VAT 5603 = VS 1 98	silver	Ašr
VAT 5392 = VS 1 92	silver	Ašr
VAT 14454 = *SAAB* 5 59	silver	Ašr
VAT 20347 = *SAAB* 5 6	silver	Ašr
VAT 20367 = *SAAB* 5 62	silver	Ašr
VAT 20372 = *SAAB* 5 60	silver	Ašr
ND 3421 = *Iraq* 15 140	copper	Aššūr-šarru-uṣur (Ašu)
ND 3452 = *Iraq* 15 pl. xii	silver	Ašu
TIM 11 8	silver	Bēl-aḫu-uṣur (Bau)
CTN 3 41	silver	Bau
VAT 20362 = *SAAB* 5 64	silver	Bau
VAT 20375	silver	Bau
VAT 20382 = *SAAB* 5 48	silver	Bau
Assur 20 = *Al-Rāfidān* 17 no. 33	silver	Bau
Assur 33A = *Al-Rāfidān* 17 no. 25	silver	Bau
TIM 11 25	silver	Bēl-iqbi (Biq)
ND 2319 = *Iraq* 16 41	silver	Biq
ND 3429 = *Iraq* 15 141	silver	[Biq]
VAT 8645	silver	Biq
VAT 9620 = *SAAB* 9 70	silver	Biq
VAT 14437 = *SAAB* 5 61	silver - mina of Carchemish	Biq
VAT 19511	silver	Biq
ADD 1 = NALDK 139	silver	Bēl-lū-dāri (Bld)
ADD 295	[silver ?]	Bld
ND 3420 = *Iraq* 15 140	silver	Bld

ADD 373 = NALDK 331	silver	Bulluṭu (Blṭ)
ADD 384+528 = NALDK 319	[copper ?]	Blṭ
TIM 11 15	silver	Blṭ
TIM 11 16	silver - mina of Carchemish	Blṭ
VAT 8274	silver	Blṭ
VAT 9332	silver	Blṭ
CT 33 17 = FNALD 40	silver	Blṭ
ND 3460 = *Iraq* 15 145	silver	Blṭ
ADD 87/88 = NALDK 199	silver	Daddî (Ddi)
ADD 210 = NALDK 378	silver	Ddi
ADD 221	silver	Ddi
TIM 11 6	silver	Ddi
CTN 3 36	silver	Ddi
CTN 3 53	silver	Ddi
ND 3427 = *Iraq* 15 141	silver	Ddi
VAT 8266	silver	Ddi
VAT 14442 = *SAAB* 9 112	silver	Ddi
VAT 14450 = *SAAB* 5 17	silver	Ddi
VAT 15457	silver	Ddi
VAT 20353 = *SAAB* 5 23	silver	Ddi
VAT 20371+20400' = *SAAB* 5 49	silver	Ddi
VAT 20377 = *SAAB* 5 50	silver	Ddi
Assur 9 = *Al-Rāfidān* 17 no. 8	silver	Ddi
TH ε = *AfO Bh.* 6 pl. 23	silver	Ddi
VAT 5395 = VS 1 99	silver	Iqbi-ilāni (Iqi)
VAT 8641	washed silver	Iqi
VAT 15532	silver	Iqi
Assur 14 = *Al-Rāfidān* 17 no. 13	silver	Iqi
As 62 (Munich expedition 1990)	silver	Iqi
SAAB 1 24 no. 10	silver	Iqi
ADD 400 = NALDK 132	silver	Kanūnāyu (Knn)
CTN 3 33	silver	Knn
ND 2089 = *Iraq* 16 35	silver	Knn
VAT 8937 = *SAAB* 9 130	silver	Knn
As 112 (Munich expedition 1990)	silver	Knn
Assur 6 = *Al-Rāfidān* 17 no. 5	silver - mina of Carchemish	Knn
ADD 50 = NALDK 388	silver	Mannu-kī-aḫḫē (Mka)
VAT 9309 = *SAAB* 9 75	silver	Mka
ADD 22 = NALDK 395	silver	Marduk-rēmanni
ADD 173 = NALDK 294	silver	Mušallim-Aššūr (MšA)
ADD 250 = NALDK 215	silver	MšA
ND 2320 = *Iraq* 16 pl. viii	silver	MšA
VAT 9700 = *SAAB* 9 88	silver	MšA
VAT 14449 = *SAAB* 5 5	silver	MšA
VAT 19497	silver	MšA
Assur 11 = *Al-Rāfidān* 17 no. 9	silver	MšA
ADD 311 = NALDK 1	silver	Marduk-šarru-uṣur (Mšu)
VAT 8653	silver	Mšu
VAT 15579	silver	Mšu
As 105 (Munich expedition 1990)	silver	Mšu
Ṣariza 146 = *SAAB* 2 24 fig. 5	silver	Mšu
ADD 329 = NALDK 107	silver	Nabû-da$^{\supset\supset}$inanni (Ndn)
VAT 19519	silver	Ndn
Assur 1 = *Al-Rāfidān* 17 no. 1	silver	Ndn
TH δ = *AfO Bh.* 6 pl. 20 no. 105	silver	Nabû-mār-šarri-uṣur (Nmš)

TH III 908a = *AfO Bh.* 6 pl. 18 no. 101	silver	Nmš
TH III 908c = *AfO Bh.* 6 pl. 19 no. 103	silver	Nmš
ADD 63 = NALDK 18	silver	Nabû-nādin-aḫi (Nna)
VAT 9693 = *SAAB* 9 100	silver	Nna
RA 65 85	silver	Nna
ADD 151 = NALDK 137	silver	Nabû-sākip (Nsg)
ND 3442 = *Iraq* 15 143	silver	Nsg
ND 3458 = *Iraq* 15 145	silver	Nsg
VAT 9319	silver	Nsg
VAT 9686 = *SAAB* 9 92	silver	Nsg
VAT 20342 = *SAAB* 5 13	silver	Nsg
VAT 20396 = *SAAB* 5 46	silver	Nsg
Assur 26 = *Al-Rāfidān* 17 no. 24	silver	Nsg
Assur 29 = *Al-Rāfidān* 17 no. 34	silver	Nsg
Assur 34A = *Al-Rāfidān* 17 no. 26	silver	Nsg
Assur 35A = *Al-Rāfidān* 17 no. 27	silver	Nsg
ADD 68 = NALDK 392	silver	Nabû-šar-aḫḫēšu (Nša)
ND 3434 = *Iraq* 15 142	silver	Nša
VAT 8663	washed silver	Nša
VAT 15533	silver	Nša
VAT 20393	silver	Nša
ADD 24/25 = NALDK 23b	silver - mina of Carchemish	Nša
CTN 3 45	silver	Nabû-šarru-uṣur (Nšu)
CTN 3 51	silver	Nšu
ND 2091 = *Iraq* 16 pl. v	silver	Nšu
ND 2322 = *Iraq* 16 41	silver	Nšu
ND 3438 = *Iraq* 15 142	silver	Nšu
VAT 8937 = *SAAB* 9 130	silver	Nšu
VAT 9398 = *SAAB* 5 35	silver	Nšu
VAT 9696 = *SAAB* 9 102	silver	Nšu
VAT 14440 = *SAAB* 5 10	silver	Nšu
VAT 14441 = *SAAB* 5 25	silver	Nšu
VAT 20343 = *SAAB* 5 56	[silver]	Nšu
VAT 20348 = *SAAB* 5 32	silver	Nšu
VAT 20395 = *SAAB* 5 45	silver	Nšu
VAT 20768	silver	Nšu
ZA 73 250 no. 7 = *SAAB* 3 69ff	silver	Nšu
VAT 9702 = *SAAB* 9 104	copper	Nšu
ADD 711 = NALDK 124	silver	Nšu GAL SAG
ND 3423 = *Iraq* 15 140	silver	Nšu GAL SAG
ADD 177 = NALDK 116	silver - mina of [...]	Nšu A.BA KUR
CTN 3 59	silver	Nšu A.BA KUR
ND 2093 = *Iraq* 16 pl. v	silver - mina of Carchemish	Nšu A.BA KUR
ND 2325 = *Iraq* 16 42	silver - mina of Carchemish	Nšu A.BA KUR
ND 2335 = *Iraq* 16 pl. ix	silver	Nšu A.BA KUR
ND 2338 = *Iraq* 16 pl. ix	washed silver	Nšu A.BA KUR
ND 3441 = *Iraq* 15 pl. xii	silver	Nšu A.BA KUR
VAT 9144 = *SAAB* 9 121	silver	Nšu A.BA KUR
VAT 9622 = *SAAB* 9 69	silver	Nšu A.BA KUR
VAT 9930	silver	Nšu A.BA KUR
VAT 20346 = *SAAB* 5 14	silver	Nšu A.BA KUR
VAT 5390 = VS 1 85	silver	after Nšu A.BA KUR
VAT 5400 = VS 1 84	silver	after Nšu A.BA KUR
VAT 9365 = *SAAB* 5 41	silver	after Nšu A.BA KUR
VAT 20335 = *SAAB* 5 19	silver	after Nšu A.BA KUR

VAT 20405 = *SAAB* 5 43	silver	after Nšu A.BA KUR
CT 33 16 = FNALD 21	silver	after Nšu A.BA KUR
CTN 3 60	good silver	Nabû-tappûtu-alik (Nta)
VAT 5384 = VS 1 87	silver	Nta
VAT 5391 = VS 1 93	silver	Nta
VAT 14445 = *SAAB* 9 114	silver	Nta
VAT 20370 = *SAAB* 5 65	silver	Nta
Assur 8 = *Al-Rāfidān* 17 no. 7	silver	Nta
Assur 15 = *Al-Rāfidān* 17 no. 14	silver	Nta
RA 24 114 no. 3 = *BaM* 15 240ff	good silver	Nta
MCS 2 19	silver	Nta
TH g =*AfO Bh.* 6 pl. 24 no. 110	silver	Nta
VAT 9606 = *SAAB* 9 115	silver	Pašî (Pši)
VAT 20383 = *SAAB* 9 117	silver	Pši
CTN 3 38	silver	Sîn-ālik-pāni (Sap)
CTN 3 39	silver	Sap
CTN 3 40	silver	Sap
CTN 3 61	silver	Sap
SAAB 1 20 no. 4	silver	Sap
VAT 20349 = *SAAB* 9 109	silver - mina of [...]	Sap
Assur 17 = *Al-Rāfidān* 17 no. 16	silver	Sap
TCL 9 63	silver	Sap
VAT 19500	silver	Sîn-kēnu-īde
VAT 5389 = VS 1 86	silver - mina of Carchemish	Sailu (Slu)
VAT 9619 = *SAAB* 9 67	silver	Slu
VAT 9771/VAT 9783	silver	Slu
VAT 15500 = *SAAB* 5 51	silver	Slu
LB 851 = *OLZ* 8 130	silver	Slu
ADD 67 = NALDK 413	silver - mina of Carchemish	Sîn-šumu-ibni
ADD 2 = NALDK 398	silver	Sîn-šarru-uṣur (Sšu)
ADD 207 = NALDK 136	silver	Sšu
ADD 325 = NALDK 123	silver	Sšu
ADD 414 = NALDK 127	silver	Sšu
ADD 623 = NALDK 128	silver	Sšu
ND 2318 = *Iraq* 16 pl. vii	silver	Sšu
ND 2327 = *Iraq* 16 42	silver	Sšu
ND 3432 = *Iraq* 15 142	good silver	Sšu
VAT 5602 = VS 1 95	silver	Sšu
VAT 8901 = *SAAB* 9 124	silver	Sšu
VAT 8915 = *SAAB* 9 127	silver	Sšu
VAT 9337 = *SAAB* 5 24	silver	Sšu
VAT 9623 = *SAAB* 9 68	silver	Sšu
VAT 9682 = *SAAB* 9 103	silver	Sšu
VAT 9825	silver	Sšu
VAT 15527	silver	Sšu
VAT 20389 = *SAAB* 9 117	silver	Sšu
AfO 32 39ff	silver	Sšu
CTNMC 68 = FNALD 18	silver	Sšu
ADD 81/82 = NALDK 352	silver	Ṣalmu-šarru-iqbi (Ṣši)
ADD 308 = NALDK 120	silver	Ṣši
ADD 309 = NALDK 133	silver	Ṣši
ADD 349 = NALDK 118	silver	Ṣši
ADD 446 = NALDK 119	silver	Ṣši
Assur 2 = *Al-Rāfidān* 17 no. 2	silver - mina of Carchemish	Ṣši
TIM 11 7	silver	Ṣši

VAT 15465	washed silver	Ṣši
RA 24 119 no. 10	silver	Ṣši
TIM 11 1	silver - mina of Carchemish	Ṣši
ADD 1160+1161	silver	Šamaš-šarru-ibni (Šši)
TIM 11 3	silver	Šši
TIM 11 4	silver	Šši
TIM 11 22	silver	Šši
VAT 8739 = *SAAB* 9 94	silver	Šši
VAT 20711	silver	Šši
Assur 18 = *Al-Rāfidān* 17 no. 17	silver	Šši
Assur 19 = *Al-Rāfidān* 17 no. 18	silver	Šši
Assur 21 = *Al-Rāfidān* 17 no. 19	silver	Šši
Assur 24 = *Al-Rāfidān* 17 no. 22	silver	Šši
Assur 28 = *Al-Rāfidān* 17 no. 10	silver	Šši
ADD 4 = NALDK 147	silver	Šamaš-daˀˀinanni (Ššd)
ADD 57 = NALDK 102	silver	Ššd
ND 2324 = *Iraq* 16 42	silver	Ššd
VAT 8738 = *SAAB* 9 96	silver	Ššd
RA 24 118 no. 7	silver	Ššd
ND 3431 = *Iraq* 15 142	silver	Šanta-dameqi
ND 2099 = *Iraq* 16 36	silver	Šamaš-mītu-uballiṭ (Šmu)
ND 3454 = *Iraq* 15 144	silver	Šmu
ND 3459 = *Iraq* 15 145	silver	Šmu
VAT 15464	silver	Šmu
Assur 23 = *Al-Rāfidān* 17 no. 21	silver	Šmu
BM 103956 = *ZA* 73 254 no. 11	silver	Šmu
ND 3462 = *Iraq* 15 145	silver	Ṭāb-ṣil-Sîn
ADD 214 = NALDK 217	silver	Upāqa-ana-Arbail (Upq)
ADD 628 = NALDK 25	silver	Upq
MADD 4	silver	Upq
ND 2094 = *Iraq* 16 pl. v	silver	Upq
ND 3433 = *Iraq* 15 142	silver	Upq
VAT 9145 = *SAAB* 9 125	silver	Upq
Assur 25 = *Al-Rāfidān* 17 no. 23	silver	Upq
ND 3422 = *Iraq* 15 140	silver	Urda-Nabû
ADD 642 = SAA 12 94	silver	Zababa-erība (Zbe)
ADD 1193 = NALDK 230	silver	Zbe
ND 2323 = *Iraq* 16 42	silver	Zbe
ND 2326 = *Iraq* 16 42	silver	Zbe
ND 3425 = *Iraq* 15 141	silver	Zbe
ND 3444 = *Iraq* 15 143	silver	Zbe
VAT 8660	silver	Zbe
VAT 9707 = *SAAB* 9 87	silver	Zbe
VAT 14443 = *SAAB* 9 106	silver	Zbe
VAT 20688	silver	Zbe
DeZ 12648 = SH 92/6349/12 = *SAAB* 7 121 no. 1	silver	603
DeZ 12650 = SH 92/6349/11 = *SAAB* 7 122 no. 2	silver	602
DeZ 12647 = SH 92/6349/21 = *SAAB* 7 123 no. 3	silver	602
DeZ 12649 = SH 92/6349/10 = *SAAB* 7 124 no. 4	silver	600

Appendix 2: The different silver standards according to the legal documents

Silver according to the king's mina: *ṣarpu ina manê ša šarri*

738	1 mina of silver	CTN 2 106
737	1 mina of silver	CTN 2 107
702	[x] minas of silver	ADD 1180 = SAA 6 115
697	1 mina of silver	BT 114 = *Iraq* 25 pl. xxii
696	8 1/2 minas of silver	ADD 241 = SAA 6 130
694	31/3 minas of silver	BT 115 = *Iraq* 25 pl. xxiii
693	3 minas of silver	ADD 243 = SAA 6 138
692	3 minas of silver	ADD 326 = SAA 6 42
692	[x] minas of silver	ADD 440 = SAA 6 65
692	1 mina of silver	ADD 242 = SAA 6 85
692	1 mina of silver	ADD 324 = SAA 6 142
692	1 mina of silver	ADD 33 = SAA 6 143
692	2 minas of silver	BT 127 = *Iraq* 25 pl. xxvi
686	1 1/2 minas of silver	ADD 9 = SAA 6 167
686	3 minas of silver	BT 124 = *Iraq* 25 pl. xxii
682	1/2 mina of silver	ADD 89 = SAA 6 180
682	5 1/2 minas of silver	ND 2080 = *Iraq* 16 pl. v
670	1 1/2 minas of silver	ADD 172 = SAA 6 301
668	1/2 mina of silver	ADD 184 = NALDK 6
659	1 mina of silver	TIM 11 18
Aššūr-gārūa-niri	1 mina of silver	A 2692 = *BaM* 18 223
[...]	10 shekels of silver	CTN 3 47
[...]	11 shekels of silver	A 1926
[...]	1/2 mina of silver	ADD 508 = SAA 6 38
[...]	1 1/2 minas of silver	ADD 196 = SAA 6 55
[...]	2 minas of silver	CTN 2 30
[...]	2 minas [+ x shekels] of silver	CTN 2 31
[...]	5 1/2 minas of silver	ADD 357 = NALDK 71
[...]	6 minas of silver	ADD 422 = SAA 6 50
[...]	6 minas of silver	ADD 423 = SAA 6 51
[...]	12 minas of silver	ADD 346 = NALDK 10
[...]	[x] minas of silver	ADD 727 = NALDK 175
[...]	[x] minas of silver	ADD 452 = NALDK 176
[...]	[x] minas of silver	ADD 517 = ARU 391
[...]	[x] minas of silver	ADD 521 = ARU 385

Silver according to the mina of Carchemish: *ṣarpu ina manê ša Gargamis*

747	[x] minas of silver	ADD 412 = SAA 6 17
711	20 minas of silver	ADD 5 = SAA 6 26
709	3 minas of silver	ADD 234 = SAA 6 34
699	1 mina of silver	ADD 1167 = SAA 6 119
694	2 minas of silver	ADD 201 = SAA 6 103
694	2 minas of silver	ADD 58 = SAA 6 81
693 or 688	[x] minas of silver	ADD 238 = SAA 6 40
693 or 688	18 minas of silver	ADD 239 = SAA 6 39
693	[x] minas of silver	ADD 240 = SAA 6 41
691 or 686	1/2 mina of silver	VAT 9697 = *SAAB* 9 101
690	[x] of silver	ADD 55 = SAA 6 104
687	[x] of silver	ADD 125 = SAA 6 158

686	3 minas of silver	ADD 28 = SAA 6 107
684	6 minas of silver	ADD 230 = SAA 6 177
684	6 minas of silver	SU 51/43A = *AnSt* 7 139
683	[x] minas of silver	ADD 447 = SAA 6 90
683	2 minas of silver	ADD 47 = SAA 6 183
683	1/2 mina of silver	ADD 51 = SAA 6 108
682	1 mina of silver	ADD 222 = SAA 6 45
681	20 minas of silver	ADD 59 = SAA 6 91
681	30 shekels of silver	ADD 279 = SAA 6 196
681	2 minas of silver	ADD 231 = SAA 6 110
681	4 minas of silver	A 2555
680	4 minas of silver	ADD 359 = SAA 6 202
680	1 mina of silver	ADD 1194 = SAA 6 257
680	1 mina of silver	ADD 3 = SAA 6 263
680	1 mina of silver	ADD 26 = SAA 6 262
679	10 minas of silver	ADD 462 = SAA 6 269
679	1 mina of silver	ADD 83 = SAA 6 223
679	1 mina of silver	ADD 84 = SAA 6 224
676	1 mina of silver	VAT 19506
676	2 minas of silver	ADD 175 = SAA 6 274
676	[x] minas of silver	ADD 330 = SAA 6 210
676	[x] shekels of silver	ADD 256 = SAA 6 239
676	5 minas minus 6 shekels of silver	ADD 37 = SAA 6 273
675	3 1/2 minas of silver	ADD 1196 = SAA 6 275
672	15 minas of silver	ADD 64 = SAA 6 245
672	3 1/2 minas of silver	ADD 15 = SAA 6 234
671	2 minas of silver	ADD 257 = SAA 6 284
671	1 mina of silver	ADD 41 = SAA 6 235
669	1 mina 16 shekels of silver	BM 73164 = A.H. 82-9-18, 13175
669	1 mina of silver	ADD 183+188 = SAA 6 305
669	1 mina of silver	ADD 187 = SAA 6 306
669	2 minas of silver[101]	ADD 310 = NALDK 149
668	1/2 mina of silver	ADD 208 = NALDK 402
668	3 minas of silver	ADD 65 = SAA 6 307
667	4 minas of silver	ADD 27 = NALDK 213
666	3 minas of silver	ADD 258 = SAA 6 313
666	[x] mina of silver	ADD 420 = SAA 6 315
666	[x] mina of silver	ADD 421 = SAA 6 316
666	3 minas of silver	ADD 801 = SAA 6 312
666	4 minas of silver	ADD 331 = SAA 6 311
665	1 mina of silver	ND 3424 = Ash. 1954.737
665	10 minas of silver	ADD 35 = SAA 6 318
664	10 minas of silver	ADD 115/116 = SAA 6 323/324
660	4 minas of silver	ADD 444 = SAA 6 329
660	4 minas of silver	ADD 445 = SAA 6 330
659	1 mina of silver	ADD 1241 = NALDK 195
658	9 minas 15 shekels of silver	ADD 48/49 = NALDK 40
658	13 1/2 minas of silver	VAT 8936 = *SAAB* 9 129
650	1/2 mina of silver	ND 3435 = *Iraq* 15 142
649	2 minas 1 shekel of silver	ND 3426 = *Iraq* 15 pl. xii
Adad-rēmanni	33 shekels of silver	Assur 4 = *Al-Rāfidān* 17 no. 4
Aššur-gārūa-niri	[x] minas 5 shekels of silver	VAT 9380 = *SAAB* 5 39

101 Carchemish is written URU.*ga-ár-sa-me-si*.

Aššūr-gimillī-tirri	1 mina minus 2 shekels of silver	VAT 20338 = *SAAB* 5 18
Bēl-iqbi	1 1/2 minas of silver	VAT 14437 = *SAAB* 5 61
Bulluṭu	1 mina of silver	TIM 11 16
Kanūnāyu	1 1/2 minas of silver	Assur 6 = *Al-Rāfidān* 17 no. 5
Nabû-šar-aḫḫēšu	1 mina of silver	ADD 24/25 = NALDK 23
Nabû-šarru-uṣur palace scribe	1 mina of silver	ND 2325 = Iraq 16 42
Nabû-šarru-uṣur palace scribe	1 talent 7 minas of silver	ND 2093 = *Iraq* 16 pl. v
Sailu	1 1/2 minas of silver	VAT 5389 = VS 1 86
Sîn-šumu-ibni	[x] minas of silver	ADD 67 = NALDK 413
Ṣalmu-šarru-iqbi	1 mina 2 1/2 shekel of silver	Assur 2 = *Al-Rāfidān* 17 no. 2
Ṣalmu-šarru-ibni	1 1/2 minas of silver	TIM 11 1
no eponym	1 mina 36 shekel of silver	TH ζ = *AfO Bh.* 6 no. 113
[...]	1/2 mina of silver	ADD 450 = ARU 549
[...]	1 mina of silver	ADD 182 = NALDK 220
[...]	1 mina of silver	ADD 236 = SAA 6 53
[...]	1 mina of silver	ADD 174 = SAA 6 347
[...]	1 mina of silver	ADD 203 = SAA 6 346
[...]	1 1/2 minas of silver	ADD 1157 = SAA 6 219
[...]	1 1/2 minas of silver	ADD 217 = NALDK 332
[...]	2 minas of silver	MADD 10
[...]	2 minas of silver	ADD 245 = SAA 6 250
[...]	2 minas of silver	A 2565
[...]	5 minas of silver	ADD 271 = SAA 6 344
[...]	5 minas of silver	ADD 270 = SAA 6 343
[...]	8 minas of silver	MADD 8
[...]	10 minas of silver	ADD 52 = SAA 6 248
[...]	10 minas of silver	ADD 253 = SAA 6 57
[...]	10 minas of silver	ADD 418 = SAA 6 335
[...]	17 1/2 minas of silver	ADD 471 = SAA 6 326
[...]	[x] minas of silver	ADD 587 = ARU 583
[...]	[x] minas of silver	ADD 519 = SAA 6 99
[...]	[x] minas of silver	ADD 725 = SAA 6 54
[...]	[x] minas of silver	ADD 260 = NALDK 218
[...]	[x] minas of silver	ADD 247 = SAA 6 342
[...]	[x] minas of silver	ADD 429 = SAA 6 334
[...]	[x] minas of silver	ADD 451 = SAA 6 333
[...]	[x] minas of silver	A 795

Silver according to the merchant's mina: *ṣarpu ina manê ša tankāri*

710	1/2 mina of silver	BT 101 = *Iraq* 25 pl. xix
695?	3 minas of silver	ADD 244 = SAA 6 96
693	17 minas of silver	ADD 66 = SAA 6 97
692	1 mina 1/2 shekel of silver	A 316
686	1/2 mina of silver	A 2650
671	1 mina of silver	ND 3479 = *Iraq* 15 147
[...]	1/2 mina of silver	ADD 254 = NALDK 219
[...]	1/2 mina of silver	VAT 9367 = *SAAB* 5 37
[...]	2 minas of silver	CTN 2 248
[...]	5 3/4 minas of silver	ADD 434 = SAA 6 27

Appendix 3: Penalty clauses stipulating the payment of processed gold and/or silver

Year	Text	Metal	To be given to
802	CTN 2 14	“red” (SA_5) gold	Inurta of Kalhu
778	CTN 2 53	washed silver and heated gold	Inurta of Kalhu
754	CTN 2 23	silver and heated gold	Inurta of Kalhu
742	ND 677 = *BaM* 24 no. 5	washed silver and heated gold	Inurta of Kalhu
736	ND 686 = *BaM* 24 no. 11	washed silver and heated gold	Issār of Nineveh
735	CTN 2 6	washed silver and heated gold	Issār of Nineveh
727	ADD 1156 = SAA 6 23	washed silver and heated gold	
717	ADD 394 = SAA 6 11	[washed silver] and heated gold	Inurta of Kalhu
709	TCL 9 58 = SAA 6 31	heated gold	Issār of Nineveh
695?	ADD 244 = SAA 6 96	washed silver and heated gold	Adad of Urakka
693	ADD 243 = SAA 6 138	washed silver and [heated gold]	Mullissu
692	ADD 242 = SAA 6 85	washed silver and heated gold	Issār of Nineveh
692	ADD 326 = SAA 6 42	washed silver and heated gold	[...]
681	MADD 6 = SAA 6 194	[washed silver] and heated gold	
680	ADD 360 = SAA 6 201	washed silver and heated gold	Issār of Nineveh
671	ADD 257 = SAA 6 284	washed silver and heated gold	Inurta of Kalhu
671	ADD 503 = SAA 6 298	washed silver and heated gold	Inurta of Kalhu
670	ADD 172 = SAA 6 301	washed silver and heated gold	Issār of Nineveh
669	ADD 310 = NALDK 149	washed silver and heated gold	Issār of Nineveh
669	BM 73164 = A.H. 82-9-18, 13175	washed silver and heated gold	[Inurta] of Kalhu
668	CTN 3 57	washed silver and heated gold	Inurta of Kalhu
666	ADD 448 = SAA 6 314	washed silver and heated gold	Issār of Nineveh
663	ADD 470 = SAA 6 325	washed silver and heated gold	Issār of Nineveh
660	ADD 444 = SAA 6 329	washed silver and [heated gold]	Issār of [Nineveh]
659	ADD 233 = NALDK 146	washed silver and heated gold	Issār of Nineveh
652	ADD 86 = NALDK 401	silver and heated gold	Issār of Nineveh
649	ND 3426 = *Iraq* 15 pl. xii	washed silver and heated gold	Inurta of Kalhu
Aššur-mātu-taqqin	ADD 361 = NALDK 121	washed silver and gold	Issār of Nineveh
Aššur-rēmanni (Ašr)	VAT 5603 = VS 1 98	washed silver and heated gold	Aššūr
Ašr	VAT 5393 = VS 1 94	washed silver and heated gold	Aššūr
Ašr	*PSBA* 30 (1908) 137f	washed silver and heated gold	Aššūr
Bulluṭu	ADD 384+528 = NALDK 319	heated gold	Issār of Arbail
Iqbi-ilāni	CTN 3 52	washed silver and heated gold	Inurta
Marduk-šarru-uṣur	ADD 311 = NALDK 1	washed silver and heated gold	Issār of Nineveh
Nabû-šarru-uṣur	CTN 3 51	washed silver	[Inurta] of Kalhu
Sîn-šarru-uṣur (Sšu)	ADD 414 = NALDK 127	washed silver and heated gold	Issār of Nineveh
Sšu	VAT 8915 = *SAAB* 9 127	washed silver and heated gold	Issār of Nineveh
Sšu	BM 103389 = *AfO* 32 39ff	heated gold and washed silver (*ma-ši-i*)	Issār of Nineveh
Sšu	ND 2327 = *Iraq* 16 42	silver and heated gold	Inurta of Kalhu
Sšu	VAT 8901 = *SAAB* 9 124	washed (LUḪ-*i*) silver and heated gold	Sîn of Harran
Sîn-ālik-pāni	TH 3 908e = *AfO Bh.* 6 no. 106	washed silver and heated gold	Adad of Guzana
Sailu	LB 851 = P 350 = *OLZ* 8 130		washed silver and heated
		(*sak-rum*) gold	Aššūr

Sailu	VAT 5389 = VS 1 86	washed silver and heated (*sak-rum*) gold	Aššūr
Ṣalmu-šarri-iqbi	TIM 11 1	washed silver and heated gold	Issār of Nineveh
Zababa-erība	ADD 642 = SAA 12 94	washed silver and heated gold	Inurta of Kalhu
Zababa-erība	ND 2323 = *Iraq* 16 42	washed silver and heated gold	Nergal of Kalhu
Zababa-erība	ND 2326 = *Iraq* 16 42	washed silver and heated gold	Inurta of Kalhu
[...]-ilā'ī	ADD 1162 = NALDK 330	washed silver and heated gold	Issār of Nineveh
[...]	ADD 289 = ARU 191	washed silver	
[...]	VAT 5388 = VS 1 89	washed silver and heated (*sak-rum*) gold	Aššūr
[...]	ADD 500 = NALDK 117	washed silver and heated gold	Adad of Dūr-Bēl
[...]	ADD 613 = NALDK 5	washed silver and heated gold	Inurta of Kalhu
[...]	ADD 477 = SAA 6 299	washed silver and heated gold	Inurta of Kalhu
[...]	ADD 1185 = NALDK 396	washed silver and heated gold	Inurta of Kalhu
[...]	CTN 3 35	washed silver and heated gold	Inurta of Kalhu
[...]	ND 705 = *BaM* 24 no. 17	heated gold	Inurta of Kalhu
[...]	ADD 422 = SAA 6 50	silver and heated gold	Issār of Nineveh
[...]	ADD 263 = SAA 6 87	washed silver and heated gold	Issār of Nineveh
[...]	ADD 804 = SAA 6 251	washed silver and [heated gold]	Issār of Nineveh
[...]	ADD 471 = SAA 6 326	washed silver and heated gold	Issār of Nineveh
[...]	ADD 418 = SAA 6 335	washed silver and heated gold	Issār of Nineveh
[...]	ADD 495 = NALDK 76	washed silver and heated gold	Issār of Nineveh
[...]	ADD 357 = NALDK 71	washed silver and heated gold	Issār of Nineveh
[...]	ADD 334 = NALDK 200	washed silver and heated gold	Issār of Nineveh
[...]	ADD 464 = NALDK 323	silver and heated gold	Issār of Nineveh
[...]	ADD 706 = ARU 343	washed silver and heated gold	Issār of Nineveh
[...]	ADD 260 = NALDK 218	washed silver and heated gold	Issār of Nineveh
[...]	ADD 1175+= NALDK 232	washed silver and heated gold	Issār of Nineveh
[...]	ADD 426 = NALDK 145	[washed silver] and heated gold	Issār of [...]
[...]	ADD 722 = ARU 575	[washed silver] and heated gold	Mullissu
[...]	ADD 585 = ARU 584	washed silver and [heated gold]	Nabû of [...]
[...]	ADD 417 = NALDK 207	washed silver and heated gold	Nergal
[...]	ADD 389 = NALDK 83	washed silver and heated gold	Nikkal
[...]	ADD 336 = NALDK 348	washed silver and heated gold	Sîn of Dūr-šarrukēn
[...]	ADD 303 = SAA 6 20	washed silver and heated gold	[...]
[...]	ADD 508 = SAA 6 38	[washed silver] and heated gold	[...]
[...]	ADD 378 = SAA 6 217	washed silver and heated gold	[...]
[...]	ADD 419 = SAA 6 336	washed silver	[...]
[...]	ADD 424 = SAA 6 341	[washed silver] and heated gold	[...]
[...]	ADD 413 = NALDK 212	washed silver and [heated gold]	[...]
[...]	ADD 578 = ARU 588	washed silver] and heated gold	[...]
[...]	ADD 564 = ARU 593	[washed silver] and heated gold	[...]
[...]	TIM 11 34	washed silver and heated gold	[...]
[...]	Kelsey 89519 = *AfO* 27 85	washed silver and heated gold	[...]

Appendix 4: Prices in the Neo-Assyrian Period

Only recently, F. M. Fales has discussed the prices and the underlying mechanisms in the Neo-Assyrian period.[102] Since I generally share his interpretation of the evidence I refer the reader to his study and restrict myself to giving up-to-date attestation lists for the key-word *maḫīru* "exchange rate" and the so-called *Getreidekursangaben*.[103]

I agree with Fales's conclusion that *maḫīru* was "a commonly recognized and accepted mechanism which provided general guidelines in space and time".[104] Correctly stating that "this is a far cry from the reality of a 'market economy' *stricto sensu*" he is nevertheless right in my opinion to stress that the situation is "equally remote from the concept and practice of uncontrolled barter".[105]

Maḫīru "exchange rate"

Attestations in texts from Nineveh:

*Legal documents:

ADD 125 = SAA 6 158 (687) - wine debt-note.
ADD 122/123 = SAA 6 182/181 (683) - wine debt-note.
ADD 124 = SAA 6 232 (675) - wine debt-note.

*Assyrian letters:

ABL 2 = SAA 10 226 (Adad-šumu-uṣur to Ashurbanipal).
CT 53 930+ (Esarhaddon to [...]lî).

*Babylonian letters:

ABL 282 (Bēl-ibni from the Sealand to Ashurbanipal).
ABL 1445 ([...] to the king).

*Astrological reports:

For attestations see *CAD* M/1, 94 *sub maḫīru* 2.c and Hunger 1992, 326b.

Attestations in texts from Kalhu:

*Legal documents:

ND 2081 = *Iraq* 16 33 (658) - silver debt-note - delivery contract for barley.
ND 2335 = *Iraq* 16 pl. ix (eponymy of Nabû-šarru-uṣur) - delivery contract for barley.
ND 3445 = *Iraq* 15 143 (eponymy of Sîn-šarru-uṣur) - debt-note - delivery contract.
CTN 3 19 (date lost) - barley debt-note.

102 Fales 1996, 11-35, see especially 20-26.
103 First recognized and named by Deller (1964, 257-261).
104 Fales 1996, 25.
105 Fales 1996, 25f, especially n. 52.

*Letters:

NL 52 (Aššūr-mātka-tēre to Sargon II or Tiglathpileser III).

CTN 2 204 (too fragmentary to assign).

Attestations in texts from Assur:

*Legal documents:

A 1805 = Ass. 21506ba (692) - silver debt-note.

A 2779 = Ass. 21506bq (eponymy of Nabû-[...]) - barley debt-note.

ZA 73 250 no. 1 (date lost) - animal debt-note.

Attestations in texts from elsewhere:

*Legal document from Ma^{c}allānāte:

LBAF Acc.no. 803 = C 39 = Grayson (1981) (eponymy of Adad-rēmanni) - judicial document.

Attestations in the royal inscriptions:

*Inscriptions of Sargon II:

Ann. 18 = Fuchs 1994:88: "I opened the sealed harbour of Egypt, mixed the people of Assyria and Egypt and" *ú-še-pi-šá ma-ḫi-ru* // Gadd 1954:179 iv 49: [*ú-še-p*]*i-šá ma-ḫi-ru.*

Ann. 233 = Fuchs 1994:131: *ma-ḫi-ri* KÙ.BABBAR *ki-ma si-pár-ri i-na qé-reb* KUR ^{d}*aš-šur*^{ki} *i-šim-mu.*

Zyl. 41 = Fuchs 1994:38: *áš-šu* ... ŠE.GIŠ.Ì *ki-i* ^{d}NISABA *i-na* KI.LAM *šá-a-mi.*

*Inscriptions of Esarhaddon:

Bab. A-G, Episode 4a: 33 = Borger 1956:13: KÙ.BABBAR [KÙ].GI *ni-siq-ti* NA$_4$.MEŠ *a-na* KUR.*elam-ma*^{ki} *ip-šu-ru ma-ḫi-riš* // Episode 4b: 7: [...] É.KUR *a-na* KUR.*e-lam-ti ip-šu-ru ma-ḫi-riš.*

*Inscriptions of Ashurbanipal:

Prism A ix 48f = Borger 1996:67: *ina qa-bal-ti* KUR-*ia* ANŠE.A.AB.BA.MEŠ *ina* 1 GÍN 1/2 GÍN *kas-pi* [49] *i-šam-mu ina* KÁ *ma-ḫi-ri* // Prism B viii 18f = Borger 1996:114: *qa-bal-ti* KUR-*ia* ANŠE.*gam-mal ina* 1 GÍN *ina* 1/2 GÍN *kas-pi* [19] *i-šam-mu ina* KÁ *ma-ḫi-ri* // VAT 5600 ii 1f = Borger 1996:77: *ina qa-bal-ti* KUR-*ia* ANŠE.*gam-mal*.MEŠ [2] *ina* 1 GÍN 1/2 GÍN *kás-pi i-šam-mu ina* KÁ *ma-ḫi-ri.*

Prism B i 36-38 = Prism C i 128-130 = Borger 1996:93: 10 (// 12) ANŠE ŠE.PAD 1 (// 3) ANŠE GEŠTIN.MEŠ [37] [(129)] 2-BÁN Ì.MEŠ 1 GÚ.UN SÍG.MEŠ [38] [(130)] *ina nap-ḫar* KUR-*ia* KI.LAM *nap-šú i-šam-mu ina* 1 GÍN *kas-pi.*

K 4449 = Lambert 1957/58:384 r. iii 12f: *šá a-na* ZÍZ.A.AN ŠE.BAR *ma-ḫi-ri* [...] [13] *šá ana* X.A.AN *ma-ḫi-ri* x [...].

Getreidekursangaben[106]

Year	Provenience	Text	Rate	*ina šatti (ukli) la bašīti*
791	Kalhu	CTN 2 15*	- -	x
791	Kalhu	CTN 2 16*	- -	x
742	Assur	VAT 9749 = *SAAB* 9 136*	[1 sql. silver] : [...] barley	
723	Assur	VAT 9764	1 mn. copper : [x *sū*] 4 *qa* barley	
698	Assur	VAT 19509	[1 mn. copper] : 4 *sū* barley	
698	Assur	VAT 9359 = *SAAB* 9 73*	1 mn. copper : 2 *sū* barley	
probably 698 (*šīāmu*, copper)				
	Assur	VAT 9842*	1 mn. copper : 2 *sū* 4 *qa* barley	
probably 698 (*šīāmu*, copper)				
	Assur	Ass. 10805ed*	1 mn. [copper] : [x *sū* barley]	
probably 698 (*šīāmu*, copper, sealing official)				
	Assur	VAT 10010	1 mn. copper : [x *sū*] barley	
probably 698 (*šīāmu*, copper, sealing official)				
	Assur	VAT 10696*	1 mn. copper : [...]	
probably 698 (archive)				
	Ninua	ADD 632 = SAA 6 285	[1 sql. silver] : 6 *sū* barley	
probably 698 (archive)				
	Huzirina	SU 51/36 = *AnSt* 7 139*	1 sql. (silver) : 2 *sū* barley	
Aššur-šarru-uṣur				
	Kalhu	ND 3421 = FNALD 8*	1 1/2 mn. copper : 1 *qa* barley	x
Nabû-mār-šarri-uṣur				
	Guzana	TH 3 908c = *AfO Bh.* 6 no. 103*	1 sql (silver) : 1 *sū* barley	
Nabû-šarru-uṣur				
	Assur	VAT 9930*	1 sql. (silver) : 1 *sū* barley	
eponymy after Nabû-šarru-uṣur				
	Assur	VAT 9365 = *SAAB* 5 41*	1 sql. silver : 1 *sū* barley	
eponymy after Nabû-šarru-uṣur				
	Assur	VAT 20405 = *SAAB* 5 43*	1 sql. silver : 1 *sū* barley	
probably Nabû-šarru-uṣur or after him (sealing officials)				
	Assur	HK 9572*	1 mn. copper : 2 *sū* barley	
[...]	Ninua	ADD 522 = ARU 380		
[...]	Kalhu	*SAAB* 1 18f. no. 2	[...]	[...]

In a recent paper, P. Vargyas compared the *Getreidekursangaben* with the tariffs as given in the royal inscriptions of the second and first millennium. Whereas the *Getreidekursangaben* obviously reflect real prices which are very low due to economic strain the tariffs in the royal inscriptions give extremely favorable prices. Vargyas,[107] essentially following J. D. Hawkins's study of the tariffs in the Assyrian, Babylonian, and Hieroglyphic Luwian sources,[108] links this with the ideal of the "fair price", a literary topos expressing prosperity and well-being.

106 The asterisk is used to mark those references already discussed by Deller (1964) and Fales (1996).

107 Vargyas 1997, 185-190.

108 Hawkins 1986, 93-102, see also Hawkins - Morpurgo-Davies 1982, 91-105.

MONEY IN THE NEO-BABYLONIAN INSTITUTIONS*

A.C.V.M. BONGENAAR (LEIDEN)

No Assyriologist will deny that silver played an important rôle in Mesopotamian institutional life. Thousands of texts in the institutional archives record the issue of silver as payment for personnel or for the purchase of commodities, and the receipt of silver by these institutions as payment of taxes, rent, gifts and the like. Again thousands of texts record loans - either private or institutional - which are due in silver. Despite the abundant evidence about silver in Mesopotamian society, many scholars hesitate to call it "money". In the present paper I would like to investigate some of the theories about money in pre-industrialized societies found in studies of Mesopotamian economics. Secondly, I will present the evidence for the use of silver in the two best known institutional archives from the later period, the Neo-Babylonian - early Achaemenid temple archives of Eanna at Uruk and Ebabbar at Sippar. Finally, I will investigate how information from these two archives relates to the theories about money.

1. *Money: Payment, Standard, Exchange and Hoarding. Polanyi and beyond*

It is the economic historian Karl Polanyi to whom scholars often refer whenever they deal with theoretical explanations for the intractable socio-economic data of the Ancient Near East, either following or refuting his theories.[1] Polanyi's theories about trade and markets in early societies made an enormous impact in the late fifties and early sixties, not in the least because he was the first to describe Mesopotamian economics by means of anthropological and economic vocabulary and insight. Although some immediately rejected his theory about a marketless Mesopotamia based on redistribution,[2] there is no reason to reject his theory about money and its uses in early societies without further examination.[3]

---

* I would like to thank H.D. Baker for her valuable comments as well as for her revision of my sometimes incomprehensible English, G. van Driel for discussing this paper with me, and M. Jursa for his remarks which are always to the point, and often prevent me from overlooking secondary literature. The research for this paper is made possible by a postdoc grant from The Netherlands Organization for Scientific Research (NWO).

1 Recently *e.g.* J.F. Robertson, 'The Social and Economic Organization of Ancient Mesopotamian Temples', in J.M. Sasson (ed.), *Civilizations of the Ancient Near East* (New York 1995), Vol. I, 443-454 (especially 447 and 454), and D.A. Warburton, *State and Economy in Ancient Egypt. Fiscal Vocabulary of the New Kingdom*, Fribourg/Göttingen 1997, 83-99.

2 *E.g.* W.F. Leemans, *JEOL* 15 (1957-58), 203-204, *RlA* 4 (1972-75), 89 (*s.v.* Handel), and the introduction of his *Foreign Trade* (1960).

3 I do not intend to write an overview of *all* theories about "early" money. For some literature, see Renger 1995, 271-324, and Powell 1996, 224-242. Note that in recent publications the redistribution theory keeps turning up in connection with the use of silver as money, *e.g.* J. Williams (ed.), *Money. A History*, London 1997, 17f.

According to Polanyi's definition of money, three different uses of money can be distinguished: payment, standard and exchange (Polanyi 1957b, 264-266). He defined payment as "the discharge of obligations in which quantifiable objects change hands", standard as "the equating of amounts of different kinds of goods for definite purposes" and exchange as the result of "a need for quantifiable objects for indirect exchange". In the case of payment one should think of the discharge of several kinds of obligations in primitive societies (blood money, bride price, and in later times taxes, rent and tribute). The standard or accounting use of money allows the interchangeability of staples, and thus is important in societies where barter and the storage and management of staples are daily routine. Polanyi called the standard use of money "essential to the elasticity of a redistributive system". The exchange use of money, *i.e.* acquiring money objects through direct exchange in order to acquire the desired objects through a further act of exchange, occurs with organized trade, especially in markets, or, in the absence of markets, in the trading ports of commercial empires, which Polanyi called "ports of trade". Polanyi distinguished two further derivatives of money in primitive societies: the ideal unit and the operational device (Polanyi 1957b, 265). Ideal units were "mere verbalizations or written symbols employed as if they were quantifiable units, mainly for payment and as standard". As examples of the use of ideal units he had in mind the Old Assyrian trade and the earliest temple economies of Mesopotamia: the practice of clearing (written debt) accounts without the intervention of money objects, which he called "common facts of primitive life, and not, as was often believed, peculiar to monetarized economies". The operational device occurs (occasionally) in societies where different quantifiable objects are used for different purposes, that is: different objects for arithmetical, statistical, taxational, administrative or other non-monetary purposes (Polanyi 1957b, 265-266; Dalton 1975, 99-100).

Two notions are crucial in Polanyi's ideas about money: present day money is "all-purpose money" ("it is used for payment and as a standard precisely because it is a means of exchange"; Polanyi 1957b, 264), as opposed to the "special-purpose money" of early societies. Secondly, all-purpose money is dependent upon the existence of markets, whereas special-purpose money occurs in the very absence of markets. Of the latter, he regarded the Old Babylonian period as a fine example, with barley as the means of payment, silver as the standard, and barley, silver, wool, and other commodities as means of exchange. Thus, Polanyi explained the special-purpose money in the Old Babylonian period as a result of the absence of markets (Polanyi 1957a, 12-26; Dalton 1968, 189).

After the appearance of *Trade and Market* in 1957, Polanyi came up with a fourth use of money which he called "hoarding" or the storage use of money, *i.e.* the accumulation of goods which can be used as payment at a later moment (Dalton 1968, 183-188). Polanyi distinguishes two types of stored wealth in early societies: treasure and staple finance. Treasure is formed of prestige goods which bestowed prestige upon both giver and recipient, and which could serve as money only in a narrow elite circle ("treasure finance") since the common staples, like most foodstuffs, were rarely used to store wealth. Staple finance, on the contrary, occurs when people or institutions start accumulating subsistence goods to use as a means of payment. Now, Mesopotamia could be described as a society where staple-economy was practised, in which the redistribution of accumulated goods as payments as well as barter in kind, and the clearing of accounts without the intervention of money objects took place. In Polanyi's view, these characteristics prevented the development of a market system in (the older periods of)

Mesopotamia. K.R. Veenhof showed that Polanyi's ideas were partly based on inaccurate information about Mesopotamia.[4] He substantiated that silver in Old Assyrian trade could be regarded as "money" according to Polanyi's definition, that is: Old Assyrian silver was used as a standard, as payment, and as an indirect means of exchange. Polanyi's fourth use of silver, hoarding, easily fits into the Old Assyrian example. The crux is, of course, that Polanyi wanted at all costs to connect modern (general-purpose) money with a market system, and primitive (special-purpose) money with the absence of a (free) market system.[5] Nevertheless, Polanyi's ideas influenced A.L. Oppenheim (1957, 27-37; about the use of silver see Oppenheim 1977, 86-87). Therefore we find in *The Chicago Assyrian Dictionary* the translation "money (as medium of exchange), price, value, payment" as the second meaning of the lemma *kaspu*, "silver" (*CAD* K, 247).

George Dalton, who explained and elaborated on Polanyi's theories, further divided special-purpose money into two classes: primitive money and primitive valuables (1975, 97-98). Neither primitive money nor primitive valuables were general-purpose money, for two reasons: they did not perform all the monetary functions (payment, exchange, hoarding and accounting), and they could not usually be used in both market and non market transactions. Primitive money he defined as consisting of "divisible and relatively uniform objects used in ordinary commercial purchase and sale in the market sector of aboriginal economies in which variants of reciprocity and redistribution were usually more important modes of transactions." Thus, in his eyes, primitive money was used to buy foodstuffs and other small consumption goods on a local marketplace, whereas land, labour, and the like, were acquired through other systems of exchange. Primitive valuables like shells, bracelets, and similar objects, on the other hand, were "less uniform and less easily divisible than primitive money", often used for certain non commercial transactions (blood money, fines, sacrifice, etc.) in stateless societies. They occur in economies in which markets are (nearly) absent, and are not, therefore, used for commercial payments. He preferred the term "treasure" for primitive valuables in state societies.

Because the price of goods, bought with primitive money or valuables, was not formed by market forces, Polanyi and Dalton used the term "equivalences" (Polanyi 1957b, 268-269; Oppenheim 1957, 32; Dalton 1975, 99), which one can define as "substitutable goods in prescribed proportions". Their idea was that the storehouses of palace (or temple) economies, which received taxes and other obligations in kind, could stipulate a staple-to-staple ratio, which made it possible to accept dates instead of barley or wool instead of dates as payment of rent, taxes, etc. Equivalences are the underlying principle of what Polanyi called a system of staple finance, *i.e.* "the dealing with staples on a large scale, involving inventories and accountancy, for the purpose of budgeting,

4 Veenhof 1972, 348-357.

5 Dalton (1975, 87-88) clarified the notion "general-purpose money" (or "all-purpose money") as follows: dollars, for example, are general-purpose money because 1) dollars perform all four monetary uses (payment, exchange, hoarding and accounting), and 2) one can make commercial exchanges and payments in dollars (*e.g.* buying goods) as well as non commercial payments (*e.g.* paying taxes and fines). Dalton calls these characteristics "a direct expression of our market dominance and market integration. Our money is what it is because our market system is what it is." However, Dalton also points to the fact that not *everything* in a market society is purchaseable or dischargeable: when convicted of murder, we cannot discharge the obligation by a cash payment, but we have to pay by going to jail or worse.

balancing, controlling, and checking" (Polanyi 1960, 343ff). Staple finance is always in kind. Instead of money, equivalences are set up between staples, and the staple which is used as a standard acts as money. To conclude: according to Polanyi and Dalton, Mesopotamia had an economy where primitive money was used to buy small goods in the local market place, where land, labour and the bulk of livelihood were acquired without primitive money (*i.e.* through redistribution or reciprocity), and where equivalences were established, either by custom, statute or proclamation, to enable the storehouses of palaces and temples to manage the array of commodities in an efficient way.

In the last decade, J. Renger has proved to be a supporter of Polanyi's theories.[6] Recently, he devoted a long article to the question of whether Mesopotamia had money or not (Renger 1995, 271-324), investigating which commodities - according to Polanyi's theory about money - served as a standard, and/or were used for payment, exchange, or hoarding in every period of Mesopotamian history (Renger 1995, 286-287, fig. 2). I will summarize here his three main conclusions. The first of these is that at least from 2500 B.C. onwards silver in Mesopotamia fulfilled the four monetary functions as defined by Polanyi, although not exclusively. Barley also performed at least three monetary functions (standard, exchange, payment), gold, copper and tin were important standards in certain periods, for hoarding precious metals and all kind of prestige goods could be used, and as medium of exchange every commodity served the purpose. The second conclusion of Renger is that these four monetary functions of silver and other commodities occurred in certain economic spheres only ("sectorial" use of silver; Renger 1995, 318). In the villages, but also in the cities to a certain extent, agricultural and other products will have served as medium of exchange on the basis of reciprocity throughout Mesopotamian history, which made the use of silver redundant. The urban elite, in close contact with the institutional households (temple and palace), was affected by the increasing use of silver as the standard of these institutions, which is why silver developed into a more and more important means of payment also. Renger's third conclusion follows from the second: the need for silver in Mesopotamia was relatively small (Renger 1995, 293, 302 and 317), not only because a large part of the population did not have a need for silver as the medium of exchange, but also because of the use of debt notes in business transactions. Without the silver actually changing hands, debt notes of silver could be discharged by balancing them with counterclaims.

For the Neo-Babylonian and Achaemenid period Renger (1995, 300-304) postulated that large parts of the farming lands were either in the hands of the crown (and given to small tenants in return for military service), or in the hands of the temples (and leased out to the so-called rent farmers who in turn leased the land out to small tenants). These small tenants, working on the domains of crown or temple, will have lived at subsistence level, and will have had little possibility of obtaining silver. On the other hand, we find entrepreneurs from the urban elite, in close contact with the institutions, who occupied themselves with the management of the agricultural production of these institutions and

---

6 In his article 'Patterns of Non-Institutional Trade' (1984), Renger described the Assyriological response to Polanyi's theories (32-42), and concluded that Polanyi's critics "did not discuss these theoretical premises sufficiently" (42). He further concluded that evidence from the Old Babylonian period proved (some of) Polanyi's ideas to be still valid (114). Renger defended Polanyi again in his article 'On Economic Structures' (1994), this time against the economist Morris Silver.

the distribution of farming produce. For these entrepreneurs, silver served as the standard, as medium of exchange and as means of payment. Whether the amount of circulating silver was large or not, is difficult to establish according to Renger. The system of counterbalancing debt notes in the business transactions of the entrepreneurs ("moneyless business") could be explained by assuming a shortage of silver, but the ample references to the different qualities of silver (colour and purity) in the texts, as well as the large quantities of silver which are reported to be sent annually to Persia during Achaemenid rule over Mesopotamia, favour the idea that a large quantity of silver was present in Babylonia. We will return to this matter after we have discussed the evidence from the institutional archives.

A completely different, rather non-theoretical and refreshing, approach towards the question of whether money existed in Mesopotamia or not, is found in a series of articles by M.A. Powell (1978b, 1990, and 1996). "Money, of course, did exist in ancient Mesopotamia" is his point of departure (Powell 1996, 225). Because Mesopotamia did not have coins before the end of the Achaemenid period, money was substance orientated, therefore it was always weighed and not counted. Every staple or commodity could be used as money, but barley in general served as the cheap, local money (institutions could store it, and feed their dependents with it or turn it into all sorts of other things), whereas silver served as the high-range money, *e.g.* for long-distance overland trade. Moreover, silver in amounts of less than one shekel probably rarely changed hands, according to Powell, because ancient technology did not permit sufficiently accurate weighing, and one shekel still constituted about a month's pay for labour.[7] Nevertheless Powell echoes Polanyi's view when he states that "Mesopotamian monies are distinguished from ordinary commodities by being exchanged, sometimes for one another, more often as payments for other tangible commodities or for other less tangible goods (...). They were used as indices or standards of value and were stockpiled as storable wealth" (Powell 1996, 227). Here the "money = exchange + payment + standard + hoarding" definition of Polanyi recurs.

Powell pays much attention to the qualities of silver which are mentioned in written documents from the Neo-Babylonian and later periods (1996, 230ff; 1978b, 222ff). Apart from certain expressions denoting the specific fineness of the silver, which one could not possibly have observed with the naked eye, some qualifications of silver in Neo-Babylonian texts are left unexplained. Powell has a point when he assumes that some authority might have mixed silver with a percentage of alloy, and then marked it with a certain imprint, so that the people who used the silver afterwards could distinguish between the different qualities. In that way, the words *nuḫḫutu* ("alloyed?") and *ginnu* ("mark denoting quality?") could be explained. Although texts from the later period mention the quality of silver with increasing frequency, Powell concludes that concern and awareness of the quality of money substances must have been present in Mesopotamia throughout its history, but that people did not feel the need to record it.

---

7 Powell 1996, 229. As far as I can see, this conflicts with what he previously wrote in 1978b, 222, notably that the term *bitqu*, literally "cutting", developed into the meaning "one-eighth of a shekel" because of the practice of cutting one-eighth pieces from a coil (ḪAR/*semeru*) especially made for that purpose. His idea at the time was that amounts of silver larger than one-eighth of a shekel were exchanged in some other form, and that smaller amounts were paid in fragments or scrap silver.

2. *Incoming Silver in the Neo-Babylonian Temple Organizations*

The Neo-Babylonian temple organizations were not involved in mining activities, so the first question should be: where did the silver in the temple organizations come from? The texts are in most cases silent about the physical origin of silver, but there is ample evidence in the archives for the receipt and the expenditure of silver. The temple organizations had four sources of incoming silver: the crown; obligations from people somehow connected with the temple (rent, tithes and the like); commercial activities, *i.e.* the sale of animals, agricultural produce and other commodities; and (votive) gifts. One could add a fifth source: the stock of silver in the temples themselves, not only stockpiled as "treasure" in the storehouses, but also the amount of outstanding working material (*ḫāṭu*) at the disposal of the smiths.[8] I intend to discuss these sources only briefly with a few examples. For those who are not familiar with the Neo-Babylonian archives: the data concerning the receipt and the expenditure of silver are so overwhelming that one could easily drown in it.

The king, perhaps to be regarded as the main provider of the temple, was certainly an important supplier of silver and other precious metals for the temples, although the written evidence for this is rather meagre compared to the other sources for incoming silver. Examples from Ebabbar at Sippar are *Nbn* 119:1-2, which records "37 minas (= ca. 18.5 kg.) of silver of the king which has been given for work in Ebabbar" in Nabonidus's third year, and VS 4 7:9'-10', recording "[x mina(s)] and 18 shekels of silver, which Ashurbanipal, the king of Assur, gave to Shamash". Apart from all sorts of gifts (sometimes called *nidintu*) of the king to the temples in kind (*e.g.* cattle and sheep for the offerings), the Neo-Babylonian royal family also paid tithes (*ešrû*) to the temples, in kind as well as in silver or gold.[9] King Nabonidus, for example, paid six minas of gold as tithes to Ebabbar shortly after his succession (*Nbn* 2), and six minas of silver on the first day of his fourth regnal year (MacGinnis, *ZA* 84 (1994), no. 5; for the collated date see Jursa 1998, 65[222]). Crown prince Belshazzar paid silver as tithe to Ebabbar (CT 56 348: [x] mina) as well as to Eanna (GCCI 1 322: one mina), and Nabonidus's daughter Ina-Esangila-rīšat[10] paid a silver bowl with the weight of 27 shekels as tithe to Ebabbar (*Nbn* 1043). I do not know of any example of an Achaemenid king paying tithes to the Babylonian temples.

The payments of house rent, tithes, and other obligations to the temples were the second source of incoming silver. Of these, house rent is the most important one. Both Eanna and Ebabbar owned houses in the inner cities as well as on the quay of the city, in most cases let to personnel of the temples. The rent of these houses had to be paid in silver. The more sophisticated houses yielded more than 20 shekels of silver annually according to the tenancy contracts, other houses between 1 and 10 shekels.[11] Ebabbar

---

8 See Bongenaar 1997, 359 for the working material at the disposal of the smiths of Ebabbar.

9 See Jursa 1998, 65ff for payments of tithes by members of the royal family.

10 H.D. Baker pointed out to me that the name of Nabonidus's daughter should be read Ina-Esangila-rīšat (so *AHw* 980a, *s.v. riāšu* 1b; compare Ina-Uruk-rīšat in Hölscher, *Personennamen*, 102) instead of Ina-Esangila-remât. Ina-Esangila-*ri-mat* has often been understood as a defective, but in fact incomprehensible, spelling for Ina-Esangila-ramât (Tallqvist, *NBN*, 77, Wiseman, *CAH* III/2^2, 244, Beaulieu, *Nabonidus*, 137; cf. Stamm, *Namengebung*, 116).

11 Sippar: *Nbn* 48 (24 shekels), CT 57 909 (2[+x] shekels); Uruk: BIN 1 118 (20 shekels), AnOr 8 58 (10 shekels), AnOr 9 17 (1, 4, 8 and 10 shekels), AnOr 8 57 (nine shekels), YOS 7 2 (three shekels).

seems to have been the owner of the local slums as is shown by BM 75208 (unpublished), in which nearly all the listed houses, let to personnel of Ebabbar, are classified as "collapsed" (ŠUB). These houses still yielded between one-third of a shekel and 10 shekels annually. It should be noted that silver was not used as an accounting unit in this case, but that the house rent was really paid in silver. This follows from a set of texts from Ebabbar, which record the delivery of the silver collected by the house rent collector (*ša muḫḫi bītāti*). The delivered amounts of silver range from a few shekels to more than 10 minas.[12] Occasionally people paid their house rent in textiles (*e.g.* CT 55 790: one TÚG.KUR.RA, the equivalent of three shekels of silver). Another obligation which was sometimes paid in silver to the temple is the tithe (*ešrû*). The nature of this phenomenon is still uncertain (who had to pay and when?), but apart from the Neo-Babylonian royal family (see above), some officials from outside the temple organizations are reported to have paid silver as tithes to the deity or the temple.[13] *Ešrû* was further levied in kind on the yield of the fields belonging to the temple, but the collector of the tithes, the *ša muḫḫi ešrî*, sometimes converted the agricultural produce into silver before handing it over to the temple (*e.g. Nbn* 382, CT 56 25 and CT 57 42; cf. Jursa 1998, 31). Yet other obligations paid to the temple in silver include the *maddattu*, the compensation paid for slaves and oblates (*širku*) owned by the temple who were hired out (*e.g.* UCP 9/I 53, UCP 9/II 37 and YOS 7 44), and fines paid by people who did not turn up in time or did not pay their debts at a certain date. The most important source of income for the temple, field rent (*sūtu* and *imittu*), was, not surprisingly, in most cases paid in agricultural produce, *i.e.* barley and dates, and to a much lesser extent sesame, vegetables and fruit.[14] We know this from the category of texts called "letter orders"[15] in which the rent farmers (those who leased the right to collect the rent of temple land and in return paid the temple a fixed amount annually), pay barley or dates as food rations or prebendary income directly to temple personnel instead of bringing them to the storehouses where they could be redistributed. It should be noted in relation to this, that in some categories of texts one cannot establish with certainty which commodity was delivered or paid in the end, a general problem in Neo-Babylonian texts. In promissory notes, for example, where silver is reported to be due from an individual, the final payment could easily have been made in barley or dates, or balanced with counterclaims. In this way, the silver mentioned in the text only served as the standard. The reverse also

Tenancy agreements in which other commodities instead of silver are mentioned as the house rent are rare (but cf. YOS 7 45 from Uruk which mentions barley as the house rent).

12 Payments by the house rent collectors of Ebabbar: *Camb* 28 and 29 (four shekels); *Nbn* 439 (seven shekels); *Camb* 27 (8.5 shekels); *Nbn* 728 (12 shekels); CT 57,72 (38 shekels); CT 57 74 (50 shekels); CT 57 71 (one mina and two shekels); *Nbn* 717 (two minas and five shekels); *Nbn* 428 (3 minas and 11 shekels); *Nbn* 234 (5 minas and 20? shekels); *Nbn* 319 (seven minas); CT 57 82 (13 minas and 1 shekel).

13 Payments of silver tithes to Ebabbar: CT 55 435 ([x] mina and 12 shekels of silver beside other commodities by the governor (*pīḫātu*) of Gubbal); CT 56 312 ([x] mina by the *šākin māti*); BM 77842 = Bertin 1325 (50 shekels by the *rab mê ša šarri*); CT 57 41 (25 shekels by an alphabet scribe (*sepīru*)). Payments of silver tithes to Eanna: GCCI 1 18 (eight shekels; profession unknown) and YOS 6 70 (2.5 shekels; profession unknown). See now Jursa 1998, 67ff for more details concerning payments of tithes by officials.

14 For Ebabbar see Jursa 1995; for Eanna see Cocquerillat 1968.

15 See J. MacGinnis, *Letter Orders from Sippar and the Administration of the Ebabbara in the Late-Babylonian Period*, Poznan 1995.

occurs. The well-known rent farmer in Sippar during the reign of Nabonidus, Ana-amat-Bēl-atkal, for example, paid [x+] 5/6 minas and four shekels of silver to Ebabbar instead of 426 *kor* of dates as (part of) the field rent (*sūtu*) of the seventh year (CT 57 22). Here, a debt of dates is discharged by paying silver.[16]

The third source of incoming silver for the temple was the sale of animals, agricultural produce and other commodities, such as textiles. Cattle, sheep, and fowl were bred by the temple organizations mainly for offering purposes, in addition to goats (not for offering purposes). There is textual evidence for the sale of these animals, but the temples also bought animals to meet the pressing demand for the daily offerings, despite the steady (but irregular?) supply of offering animals by the king. If we had the complete administrative archives of the temples, and could thus calculate the total number of the animals which were sold and bought for silver over a certain period, it is doubtful whether the outcome would be that the temples made much profit out of this trade. Dead animals, especially those which died in the fattening house before they could be slaughtered for offerings, were sold locally.[17] More important were the saleable products of animal husbandry: wool and hides.[18] According to the herding contracts one sheep yielded 1.5 mina of wool annually. The prices for wool vary but if we, for convenience's sake, suppose that five minas of wool were the equivalent of one shekel of silver,[19] then the profit amounted to 5 minas of silver per 1000 sheep annually (1500 minas of wool : 5 = 300 shekels = 5 minas of silver). A large amount of the wool, however, was used to manufacture textiles locally. We suppose that the manufacture and subsequent sale of these textiles was a source of income for the temples, but also in this case the organizations seem to have 'consumed' most of their production themselves. The statues of the gods frequently required new (and rather complex) clothing, and for the moment there is more evidence for the *purchase* of textiles than for the sale of textiles.[20] As for agricultural produce, dates, barley and sesame could be sold (for silver) or exchanged for other commodities. The latter occurs fairly frequently. A shortage of a certain commodity caused the temple to provide a substitute, because an interruption in the offerings was regarded a major disaster. In Sippar, for example, we find the issue of "200 *kor* of barley for sesame (as) offering" (*Cyr* 31). In this case, the prebendaries of the temple apparently had to barter the barley for sesame (on the local market?), before they could prepare the

---

16 Similarly *Nbn* 921, the payment of one mina and eight shekels instead of 91 *kor* of dates by him (cf. Jursa 1995, 92). Note further *Cyr* 28, which reads "Of the debt (note) of 60 *kor* of dates, property of Šamaš, which is due from PN, twenty shekels of silver for 22;3.2.0 *kor* of dates is paid for".

17 Prices of dead sheep ranged from less than half a shekel to two shekels in Ebabbar, see Bongenaar 1997, 64.

18 See G. van Driel, 'Neo-Babylonian Sheep and Goats', *BSA* 7 (1993), 219-258, and 'Cattle in the Neo-Babylonian Period', *BSA* 8 (1995), 215-240 (including discussion of many texts from the two institutional archives).

19 I do not intend to discuss prices, which were subject to seasonal as well as to accidental fluctuations over the years, in detail in this article. Note the following extremes for Uruk: 2.5 minas of wool for one shekel of silver (Durand, EHE 165), 3 1/3 minas (BIN 2 121), 6 minas (GCCI 1 402) and 9 minas (GCCI 2 355). Sippar: 4.5 minas for one shekel of silver (CT 55 763), 5 minas (CT 55 779) and 6.5 minas (CT 55 768).

20 The so-called TÚG.KUR.RA garment, a kind of poncho or blanket, which temple personnel received when they had to go outside the town to perform work (*e.g.* the bowmen, herdsmen and messengers), often had to be bought (Sippar: Evetts *Ner* 28, *Nbn* 661, *Camb* 27, 154 and 340; Uruk: GCCI 1 114, 192 and 415).

offerings. In other cases silver is used as a standard only, *e.g.* GCCI 1 259 (from Uruk), in which sesame, the equivalence of eight shekels of silver, is used for the purchase of one [...] (commodity broken). To conclude: the temples produced (*i.e.* bred, cultivated and manufactured) animals, crops and commodities, the largest part of which was used for the maintenance of the gods as well as for the maintenance of the organization and its personnel. A certain surplus could be sold, but quantification is impossible. Most of the commodities and animals which are recorded as being sold, can be matched up with commodities and animals bought in other texts.

Votive gifts were the fourth source of incoming silver. These gifts are rarely recorded as such,[21] because they are hidden behind the word *irbu* (*ša bābi*). *Irbu* is in itself a neutral term for everything that entered the temple, ranging from donations to payments of rent and tithes.[22] The *irbu ša bābi* consisted of the offerings (often in silver) made by people upon entering and leaving the gate(s) of the sanctuary, perhaps comparable to the offertory box in a modern church.[23] The silver collected in this way recurs in texts in which silver is issued. These texts simply state "x silver 'which entered (the gate)', is given to PN/is given for purpose y" (x *kaspu* (*ultu*) *irbu* (*ša bābi*) *ša ana* PN/y *nadnu*). The frequent use of this phrase suggests that these offerings were a substantial means of income for the temple.

3. *Outgoing Silver in the Neo-Babylonian Temple Organizations*

Probably the main reason why the temples seem keen to acquire silver, demanding substantial amounts of it from their personnel as house rent and for offerings at the entrance gate of the sanctuary, is simply that large amounts of silver were required to keep the organizations going. Every shekel of silver that went out of the temple first had to enter it, supposing that the temples tried to maintain their stock of silver. The temples had to acquire their basic materials for a large part through "long-distance trade", clay and reed being the only materials readily available in Babylonia. Due to transportation costs and the fact that most food stuffs are perishable, silver rather than farming produce was necessary to pay for these basic materials. In addition, the crown demanded silver, and when the storehouses were empty, personnel had to be paid in silver. We can distinguish four different purposes for which the temple needed silver: the crown; payments to temple personnel (prebendary income and food rations in addition to hired labour); commercial activities, *i.e.* the purchase of basic materials, finished products, animals and sometimes land or houses; and silver for the repair and the manufacture of the jewellery and utensils of the gods.

One of the purposes for which the temple needed silver was for the dues to the king or to the state administration. Unfortunately these dues are hardly recorded in the

21 The Akkadian word *šagigurû*, "votive (or voluntary) offering", does not occur in Neo-Babylonian economical texts.

22 See Oppenheim 1947, 117; Joannès 1982, 235-236; van Driel 1986, 17.

23 That *irbu* in some cases should be understood more specifically as "gift, offering" is clear from the passages cited in *CAD* I/J, 175 *s.v. irbu*, meaning 3b-1', "offering (presented at the gate when entering a temple, made in silver)". Cf. text no. 7 (from Uruk) in R.H. Sack, *Cuneiform Documents from the Chaldean and Persian Periods*, Selinsgrove 1994, which records the receipt of "one shekel of gold, *irbu* of PN, the head of the (prebendary) butchers".

archives. We know that an official designated "courtier in charge of the cash box of the king" (*ša-rēš šarri ša ina muḫḫi quppi ša šarri*) was present in the temples and supposedly collected the contents of the cash box of the king to send these at intervals to Babylon, but no archival material belonging to him has been found (as yet) within the main body of the Eanna and Ebabbar archives.[24] Part of the "1000 talents" of silver which Babylonia and Assyria had to pay annually as tribute to the Achaemenid kings (Herodotus III 92), could have been collected in this way. But what exactly was collected in the cash box of the king? In Eanna texts there are references to silver "which entered the cash box of the king at the gate" (*irbu ša* ^{gi}*quppi šarri ša bābi*; YOS 6 13:1-3), from which we may conclude that (part of) the king's revenues was collected at the gates of the temples. In the previous section I argued that the temples benefitted as well from the offering called *irbu ša bābi*, "which entered the gate". Although the presence of two cash boxes at each temple gate cannot be excluded (one for the king and one for the temple),[25] it is perhaps more likely that the offerings were collected in one cash box, and that its contents were divided between the king and the temple according to a fixed distribution code. The courtier in charge of the cash box of the king was probably responsible for the division of the contents of this cash box, and only the share of the temple entered the administration (and, thus, our texts). The king derived a further income from the temples as a (honorary?) prebendary. Like any other prebendary of the temple he was entitled to a prebendary income as well as to the remainders of the divine meal. Many texts in H. Freydank, *SWU*, mention prebendary days owned by the king in Eanna. In Ebabbar no specific prebendary days belonging to the king are recorded, but from the Nabû-apla-iddina Stone Tablet (King, *BBSt.* 36) we know that he also owned a share in Ebabbar. According to YOS 6 10:12-13, pieces of meat, after being "consumed" by the gods, were dropped into the cash box of the king. It is doubtful whether this passage refers to the cash box that was present in the entrance gate of the sanctuary.[26] Oppenheim (1947, 118-119) is probably right in his assumption that the officials in charge of the cash boxes were some kind of assayers, who evaluated the contents (silver, pieces of meat, barley, etc.) of the cash boxes. I further suspect that the officials called "in charge of the food rations of the king" (*ša kurrumat šarri*) in Sippar converted the different commodities into silver locally. Eventually this silver was brought in a cash box (*quppu*) to the king (*e.g. Nbn* 1058), since it is hard to believe that the leftovers of the divine meal were actually sent to Babylon.[27] To conclude: The king probably received two different revenues in silver

---

24 See Bongenaar 1997, 104-105 (with previous literature).

25 There was certainly more than one cash box present in both Eanna and Ebabbar. GCCI 1 360 from Uruk, for example, mentions "the cash boxes of the gate" (*quppū ša bābi*), presumably because the sanctuary had more than one entrance gate. In Sippar we have references to separate cash boxes of the minor deities, *e.g.* the cash box of Gula (Evetts *Ner* 40) and the cash box of Bēlet-Akkad (CT 57 100 and *Cyr* 267).

26 Oppenheim 1947, 117-118^{+7}, also struggled with this problem. He suspected that the cash box (*quppu*), into which incoming payments were dropped, was placed near the gate of the santuary. Another box, called the "cash box of the king" (*quppu ša šarri*), was present in the temple, wherein the royal share of the sacrificed animals was dropped. From YOS 6 13, which mentions the cash box of the king at the gate, we may conclude that this is not true.

27 Note, however, the unpublished text BM 74876, which records the issue of silver as the rent of the boat which brought the "meat of the food rations of the king" (UZU *šá* ŠUG.ḪI.A LUGAL) to the military camp (*ma-dak-ku*, for *madāktu*).

from the Babylonian temples, a fixed percentage of the offerings collected at the gate(s) of the sanctuaries, and his legitimate share as a prebendary of the temple.

The second purpose for which the temple needed silver was the payment of its personnel. The prebendaries of the temple received prebendary income (*pappasu*) and the ordinary workmen rations (*kurummatu*), either in silver or in kind. It is not altogether clear from the texts whether silver was only paid in case of a shortage of barley or dates in the storehouses, *e.g.* just before the harvest. The picture obtained from the Ebabbar archive differs from that of Eanna. Eanna more often paid silver to ordinary workmen as their food ration, generally between one shekel and one and a half monthly.[28] In Ebabbar this was rarely the case (but cf. *Nbk* 340 and CT 57 172). On the other hand, prebendary income in Ebabbar was often paid in silver to the prebendaries,[29] whereas this seems less frequent in Eanna. Apart from the payments in silver to their personnel, the temples had to hire labour, often for silver. Unspecified workmen (^{lú}ḪUN.GÁ.MEŠ, "hirelings") for digging and construction work are recorded in substantial numbers, sometimes by the hundreds.[30] The level of the monthly wages of these hirelings cannot be deduced from the texts, since the hirelings were often paid to perform a certain job (and not for a certain period of time), *e.g.* to move a specified amount of earth (GCCI 1 268), to tow a boat to another city (GCCI 1 350) or to fetch materials (GCCI 1 306). The hire of craftsmen also occurs.[31] In addition to labour, means of transport sometimes had to be hired (for silver) by the temples, especially boats.[32] If personnel of the temple had to leave the town in order to perform their work, they received silver as part of their travel provisions (*ṣidītu*) or their fitting-out (*rikis qabli*; *e.g.* CT 55 286).

The third purpose for which the temple needed silver was the purchase of everything which the temple organization could not provide, but which was required to maintain the cult of the gods as well as the organization and its personnel. When there was a shortage of sacrificial animals, the temples had to use silver to buy animals from traders or local herdsmen. The food of the gods required a continuous supply of barley, dates, sesame and other food stuffs, which were not always available in the storehouses.[33] Wool, which

---

28 *E.g.* VS NF 4 8; GCCI 1 30; YOS 6 27 (one shekel); YOS 17 341; UCP 9/II 15; GCCI 1 181 (1 1/2 shekel); cf. UCP 9/I 19 and 21; YOS 6 51; YOS 17 222 and 228; GCCI 1 163, 318, 354 and 402. Note the continued payment of wages in the event of sickness: BIN 1 140; UCP 9/I 29 (from Uruk) and *Nbn* 161 (from Sippar).

29 *E.g. Nbn* 27, 302, 424, 456, 465, 544, 588, 607, 705, 712; CT 57 95, 148, 164, 168; *Cyr* 296.

30 Payments of silver to hirelings in Uruk include VS NF 4 10; Joannès 1982 no. 46; YOS 6 7; GCCI 1 268, 270, 280, 282, 283, 284, 295, 306, 312, 323, 350, 364, 365, 369, 376, 377, 393, 414. From Sippar we have a set of texts listing the number of hirelings under supervision of certain individuals who perform work on the dike (*mušannītu*) at Gilūšu (see Jursa 1995, 184ff), who cut a weed (or reed?) called *ṣapītu* (*e.g.* CT 56 589), and who lay the foundations (*uššu*) of the city or temple gate (*e.g.* CT 56 573-574, 578 and 581). These texts are "staff-files" without mention of wages. Only occasionally payments to these hirelings are recorded (*e.g.* barley and dates in CT 56 582 and 588, silver in CT 56 585, 590, 592, 593, 598-601).

31 *E.g.* wages for hired smiths in Ebabbar (see Bongenaar 1997, 357[311]), carpenters in Ebabbar (CT 56 284 and BM 64140 = Bertin 2951) and in Eanna (GCCI 1 402), a bow maker in Eanna (YOS 17 226) and a brewer and a baker (for non-cultic purposes) in Ebabbar (CT 56 159 and CT 57 150 resp.).

32 *E.g.* VS 6 190; *Nbk* 282; *Nbn* 782, *Nbn* 862; BM 64141 = Bertin 1235 (hire of boats by Ebabbar); UCP 9/II 30 (hire of a boat and a donkey by Eanna).

33 A few examples: Issues of silver to buy food stuffs, *e.g.* for the regular offerings, in Ebabbar: CT 57 120a, 123, 441 and *Cyr* 33 (barley); *Nbk* 277, 287, 349, CT 56 165, *Camb* 249 (sesame); and *Nbn*

also served as money, *e.g.* YOS 17 352 (wool for the purchase of cress) and YOS 17 339 (wool for the purchase of a bow), nevertheless had to be bought sometimes as well (*e.g.* GCCI 2 30 and 72 from Uruk). The temples could probably obtain food stuffs and animals to some extent locally, but many finished products as well as basic materials had to be obtained through trade, traditionally divided into local trade and long-distance trade. Unfortunately the archival texts in general do not offer much information about the locality where commodities were bought, nor from whom they were bought. *Nbn* 61 (Nbn 13-II-02) from Sippar, for example, just lists three items (grinding slabs, a garment called ^{túg}*midatatu*, and lead), and the corresponding amounts of silver paid for them. We can only speculate about the story behind this text. Perhaps a temple official went to the local market, returned with the required necessities, claimed the expenses, and subsequently had a tablet written to account for the silver spent. Or the (rarely attested) merchant of the king (*tamkār šarri*) happened to arrive on that date at Sippar and sold these items, but the scribe of the text saw no need to mention the merchant's name or profession. One can think of yet other options: someone sent to Babylon or another city to acquire the items on behalf of Ebabbar, or a foreign ship arriving at Sippar with merchandise. More is known from the Eanna archive.[34] The *mēreštu*, "consignment of merchandise" texts from the Eanna archive offer some insight into the so-called long-distance trade.[35] Silver was given to certain individuals - whether professional merchants or not is not clear from the texts - who in due course returned to Eanna with the requested merchandise from the west. In this way bronze, tin, iron, lapis lazuli, dyes and mordant for the dyeing of textiles, linen fabrics, coloured wool, honey, wine, spices and aromatics were acquired by Eanna. Since there are only a few of these *mēreštu* texts from Eanna available and none from Ebabbar at present, quantification of this kind of trade is impossible for the moment. Closer at home, Babylon was an important national shopping centre. Officials of Eanna regularly went to Babylon to obtain the necessities (*ḫišiḫtu*) of Eanna, like aromatics, wine, wax, sheep, linen fabrics, gold, iron and bitumen.[36] Joannès (1982, 248-251 and 256) suspected that individuals connected with the temple (like the goldsmith and the jeweller in Joannès 1982 no. 59 and YOS 6 112) acted as merchants, not because they were connected with the temple, but merely because they were "free citizens" (*mār banî*). This cannot be proven, but it should be noted that also the private archival texts from Sippar suggest that the local upper class, consisting of "free citizens" who often owned many prebends in the temple, was involved in trading activities. In addition to the purchase of commodities, either through local or through long-distance trade, the temples bought slaves (BIN 1 120), donkeys (GCCI 1 402) and real estate with

161 (emmer). Similarly in Eanna: YOS 7 197 (dates); UCP 9/I 73 (barley and dates); GCCI 1 362 and Moore, Michigan Coll. 6 (emmer); GCCI 1 293, 329 and 378 (sesame); UCP 9/II 8 and GCCI 1 344 (cress); GCCI 349 (oil); GCCI 1 305 (figs); and YOS 17 113 (wool instead of barley and dates for the regular offerings + the prebendary income).

34 See Joannès 1982, 235-256, 'Les activités commerciales de l'Eanna'.

35 A.L. Oppenheim discussed two of these *mēreštu* texts (YOS 6 168 and TCL 12 84) in his article 'Essay on Overland Trade in the First Millennium B.C.' in *JCS* 21 (1967), 236-254. Further YOS 6 52, 61, 63; TCL 12 104 and other texts cited in *CAD* M/2, 23.

36 The officials of Eanna sent to Babylon were the resident (*qīpu*) of Eanna (Joannès 1982 no. 60, BIN 1 124 and Sack, *ZA* 77, 287), a goldsmith and a jeweller (Joannès 1982, no. 59 and YOS 6 112), and the supervisor (*bēl piqitti*) of Eanna together with the scribes (GCCI 1 332, 367, 411 and YOS 6 115). All these texts are extensively treated in Joannès 1982, 238-255. See also van Driel 1986, 16f^{+40}.

silver. In particular in the early Neo-Babylonian period, the temples expanded their territory through buying land.[37] The temples further bought houses in the city, sometimes from their indebted owners.[38] These houses could subsequently be let.

The fourth purpose for which the temple needed silver was the manufacture and the repair of the jewellery of the gods and the utensils and silverware used in the cult. The terminology of the cultic utensils in Eanna is known from a set of texts discussed by F. Joannès,[39] but the weight of these utensils is not recorded in the texts. In the Ebabbar archive many texts survive, in which working material is given for the making and the repair of objects or in which manufactured objects are delivered to Ebabbar by the smiths (Bongenaar 1997, 357ff). These texts are careful to mention the amount of silver spent on each object. Judging from these texts, substantial amounts of silver were withdrawn from the temple's general resources to manufacture objects.[40] Probably the nicest example from Sippar is *Nbn* 119, which neatly specifies the origin and destination of more than 50 minas of silver.[41]

Nbn 119 (BM 74343)

37 m.	gift of the king for work in Ebabbar (lines 1-2)
8 m. 20 sh.	tithes (*ešrû*) of the king for the barley in Ḫabūru (lines 3-6)
3 m. 30 sh.	sale of birds (line 7)
+ 1 m 10 sh.	which "entered the gate" (*irbu ša* KÁ; line 8)
---------------	
50 minas	total of silver given for refining (*ana ṭubbu*; lines 9-10)
6 m 20 sh.	lost during refining (lines 11-12)
- 1 m.10 sh.	"withdrawn" (*ṭuḫḫu itteḫis*), *i.e.* probably returned to the cash box of the gate, mentioned in line 8 (lines 13-14)
-----------------	
42 m 30 sh.	subtotal of refined silver (lines 14-15)
+ 2 m.	brought in from the supply (*ḫāṭu*) at the disposal of PN and the smiths (lines 15-16)
---------------	
44 m. 30 sh.	subtotal (line 17)
- 1 m.	lost during the (second) melting and casting process (*petēqu*; line 18)
---------------	
43 m. 30 sh.	the weight of four ingots (*kušru*; lines 19-20), given (to the smiths) for (the making of) two censers (*nignakku*) and two parts of a censer (*kusibirītu*) (lines 20 and following)

---

37 *E.g.* de Jong-Ellis, *JCS* 36 (1984) no. 8 (purchase of three fields by Eanna in Kand 6); BIN 1 130 (purchase of one field by Eanna in Nbp 15); Coll. Smit 110 (unpublished; purchase of a huge plot of land by Ebabbar in Nbp 1).

38 Purchase of houses by Eanna: AnOr 8 51 and Stigers, *JCS* 28, no. 12. Caused by debts of the owners: AnOr 8 57 and 58, AnOr 9 15, BIN 2 130 and YOS 7 2. Purchase of a house by Ebabbar: *Dar* 516.

39 'Un inventaire de mobilier sacré d'époque néo-babylonienne' in *RA* 75 (1981), 143-150. These texts from Eanna list exactly which (golden and silver) utensils and silverware were taken out of a certain treasure room (*bīt urinni*) for the Greeting-of-the-Temple (*šalām bīti*) ceremonies.

40 A few examples from the smiths' file: *Nbn* 10, delivery of a censer (*nignakku*) with the weight of 25 minas and 15 shekels of silver; BM 60821, issue of 45.5 minas of silver for the making of two censers (*nignakku*) and one basket (*nasḫapu*); *Nbn* 301, issue of 2 minas and 59 shekels of silver for the making of a container with stand (?; *sip karû*) and a box (*šusullu*); *Nbn* 598 and 673, issue of 25 minas and 22 shekels and 12 minas and 38 shekels of silver respectively for work (*ana dullu*).

41 *Nbn* 119 is edited in Zawadzki, *EOS* 73 (1985), 110 and in Bongenaar 1997, 362-363.

The first four entries correspond with the four sources of incoming silver in the temple organizations as discussed above: the crown, obligations, commercial activities and gifts. The last entry of the text corresponds with the fourth purpose for which the temples needed silver: the manufacture of cultic utensils. When discussing the qualities of Neo-Babylonian silver, we should keep this text in mind.

4. *Qualities of Silver*

A.L. Oppenheim (1947, 116-117) assumed that all the incoming silver (*irbu*) was handed over to the smiths of the temple at the end of each month to be melted and cast into ingots of a standard size and quality. This assumption was based on Ebabbar texts which record the handing over of silver "revenue of the current month" (*irbu ša arḫi*) to the smiths to be melted down and cast (*ana petēqi*; *e.g. Camb* 59). Although *Nbn* 119 above seems to confirm this, Oppenheim's assumption probably does not hold true. In my view it is unlikely that the temple management accepted alloyed silver and refined it (thus losing a certain percentage of the silver) in order to pay its personnel with the refined silver. How could one have prevented people from alloying the silver again (thus gaining a certain percentage of the silver) when they had to discharge their obligations to the temple? It should be noted in relation to this that the Ebabbar texts recording the receipt of silver *and* the issue of silver on the same day, by far outnumber the texts in which silver is given to the smiths for refining or smelting and casting. Most of the incoming silver was spent the very same day on payments, purchases, etc. In *Nbn* 119 summarized above the silver is not refined and cast to use for any future payment. The refined silver was intended for the manufacture of cultic utensils. Since only the best quality of each commodity could be used for the gods, it is fully understandable that only silver in its purest form served this purpose. We may conclude that the smiths of the temple refined the silver intended for the manufacture of cultic utensils and jewellery,[42] and in addition possibly the silver stockpiled as treasure. All other incoming silver probably left the temple in the same state as when it came in.

A second assumption with regard to Neo-Babylonian silver, notably the increasingly frequent mention of the quality of silver in the Chaldean and Achaemenid period texts (Joannès 1994, 137ff; Renger 1995, 301; Powell 1996, 231) deserves some further attention. The most common phrase denoting the quality of Neo-Babylonian silver is KÙ.BABBAR *ša ina* 1 GÍN *bitqa*, "silver which has a one-eighth (percentage of alloy) per shekel".[43] This corresponds with the percentage of lost silver in *Nbn* 119 above. Of the 50 minas of silver given for refining, 6 minas and 20 shekels are lost (= ca. 12.6 per cent or one-eighth of the total). The second loss of silver reported in *Nbn* 119 might be caused by the process of melting and casting again. We may assume that Neo-Babylonian silver generally had a one-eighth percentage of alloy, but this figure is hardly ever mentioned in

42 F. Joannès also expressed this view: see 1982, 265 and his article 'Private Commerce and Banking in Achaemenid Babylon', in J.M. Sasson (ed.), *Civilizations of the Ancient Near East*, Vol. III, New York 1995, 1478.

43 Powell (1996, 231) assumes that this phrase is an abbreviation of KÙ.BABBAR *ša ina* 1 GÍN *bitqa nuḫḫutu*, *nuḫḫutu* being the word for "alloying". Joannès (1994, 139-140), however, understands *nuḫḫutu* as an average quality of silver, used for exchange only.

the institutional archives. The temple's administration of incoming and outgoing silver simply records "silver" in its texts. The *bitqa* phrase mainly occurs in loan documents which often belong to private archives.[44]

Other qualities of silver hardly occur in the institutional archives before the beginning of the reign of Darius.[45] Probably as a result of the tax reform and the introduction of a fixed standard between Babylonian silver and Euboian gold by Darius I (Herodotus III 89-97) the temple's administration of silver changed.[46] Although "silver" without mention of a quality still occurs in the administrative texts from Darius's reign, one suddenly finds white silver (*kaspu peṣû*) in contrast with silver with a *ginnu* mark (*kaspu* (*ša*) *ginnu*). Since the Eanna archive as we know it comes to an end early in Darius's reign, the evidence is based on the Ebabbar archive. White silver is attested on a regular basis in Ebabbar texts from the third regnal year of Darius,[47] *ginnu*-silver from the eleventh year of Darius.[48] *Ginnu*-silver is attested earlier in private archival context, *e.g. Dar* 142 (Dar 4) and other texts cited in *CAD* G, 79.[49] F. Joannès (1982, 265 and 1994, 140) argues that we should distinguish between three different qualities of Neo-Babylonian silver: a superior quality (only used by the smiths), the average quality (used for exchange purposes), and an inferior quality (improper for exchange purposes and, thus, hardly ever mentioned in the texts). This division into three qualities of silver, however, still does not account for the many designations of silver used in the texts. Joannès (1994, 140ff) explains this by assuming that these designations are in fact subdivisions of the average quality of silver, all used for exchange purposes. Indeed, when we examine the Ebabbar texts which contrast white silver (*kaspu peṣû*) and silver with a mark (*kaspu ša ginnu*), there is no reason to assume a distinguishing difference in quality between the two. CT 57 110 ([Dar] 19), for example, records the purchase of wool and bitumen for *ginnu*-silver, beside the purchase of barley for white silver. In the same text *ginnu*-silver is given for mounting (*ana aḫāzi*), something one would not

44 Loan documents from the Eanna archive start mentioning the percentage of alloy towards the end of the reign of Nebuchadnezzar, *e.g.* GCCI 1 236 (Nbk 35); AnOr 8 16 (Nbk 36); GCCI 1 262 (Nbk 37); GCCI 1 233, and 261 (Nbk 38). These texts mention a one-sixth percentage of alloy (= roughly 16.5 per cent).

45 For the different percentages of alloy and other qualities of silver mentioned in Neo-Babylonian texts, see Joannès 1982, 264-265; Joannès 1994, 139-144; Joannès, *RlA* 8 (1993-), 104 and 108-109; Powell 1978b, 222-225; Powell 1990, 80; Powell 1996, 231-234; S. Zawadzki, *EOS* 73 (1985), 109.

46 For the impact of Darius's fiscal policy on Babylonia, see also Stolper 1985, 143ff.

47 CT 55 286 (Dar 3). Other examples from Ebabbar include *Dar* 190 (Dar 5); CT 57 120a (Dar 7); CT 57 120b (Dar 11); CT 57 146 (Dar 12); *Dar* 394 (Dar 14); *Dar* 436 (Dar 16); CT 55 389 and CT 57 119 (Dar 18); CT 57 110 ([Dar] 19); *Dar* 513 and CT 57 123 (Dar 20); *Dar* 548 and *Dar* 555 (Dar 22); *Dar* 570 and *Dar* 574 (Dar 23); CT 57 106 ,124 and 128 (Dar 24); CT 55 275 (Dar 25); CT 55 142 and Stevenson, *ABC* 39 (Dar 27); BM 60851 (Dar 28); CT 55 435 and CT 57 684 (Dar x). White silver is not completely unknown before Darius's third year. Note *Nbn* 173 (Nbn 4) from Ebabbar, and BIN 2 130 (Camb 0) and Pinches, *ET* 25 (1913-4), 422 (Dar 2) from Eanna.

48 CT 57 120b (Dar 11). Other examples from Ebabbar include *Dar* 394 (Dar 14); Stevenson, *ABC* 36 (Dar 17); CT 57 110 ([Dar] 19); *Dar* 512, 513, 516 and CT 57 123 (Dar 20); *Dar* 518 and CT 57 122 (Dar 21); *Dar* 570 (Dar 23); CT 57 124 and 128 (Dar 24); Stevenson, *ABC* 39 (Dar 27); CT 55 767 and CT 57 255 (Dar x). Note further the occurrence of *ginnu*-silver in private archival texts from Sippar: CT 4 pl. 21a (Dar 19); VS 5 95 (Dar 23); BM 74517 = Bertin 2523, and Stigers, *JCS* 28, no. 49 (Dar 24).

49 *CAD* G, 80 considers silver with a *ginnu*-mark to be an inferior (currency) quality of silver. This is refuted by Powell 1978b, 224.

expect of silver of an inferior quality. Another example, CT 57 123 (Dar 20), records the purchase of sheep for white silver and *ginnu*-silver, in addition to the purchase of barley and emmer for white silver.

5. *Silver or Money*?

The evidence for the use of silver in the Neo-Babylonian institutional archives, which has been the subject of this paper, permits only one conclusion: silver served as money, although not exclusively. Other commodities, in particular barley, dates and wool, served to some extent as money. The four different uses of money which Polanyi distinguished all apply to Neo-Babylonian silver: it was used to discharge obligations, it served as a standard, it was a means of exchange, and it was suitable and used (more than other commodities) for hoarding. J. Renger (1995, 286-287) already noted this. Contrary to Polanyi's assumption, the existence of money does not necessarily imply a free market system in Babylonia. The use of silver in the Neo-Babylonian institutions certainly does not fit Dalton's definition of primitive money, nor his (and Polanyi's) description of a staple-financed society. And yet, to define Neo-Babylonian silver as "all-purpose money" is too far-fetched. Contrary to present-day money, Neo-Babylonian silver was never a universally acceptable currency. One could not go to a bakery in Sippar and buy half a loaf of bread with silver, so to speak. Renger explained this by assuming that the need for silver in Mesopotamia was relatively small, because a large part of the population used agricultural and other products as a medium of exchange on the basis of reciprocity. It is questionable whether the availability of silver decisively explains the relatively small need for silver. Silver could never develop into an everyday money because its value was too high in comparison with other commodities. As long as one shekel of silver still constituted a month's pay, small products at the local market had to be bought with other, "cheaper" commodities. Whether the high value of silver was caused by a certain scarcity of the metal (Mesopotamia did not have silver mines), cannot be judged from the texts. We should conclude, with Powell (1996, 228), that silver was a high-range money.

Summer 1998

STRUCTURES ET OPÉRATIONS COMMERCIALES EN BABYLONIE À L'ÉPOQUE NÉO-BABYLONIENNE

FRANCIS JOANNÈS (PARIS)

Les données fournies par les archives des temples et les archives privées, en l'absence de véritables archives officielles à cette époque, nous permettent d'avoir quelques renseignements sur la pratique du commerce en Babylonie, du 7e au 4e siècle av. J.-C.; il n'existe cependant aucun lot d'archive commerciale véritable, et les éléments que l'on peut collecter sont donc souvent épars et indirects.[1]

Une différence de nature assez nette peut être établie entre les données concernant le commerce local et le commerce international. On a donc dans ce qui suit envisagé d'abord le fonctionnement du commerce local, ses structures, ses agents, ses produits et ses lieux, avant de passer au commerce international, surtout le commerce avec l'ouest méditerranéen.

LE COMMERCE LOCAL

Les structures

Les sanctuaires

En tant que grands fournisseurs d'archives comptables, les temples ont leur place dans une reconstitution des circuits et des opérations de type commercial. Telles qu'elles sont connues, leurs ressources proviennent cependant souvent d'autres circuits: d'abord celui de leurs domaines propres, qui sont censés leur permettre de pourvoir à l'essentiel des besoins en matière de culte et d'entretien du personnel. Ce système a désormais été bien étudié pour Uruk[2] et pour Sippar,[3] et les données disponibles montrent que les temples couvrent sous la dynastie néo-babylonienne largement leurs besoins, dégageant même des surplus; les éventuelles difficultés rencontrées sont plus liées aux pratiques administratives des modes de gestion qu'à un manque de ressources.

La seconde source, également conséquente, est constituée par les donations royales, en particulier les attributions en hommes et en produits issus de la conquête: dans le cas de Sippar on peut ainsi mettre directement en relation la présence de contingents

---

1 Les abréviations utilisées ici sont celles du *Chicago Assyrian Dictionary*; ainsi que: MacGinnis = *Letter Orders from Sippar and the Administration of the Ebabbara in the Late-Babylonian Period*, Poznan 1995; Stigers = 'Neo- and Late-Babylonian Business Documents from the John Frederick Lewis Collection', *JCS* 28 (1976), 3-59.

2 Cocquerillat 1968, ainsi que les compléments parus dans la *RA* 77 (1983), 163-168; 78 (1984), 49-70 et 143-167; et 79 (1985), 51-59.

3 Les dernières synthèses en date fournissent la bibliographie antérieure: Zawadzki 1990; *id.* 1991; Jursa 1995; Bongenaar 1997.

d'esclaves du temple d'origine égyptienne avec les campagnes de Nabuchodonosor II,[4] ou les attributions de fer cilicien avec celles de Nériglissar et de Nabonide.[5] Le texte FLP 1595 [n°1][6] est un exemple parmi d'autres de la variété des produits ainsi fournis.

Dans les opérations commerciales proprement dites, la part des sanctuaires est liée à deux types d'opérations: d'une part la commercialisation de certains surplus, en particulier ceux provenant de l'agriculture et de l'élevage, d'autre part la satisfaction des besoins en produits rares ou exotiques, que les donations royales ne suffiraient pas à couvrir. Le premier type d'opération inclut aussi une commercialisation interne, le sanctuaire revendant à son propre personnel des moutons ou des céréales. Certains membres du personnel du temple procèdent par ailleurs à des ventes directes, mais dans un contexte qui n'est pas toujours légal, et qui leur vaut d'être soumis à des enquêtes ou des instructions judiciaires.[7] Mais on constate également la présence de transactions entre le temple et de véritables marchands, ceux qui portent le titre de *tamkâru* (voir ci-dessous).

D'une manière générale, ce sont les métaux précieux qui semblent être ce que les temples recherchent le plus, à la fois comme moyen de paiement pour des opérations commerciales ultérieures, comme réserve pour le versement du salaire des travailleurs loués (*agrû*), enfin comme matière première pour la réalisation des objets précieux et des bijoux utilisés pour le culte.

Il faut noter que les temples n'ont pas pour autant mis sur pied de structures commerciales propres: en particulier, nul personnel spécialisé dans ce type d'opérations n'apparaît dans les nombreuses listes de distribution de rations d'entretien qui nous permettent d'avoir une vue relativement exhaustive du personnel des temples néo-babyloniens.[8] On peut, à titre d'exemple, examiner ce qui se passe dans le «bureau de la laine» de l'Ekur de Nippur à l'époque achéménide[9] et comment y fonctionne le système de commercialisation: les scribes du Trésor chargés de la gestion du temple enregistrent un certain nombre de donations et de versements de taxes; ils envoient des ordres écrits d'attribution de rations de laine par l'entrepôt central à des membres du clergé ou des gens travaillant au service de l'Ekur. Ils organisent la revente de la laine au personnel du temple, ou à des individus extérieurs, ainsi que l'achat de divers produits auprès de l'administration royale ou auprès de marchands privés. Les divers transferts sont éclairés par le texte ROMCT 2 50 [n°2].

Il apparaît donc que le service chargé originellement de la simple gestion de la laine pour les besoins du temple a été intégré dans une structure plus vaste, sorte de service gestionnaire central qui ajoute à ses fonctions de réception et de distribution une activité commerciale permettant d'écouler les surplus de laine et les donations diverses contre

4 Bongenaar - Haring 1994.

5 Cf. Joannès 1991.

6 Dillard 1975. Le numéro entre crochets renvoie aux textes placés en annexe à la fin de cet article.

7 Cf. le dossier concernant l'oblat Gimillu à Uruk, dans Cocquerillat 1968.

8 Pour Uruk, cf. Kümmel 1979; pour Sippar, cf. Bongenaar 1997, 138.

9 Le dossier du bureau de la laine de l'Ekur est actuellement composé de 11 textes: FLP 1480 (17-iii-Artaxerxès 21), *NABU* 1997/13b (30-ix-Artaxerxès 35), FLP 1455 (4-x-Artaxerxès 35), ROMCT 2 48 (8-x-Artaxerxès 35), Stigers 24 (26-x-Artaxerxès 35), ROMCT 2 51 (12-xi-Artaxerxès 35), Stigers 3 (20-xi-Artaxerxès 35), *NABU* 1997/13a (23-I-Artaxerxès 36), ROMCT 2 n°49 (27-v-Artaxerxès 36), ROMCT 2 50 (20-xi-Artaxerxès 36), ROMCT 2 47 (28-xi-Artaxerxès 36). Un premier commentaire en a été proposé par M.W. Stolper (1988), qui penche en faveur d'une attribution au règne d'Artaxerxès Ier.

argent et d'acquérir des produits rares. Mais les membres de cette structure de gestion ne sont pas pour autant des marchands.

Les tamkâru

Il n'existe pas de véritable archive de *tamkâru* pour l'époque néo-babylonienne mais un assez grand nombre des mentions dispersées, qui nous renseignent surtout sur les types de produits qui passent par les mains des gens portant ce titre.

L'activité des *tamkâru* peut se reconstituer de la manière suivante:

— ils apparaissent comme achetant contre argent des produits bruts ou des animaux au temple: des dattes (*Nbn* 612, *Nbn* 887, MacGinnis 118), de l'orge (VS 6 238: l'orge est payée en moutons), de la laine (CT 55 763), des moutons (CT 22 3). Les textes cités appartiennent aux archives comptables de l'Ebabbar. On peut considérer qu'il s'agit là de surplus du temple qui sont revendus pour procurer de l'argent au sanctuaire. Ces produits sont utilisés par les *tamkâru* pour des opérations commerciales qui leur sont propres, comme semble le montrer CT 22 3:1-10: «Les bergers qui ont vendu du petit bétail et les *tamkâru* qui l'ont emmené de leurs mains, assurent le service de mon seigneur (= le *qîpu* de l'Ebabbar) dans la ville d'Opis», où l'on peut supposer que les marchands-*tamkâru* ont pour dessein de revendre les moutons achetés à l'Ebabbar dans le centre commercial d'Opis. On constate aussi que certains marchands procèdent à des prêts de céréales envers des personnes privées. Il peut s'agir ici aussi d'un débouché de leurs acquisitions de produits agricoles auprès des sanctuaires. On trouve ainsi dans les archives de l'Ebabbar trois textes illustrant les activités de Sîn-aḫ-iddin fils d'Innudaʾinaʾ. Ce personnage est cité dès l'an 36 de Nabuchodonosor II avec son collègue Nabû-zêr-ukîn, où il achète de la laine au temple (CT 55 763). En l'an 2 de Nabonide (CT 55 96), son subordonné[10] Šamaš-iqîša, fils de Šamaš-aḫ-iddin consent un prêt de 3 *kur* d'orge à un couple; en l'an 5 de Nabonide (CT 55 173), le même Šamaš-iqîša est créditeur d'une certaine quantité d'orge sur un dénommé Kalbaia. Le texte précise que l'orge provient de l'association commerciale (*ḫarrânu*) de Sîn-aḫ-iddin, qui porte le titre de *tamkâr šarri*. A une date indéterminée du règne de Nabonide, enfin, a lieu un nouveau prêt d'orge de Šamaš-iqîša dans le cadre de l'association commerciale de Sîn-aḫ-iddin à un nommé Nabû-mîta-uballiṭ. Il s'agit dans les trois cas de prêts d'une durée inférieure à une année, à rembourser en orge au moment de la récolte.

— dans l'autre sens, les *tamkâru* apparaissent également comme fournisseurs des sanctuaire en produits rares: par exemple de l'or à l'Eanna d'Uruk (GC 2 39) sous Nabopolassar, ou de la résine de genévrier (ŠIM.LI) au temple de Nippur sous Artaxerxès (Stiggers 24). Le texte TuM 2/3 251 enregistre la fourniture par un *tamkâru* d'au moins 114 mines d'alun, mais il n'est pas sûr que le récipiendaire soit un agent du temple; il pourrait aussi s'agir d'une transaction privée. On remarque que les *tamkâru* sont par ailleurs toujours à même de fournir au temple des animaux: des moutons (CT 55 483,

10 Sîn-aḫ-iddin n'est pas le contractant direct de ces textes, mais y apparaît comme propriétaire ultime du produit prêté, et porte seul le titre de *tamkâru*. Le Šamaš-iqîša mentionné ici n'est vraisemblablement pas le *rab bûli* attesté au début du règne de Nabonide: cf. Bongenaar 1997, 130.

608; VS 6 238), ou des poissons (YOS 7 151), mais il semble s'agir dans chaque cas de besoins ponctuels, portant sur quelques têtes, et non sur des troupeaux entiers.

— le texte CT 55 823 [n°3] semble prouver enfin que les *tamkâru* peuvent avoir à verser au temple une dîme (*ešrû*). L'origine souvent occidentale du lin importé en Babylonie place ce document dans le contexte du commerce international (voir ci-dessous) et pose la question de la nature de l'obligation contractée par les marchands envers l'Ebabbar de Sippar qui se traduit par l'acquittement d'une telle dîme.

— le cercle d'activité des *tamkâru* n'est pas restreint aux sanctuaires, car ils sont à même de fournir à des individus privés toutes sortes de biens: le texte TCL 12 32 montre ainsi que l'on peut acheter un esclave à des *tamkâru*.[11] On les trouve enfin mentionnés comme témoins dans des actes officiels ou privés, dont la nature n'est pas toujours commerciale.[12]

— toutes ces mentions éparses ne permettent pas véritablement de savoir si l'on a affaire avec les *tamkâru* à un corps structuré de marchands, possédant sa propre hiérarchie comme à l'époque paléo-babylonienne. Aucun *tamkâru* n'est cité comme rattaché explicitement à un temple;[13] quand il y a rattachement à un organisme officiel, c'est avec le palais royal, d'où les titres de *tamkâr šarri* attribué à plusieurs d'entre eux,[14] sans parler du célèbre cas de Ḫanunu, chef des marchands royaux.[15] Cependant le titre de *tamkâr šarri* n'indique pas forcément en lui-même que l'on a affaire à des membres de l'administration: il peut s'agir d'organismes commerciaux ou d'individus dont l'une des activités est la fourniture des besoins du palais, ou la commercialisation de certains de ses biens, sans qu'ils soient pour autant intégrés dans la structure de l'administration palatiale.

— on ne décèle, par ailleurs, aucune hiérarchie interne autre que celle mettant les *tamkâru* sous l'autorité d'un chef des marchands (LÚ GAL DAM.GÀR.MEŠ: CT 55 823, MacGinnis 118, cf. Bongenaar 1997, 138-139), ou faisant apparaître des subordonnés agissant en leur nom, mais dépourvus eux-même du titre de *tamkâru* (cf. ci-dessus, le cas de Šamaš-iqîša). La mention dans les archives des Murašû d'un «préposé des marchands» (LÚ *šaknu ša* LÚ DAM.GÀR.MEŠ: PBS 2/1 195) renvoie à un contexte particulier, puisqu'il

---

11 TCL 12 32:37-38: LÚ-*tú ina* ŠU^{II} LÚ.DAM.GÀR *ab-kam-ma šup-ra*.

12 Dans le texte 26 de M.T. Roth, *Babylonian Marriage Agreements 7th-3rd Centuries B.C. AOAT* 222 (Neukirchen-Vluyn, 1989), on trouve 4 *tamkâr šarri* cités comme témoins à Sippar, en l'an 5 d'un roi achéménide.

13 Le texte *Nbn* 464 pourrait être interprété comme mentionnant des rations d'entretien versées par l'Ebabbar de Sippar à des marchands, mais il pose des problèmes de lecture que seule une collation précise pourra résoudre. En particulier l. 2, faut-il lire: NINDA.ḪÁ KURUM$_6$.ḪÁ LÚ.DAM.<GÀR>.MEŠ ? Cf. Bongenaar 1997, 139, et J. MacGinnis, 'The Royal Establishment at Sippar in the 6th Century BC', *ZA* 84 (1994), 205 note 38.

14 Sîn-aḫ-iddin, fils d'Innudaʾinaʾ, LÚ DAM.GÀR LUGAL: CT 55 96, [118?], 173(!); Lûṣî-ana-nûri, fils d'Arrabi, LÚ DAM.GÀR LUGAL (VS 6 238); Aḫî-nûrî, fils de Šulum-Adad, LÚ DAM.GÀR LUGAL (VS 6 252); Nabû-nâʾid, LÚ *dam-ga-ar*^{sic} LUGAL (VS 3 18); Ardiya, fils de Nabû-aḫ-iddin, LÚ DAM.<GÀR> LUGAL (*Nbn* 17). Le texte VS 6 252 mentionne également un *tamkâru* du gouverneur (l. 15': LÚ DAM.GÀR *šá* LÚ GAR.KUR).

15 Oppenheim 1967, 253.

existe à Nippur un *ḫaṭru ša tamkarê*, qui n'est pas cité pour ses activités commerciales, mais en tant que communauté de feudataires. Le préposé ainsi nommé a d'ailleurs des activités fiscales dans le texte où il apparaît, et non commerciales.

— il semble enfin que certains *tamkâru* soient spécialisés dans certains domaines, si c'est bien ainsi qu'il faut comprendre des mentions comme LÚ DAM.<GÀR> UDU.NÍTA («marchand de moutons», VS 6 238; le terme est attesté en entier dans *Dar* 141), ou LÚ DAM.GÀR ZÚ.LUM.MA («marchands de dattes», *Nbn* 887), mais leur rareté même amène à penser que la norme est plutôt dans la non spécialisation.

On retiendra, au total, qu'il existe de manière indubitable, des groupes d'agents commerciaux portant le titre explicite de «marchand-*tamkâru*», qui paraissent intervenir de manière privilégiée dans les processus de commercialisation des temples ou du palais royal, soit pour écouler une partie de leurs réserves en produits bruts, soit pour leur procurer des marchandises rares ou satisfaire des besoins ponctuels. Le champ d'activité de ces *tamkâru* n'est cependant pas restreint à ce cercle officiel mais s'étend aussi au domaine des transactions privées. On considèrera donc que, comme à d'autres époques, les marchands fonctionnent de manière indépendante, avec leur circuits propres de commercialisation, dont peuvent profiter temple, palais, ou individus privés.

Les données des archives privées

Il reste pourtant difficile de faire la liaison entre les *tamkâru* et les archives privées, pourtant abondantes à l'époque néo-babylonienne, et qui illustrent elles aussi les relations commerciales. La structure la plus directement identifiable est l'association commerciale réalisée par les contrats *ana ḫarrâni* (KASKAL^{II}), qui associe deux ou plusieurs personnes, avec toute une série de cas de figure, dont l'inventaire précis a été réalisé par H. Lanz.[16] L'apport de capital peut y être unique ou partagé entre plusieurs investisseurs, les opérations commerciales peuvent être réalisées par un mandataire ou par l'un des bailleurs de fonds.

Mais, comme l'a nettement marqué H. Lanz, le champ d'application de ces associations déborde largement du cadre commercial *stricto sensu*: il touche aussi bien ce que l'on pourrait appeler la «sphère de production» (contrats *ana ḫarrâni* pour l'exploitation d'une terre ou celle d'une brasserie), que la «sphère financière» (certains contrats *ana ḫarrâni* ont pour objet essentiel des opérations de prêt), ou la véritable «sphère commerciale».[17] Dès lors, il apparaît que si leur but reste relativement indéterminé, c'est la nature juridique même de ces contrats qui est l'essentiel. Il s'agit avant tout de fixer de manière précise les modalités d'investissement et de partage des bénéfices, et l'on a ici un cas identique à celui du contrat écrit de reconnaissance de dette,

[16] Lanz 1976.

[17] Lanz 1976, 139: «Trotzdem ist das *ḫarrânu*-Geschäft in chaldäischer und frühpersischer Zeit wohl nicht mehr überwiegend mit dem überlandhandel verbunden, sondern hat auch in vielen anderen Wirtschaftszweigen Eingang gefunden. Möglicherweise waren die bedeutenderen und langdauernden *ḫarrânu*-Gesellschaften nicht mehr auf einen engen Gewerbezweig spezialisiert, sondern traten immer dort in Erscheinung, wo gerade günstige Gewinne erzielt werden konnten.»

dont le champ d'application apparaît lui aussi particulièrement large, ou à celui des contrats de dépôt récemment étudiés par M. Stolper.[18] Le but premier des contrats *ana ḫarrâni* est de fixer les relations entre associés, quel que soit le but de l'association commerciale ainsi constituée.

Si c'est en amont et en aval de l'opération commerciale, c'est-à-dire au moment du rassemblement des fonds puis du partage des bénéfices, que le contrat *ana ḫarrâni* prend toute sa signification, les données que fournit leur corpus n'éclairent donc finalement qu'assez peu la réalité des opérations commerciales réalisées. Elles illustrent par contre de manière précise les possibilités de circulation de l'argent: de même que certaines reconnaissances de dette entrent dans le cadre des relations de sociabilité, et ne procurent pas de bénéfice substantiel au créancier autre que l'obligation morale contractée par le débiteur, il semble que les contrats d'association commerciale *ana ḫarrâni* permettent d'associer à un noyau familial des membres éloignés ou des gens n'appartenant pas au cercle familial strict.

Une illustration de cette hypothèse peut être trouvée dans la carrière d'Iddin-Marduk descendant de Nûr-Sîn, telle qu'elle a été reconstituée par C. Wunsch.[19] Elle observe que ce personnage bâtit sa fortune sur le transport et la commercialisation de produits agricoles: dattes, orge, et surtout oignons. Il joue ainsi le rôle d'intermédiaire entre les petits producteurs des bords du Canal de Borsippa qui relie cette ville aux quartier du sud de Babylone et la population de la capitale qui a tendance à croître à partir de la reconstruction, de l'extension et de l'embellissement de la ville par Nabuchodonosor II. C. Wunsch suppose avec raison que l'augmentation de cette population urbaine va de pair avec une stagnation, sinon même une diminution des surfaces agricoles dans la ville même de Babylone et ses environs immédiats. Les petits producteurs campagnards ne disposant pas des ressources personnelles suffisantes pour assurer eux-même la commercialisation des surplus que dégageaient leurs exploitations, Iddin-Marduk d'abord par le biais de sociétés commerciales en partenariat, puis de manière indépendante, a profité de cette situation pour assurer un débouché aux exploitants et fournir le marché de la capitale. Les données dont dispose C. Wunsch ne permettent pas de déterminer exactement le montant du bénéfice réalisé par Iddin-Marduk sur ses opérations commerciales, ni la manière dont est écoulée la marchandise qu'il achète. Mais on voit ainsi apparaître dès cette époque le prototype d'un genre d'homme d'affaires qui bâtit sa fortune sur l'existence d'un marché relativement important pour les produits agricoles, qu'il est en mesure de transporter et de livrer avec un équipement (moyen de transport, main d'œuvre) hors de portée des petits producteurs de la campagne.

Peut-on définir ce type d'entreprise comme essentiellement *commerciale*? L'achat et la revente de produits agricoles sont bien présents, mais comme l'observe C. Wunsch,[20] on trouve aussi chez Iddin-Marduk et ses associés d'autres activités: par exemple un système de prêt aux exploitants en cours d'année, remboursable au moment de la récolte et qui permet de «réserver» celle-ci au bénéfice du créancier-acheteur; ou bien l'achat aux responsables administratifs royaux du produit des taxes, versées en *naturalia*, alors qu'ils ont surtout besoin d'argent. En échange, les agents du roi assurent le transport à faible coût jusqu'à Babylone; et le cercle d'hommes d'affaires auquel appartient Iddin-Marduk

18 Stolper 1993.
19 Wunsch 1993.
20 Wunsch 1993, 21-37.

peut même être amené à assurer certains aspects de la perception de ces taxes. Au total, il y a beaucoup de points communs entre les *tamkâru* proprement dits et les hommes d'affaires comme Iddin-Marduk, mais ces derniers ont un champ d'activité plus large, qui ne peut être réduit aux seules opérations commerciales. Le stade supérieur, représenté par les familles Egibi[21] ou Murašû,[22] ou l'entourage du gouverneur Bêlšunu[23] consiste à contrôler de surcroît la production agricole elle-même.

Dans le cas d'Iddin-Marduk joue aussi le fait qu'il a probablement eu besoin d'un capital de départ qu'il ne pouvait rassembler sur ses ressources propres, et qu'il a trouvé dans les associations commerciales auxquelles il participe. Lorsque son entreprise réussit, il mène certaines opérations sur ses fonds propres, et le fait de participer à des associations commerciales est surtout dû à l'impossibilité de couvrir un champ d'opérations devenu très vaste. La phase ultime est l'intégration de son activité dans celle de la famille Egibi, et le recours à des agents (essentiellement des esclaves) propres à sa firme.

Types de commerce

La commercialisation des produits de base

La plupart des produits agricoles provenaient de terres régies par des contrats privés ou publics. Leur destination première était la nourriture ou l'entretien des tenanciers et des propriétaires, d'où l'obligation pour les premiers de les livrer dans la maison ou l'entrepôt des seconds, en prenant souvent à leur charge les frais de transport (*gimru*).[24] Il est probable qu'une partie excédait les besoins personnels des propriétaires et pouvait ensuite être mise sur le marché, soit par le biais de prêts, soit pour être vendue. Mais aucune source écrite ne documente explicitement le circuit commercial des céréales: le problème se pose en particulier de savoir comment il faut interpréter les relevés de prix consignés dans les *Astronomical Diaries* de Babylone. S'agit-il du cours réel, sur le marché, des principaux produits agricoles (orge, dattes, laine, sésame), ce qui établirait non seulement l'existence d'un «marché», mais en attesterait sa régularité mensuelle? S'agit-il d'une compilation tirée de transactions d'ordre privé, mais dont on ne voit pas très bien comment on aurait pu établir la synthèse? Ou bien s'agit-il de données extraites de la comptabilité du temple, soit pour satisfaire ses propres besoins, soit pour écouler au contraire ses surplus? En tout état de cause, ces enregistrements de prix donnent de réelles indications quantitatives, mais ne nous renseignent pas sur les structures de commercialisation des céréales ou des autres produits agricoles.

---

21 Van Driel 1985-86; Krecher 1970; Martirossian 1977a; *id.* 1977b; *id.* 1978; *id.* 1983; Ungnad 1941-44; Weingort 1939.

22 Cardascia 1951; Stolper 1985; van Driel 1989.

23 Stolper 1987; *id.* 1990a.

24 Les frais de transport des produits agricoles peuvent être énormes par rapport à la valeur de base. Bongenaar 1997, 39, cite plusieurs attestations où les frais de transport de farine pour le compte du temple représentent 1/3 de la quantité initiale.

La même question se pose pour la référence assez souvent fait à un «cours du marché» (GANBA/*maḫîru*) de telle ou telle ville,[25] qui sert de référence pour le remboursement de certaines dettes. Il reste enfin problématique de savoir comment étaient payés ces produits du marché, alors qu'on sait que la circulation de l'argent restait relativement restreinte, et qu'en l'absence de véritable monnaie divisionnaire, un achat au détail mettait en jeu une quantité infime d'argent, nécessitant une pesée très fine.

Le cas d'Iddin-Marduk, tel qu'il a été présenté par C. Wunsch, milite en faveur d'une commercialisation de certains produits agricoles: dans son cas essentiellement les oignons. L'hypothèse la plus vraisemblable est donc qu'il existait dans les villes, un ou plusieurs marchés de quartier, servant à l'écoulement de la production des jardins potagers et des champs de la périphérie, et que recouvre sans doute l'expression *ina sûqi*. Mais ce marché ne fonctionnait que comme un complément à l'accès aux ressources alimentaires, qui provenaient normalement des propriétés foncières d'une partie de la population urbaine, ou des distributions de rations d'entretien de la part des grands organismes.

Il est par contre plus douteux qu'il ait existé un système aussi élaboré d'encadrement du commerce des produits agricoles que ceux que l'on trouve autour de l'agora athénienne, ou avec la préfecture romaine de l'annone. Ces «marchés» de quartier répondraient à deux nécessités: compléter ce que la gestion directe ne pouvait assurer, compenser, pour une partie de la population urbaine l'éloignement, ou l'absence d'accès à ces ressources.

Si l'on pense naturellement en premier aux produits alimentaires, il faut leur adjoindre aussi les animaux. Même si les achats de moutons par les temples sont abondamment attestés, de même que les contrats privés d'achats de mules ou d'ânes, il est probable que la transaction s'effectuait le plus souvent de manière privée, sans passer par un lieu de marché des animaux, comme le montrent TCL 13 132 [n°4] et 133 [n°5].

Pour récapituler, il existe probablement un commerce de détail, qui permet l'écoulement direct d'une production de type privé. Il semble que certains entrepreneurs privés réalisent des associations commerciales pour profiter des opportunités liées au développement de Babylone. Mais tout cela reste de type local. On ne discerne pas de commerce de type régional à l'intérieur de la Babylonie elle-même, sauf quelques cas particuliers. Les grands organismes subviennent à leurs besoins d'une autre manière: soit par la possession de propriétés dans les endroits de production des produits dont ils ont besoin, soit par l'envoi de caravanes chargées d'aller chercher à l'extérieur ces produits nécessaires. Ces opérations commerciales relèvent alors du personnel du temple issu des cercles d'artisans spécialisés, et des *tamkâru* royaux.

---

25 Par exemple: *BBSt* 9: «à ce moment-là, pour 1 sicle d'or, on avait 1 *kur* de grain aux marchés du pays d'Akkad»; *Nbk* 59: argent à rembourser en dattes selon les cours de Babylone (*kî maḫîri ša Bâbili*) au mois d'Araḫšamnu; *Nbn* 103: argent à rembourser au mois vii, avec un intérêt calculé en dattes, selon le tarif de la ville de Šaḫrînu (*akî maḫîri ša Šaḫrîn(i) itti* 1 *šiqli* 1 *pi akî ḫubulli inamdin*); *Cyr* 60: emprunt d'argent à rendre dans un délai maximum de 2 mois, avec un intérêt calculé en dattes (*akî maḫîri ša Bâbili itti* 1 GÍN 0,0.2 *suluppê inandin*); BV 106: *akî maḫîri ša Babili itti* 1 *manê* 2 GUR ŠE.BAR (au mois de Tašrîtu); *Dar* 309: orge à rembourser en argent au mois de Ṭebêtu *akî maḫîri ša Bâbili;* TCL 13 186: orge remboursée en argent *akî maḫîri ša Bâbili.*

Formes du commerce de détail

Notre méconnaissance encore profonde des réalités de la vie quotidienne fait qu'il est difficile de présenter ici autre chose qu'un certain nombre d'exemples ponctuels, qui illustrent ce phénomène sans pour autant en rendre compte intégralement.

Dans la pratique de l'artisanat, l'artisan spécialisé écoule lui-même ce qu'il fabrique, et travaille dans certains cas à la commande. De ce fait, les contrats passés avec les clients peuvent prendre des formes juridiques qui nous semblent *a priori* peu conformes: c'est ainsi que plusieurs commandes passées à des artisans très spécialisés se présentent comme des reconnaissances de dette.[26] De même l'on intégrera dans des contrats de location de maison des clauses qui prévoient la reconstruction d'éléments annexes,[27] et qui montrent que le domaine des travaux publics ne génère pas de commercialisation au sens strict.

Il est intéressant de remarquer que la pratique de formation par apprentissage d'un esclave à un travail artisanal spécialisé peut tout à la fois satisfaire les besoins de certaines familles assez riches pour disposer dans leur personnel domestique d'esclaves hautement spécialisés, et permettre d'utiliser le savoir-faire de ces esclaves placés en apprentissage pour commercialiser leur production, parfois sous leur propre responsabilité. Il vaudrait la peine, de ce point de vue, de collecter systématiquement les attestations de *bît kâri*, qui semblent souvent fonctionner comme des échoppes dépendant d'une maison de notable, dont le revenu commercial est partagé entre un esclave tenancier et son propriétaire.

Dans un domaine au moins, on peut avoir une vue un peu précise, celui de la fabrication de l'alcool ou de la bière. Les archives des Egibi en particulier montrent que le matériel de brasserie, et les récipients de conservation, peut-être parce qu'ils avaient du mal à trouver leur place dans l'architecture habituelle de la maison, pouvaient être loués, ou prêtés à des individus disposant d'installations spécifiques; le produit de la commercialisation de cette bière ou de cet alcool revenait alors en partie à l'investisseur. On constate que plusieurs sociétés commerciales *ana ḫarrâni* ont été constituées à cet effet.[28] Le stade ultime semble avoir été l'installation d'esclaves domestiques comme gérants (ou gérantes: la profession paraît comporter un fort effectif féminin) d'établissements du type cabaret, qui sont un des lieux traditionnels de la sociabilité babylonienne.[29]

La question peut également être posée de la place tenue par certains prébendiers dans un éventuel circuit commercial de détail. Lorsque l'on examine les archives d'Iddin-Nabû de la famille du Forgeron à Babylone,[30] il apparaît que sa possession d'une prébende de *ṭâbiḫu* dans le temple d'Išḫara, lui assurait un revenu de viande et d'abats de moutons assez important et régulier. Il n'est pas sûr que ce revenu aît tout entier été consommé par Iddin-Nabû et sa famille, et peut-être faut-il envisager qu'une partie en était revendue dans

---

26 Cf. en particulier la série *Nbk* 307; *Nbn* 131, 171, 204, 216, 267, 501, 566; BRM 1 59; TCL 12 101.

27 Cf. ainsi: Walker 1978, 237-240 (text G); VS 5 50 et 117; TBER Pl. 88 (MNB 1907); *Nbn* 845; CT 44 76.

28 Cf. *Dar* 280, 359, 395 = 396; pour le vin, cf. *Nbn* 1013.

29 Pour la mise sur pied d'un tel établissement dans les archives des Egibi, cf. Joannès 1992.

30 Peiser 1890; MacGinnis 1991-92.

le commerce. Les données précises qui confirmeraient cette hypothèse n'ont cependant pas encore été rassemblées.

LE COMMERCE INTERNATIONAL

Les degrés d'accès

L'accès au commerce international peut être étudié de manière significative à travers les archives de l'Eanna d'Uruk, de Nabopolassar à Cambyse. Tel qu'on peut le reconstituer, le système présente un horizon souvent limité à la seule ville de Babylone: des agents de l'Eanna, ou des membres haut placés de son administration se fournissaient en produits rares dans la capitale, au cours de séjours qui n'étaient pas toujours dictés par des nécessités commerciales. Il apparaît ainsi que la période du début de l'année, au cours de laquelle était célébrée la fête de l'Akîtu, nécessitant la présence à Babylone de la statue d'Ištar d'Uruk et d'une partie des dignitaires de l'Eanna, était également le moment où avaient lieu certaines des transactions commerciales.

Les agents de ces transactions sont soit des membres de l'administration, en particulier le *qîpu* du temple ou le *ša rêš šarri bêl piqitti ša Eanna*, soit des membres du collège des artisans parmi les plus spécialisés (en particuliers orfèvres et joailliers, lorsqu'il s'agit de l'achat d'or[31]), soit des agents commerciaux dont il est probable alors que malgré l'absence de mention explicite, il s'agisse de *tamkâru*: le domaine d'action de Bêl-êṭir fils d'Amêl-Nabû[32] correspond étroitement à ce qui a été dit plus haut des marchands lorsqu'ils sont en relation avec le temple.

Les produits acquis au cours de ces transactions peuvent être d'origine locale (moutons ou laine), ou régionale (bitume, cire, vin), ou internationale (pierres précieuses, or, fer, lin, alun, produits tinctoriaux, produits de parfumerie). La raison de l'achat en Babylonie du nord de moutons ou de laine est difficile à déterminer: il peut s'agir d'espèces ou de qualités particulières, ou d'un besoin immédiat lié à la présence à Babylone. Le commerce régional est, lui, plus compréhensible. Par ce terme, on peut désigner l'environnement immédiat de la Babylonie proprement dite, en particulier la région du Moyen Euphrate et la Haute Mésopotamie. La première est bien documentée comme source privilégiée de bitume depuis la ville de Hît, ou comme lieu d'élevage des abeilles dans la région de Hanat. Si l'Ebabbar de Sippar a la possibilité, par sa situation géographique, d'organiser lui-même des expéditions fluviales pour aller chercher bitume et asphalte à Hît, les sanctuaires plus éloignés préféraient s'approvisionner à Babylone. Il y avait donc clairement un système de transport par l'Euphrate de ce produit depuis le Moyen-Euphrate jusqu'à la capitale. La même pratique est d'ailleurs attestée par Xénophon dans l'*Anabase* en ce qui concerne les pierres de meule,[33] et s'inscrit dans une tradition que l'on voit attestée dès le début du second millénaire. De même, pour le vin une origine sur le Moyen-Euphrate, dans la vallée de la Diyala, et en Haute-Mésopotamie est attestée sur une longue période: on peut donc supposer que son commerce par le Tigre

---

31 Surtout Bêl-ibni, fils de Nâdinu, et son fils Ḫašdaia, descendants de Babûtu, orfèvres, ainsi que Marduk-šum-lišir, fils de Balâssu, descendant de Nûr-Sîn, joaillier: cf. Kümmel 1979, 24-30.

32 Cf. TEBR, 249-250.

33 *Anabase*, Livre I.

et l'Euphrate avait continué de prospérer, permettant ainsi d'approvisionner ses deux principaux débouchés: les sanctuaires et la Cour royale.

Entrent enfin dans ce que l'on peut appeler le véritable commerce international, des produits venant en majorité de l'ouest, que recouvre la dénomination d'*Ebir nâri*. Cela ne signifie pas qu'il s'agisse de la seule origine attestée, car un commerce d'origine orientale est également mentionné, et s'est sans doute renforcé à partir de la mise en place de l'empire achéménide. Il convient donc d'examiner, à travers les sources disponibles, ce que l'on peut dire d'abord du commerce d'origine orientale, puis du commerce d'origine occidentale.

Le commerce oriental

La principale «porte d'entrée» en Babylonie de ce commerce semble avoir été la ville d'Opis, au débouché du confluent du Tigre et de la Diyala. Cette ville apparaît à la fois dans les archives des sanctuaires et dans celles de la famille Egibi, lorsque ses membres avaient en charge la gestion des domaines de Nergal-šar-uṣur situés dans cette région. Le texte *Nbk* 361,[34] éclaire ainsi le rôle de tête de pont commerciale que revêt Opis.

L'un des dossiers les plus intéressants dans ce contexte des relations avec l'Est est celui des voyages effectués par Itti-Marduk-balâṭu depuis le début du règne de Cyrus jusqu'à la fin de celui de Cambyse en Iran. On a souvent interprété ces voyages comme le signe d'une expansion financière, et surtout commerciale des Egibi vers l'est.[35] En fait, on remarque que ces voyages sont les seuls à avoir jamais entraîné un déplacement prolongé d'Itti-Marduk-balâṭu en dehors de sa zone traditionnelle d'activité qui se restreint au triangle Kiš-Babylone-Borsippa.[36] Les neuf voyages, en majorité vers l'Iran, qu'a accomplis Itti-Marduk-balâṭu sont à mettre en rapport avec le rôle de gestionnaires de domaines de la Couronne que les Egibi avaient assumé de Nabuchodonosor II à Nabonide, et qui les mettait, à partir du règne de Cyrus, soit en relation avec la nouvelle famille royale, soit avec de hauts dignitaires perses.[37] Les opérations financières conclues à cette occasion n'étaient donc pas la raison d'être des voyages d'Itti-Marduk-balâṭu. Il est d'autant plus intéressant de remarquer que le chef de la famille Egibi a noué au cours de l'un de ces voyages des liens avec la structure commerciale officielle en poste en Iran, qui lui valut le cadeau d'une servante. Les textes *Camb* 384 et T. Pinches, *Hebraica* 8 nous fournissent ainsi le nom du chef des marchands local: Artaruš(u) (LÚ GAL DAM.GÀR.MEŠ / GAL LÚ DAM.GÀR).

Cette interprétation des voyages de la famille Egibi en Iran, déjà mise en avant par M. Stolper,[38] rejoint l'interprétation qu'il donne de la présence à plusieurs reprises à Suse du chef de la famille Murašû, un siècle plus tard. Il ne s'agit pas de voyages d'affaires, mais d'un accès à la Cour royale lié à la gestion des domaines de Babylonie. La conséquence

---

34 Cf. le commentaire de G. van Driel (1985-86, 55).

35 Zadok 1976; Zawadzki 1994.

36 A l'exception d'un déplacement à Uruk en l'an 6 de Cyrus (*Cyr* 219), et d'un autre à Opis en l'an 2 de Cambyse (*Camb* 143).

37 Cette hypothèse est développée et justifiée dans un article en cours d'élaboration, à paraître, sous le titre «Les voyages d'Itti-Marduk-balâṭu».

38 Stolper 1990b; *id.* 1992.

globale est donc que les relations commerciales avec l'est n'ont pratiquement pas laissé de traces dans les archives privées babyloniennes actuellement connues, et que les mentions d'Opis fournissent pour le moment la seule véritable documentation liée à ce courant oriental.

Il est probable par ailleurs que les relations attestées de la Babylonie du sud avec la Susiane sous les Achéménides ont eu aussi une tonalité commerciale, même si, pour l'instant le seul mouvement bien attesté soit celui des fournitures en hommes et main d'œuvre découlant des obligations envers la Cour de Suse.[39] La présence en Iran d'une organisation commerciale hierarchisée montre que la Cour royale était une destination commerciale naturelle, et l'on peut penser que des marchands se joignaient aux convoiements de produits et d'hommes partant de Babylonie vers l'Elam.

Le commerce occidental

La reconstitution du commerce avec l'ouest que l'on peut proposer repose encore actuellement sur l'article de référence de L. Oppenheim.[40] Les développements qu'il y a consacrés aux divers produits importés dispensent, me semble-t-il, de revenir sur la question de la nature et de l'origine précise de ces produits. Tout au plus peut-on noter qu'à propos du vin syrien, la question peut se poser du statut exact des lieux de production. La fourniture régulière de vin de Hilbunu, de Simyra et de Tuʾimmu est peut-être le fait d'une structure commerciale, mais pourrait provenir aussi de domaines royaux administrés par des agents de la Couronne.[41] L'acheminement de ce produit vers la Babylonie relèverait alors moins du commerce que du système de livraison au palais, puis aux temples par redistribution.

Pour le reste, le fonctionnement que l'on peut reconstituer est le suivant: le temple met à la disposition de certaines personnes une somme d'argent souvent assez importante (de 10 à 20 mines en général), à charge pour eux de constituer une cargaison de produits importés (*mêreštu*) et de la faire parvenir à l'Eanna. Il semble que les besoins soient définis de manière très générale, et que l'achat soit conditionné à la fois par la disponibilité et le prix des produits demandés. Les textes qui évoquent ces transactions commerciales insistent d'ailleurs sur le fait que les acheteurs doivent payer selon que la marchandise est disponible ou non (YOS 7 63: «selon la cargaison qu'ils auront pu constituer dans l'*Ebir nâri*, et qu'ils auront fait parvenir à Babylone, ils livreront dans l'Eanna du vin pur, du miel pur, du cuivre, du fer, de l'étain, de la laine bleue, et (d'autres produits) nécessaires à

---

39 Les textes mentionant un «service» à accomplir en Elam ne sont pas rares, bien qu'ils n'aient pas fait l'objet d'un rassemblement systématique. Le dernier en date à avoir été publié est celui de R. Zadok, *NABU* 1995/04. Cf. également pour la ville d'Ur, F. Joannès, *NABU* 1988/01. La mobilisation ordonnée à Uruk en l'an 2 de Darius II attestée par les archives des Murašû semble illustrer le rôle de débouché immédiat de l'Elam que tient le sud mésopotamien à cette époque.

40 Oppenheim 1967.

41 Cf. Joannès 1997. Que du vin soit acheté directement en Syrie par les temples est cependant prouvé par CT 57 206:11-14: [x MA.NA K]Ù.BABBAR *a-na* 10.TA *šap-pat* ^{giš}GEŠTIN KÙ *šá e-bir* I_7 *a-na sat-tuk* ^{m}*na-ṣir u* ^{m}*šu-la-a it-tan-nu*.

l'Eanna»),[42] et ne pas prendre de bénéfice par rapport au prix d'acquisition entre l'*Ebir nâri* et la Babylonie (YOS 6 52: «là-dessus (= sur une somme originelle de 10 mines), pour 5 mines d'argent, selon la reconnaissance de dette qui a été produite dans l'Eanna à la charge d'Innin-zêr-ušabši et Innin-aḫḫê-iddin, ils livreront une cargaison selon le marché de l'*Ebir nâri* à la Dame d'Uruk»[43]).

Il en ressort que les expéditions commerciales de ces personnes sont financées pour l'essentiel par l'Eanna, qui met à leur disposition des fonds utilisables soit pour l'achat direct des produits, soit comme une somme d'argent dont ils auraient le libre emploi, mais qui porte alors un intérêt.[44] Ils sont chargés de prospecter dans l'*Ebir nâri*[45] et de faire acheminer vers Babylone, puis Uruk, les produits achetés.

Les textes étudiés par Oppenheim (YOS 6 168 [n°6] // PTS 2098 [n°7] et TCL 12 84 [n°8]) doivent être rattachés à ce système. L'un des problèmes qu'ils posent est celui de leur date: YOS 6 168[46] est daté du 7-vii de l'an 6 de Nabonide, TCL 12 84 du 5-vii de l'an 5 de Nabonide. Ce qui frappe est la reproduction presque exacte des quantités de produits cités (voir le tableau dans Oppenheim 1967, 238) d'un texte à l'autre. L. Oppenheim a choisi d'interpréter cette répétition comme l'indice que les marchands se constituaient d'une année à l'autre un contingent de marchandise identique; je préfèrerais y voir la preuve qu'il s'agit en fait d'une seule et même opération, et qu'une correction de la date s'impose, soit sur YOS 6 168, soit sur TCL 12 84. Dans une seule et même année (l'an 5 ou l'an 6 de Nabonide), les deux personnages nommés Šamaš-zêr-ibni, fils de Nanaia-iddin, et Nâdin-aḫi, fils d'Innin-aḫ-uṣur auraient fait parvenir dans l'Eanna un ensemble de produits, dont on a dressé l'inventaire le 5-vii par poids, au seul nom de Nâdin-aḫi (TCL 12 84),[47] puis dont on a déterminé la valeur 2 jours plus tard au moment de l'apurement des comptes avec les deux hommes d'affaires, en précisant le contingent de chacun (YOS 6 168 // PTS 2098).

Le versement personnel par Nâdin-aḫi le 5-vii de 2 pièces de tissu de lin, enregistré comme donation au temple (*irbu*), est requalifié le 7-vii comme dîme payée au temple (*ešrû*), et modifié pour chacune des deux personnes en ce qui concerne les produits fournis. On peut alors rapprocher ce versement de dîme de celui attesté en CT 55 823, où le chef des marchands offrait 1 *šalḫu* de lin au dieu Šamaš.[48]

---

42 YOS 7 63:5-9: *lìb-bu-ú mi-riš-*tu_4 *šá ina e-bir-*I_7 *i-maḫ-ḫa-ru-nim-ma a-na* TIN.TIR^{ki} *ú-šá-ak-šá-d*[*u*]*-nu* GEŠTIN KÙ LÀL KÙ ZABAR AN.BAR AN.NA SÍG ZA.GÌN.KUR.RA *u ḫi-šiḫ-*[tu_4] *šá* É.AN.NA *ina* É.AN.NA *i-na*[*m-din-nu*].

43 YOS 6 52:8-12: *ina lìb-bi šá* 5 MA.NA KÙ.BABBAR *a-ki-i ú-ìl-tì šá ina* É.AN.NA *ina* UGU ^{md}IN.NIN-NUMUN-GÁL-*ši u* ^{md}IN.NIN-ŠEŠ.MEŠ-MU *e-li-tu mi-riš-*tu_4 *a-ki-i* GANBA *šá e-bir-*I_7 *a-na* ^{d}GAŠAN *šá* UNUG^{ki} *i-nam-di-nu.*

44 Cette double possibilité est bien présente dans YOS 6 52; la partie constituée en dette porte un intérêt de 20% annuel.

45 La mention de YOS 7 63 *lìb-bu-ú mi-riš-*tu_4 *šá ina e-bir-*I_7 *i-maḫ-ḫa-ru-nim-ma* «selon la cargaison qu'ils auront pu constituer dans l'*Ebir nâri*», prouve qu'il y a déplacement effectif dans cette région. De même, l'interdiction de modifier le prix des denrées (YOS 6 52) ne se justifie que si elles ont été acquises sur place.

46 PTS 2098 n'est pas daté, mais peut, vu le parallélisme, être ramené à la date d'YOS 6 168.

47 Les lignes 1 à 8 de TCL 12 84 représentent une partie du contingent attribué à Nâdin-aḫi; les lignes 9 à 16 correspondent à une partie du contingent de Šamaš-zêr-ibni.

48 Cette dîme évoque les contributions des marchands d'Ur de la fin du IIIème millénaire et du début du IIème qui offraient des bateaux en métal précieux à la déesse Nikkal. Il s'agit donc probablement d'une

Si l'on reprend l'ensemble des données, les agents commerciaux attestés ici apparaissent comme pourvus par le temple d'une certaine somme de métal précieux, et d'une liste globale de produits à acheter. Ils prospectent l'ouest (*Ebir nâri*), pour se les procurer, et les ramènent à Uruk, via Babylone. Au moment de la livraison finale, on apure les comptes pour faire correspondre d'une part le versement initial avec la dépense réelle, et vérifier d'autre part que les prix des produits ou des objets ne sont pas exagérés. Les marchands fournissent enfin une contribution personnelle symbolique à la divinité pour la remercier du succès de l'entreprise. Aucun de ces textes n'inclut donc l'évaluation du bénéfice que l'on suppose réalisé par les marchands. Il se peut que la clé soit à chercher dans le texte YOS 6 52: à côté de la somme destinée aux achats du temple, les marchands disposaient d'un fonds en argent mis à leur disposition par le sanctuaire à intérêt, et devaient pouvoir l'utiliser pour leurs opérations personnelles. Cela implique que le bénéfice tiré d'une expédition commerciale à l'ouest était largement supérieur aux 20% d'intérêt à verser et aux coûts du transport, et explique qu'il s'agisse de produits en général rares. Ce système permet aux marchands de disposer de fonds extérieurs, mais ne génère pas a priori de commerce portant sur de grosses quantités.[49]

La question se pose naturellement de savoir si, réciproquement, il n'existait pas en Babylonie, des représentants de «maisons de commerce» occidentales, fournisseurs directs de produits importés. Le texte CT 2 2 mentionne ainsi la vente par un égyptien devant des témoins babyloniens, d'une pièce de lin à un membre du personnel du temple de Šamaš de Sippar. De même, les textes d'achats d'or réalisés pour le compte de l'Eanna d'Uruk par des membres de son personnel mandatés à cet effet, citent à Babylone un certain nombre de gens, dont plusieurs ont des noms non-babyloniens, et qui semblent installés à demeure dans la capitale. La présence en Babylonie de plusieurs importantes communautés ethniques d'origine occidentale, d'un palais royal aux besoins considérables sous les rois néo-babyloniens, et encore conséquents sous les Achéménides, ainsi que celle des représentants des principaux sanctuaires babyloniens à intervalles plus ou moins réguliers, justifiaient l'envoi de caravanes commerciales organisées par les communautés marchandes de l'ouest. Il est donc peu probable qu'il y ait eu, à proximité des frontières naturelles de la Babylonie, un ou plusieurs centres de redistribution du type *emporium* où seraient venus s'approvisionner les marchands babyloniens, comme le suppose L. Oppenheim. On assiste plutôt à deux mouvements opposés: de la Babylonie vers l'extérieur pour satisfaire certains besoins des grands organismes (palais et temples), de l'extérieur vers la Babylonie pour tirer parti du marché que représente à cette époque le pays. En l'état actuel des recherches, il est pratiquement impossible de juger de la valeur quantitative de ces mouvements, et de leurs rapport, mais le besoin ressenti d'aller s'approvisionner à l'ouest montre que les bénéfices générés justifiaient d'aller chercher sur place certains produits.

---

contribution volontaire de la part des marchands néo-babyloniens pour remercier la divinité du succès de l'entreprise.

[49] Les personnes actuellement connues qui apparaissent spécialisées dans la fourniture du temple d'Uruk en produits occidentaux sont: Bêl-êṭir fils d'Amêl-Nabû; Šamaš-zêr-ibni, fils de Nanaia-iddin; Nâdin-aḫi, fils d'Innin-aḫ-uṣur; Iqîšaia et Balâṭu, fils de Lâbâši, descendants de Šum-libši.

Un commerce local sur la production agricole et l'élevage, passant par les mains d'entrepreneurs privés et d'agents commerciaux spécialisés (*tamkâru*), existe bien en Babylonie à l'époque néo-babylonienne; il s'appuie sur les besoins d'une population urbaine croissante, mais son extension est limitée à la fois par le coût du transport (y compris les taxes de passage) et par le fait qu'il ne représente qu'un complément par rapport à un mode de production directe des propriétaires et de leurs exploitants. L'horizon géographique de ce commerce est donc vite limité.

Les associations commerciales mises sur pied par les entrepreneurs urbains ont de ce fait un champ d'application très général, même en dehors du commerce proprement dit, et ne débouchent pas sur la fondation de véritables «maisons de commerce».

C'est dans le commerce international que ce genre de structure s'est probablement mis en place, mais il n'est pas sûr que la part des babyloniens y ait été prépondérante. Des contacts directs avec l'est et l'ouest du Proche-Orient sont attestés, mais une ville comme Babylone paraît plus avoir fonctionné comme un marché régional d'importation et de redistribution vers les autres villes babyloniennes que comme une place majeure du commerce proche-oriental.

Annexe: textes cités

[n°1]

FLP 1595

	2 MA.NA KÙ.GI 4 EME.ME	2 mines d'or (sous forme de) 4 plaquettes
2	1 MA.NA KÙ.GI 2 *mu-kár-ri-šá-nu*	1 mine d'or (sous forme de) 2 bols
	5 GUN ^{giš}*ki-sit-ti* ^{giš}ERIN	5 talents de copeaux de cèdre
4	5 GUR ^{giš}ŠIM.LI	5 *kur* de genévrier
	2 GADA *sal-ḫu*	2 pièces de lin
6	*ir-bi šá* LUGAL	– donation du roi –
	šá ^{md}30-SIG$_5$-*iq*	que Sîn-mudammiq
8	LÚ.SAG LUGAL *iš-šá-a*	l'officier royal a apportée,
	ina É ^{d}UTU IGI-*ir*	(et qui) a été reçue dans le temple de Šamaš
10	ITI ŠE U$_4$ 3.KAM MU 13.KAM	3 Addaru de l'an 13
	^{d}NÀ-NÍ.TUK LUGAL TIN.TIR^{ki}	de Nabonide, roi de Babylone.

[n°2]

ROMCT 2 50

a-[*na* ^{md}EN.LÍL]-MU-GIN ^{m}*ba-la-ṭu* [*šá* UGU SÍG.ḪÁ]
2 *en*-[*na ina* KÙ.BABBAR] ŠÁM SÍG *šá ina* IGI-*ku-nu ina lìb-b*[*i*]
1 M[A.N]A KÙ.BABBAR ⌜*ku*⌝-*um* 1 MA.NA KÙ.BABBAR *šá* ^{md}EN-*it*-[*tan-nu*]
4 *šá* UGU ^{giš}BÁN *šá* I$_{7}$ ^{d}30 *a-na* 1+*en* ANŠE.KUR.RA
ir-bi šá KÁ *ana* É NÍG.GA SÌ-*in*
6 *ù ina* É-*šú* UG$_{6}^{!}$ *a-na* ^{md}EN-*it-tan-nu*
SÌ-*ʾa* ITI GAN U$_{4}$ 20.KAM MU 36.KAM
8 [^{m}*aš*]-*taḫ-šá-as-su* LUGAL U$_{4}$.BI 5 GÍN [KÙ.BABBAR]
ŠÁM 1+*et* TÚG *šu-pal-li-tu*$_{4}$ *a-na*
10 [^{m}]*man-nu-ki-i*-^{d}DIL.BAT ⌜x x x⌝
[LÚ].⌜UMBISAG KÁ⌝ *ina* ŠU^{II}-*šú* IGI

sceaux NA$_{4}$.KIŠIB NA$_{4}$.[KIŠIB]
^{md}MAŠ-MU ^{m}[...............]

A Enlil-šum-ukîn (et) Balâṭu, [les responsables de la laine]: "sur l'argent provenant de la vente de laine, qui est à votre disposition, là-dessus versez à Bêl-ittannu 1 mine d'argent, équivalent de la mine que Bêl-ittannu, Fermier Général du Canal de Sîn avait donnée au Trésor (du temple) pour l'achet d'un cheval – donation à la Porte (du temple) – qui est ensuite mort dans sa maison. Le 20 Kislîmu de l'an 36 d'Artaxerxès le roi. Ce même jour, recevez 5 sicles d'argent, prix d'un vêtement de dessous qui lui a été vendu, des mains de Mannu-kî-Dilbat, le scribe de la Porte". Sceau de Ninurta-iddin; sceau de [Sîn-nadin-šumi].[50]

[n°3]

CT 55 823

	1 GADA *šal-ḫi* [10]-*ú*	Une pièce de lin, dîme
2	*šá* LÚ GAL DAM.[GÀR.MEŠ]	que le Chef des marchands
	a-na ^{d}UTU *id-din-nu*	a donnée pour le dieu Šamaš,
4	*ina pa-ni* ^{md}SÁGGAR-*šì-man-ni*	(a été mise) à la disposition de Bunene-šîmanni,
	LÚ *mu-ka-bu-ú*	le ravaudeur.
6	ITI IZI U$_{4}$ 21.KÁM	21 Abu
	MU 13.KÁM ^{md}NÀ-I	de l'an 13 de Nabonide,
8	LUGAL E^{ki}	roi de Babylone.

50 Un cheval offert au temple avait été revendu pour 1 mine d'argent au Fermier Général du Canal de Sîn; mais il est mort prématurément et le temple doit rembourser son prix: l'argent est prélevé sur le produit de la vente de laine par le «bureau» qui en a la gestion; celui-ci encaisse par ailleurs le prix d'une pièce de lin vendue à un portier du temple par le sanctuaire.

[n°4]

TCL 13 132

1 U$_8$ 1 UD$_5$ PAP 2 *ṣe-e-nu šá* AN *mar-ri ù qa-an-ṭup-pu še-en-du*
2 *šá qa-bu-ut-tu*$_4$ *šá* ^{md}UTU-MU A-*šú šá* ^{m}*šul-lu-mu* LÚ.NA.GAD *šá* ^{d}PA
šá ul-tu É ^{md}IN.NIN-MU-URI$_3$ A-*šú šá* ^{m}DÙ-^{d}15 *ab-ka-na*
4 ^{md}IN.NIN-MU-URI$_3$ *i-bu-ku-nim-ma iq-bi um-ma* U$_4$ 6.KAM *šá* ITI IZI MU 4.KAM
^{m}*ku-ra-áš* LUGAL TIN.TIR^{ki} LUGAL KUR.KUR *ṣe-en a*$_4$ 2 *a-na* 3 GÍN 4-*tú*-LÁ^{ti}
KÙ.BABBAR
6 ^{md}UTU-MU LÚ.NA.GAD *šá* ^{d}PA *ina* É ^{m}*ki-na-a* A-*šú šá* ^{m}DÙ-^{d}15
A ^{m}*su-pe-e*-^{d}EN *it-tan-ni* ^{md}UTU-MU LÚ.NA.GAD *šá* ^{d}NÀ *i-bu-ku-nim-ma*
8 *iq-bi um-ma* 1 U$_8$ 1 UD$_5$ *šá* AN *mar-ri ù qa-an-ṭup-pu še-en-du*
a-na 3 GÍN 4-*tú*-LÁ^{ti} KÙ.BABBAR *a-na* ^{md}IN.NIN-MU-URI$_3$ A-*šú šá* ^{m}DÙ-^{d}15
10 *at-ta-din ù* ^{md}UTU-MU *niš* DINGIR *u* LUGAL *iz-ku-ru ki-i ṣe-e-nu a*$_4$ 2
ina É ^{m}*ki-na-a* A-*šú šá* ^{m}DÙ-^{d}15 A ^{m}*su-pe-e*-^{d}EN *a-na* ^{md}IN.NIN-MU-URI$_3$
12 A-*šú šá* ^{m}DÙ-^{d}15 *a-na* KÙ.BABBAR *ad-di-ni ù man-ma šá-nam-ma*
it-ti ^{md}IN.NIN-MU-URI$_3$ GANBA *ina ṣe-e-nu a*$_4$ 2 *it-ti-ia*
14 *i-pu-šu* KÙ.BABBAR *a*$_4$ 3 GÍN 4-*tú*-LÁ^{ti} *šá ina* ŠU^{II}
^{md}IN.NIN-MU-URI$_3$ *áš-šá-ʾa a-na* ^{m}*lu-la-ʾa*-^{d}NÀ
16 LÚ.GAL 1.ME-*ia at-ta-din*
(...)

1 brebis, 1 chèvre: total 2 têtes de petit bétail marquées de la bêche et du calame, du troupeau de Šamaš-iddin, fils de Šullumu, berger de Nabû, qui ont été emportées de la maison d'Innin-šum-uṣur. On a convoqué Innin-šum-uṣur et il a fait la déclaration suivante: «le 6-v de l'an 4 de Cyrus, roi de Babylone, roi des pays, ces 2 têtes de petit bétail, Šamaš-iddin, berger de Nabû, me les a vendues pour 2 sicles 3/4 d'argent, dans la maison de Kînaia, fils d'Ibni-Ištar, descendant de Supê-Bêl».

On a convoqué Šamaš-iddin et il a fait la déclaration suivante: «1 brebis et 1 chèvre marquées de la bêche et du calame, je les ai vendues pour 2 sicles 3/4 d'argent à Innin-šum-uṣur, fils d'Ibni-Ištar». Alors Šamaš-iddin a prononcé le serment du dieu et du roi: «(Je jure) que j'ai vendu ces 2 têtes de petit bétail, dans la maison de Kînaia, fils d'Ibni-Ištar, descendant de Supê-Bêl, contre argent à Innin-šum-uṣur, fils d'Ibni-Ištar et qui que ce soit d'autre qui ait pu être avec Innin-šum-uṣur pour négocier ces 2 têtes de petit bétail; ces 2 sicles 3/4 d'argent que j'avais reçus des mains de Innin-šum-uṣur, je les ai donnés à Lulaʾ-Nabû, mon chef de centurie». (...)

[n°5]

TCL 13 133

(...)
8 LÚ.DUMU.DÙ.MEŠ *šá ina pa-ni-šú-nu* ^{md}UTU-MU
A-*šú šá* ^{m}*šul-lu-mu* LÚ.NA.GAD *šá* ^{d}NÀ
10 *iq-bu-ú um-ma* 1 UDU.U$_8$ 1 UD$_5$
šá mar-ri u qa-an-ṭup-pi še-en-du
12 *a-na* ^{md}IN.NIN-MU-URI$_3$ A-*šú šá* ^{m}DÙ-^{d}15
u ^{m}ŠEŠ-MU A-*šú šá* ^{md}NÀ-GIN-IBILA
14 *a-na* KÙ.BABBAR *at-ta-din*

u ^{md}IN.NIN-MU-URI$_3$ *ina la qer-re-bu*
16 *šá* ^{m}ŠEŠ-MU *ina* UKKIN *iq-bu-ú*
um-ma a-na-ku u ^{m}ŠEŠ-MU
18 GANBA *it-ti* ^{md}UTU-SÌ-*na*
ni-te-pu-uš
(...)

(...) *mâr bânî* en présence desquels Šamaš-iddin, fils de Šullumu, berger de Nabû a fait la déclaration suivante: «1 brebis et 1 chèvre, marquées de la bêche et du calame, je les ai vendues contre argent à Innin-šum-uṣur, fils d'Ibni-Ištar et à Aḫ-iddin, fils de Nabu-mukîn-apli». Et Innin-šum-uṣur, Aḫ-iddin étant absent, a déclaré dans l'assemblée: «Moi et Aḫ-iddin, nous avons conclu un marché avec Šamaš-iddin». (...)

Le temple de Nabû ayant confié un troupeau au berger Šamaš-iddin, on retrouve deux des bêtes chez Innin-šum-uṣur. Celui-ci prétend les avoir achetées régulièrement au berger, chez un tiers, Kînaia. Le berger confirme sous serment et assure avoir remis le produit de la vente à son supérieur hiérarchique, le chef de centurie Lulaʾ-Nabû. Mais une seconde déposition est enregistrée quatre jours après. La teneur des propos de Šamaš-iddin étant pratiquement la même, cette nouvelle séance s'explique par le fait que l'acolyte de l'acheteur a été identifié. Il s'agit d'un nommé Aḫ-iddin, qui n'est pas présent. L'insistance mise par les *mâr bânî* à connaître les personnes concernées indique que l'affaire n'est certainement pas aussi limpide que l'indiquent les dépositions.

[n°6]

YOS 6 168
10 GÚ.UN ZABAR *šá* KUR *ia-a-ma-na a-na* 3 MA.NA 1/3 GÍN KÙ.BABBAR
2 1 (GÚ.UN) 21 MA.NA 1/3 GÍN *in-za-ḫu-re-e-ti*
a-na 2 MA.NA 2 GÍN
4 37 MA.NA AN.NA *a-na* 55 1/2 GÍN KÙ.BABBAR
16 MA.NA 15 GÍN SÍG ZA.GÌN.KUR.RA *a-na* 2 MA.NA 2/3 GÍN
6 PAP *šá* ^{md}UTU-NUMUN-DÙ A ^{md}*na-na-a*-MU

---

4 (GÚ.UN) 55 MA.NA ZABAR *šá* KUR *ia-a-ma-na*
8 *a-na* 1 1/2 MA.NA 8 GÍN *šal-šú* 1 GÍN KÙ.BABBAR
55 MA.NA NA$_4$ ZA.GÌN *a-na* 1/2 MA.NA 6 GÍN 2.TA.⌈ŠU^{II}⌉.ME
10 2 (GÚ.UN) 33 MA.NA GADA *ṭu-man a-na* 1 2/3 MA.NA 2 GÍN
3 (GÚ.UN) 53 MA.NA NA$_4$ *gab-ú šá* KUR *mi-ṣir*
12 *a-na* 1 MA.NA 17 GÍN 2.TA.⌈ŠU^{II}⌉.MEŠ
32 MA.NA 1/3 GÍN *in-za-ḫu-re-e-ti*
14 *a-na* 2/3 MA.NA 8 1/2 GÍN
2 (GÚ.UN) 10 MA.NA AN.BAR *šá* KUR *ia-a-ma-na*
16 *a-na* 1/2 MA.NA 2 1/2 GÍN
4 (GÚ.UN) 17 MA.NA AN.BAR *šá* KUR *la-ab-na-nu*
18 *a-na* 2/3 MA.NA 2 GÍN 2.TA.⌈ŠU^{II}⌉.MEŠ

0,3.4 LÀL.ḪÁ *a-na* 1/3 6 GÍN
20 20 DUG *kan-da-a-nu šá* ^{giš}GEŠTIN KÙ *a-na* 1 MA.NA
2 GÚ.UN ŠIM.ḪAB *a-na* 1/2 MA.NA
22 40 MA.NA ŠIM *ḫas-ḫal-ti a-na* 2 GÍN
1 GUR *ta-tur-ru a-na* 10 GÍN
24 1 GUR ŠIM.LI *a-na* 3 GÍN
PAP *šá* ^{m}SÌ-*na*-ŠEŠ
26 ITI DU$_6$ U$_4$ 7.KAM MU 6(?).KAM ^{d}NÀ-NÍ-TUK LUGAL TIN.TIR^{ki}
3 MA.NA 10 GÍN SÍG ZA.GÌN.KUR.RA 10-*ú šá* ^{m}SÌ-*na*-ŠEŠ
28 5 MA.NA SÍG ZA.GÌN.KUR.RA 40 MA.NA
AN.BAR 10-*ú šá* ^{md}UTU-NUMUN-DÙ

[n°7]

PTS 2098[51]

10 GÚ.UN ZABAR *šá* K[UR *ia-a-ma-na]*
2 *a-na* 3 MA.NA 1/3 GÍN [KÙ.BABBAR]
1 GÚ.UN 21 MA.NA 1/3 GÍN ⸢Ú⸣ *i[n-za-ḫu-re-e-ti]*
4 37 MA.NA AN.N[A]
a-na 2 MA.NA 2/3 GÍN K[Ù.BABBAR]
6 16 MA.NA 15 GÍN SÍG ZA.GÌN.KUR.R[A]
a-na 2 MA.NA 2/3 GÍN K[Ù.BABBAR]
8 – une ligne non inscrite –
PAP *šá* ^{md}UTU-NUMUN-DÙ
10 4 (GÚ.UN) 55 MA.NA ZABAR
a-na 1 1/2 MA.NA 8 GÍN *šul-lul-tú* 1 GÍN KÙ.BABBAR
12 55 MA.NA NA$_4$ ZA.GÌN
a-na 1/2 MA.NA 6 GÍN 2.TA.ŠU^{II}.ME
14 2 (GÚ.UN) 33 MA.NA GADA *ṭu-man*
a-na 1 5/6 MA.NA 2 GÍN KÙ.BABBAR
16 3 (GÚ.UN) 53 MA.NA NA$_4$ *gab-ú šá* KUR *mi-ṣir / gu-ra-bi ina* IGI-*šú*
a-na 1 MA.NA 17 GÍN 2.TA.ŠU^{II}.ME KÙ.BABBAR
18 32 MA.<NA> 1/3 GÍN Ú *in-za-ḫu-re-e-tú*
a-na 2/3 MA.NA 8 1/2 GÍN KÙ.BABBAR
20 2 (GÚ.UN) 10 MA.NA AN.BAR *šá* KUR *ia-a-ma-na*
a-na 1/2 MA.NA 2 1/2 GÍN
22 4 (GÚ.UN) 17 MA.NA AN.BAR *šá* KUR *la-ab-na-na*
a-na 5/6 MA.NA 2 GÍN 2.TA.ŠU^{II}.ME
24 0,3.4 LÀL *a-na* 1/3 6 GÍN KÙ.BABBAR
20 DUG *kan-da-a-nu šá* ^{giš}GEŠTIN KÙ *a-na* 1 MA.NA KÙ.BABBAR
26 3 GÚ.UN ŠIM.ḪAB *a-na* 1/2 MA.NA KÙ.BABBAR
40 MA.NA ŠIM *ḫa-as-ḫal-tu a-na* ⸢2⸣ [GÍN KÙ.BABBAR]
28 1 GUR KI *ta-tur-ru a-na* [10 GÍN KÙ.BABBAR]
2 GUR ŠIM.LI *a-[na* 3 GÍN KÙ.BABBAR]
30 PAP *šá* ^{m}SÌ-*na*-[ŠEŠ]
3 MA.NA 10 GÍN SÍG ZA.GÌN.KUR.RA *ir-bi šá* ^{m}SÌ-*na*-ŠEŠ

51 La transcription suit celle que donne Oppenheim 1967, 236 note 1.

[n°8]

TCL 12 84

4 GÚ.UN 55 MA.NA ZABAR
2 *šá* KUR *ia-a-ma-na*
45 MA.NA NA$_4$ ZA.GÌN
4 2 (GÚ.UN) 33 MA.NA GADA *ṭu-ma-nu*
3 GÚ.UN 43 MA.NA NA$_4$ *gab-ú*
6 *šá* KUR *mi-ṣir a-di gu-ra-pu*
2 (GÚ.UN) 10 MA.NA AN.BAR *šá* KUR *ia-a-ma-nu*
8 4 (GÚ.UN) 17 MA.NA AN.BAR *šá* KUR *lab-na-nu*
37 MA.NA AN.NA
10 8 *tak-pu šá* ZABAR
šá re-eš-su-nu la ⸢*na*⸣*-šu-ú*
12 11 MA.NA 1/3 GÍN [SÍG] ZA.GÌN.KUR.RA
a-di 2 GADA ⸢*na-aṣ*⸣*-ra-pa-a-tú gu-*⸢*ra*⸣*-*[*pu*]?
14 3 DUG *kan-da-a-nu šá* ⸢ŠIM⸣.ḪAB 2 (GÚ.UN) 6 ⸢MA.NA⸣ [...
2 DUG ŠAGAN.{LÁ}.MEŠ *šá in-ẓa-ḫu-re-e-tú*
16 2 *na-aṣ-ra-pa-a-tú šá* SÍG.ZA.GÌN.KUR.A
ir-bi ⸢*šá* ^{m}SÌ⸣*-na-*ŠEŠ
18 PAP *mi-riš-tú* ⸢*šá* ^{m}SÌ*-na*⸣-ŠEŠ
A ^{md}IN.NIN-MU-URI$_3$
20 ITI DU$_6$ U$_4$ 5.KAM MU 5(?).KAM ^{d}NÀ-NÍ-TUK
LUGAL TIN.TIR^{ki}

BIBLIOGRAPHY

The bibliographic abbreviations used here follow Assyriological practice and can be found in *Akkadisches Handwörterbuch* (*AHw*), *Chicago Assyrian Dictionary* (*CAD*), and *Reallexikon der Assyriologie* (*RlA*).

Adams, R. McC., 1981: *Heartland of Cities. Surveys of Ancient Settlement and Land Use on the Central Floodplain of the Euphrates*, Chicago.

Albenda, P., 1986: *The Palace of Sargon, King of Assyria*, ERC Synthèse n° 22, Paris.

Ali, F.A., 1964: *Sumerian Letters: Two Collections from the Old Babylonian Schools*, PhD. University of Pennsylvania, Philadelphia.

Bär, J., 1996: *Der assyrische Tribut und seine Darstellung. Eine Untersuchung zur imperialen Ideologie im neuassyrischen Reich*, AOAT 243, Neukirchen-Vluyn.

Bongenaar, A.C.V.M., 1997: *The Neo-Babylonian Ebabbar Temple at Sippar: its Administration and its Prosopography*, PIHANS 80, Istanbul.

Bongenaar, A.C.V.M. - Haring, B.J.J., 1994: 'Egyptians in Neo-Babylonian Sippar', *JCS* 46, 59-72.

Borger, R., 1956: *Die Inschriften Asarhaddons Königs von Assyrien*, *AfO Beiheft* 9, Graz.

Borger, R., 1996: *Beiträge zum Inschriftenwerk Assurbanipals*, Wiesbaden.

Born, H. - Seidl, U., 1995: *Schutzwaffen aus Assyrien und Urartu. Band IV Sammlung Axel Guttmann*, Mainz.

Botta, P.E. - Flandin, E., 1849-50: *Monument de Ninive* 2, Paris.

Breckwoldt, T., 1995-96: 'Management of Grain Storage in Old Babylonian Larsa', *AfO* 42/43, 64-88.

Brinkman, J.A., 1987: 'Twenty Minas of Copper', in F. Rochberg-Halton (ed.), *Language, Literature, and History: Philological and Historical Studies Presented to Erica Reiner*, AOS 67, New Haven, 33-36.

Calmeyer, P. - Naster, P., 1995: 'Münzen', *RlA* 8/5-6, 404-406.

Cardascia, G., 1951: *Les Archives des Murašû. Une famille d'hommes d'affaires babyloniens à l'époque perse (455-403 av. J.-C.)*, Paris.

Charpin, D., 1982: 'Marchands du Palais et Marchands du Temple à la Fin de la Ire Dynastie de Babylone', *JA* 270, 25-65.

Civil, M., 1990: 'The verb šu-tak$_4$ 'to send'', *Aula Orientalis* 8, 109-111.

Cole, S.W., 1996: *Nippur in Late Assyrian Times, c. 755-612 BC*, SAAS 4, Helsinki.

Cocquerillat, D., 1968: *Palmeraies et cultures de l'Eanna d'Uruk (559-520)*, Ausgrabungen der Deutschen Forschungsgemeinschaft in Uruk-Warka 8, Berlin.

Dalley, S. - Postgate, J.N., 1984: *The Tablets from Fort Shalmaneser*, CTN 3, British School of Archaeology in Iraq.

Dalley, S.M., 1988: 'Neo-Assyrian Textual Evidence for Bronzeworking Centres', in J. Curtis (ed.), *Bronzeworking Centres of Western Asia c. 1000-539 B.C.*, London, 97-110.

Dalton, G. (ed.), 1968: *Primitive, Archaic, and Modern Economies: Essays of Karl Polanyi*, New York.

Dalton, G., 1975: 'Karl Polanyi's Analysis of Long-Distance Trade and His Wider Paradigm', in J.A. Sabloff and C.C. Lamberg-Karlovsky (eds.), *Ancient Civilization and Trade*, Albuquerque, 63-132.

Deller, K., 1964: 'Getreidekursangaben in neuassyrischen Rechtsurkunden', *OrNS* 33, 257-261.

Deller, K., 1983: '*Midlu* "Pökelfleisch"', *Assur* 3, 169-175.

Deller, K., 1984: 'Drei wiederentdeckte neuassyrische Rechtsurkunden aus Aššur', *BaM* 15, 225-251.

Deller, K., 1985: '*Kurru* "Mehlbrei"', *OrNS* 54, 327-330.

Deller, K., 1987: '*Tamkāru*-Kredite in neuassyrischer Zeit', *JESHO* 30, 1-29.

Deller, K., 1991: '*Kurru(m)* "Mehlbrei" (Fortschreibung von *Or* 54, 327-330)', *NABU* 1991 no. 75.

Deller, K. - Fales, F.M. - Jakob-Rost, L., 1995: 'Neo-Assyrian Texts from Assur. Private Archives in the Vorderasiatisches Museum of Berlin', *SAAB* 9, 3-137.

Deller, K. - Finkel, I.L., 1984: 'A Neo-Assyrian Inventory Tablet of Unknown Provenance', *ZA* 74, 76-91.

Deller, K. - Mayer, W.R., 1984: 'Akkadische Lexikographie: *CAD* M', *OrNS* 53, 72-124.

Deller, K. - Millard, A.R., 1993: 'Die Bestallungsurkunde des Nergal-āpil-kūmūja von Kalḫu', *BaM* 24, 217-242.

Dercksen, J.G., 1996: *The Old Assyrian Copper Trade in Anatolia.* PIHANS 75, Istanbul.

Dillard, R.B., 1975: *Neo-Babylonian Texts from the John Frederick Lewis Collection of the Free Library of Philadelphia*, Dissertation, The Dropsie College, Philadelphie.

Donbaz, V., 1988: 'Some Neo-Assyrian Contracts from Girnavaz and Vicinity', *SAAB* 2, 3-30.

Driel, G. van, 1985-86: 'The Rise of the House of Egibi: Nabû-aḫḫē-iddina', *JEOL* 29, 50-67.

Driel, G. van, 1986: 'Neo-Babylonian texts from the Louvre', *BiOr* 43, 5-20.

Driel, G. van, 1989: 'The Murašûs in Context', *JESHO* 32, 203-229.

Driel, G. van, 1994: 'Private or not-so-private: Nippur Ur III Files', in H. Gasche, M. Tanret, C. Janssen and A. Degraeve (eds.), *Cinquante-deux reflexions sur le Proche-Orient ancien, offertes en hommage à Léon De Meyer*, Leuven, 181-192.

Driel, G. van, 1995: 'Nippur and the Inanna Temple during the Ur III Period', *JESHO* 38, 393-406.

Driel, G. van, 1998a: 'Care of the Elderly: the Neo-Babylonian Period', in M. Stol and S.P. Vleeming (eds.), *The Care of the Elderly in the Ancient Near East*, Studies in the History and Culture of the Ancient Near East, Vol. XIV, Leiden, 161-197.

Driel, G. van, 1998b: 'Land in Ancient Mesopotamia: "That what remains undocumented does not exist"', in B. Haring and R. de Maaijer (eds.), *Landless and Hungry? Access to Land in Early and Traditional Societies*, Leiden, 19-49.

Elat, M., 1978: 'The Economic Relations of the Neo-Assyrian Empire with Egypt', *JAOS* 98, 20-34.

Elat, M., 1979: 'The Monarchy and the Developement of Trade in Ancient Israel', in E. Lipinski (ed.), *State and Temple Economy in the Ancient Near East*, OLA 6/II, Leuven, 527-546.

Elat, M., 1982: 'The Impact of Tribute and Booty on Countries and People within the Assyrian Empire', in H. Hirsch and H. Hunger (eds.), *AfO Beiheft* 19 (= CRRAI 28), Horn, 244-251.

Elat, M., 1987: 'Der *tamkāru* im neuassyrischen Reich', *JESHO* 30, 233-254.

Elat, M., 1991: 'Phoenician Overland Trade within the Mesopotamian Empires', in M. Cogan and I. Ephᶜal (eds.), *Ah, Assyria ... Studies in Assyrian History and Ancient Near Eastern Historiography presented to H. Tadmor*, Scripta Hierosolymitana 33, Jerusalem, 21-35.

Engel, B.J., 1987: *Darstellungen von Dämonen und Tieren in assyrischen Palästen und Tempeln nach den schriftlichen Quellen*, Münchengladbach.

Englund, R.K., 1990: *Organisation und Verwaltung der Ur III-Fischerei*, BBVO 10, Berlin.
Englund, R.K., 1992: 'Ur III Sundries', *Acta Sumerologica* 14, 77-102.
Fales, F.M., 1995: 'Assyro-Aramaica: The Assyrian Lion-Weights', in K. Van Lerberghe and A. Schoors (eds.), *Immigration and Emigration within the Ancient Near East. Festschrift E. Lipinski*, OLA 65, Leuven, 33-55.
Fales, F.M., 1984: 'The Neo-Assyrian Period', in A. Archi (ed.), *Circulation of Goods in Non-Palatial Context in the Ancient Near East*, Incunabula Graeca 82, Roma, 207-220.
Fales, F.M., 1996: 'Prices in Neo-Assyrian Sources', *SAAB* 10, 11-53.
Fales, F.M. - Postgate, J.N., 1992: *Imperial Administrative Records, Part I. Palace and Temple Administration*, SAA 7, Helsinki.
Farber, H., 1978: 'A Price and Wage Study for Northern Babylonia during the Old Babylonian Period', *JESHO* 21, 1-51.
Frahm, E., 1997: *Einleitung in die Sanherib-Inschriften*, *AfO Beiheft* 26, Horn.
Fuchs, A., 1994: *Die Inschriften Sargons II. aus Khorsabad*, Göttingen.
Gadd, C.J., 1936: *The Stones of Assyria*, London.
Gadd, C.J., 1954: 'Inscribed Prisms of Sargon II from Nimrud', *Iraq* 16, 173-201.
Garelli, P., 1963: *Les Assyriens en Cappadoce*, Paris.
Garelli, P., 1977: 'Marchands et *tamkārū* assyriens en Cappadoce', *Iraq* 39, 99-107.
Garelli, P., 1979: 'Le système fiscal de l'Empire assyrien', in H. van Effentere (ed.), *Points de vue sur la fiscalité antique*, Paris, 7-18.
Gasche *et al.* 1998: H. Gasche, J. A. Armstrong, S. W. Cole, V. G. Gurzadyan, *Dating the Fall of Babylon, A Reappraisal of the Second-Millennium Chronology*. MHEM IV, University of Ghent and the Oriental Institute of the University of Chicago.
Gelb *et al.* 1991: I. J. Gelb, P. Steinkeller, R. M. Whiting, Jr., *Earliest Land Tenure Systems in the Near East: Ancient Kudurrus*, OIP 104, Chicago.
George, A. R., 1992: *Babylonian Topographical Texts*, OLA 40, Leuven.
Gitin, S., 1997: 'The Neo-Assyrian Empire and its Western Periphery: The Levant, with a Focus on Philistine Ekron', in S. Parpola and R. M. Whiting (eds.), *Assyria 1995*, Helsinki, 77-103.
Goiten, S.D., 1967: *A Mediterranean Society*, I. *Economic Foundations*, Berkeley.
Grayson, K.A., 1981: 'No. 84', in O.W. Muscarella (ed.), *Ladders to Heaven. Art Treasures from Lands of the Bible*, Toronto, 126-127.
Grégoire, J.-P., 1996: *Archives administratives et inscriptions cunéiformes de l'Ashmolean Museum et de la Bodleian Collection d'Oxford*, AAICAB I/1, Paris.
Hallo, W. W., 1992: 'Trade and Traders in the Ancient Near East: Some New Perspectives', in D. Charpin and F. Joannès (eds.), *La circulation des biens, des personnes et des idées dans la Proche-Orient ancien* (= CRRAI 38), Paris, 351-356.
Haring, B.J.J., 1997: *Divine Households. Administrative and Economic Aspects of the New Kingdom Royal Memorial Temples in Western Thebes*, Egyptologische Uitgaven 12, Leiden.
Hawkins, J.D., 1986: 'Royal Statements of Ideal Prices: Assyrian, Babylonian, and Hittite', in J. V. Canby, E. Porada, B. S. Ridgway and T. Stech (eds.), *Ancient Anatolia. Aspects of Change and Cultural Development. Essays in Honor of M. J. Mellink*, Madison, 93-102.
Hawkins, J.D. - Morpurgo-Davies, A., 1982: 'Buying and Selling in Hieroglyphic Luwian', in J. Tischler (ed.), *Serta Indogermanistica. Festschrift für G. Neumann*, Innsbrucker Beiträge zur Sprachwissenschaft 40, Innsbruck, 91-105.
Hecker, K., 1991: 'Zu den Keilschrifttexten der Grabung Frühjahr 1990 in Assur', *MDOG* 123, 111-114.

Heimpel, W., 1997: 'Disposition of Households of Officials in Ur III and Mari', *Acta Sumerologica* 19, 63-82.

Hrouda, B., 1965: *Die Kulturgeschichte des assyrischen Flachbildes*, Saarbrücker Beiträge zur Altertumskunde 2, Bonn.

Hunger, H., 1992: *Astrological Reports to Assyrian Kings*, SAA 8, Helsinki.

Hurowitz, V.A., 1986: 'Another Fiscal Practice in the Ancient Near East: 2 Kings 12:5-17 and a Letter to Esarhaddon (LAS 277)', *JNES* 45, 289-294.

Jankowska, N.B., 1969: 'Some Problems of the Economy of the Assyrian Empire', in I. M. Diakonoff (ed.), *Ancient Mesopotamia. Socio-Economic History*, Moskva, 253-276.

Jansen-Winkeln, K., 1995: 'Die Plünderung der Königsgräber des Neuen Reiches', *ZAeS* 122, 62-78.

Jas, R., 1990: 'A Neo-Assyrian Letter without Address', *SAAB* 4, 3-5.

Jas, R., 1996: *Neo-Assyrian Judicial Procedures*, SAAS 5, Helsinki.

Joannès, F., 1982: *Textes économiques de la Babylonie récente*, ERC Cahier n° 5, Paris.

Joannès, F., 1991: 'L'Asie Mineure méridionale d'après la documentation cunéiforme d'époque néo-babylonienne', *Anatolica antiqua* 1, Paris, 261-266.

Joannès, F., 1992: 'Inventaire d'un cabaret', *NABU* 1992 nos. 64 and 89.

Joannès, F., 1994: 'Métaux précieux et moyens de paiement en Babylonie achéménide et hellénistique', *Transeuphratène* 8, 137-144.

Joannès, F., 1997: 'Le monde occidental vu de Mésopotamie, de l'époque néo-babylonienne à l'époque hellénistique', *Transeuphratène* 13, 141-153.

Jursa, M., 1995: *Die Landwirtschaft in Sippar in neubabylonischer Zeit, AfO Beiheft* 25, Horn.

Jursa, M., 1998: *Der Tempelzehnt in Babylonien vom siebenten bis zum dritten Jahrhundert v. Chr.*, AOAT 254, Münster.

Karwiese, S., 1995: *Die Münzprägung von Ephesos. 1. Die Anfänge: die ältesten Prägungen und der Beginn der Münzprägung überhaupt*, Wien.

Kataja, L. - Whiting, R., 1995: *Grants, Decrees and Gifts of the Neo-Assyrian Period*, SAA 12, Helsinki.

Kienast, B., 1975-76: 'Bemerkungen zum altassyrischen Pfandrecht', *WO* 8, 218-227.

Kienast, B., 1984: *Das altassyrische Kaufvertragsrecht*, FAOS Beiheft 1, Stuttgart.

Kienast, B., 1989: 'The Old Assyrian *beʾūlātum*', *JCS* 41, 87-95.

Kinnier Wilson, J.V., 1972: *The Nimrud Wine Lists*, CTN 1, British School of Archaeology in Iraq.

Kisch, B., 1965: *Scales and Weights: A Historical Outline*, New Haven.

Koppen, F. van, 1997: *De Koning geeft, de Koning neemt. Landgoederen van hof-dignitarissen in Oud-Babylonisch Mari*, unpublished MA thesis Leiden University.

Kraus, F.R., 1958: *Ein Edikt des Königs Ammi-ṣaduqa von Babylon*, SD 5, Leiden.

Kraus, F.R., 1982: '"*Kārum*", ein Organ städtischer Selbstverwaltung der altbabylonischen Zeit', in A. Finet (ed.), *Les pouvoirs locaux en Mésopotamie et dans les régions adjacentes*, Brussels, 29-42.

Kraus, F.R., 1984: *Königliche Verfügungen in Altbabylonischer Zeit*, SD 11, Leiden.

Krecher, J., 1970: *Das Geschäftshaus Egibi in Babylon in neubabylonischer und achämenidischer Zeit,* Habilitationsschrift, Münster.

Kümmel, H.M., 1979: *Familie, Beruf und Amt im spätbabylonischen Uruk. Prosopographische Untersuchungen zu Berufsgruppen des 6. Jahrhunderts v. Chr. in Uruk*, Berlin.

Kwasman, T., 1988: *Neo-Assyrian Legal Documents in the Kouyunjik Collection of the British Museum*, Studia Pohl SM 14, Roma.

Kwasman, T. - Parpola, S., 1991: *Legal Transactions of the Royal Court of Nineveh, Part I. Tiglath-Pileser III through Esarhaddon*, SAA 6, Helsinki.

Lambert, W.G., 1957-58: 'Two Texts from the Early Part of the Reign of Ashurbanipal', *AfO* 18, 382-387.

Landsberger, B., 1967: 'Akkadisch-Hebräische Wortgleichungen', *Festschrift für W. Baumgartner. Suppl. Vetus Testamentum* 16, 176-204.

Larsen, M.T., 1967: *Old Assyrian Caravan Procedures*, Istanbul.

Larsen, M.T., 1976: *The Old Asyrian City-state and its Colonies*, Copenhagen.

Larsen, M.T., 1977: 'Partnerships in the Old Assyrian Trade', *Iraq* 39, 119-145.

Lanz, H., 1976: *Die neubabylonischen* ḫarrânu-*Geschäftsunternehmen*, Münchener Universitätsschriften. Juristische Fakultät. Abhandlungen zur rechtswissenschaftlichen Grundlagenforschung 18, Berlin.

Leemans, W.F., 1960: *Foreign Trade in the Old Babylonian Period*, SD 6, Leiden.

Limet, H., 1977: 'Les schemas du commerce néo-sumériens', *Iraq* 39, 51-58.

Lipinski, E., 1979: 'Les temples néo-assyriens et les origines du monnayage', in E. Lipinski (ed.), *State and Temple Economy in the Ancient Near East*, OLA 6/II, Leuven, 565-588.

Lipinski, E., 1997: 'The Personal Names Handî, Harrānay, and Kurillay in Neo-Assyrian Sources', in H. Waetzoldt and H. Hauptmann (eds.), *Assyrien im Wandel der Zeiten* (= CRRAI 39), HSAO 6, Heidelberg, 89-93.

Liverani, M., 1990: 'The Shape of Neo-Sumerian Fields', *BSA* 5, 147-181.

Liverani, M., 1991: 'The Trade Network of Tyre according to Ezek. 27', in M. Cogan and I. Eph^{c}al (eds.), *Ah, Assyria ... Studies in Assyrian History and Ancient Near Eastern Historiography presented to H. Tadmor*, Scripta Hierosolymitana 33, Jerusalem, 65-79.

Liverani, M., 1992: *Studies on the Annals of Ashurnasirpal II. 2: Topographical Analysis*, QGS 4, Roma.

MacGinnes, J., 1991-92: 'Neo-Babylonian Prebend Texts from the British Museum', *AfO* 38/39, 74-100.

Maekawa, K., 1974: 'Agricultural Production in Ancient Sumer', *Zinbun* 13, 1-60.

Martin, W., 1939: *Tribut und Tributleistungen bei den Assyrern*, StOr 8/I, Helsinki.

Martirossian, A., 1977a: 'Der Vermögenserwerb im neubabylonischen Geschäftshaus Egibi (555-522)', *IFZ* 4, 183-190.

Martirossian, A., 1977b: 'Die Pachtunternehmungen im Geschäftshaus Egibi in den Jahren 543-522', *YONA* 7, 84-91.

Martirossian, A., 1978: 'The Property of the House of Egibi (555-522 B.C.)', *DV* 3, 179-211.

Martirossian, A., 1983: 'Credit Operations of the Business House Egibi', *DV* 4, 232-253.

Matouš, L., 1969: 'Der Streit um den Nachlass des Puzur-Aššur', *ArOr* 37, 156-180.

Maxwell-Hyslop, K.R., 1974: 'Assyrian Sources of Iron. A Preliminary Survey of the Historical and Geographical Evidence', *Iraq* 36, 139-154.

Mayr, R.H., 1997: *The Seal Impressions of Ur III Umma*, Proefschrift Leiden.

Menzel, B., 1981: *Assyrische Tempel*, Studia Pohl SM 10, Roma.

Menzel-Wortmann, B., 1986: 'Der ^{LÚ}GAL *danibata* in neuassyrischer Zeit', *Mesopotamia* 21, 213-227.

Michalowski , P., 1976: *The Royal Correspondence of Ur*, PhD. Yale University, New Haven.

Michel, C., 1991: *Innāya dans les tablettes paléo-assyriennes*, Paris.

Michel, C., 1995: 'Validité et durée de vie des contrats et reconnaissances de dettes paléo-assyriennes', *RA* 89, 15-27.

Michel, C., 1996: 'Propriétés immobilières dans les tablettes paléo-assyriennes', in K. R. Veenhof (ed.), *Houses and Households in Ancient Mesopotamia* (= CRRAI 40), PIHANS 78, Istanbul, 285-300.

Mieroop, M. van de, 1986: 'Tūram-ilī: An Ur III Merchant', *JCS* 38, 1-80.
Mieroop, M. van de, 1987: *Crafts in the Early Isin Period: a Study of the Isin Craft Archive from the Reigns of Išbi-Erra and Šū-ilišu*, OLA 24, Leuven.
Mieroop, M. van de, 1992: *Society and Enterprise in Old Babylonian Ur*, BBVO 12. Berlin.
Millard, A., 1994: *The Eponyms of the Assyrian Empire 910-612 BC*, SAAS 2, Helsinki.
Mitchell, T.C., 1990: 'The Bronze Lion Weights from Nimrud', *Res Orientales* 2, 129-138.
Molina, M., 1996: *Tablillas administrativas neosumerias de la Abadía de Montserrat (Barcelona), Aula Orientalis Supplementa* 11, Barcelona.
Muhly, J.D., 1973: *Copper and Tin. The Distribution of Mineral Resources and the Nature of the Metals Trade in the Bronze Age*, New Haven.
Muhly, J. D., 1980: Review of J. D. Hawkins (ed.), *Trade in the Ancient Near East* (1977), *JAOS* 100, 173-175.
Müller, G., 1997: 'Gedanken zur neuassyrischen Geldwirtschaft', in H. Waetzoldt and H. Hauptmann (eds.), *Assyrien im Wandel der Zeiten* (= CRRAI 39), HSAO 6, Heidelberg, 115-121.
Neumann, H., 1979: 'Handel und Händler in der Zeit der III. Dynastie von Ur', *AoF* 6, 15-67.
Neumann, H., 1992a: 'Nochmals zum Kaufmann in neusumerischer Zeit: Die Geschäfte des Ur-DUN und anderer Kaufleute aus Nippur', in D. Charpin and F. Joannès (eds.), *La circulation des biens, des personnes et des idées dans le Proche-Orient ancien* (= CRRAI 38), Paris, 83-94.
Neumann, H., 1992b: 'Zur privaten Geschäftstätigkeit in Nippur in der Ur III-Zeit', in M. deJong Ellis (ed.), *Nippur at the Centennial* (= CRRAI 35), Philadelphia, 161-176.
Neumann, H., 1993: 'Zu den Geschäften des Kaufmanns Ur-Dumuzida aus Umma', *AoF* 20, 69-86.
Neumann, H., 1997: 'Gläubiger oder Schuldner? Anmerkungen zu einem neuassyrischen Privatbrief', in H. Kühne, B. Pongratz-Leisten and P. Xella (eds.), *Ana šadî Labnāni lū allik. Beiträge zu altorientalischen und mittelmeerischen Kulturen. Festschrift für W. Röllig*, AOAT 247, Neukirchen-Vluyn, 281-293.
Oppenheim, A.L., 1947: 'A Fiscal Practice of the Ancient Near East', *JNES* 6, 116-120.
Oppenheim, A.L., 1950: 'Babylonian and Assyrian Historical Texts', in J. B. Pritchard (ed.), *Ancient Near Eastern Texts relating to the Old Testament*, Princeton, 265-317.
Oppenheim, A.L., 1957: 'A Bird's-Eye View of Mesopotamian Economic History', in K. Polanyi, C.M. Arensberg and H.W. Pearson (eds.), *Trade and Market in the Early Empires. Economies in History and Theory*, New York, 27-37.
Oppenheim, A.L., 1964: *Ancient Mesopotamia. Portrait of a Dead Civilization*, Chicago.
Oppenheim, A.L. 1967: 'Essay on Overland Trade in the First Millennium B.C.', *JCS* 21, 236-254.
Oppenheim, A.L., 1970: 'Trade in the Ancient Near East.' *Fifth International Congress of Economic History*, Moskva.
Oppenheim, A.L., 1977: *Ancient Mesopotamia. Portrait of a Dead Civilization*, (second edition, revised by E. Reiner), Chicago.
Owen, D.I., 1980: 'Widows' rights in Ur III Sumer', *ZA* 70, 170-184.
Parise, N.F., 1987: 'Fra Assiri e Greci: dall'argento di Ishtar alla moneta', Dialoghi di Archeologia 3. Ser. 5/2, 37-39.
Parpola, S., 1980: 'The Murderer of Sennacherib', in B. Alster (ed.), *Death in Mesopotamia* (= CRRAI 26), Mesopotamia 8, Copenhagen, 171-182.
Peiser, F., 1890: *Babylonische Verträge des Berliner Museums*, Berlin.

Pettinato, G., 1969: *Texte zur Verwaltung der Landwirtschaft in der Ur-III Zeit*, AnOr 45, Roma.

Pettinato, G., 1970-71: 'I$_7$-Idigna-ta I$_7$-Nun-še. Il Conflitto tra Lagaš ed Umma per la 'Frontiera Divina' e la sua Soluzione Durante la Terzia Dinastia di Ur', *Mesopotamia* 5/6, 281-320.

Pleiner, R. - Bjorkman, J.K., 1974: 'The Assyrian Iron Age: the History of Iron in the Assyrian Civilization', *PAPS* 118/3, 283-313.

Polanyi, K., 1957a: 'Marketless Trading in Hammurabi's Time', in K. Polanyi, C.W. Arensberg and H.N. Pearson (eds.), *Trade and Market in the Early Empires*, New York, 12-26.

Polanyi, K., 1957b: 'The Economy as Instituted Process', in K. Polanyi, C.W. Arensberg and H.N. Pearson (eds.), *Trade and Market in the Early Empires*, New York, 243-270 (= G. Dalton, *Essays of Karl Polanyi*, ch. 7, pp. 139-174).

Polanyi, K., 1960: 'On the Comparative Treatment of Economic Institutions in Antiquity with Illustrations from Athens, Mycenae, and Alalakh', in C.H. Kraeling and R.M. Adams (eds.), *City Invincible. A Symposium on Urbanization and Cultural Development in the Ancient Near East*, Chicago, 329-350.

Ponchia, S., 1990: 'Neo-Assyrian Corn-Loans: Preliminary Notes', *SAAB* 4, 39-60.

Postgate, J.N., 1973: *The Governor's Palace Archive.* CTN 2, British School of Archaeology in Iraq.

Postgate, J.N., 1974: *Taxation and Conscription in the Assyrian Empire*, *Studia Pohl SM* 3, Roma.

Postgate, J.N., 1976: *Fifty Neo-Assyrian Legal Documents*, Warminster.

Postgate, J.N., 1979: 'The Economic Structure of the Assyrian Empire', in M. T. Larsen (ed.), *Power and Propaganda. A Symposium on Ancient Empires*, Mesopotamia 7, Copenhagen, 193-221.

Postgate, J.N., 1994: 'Rings, Torcs and Bracelets', in P. Calmeyer, K. Hecker, L. Jakob-Rost, and C. B. F. Walker (eds.), *Beiträge zur Altorientalischen Archäologie und Altertumskunde. Festschrift für B. Hrouda*, Wiesbaden, 235-245.

Postgate, J.N., 1995: 'Some Latter-Day Merchants of Aššur', in M. Dietrich and O. Loretz (eds.), *Vom Alten Orient zum Alten Testament. Festschrift für W. von Soden*, AOAT 240, Neukirchen-Vluyn, 403-406.

Powell, M. A., 1971: *Sumerian Numeration and Metrology.* Dissertation. University of Minnesota, Minneapolis.

Powell, M.A., 1977: 'Sumerian Merchants and the Problem of Profit', *Iraq* 39, 23-29.

Powell, M.A., 1978a: 'Götter, Könige und 'Kapitalisten' im Mesopotamien des 3. Jahrtausends v. u. Z.', *Oikumene* (Budapest) 2, 127-144.

Powell, M.A., 1978b: 'A Contribution to the History of Money in Mesopotamia prior to the Invention of Coinage', in B. Hruška and G. Komoróczy (eds.), *Festschrift Lubor Matouš II*, Budapest, 211-243.

Powell, M.A., 1979: 'Ancient Mesopotamian Weight Metrology: Methods, Problems and Perspectives', in M. A. Powell and R. H. Sack (eds.), *Studies in Honor of Tom B. Jones*, AOAT 203, Kevelaer/Neukirchen-Vluyn, 71-109.

Powell, M.A., 1989-90: 'Maße und Gewichte', *RlA* 7, 457-517.

Powell, M.A., 1990: 'Identification and Interpretation of Long Term Price Fluctuations in Babylonia: More on the History of Money in Mesopotamia', *AoF* 17, 76-99.

Powell, M.A., 1996: 'Money in Mesopotamia', *JESHO* 39, 224-242.

Pritchard, J.B., 1954: *The Ancient Near East in Pictures*, Princeton.

Radner, K., 1997: *Die neuassyrischen Privatrechtsurkunden als Quelle für Mensch und Umwelt.*, SAAS 6, Helsinki.

Radner, K., 1998: 'Der Gott Salmānu ("Šulmānu") und seine Beziehung zur Stadt Dūr-Katlimmu', *WO* 29, 33-51.

Reiter, K., 1997: *Die Metalle im Alten Orient unter besonderer Berücksichtigung altbabylonischer Quellen*, AOAT 249, Münster.

Renger, J., 1984: 'Patterns of Non-Institutional Trade and Non-commercial Exchange in Ancient Mesopotamia at the Beginning of the Second Millennium B.C.', in A. Archi (ed.), *Circulation of Goods in Non-Palatial Context in the Ancient Near East*, Incunabula Graeca Vol. 82, Roma, 31-123.

Renger, J., 1989: 'Zur Rolle von Preisen und Löhnen im Wirtschaftssystem des alten Mesopotamien an der Wende vom 3. zum 2. Jahrtausend v. Chr. - Grundsätzliche Fragen und Überlegungen', *AoF* 16, 234-252.

Renger, J., 1994: 'On Economic Structures in Ancient Mesopotamia', *OrNS* 63, 157-208.

Renger, J., 1995: 'Subsistenzproduktion und redistributive Palastwirtschaft: Wo bleibt die Nische für das Geld? Grenzen und Möglichkeiten für die Verwendung von Geld im alten Mesopotamien', in W. Schelkle and M. Nitsch (eds.), *Rätsel Geld. Annäherungen aus ökonomischer, soziologischer und historischer Sicht*, Marburg, 271-324.

Röllig, W., 1975-76: 'Der altmesopotamische Markt', *WO* 8, 286-295.

Röllig, W., 1997: 'Aramaica Haburensia II. Zwei datierte aramäische Urkunden aus Tall Šēḫ Ḥamad', *AoF* 24, 366-374.

Rosen, B.L., 1977: *Studies in Old Assyrian Loan Contracts*, unpublished dissertation Brandeis Univertsity, UM no. 77-22.827.

Saggs, H.W.F., 1984: *The Might that was Assyria.* Great Civilizations Series, London.

Sallaberger, W., 1994: Review of Zettler 1992, *ZA* 84, 136-144.

Selz, G.J., 1989: *Altsumerische Verwaltungstexte aus Lagaš*, Teil I, FAOS 15/1, Stuttgart.

Sever, H., 1992: 'Eine neue Ehescheidungsurkunde', in H. Otten *et al.* (eds.), *Hittite and Other Anatolian and Near Eastern Studies in Honour of Sedat Alp*, Ankara, 483-486.

Sigrist, M. - Butz, K., 1986: 'Wirtschaftliche Beziehungen zwischen der Susiana und Südmesopotamien in der Ur-III-Zeit', *AMI* 19, 27-31.

Skaist, A., 1994: *The Old Babylonian Loan Contract. Its History and Geograph*y, Ramat Gan.

Skinner, F. G., 1967: *Weights and Measures: Their Ancient Origins and Their Development in Great Britain up to A.D. 1855*, London.

Smith, S., 1924: *Babylonian Historical Texts Relating to the Capture and Downfall of Babylon*, London.

Snell, D.C., 1977: 'The Activities of Some Merchants of Umma', *Iraq* 39, 45-50.

Snell, D.C., 1982: *Ledgers and Prices. Early Mesopotamian Merchant Accounts*, YNER 8, New Haven - London.

Snell, D.C., 1988: 'The Allocation of Resources in the Umma Silver Account System', *JESHO* 31, 1-13.

Snell, D.C., 1991: 'Marktless Trading in our Time', *JESHO* 34, 129-141.

Snell, D.C., 1993: 'Ancient Israelite and Neo-Assyrian Societies and Economies. A Comparative Approach', in M. E. Cohen, D. C. Snell, and D. B. Weisberg (eds.), *The Tablet and the Scroll. Near Eastern Studies in Honor of W.W. Hallo*, Bethesda, 221-224.

Snell, D.C., 1995: 'Methods of Exchange and Coinage in Ancient Western Asia', in J. Sasson (ed.), *Civilizations of the Ancient Near East* III, New York, 1487-1497.

Snell, D. C., 1997: *Life in the Ancient Near East, 3100-332 B.C.E.*, New Haven and London.

Steinkeller, P., 1981: 'The Renting of Fields in Early Mesopotamia and the Development of the Concept of "Interest" in Sumerian', *JESHO* 24, 113-145.

Steinkeller, P., 1986: *Commercial Activity in the Ur III Period and the Issue of Prices*. Paper for the 9th International Congress of Economic History, Bern, Session "Löhne und Preise im orientalischen Altertum" *(distributed during the congress)*.
Steinkeller, P., 1989: *Sale Documents of the Ur-III-Period*, FAOS 17, Stuttgart.
Stolper, M., 1985: *Entrepreneurs and Empire. The Murašû Archive, the Murašû Firm, and Persian Rule in Babylonia*, PIHANS 54, Istanbul.
Stolper, M., 1987: 'Bēlšunu the Satrap', in F. Rochberg-Halton (ed.), *Language, Literature, and History: Philological and Historical Studies Presented to Erica Reiner*, AOS 67, New Haven, 389-402.
Stolper, M.W., 1988: 'The *šaknu* of Nippur', *JCS* 40, 127-155.
Stolper, M., 1990a: 'The Kasr Archive', in H. Sancisi-Weerdenburg and A. Kuhrt (eds.), *Achaemenid History* 4. *Centre and Periphery*, 195-205.
Stolper, M., 1990b: 'Tobits in reverse: more Babylonians in Ecbatana', *AMI* 23, 161-176.
Stolper, M.W., 1992: 'The Murašû Texts from Susa', *RA* 86, 69-77.
Stolper, M., 1993: *Late Achaemenid, Early Macedonian, and Early Seleucid Records of Deposit and Related Texts*, AIUO Suppl. no. 77, Naples.
Ungnad, A., 1941-44: 'Das Haus Egibi', *AfO* 14, 57-64.
Vaan, J.M.C.T. de, 1995: *"Ich bin eine Schwertklinge des Königs". Die Sprache des Bēl-ibni*, AOAT 242, Neukirchen-Vluyn.
Vargyas, P., 1997: 'Getreidekursangaben und Preistarife im Assyrien und Babylonien des 2. und 1. Jahrtausends', in H. Waetzoldt and H. Hauptmann (eds.), *Assyrien im Wandel der Zeiten* (= CRRAI 39), HSAO 6, Heidelberg, 185-190.
Veenhof, K.R., 1972: *Aspects of Old Assyrian Trade and its Terminology*, SD 10, Leiden.
Veenhof, K.R., 1983-84: 'Observations on Old Assyrian Memorandums', *JEOL* 28, 10-23.
Veenhof, K.R., 1985: 'SAG.ÍL.LA = *saggilû*, "Difference assessed". On Measuring and Accounting in some Old Babylonian Texts', in J.-M. Durand and J.-R. Kupper (eds.), *Miscellanea Babylonica. Mélanges offerts à Maurice Birot*, Paris, 285-306.
Veenhof, K.R., 1987: ''Dying Tablets' and 'Hungry Silver'. Elements of Figurative Language in Akkadian Commercial Terminology', in M. Mindlin, M.J. Geller, J.E. Wansbrough (eds.), *Figurative Language in the Ancient Near East*, London, 41-75.
Veenhof, K.R., 1994: 'Miete. C. Altassyrisch', *RlA* 8, 181-184.
Veenhof, K.R., 1995a: '"In Accordance with the Words of the Stele": Evidence for Old Assyrian Legislation', *Chicago-Kent Law Review* 70, 1717-1744.
Veenhof, K.R., 1995b: 'Old Assyrian *iṣurtum*, Akkadian *eṣērum* and Hittite GIŠ.ḪUR', in T.P.J. van den Hout and J. de Roos (eds.), *Studio Historiae Ardens. Ancient Near Eastern Studies Presented to Philo H.J. Houwink ten Cate*, PIHANS 74, Istanbul, 311-332.
Veenhof, K.R., 1997: '"Modern Features" in Old Assyrian Trade', *JESHO* 40, 336-366.
Waetzoldt, H., 1984: ''Diplomaten', Boten, Kaufleute und Verwandtes in Ebla', in L. Cagni (ed.), *Il Bilinguismo a Ebla*, Naples, 405-437.
Waetzoldt, H., 1986: Review of Snell 1982, *OrNS* 55, 327-336.
Walker, C.B.F., 1973: 'Cuneiform Tablets in the County Museum and Art Galery, Truro, Cornwall', *AfO* 24, 122-127.
Walker, C.B.F., 1978: 'Texts and Fragments', *JCS* 30, 234-249.
Walker, C.B.F., 1988: 'Further Notes on Assyrian Bronzeworking', in J. Curtis (ed.), *Bronzeworking Centres of Western Asia c. 1000-539 B.C.*, London, 111-118.
Weidner, E., 1966: 'Neuassyrische Rechtsurkunden aus Assur', *AfO* 21, 69.
Weingort, S., 1939: *Das Haus Egibi in neubabylonischen Rechtsurkunden*, Berlin-Charlottenburg.

Wilcke, C., 1990: Review of H. Klengel, *Vorderasiatische Schriftdenkmäler der Staatlichen Museen zu Berlin, Neue Folge VI* (Heft XXII), *ZA* 80, 297-306.
Wilcke C., 1996: 'Neue Rechtsurkunden der Altsumerischen Zeit', *ZA* 86, 1-67.
Wunsch, C., 1993: *Die Urkunden des babylonischen Geschäftsmannes Iddin-Marduk. Zum Handel mit Naturalien im 6. Jahrhundert v. Chr.*, Cuneiform Monographs 3a/b, Groningen.
Yoffee, N., 1981: *Explaining Trade in Ancient Western Asia*, Monographs on the Ancient Near East 2/2, Malibu.
Young, G.D., 1979: 'A Merchant's Balanced Account and Neosumerian Gold', in M.A. Powell and R.H. Sack (eds.), *Studies in Honor of Tom B. Jones*, AOAT 203, Kevelaer - Neukirchen-Vluyn, 195-217.
Zaccagnini, C., 1971: 'La terminologia accadica del rame e del bronzo nel I millennio', *OA* 10, 123-144.
Zaccagnini, C., 1989: 'Prehistory of the Achaemenid Tributary System', in P. Briant and C. Herrenschmidt (eds.), *Le tribut dans l'empire perse. Travaux de l'Institut d'études Iraniennes de l'Université de la Sorbonne Nouvelle* 13, Paris, 193-215.
Zadok, R., 1976: 'On the Connections between Iran and Babylonia in the Sixth Century B.C.', *Iran* 14, 61-78.
Zadok, R., 1994: 'On Some Anthroponyms and Toponyms', *NABU* 1994 no. 14.
Zawadzki, S., 1990: 'Great Families of Sippar during the Chaldean and Early Persian Periods (626-482 BC)', *RA* 84, 17-25.
Zawadzki, S., 1991: 'Ironsmiths, Bronzesmiths and Goldsmiths in the Neo-Babylonian Texts from Sippar', *WO* 22, 21-47.
Zawadzki, S., 1994: 'The first Persian Journey of Itti-Marduk-balāṭu', *AMI* 27, 123-126.
Zettler, R.L., 1992: *The Ur III Temple of Inanna at Nippur. The Operation and Organization of Urban Religious Institutions in Mesopotamia in the Late Third Millennium B.C.*, BBVO 11, Berlin.

Fig. 1 The weighing of metal ingots at the time of Ashurnasirpal II (BM 118800)
From: C.J. Gadd, *The Stones of Assyria*, pl. 6. *See p. 135*

Fig. 2 Assyrians plundering Muṣaṣir. From: P.E. Botta - E. Flandin, *Monument de Ninive. Tome II*, pl. 140. *See p. 135*